# HAUNTED
# SECOND
# WORLD WAR
# AIRFIELDS

**The Battle of Britain Memorial Statue**
Built overlooking the English Channel at Capel le Ferne near Folkestone, the memorial includes replicas of a Hurricane and a Spitfire together with the seated statue and the names of the pilots who were killed in the battle. It is free to visit, has ample parking and a café/shop is on site. It is located off New Dover Road at OS TL 2738 8346. (© *Chris Huff*)

*Overleaf:*
**The Battle of Britain Memorial Wall of Remembrance**
The names of the pilots who were killed during the Battle of Britain are recorded on the 14 black slabs of the memorial. It is located off the New Dover Road at OS TL 2738 8346. (© *Chris Huff*)

# HAUNTED SECOND WORLD WAR AIRFIELDS

## VOLUME ONE: SOUTHERN ENGLAND

### CHRISTOPHER HUFF

FONTHILL

*This book is dedicated, with thanks, to all those men and women who served on the airfields of Britain during the Second World War.*

Fonthill Media
www.fonthillmedia.com

First published by Fonthill Media 2012

A CIP catalogue record for this book is available from the British Library

ISBN 978-1-78155-097-7 (print)
ISBN 978-1-78155-212-4 (e-book)

Typeset in 10pt on 12pt Sabon LT
Typesetting by Fonthill Media
Printed in the UK

Connect with us
 facebook.com/fonthillmedia     twitter.com/fonthillmedia

# CONTENTS

# Introduction

This book and its two companion volumes are the product of fifteen years' research into accounts of paranormal manifestation at airfields that were in use during the Second World War. They should not under any circumstances be considered a definitive study – there are many more accounts to be found, and I do so almost on a daily basis. Instead these books offer an insight into my research as it currently stands and demonstrate clearly that there is a lot of haunting going on at these usually ignored places. This first volume is a loose area which covers roughly the south of England and includes airfields from the counties of Bedfordshire, Berkshire, Buckinghamshire, Cambridgeshire, Cornwall, Devon, Dorset, Essex, Gloucestershire, Hampshire, Hertfordshire, Huntingdonshire, Kent, Middlesex, Oxfordshire, Somerset, Surrey, Sussex, and Wiltshire.

I started actively researching and documenting the accounts some fifteen years ago; however, I have been looking at haunted airfields for a much longer time and first developed an interest in all things RAF from my father who would take me to the old deserted airfields to wander around from about the age of five. Later, in my teenage years as a member of 241 ATC (Wanstead & Woodford), I continued with the RAF theme and gained access to more airfields.

It is only in the past few years, following a BA and an MA in archaeology at York then Durham universities, that I felt confident enough to study these old airfields properly and the paranormal phenomena that has been reported from them. The reason for this study seemed logical at the time of starting out. I thought to make a corpus of all the accounts that I could find (thinking that there wasn't too much scope in the topic) and it should be easy to update when I found more accounts. A bad mistake, for to date I have accounts from over 260 haunted RAF airfields in the UK, many of which have both multiple and diverse accounts and latterly include data from investigations. I have long ceased to be amazed at how these very haunted places have been largely ignored or omitted from the usual ghost books that are available.

The accounts that I present in these volumes have been obtained from a variety of sources; books, of course, were the starting point, especially Bruce Barrymore Halpenny's *Ghost Stations* series and Jack Currie's *Echoes in the Air*. Both of these, together with Kevin Desmond's *Aviation Ghosts*, inspired me to seek out further accounts. Once the available literature was exhausted, much time was spent scouring websites and forums. In the latter stages, having placed some of my research on a website that I had created, I received personal accounts from witnesses who contacted me via email. The accounts from all sources have been abridged and rewritten to keep within the confines of a word limit, and indeed avoid plagiarism. Because of my rewriting of the accounts I strongly urge anyone with a particular interest in the topic to read the originals, as they contain nuances which are missed from this work. Of particular importance are investigations that have taken place by paranormal groups, where I have summarised the findings and missed much interesting information out. The web address is given in every case should the reader wish to pursue the details further, or perhaps apply to join a group active in their area.

Right from the outset of this project, two things that I have felt necessary were a chronological history of the airfield, together with an airfield plan in order to give the accounts of hauntings some context. I have always experienced a certain frustration at never having all the information in one place and having to bury myself in a string of books to find the details that I wanted. Looking at modern photographs from the air or using Google Earth to view the modern airfield does not convey in many cases what it originally looked like. Much on these airfields was destroyed when no longer required and sold off after the war to be returned to agriculture, leaving a ghost of their former grandeur faintly visible upon the landscape. Some have fared even worse. Hawkinge and Gravesend, for example, are completely buried under housing, Usworth and Greatham (see Vol. 2) are the sites for Nissan and Tata steel respectively. Others have been turned into motor racing circuits and industrial parks, one or two for poultry farming, all of which obscures their former shape. The plans in these volumes are not to scale but depict what the airfield would have looked like during or just after the Second World War.

There are actually a number of airfields which didn't make the book. Ford and Fowlmere, for example, have a rumour that a Spitfire is heard circling the field, but in both cases I was unable to find an eyewitness or statement about the phenomena and so they were excluded. Other airfields didn't make the book because of the self-imposed date range of 1938 to 1945 for operational use, to fit them into the overall title of Second World War. Whilst the accounts from Drem, Montrose, and Scampton (see Vol. 2) are included because the airfields continued in use through the Second World War, others dating solely from the First World War, such as Throwley and South Carlton, are not included simply because they were not operational beyond that conflict. A final category for exclusion relates to airfields that opened post-1946. I have accounts of hauntings occurring at them, but they miss the cut-off date.

Other hauntings that have not been included concern shadow factories with an attached airfield but without a true military presence such as Hanwell, Leavesden, and South Marston, even though accounts of hauntings have been uncovered from them. Also conspicuous by their absence in these volumes are the accounts of airmen haunting stretches of British roads, hitching lifts, haunting pubs and private houses, and indeed the wreckage of crashed aircraft. Neither are the accounts of phantom aircraft in the skies at locations other than airfields included, although it is hoped that a separate volume may be forthcoming in the future which will deal with these and other RAF locations.

As a quick introduction to the topic, the accounts of paranormal activity at airfields start almost as soon as military men took to the air. In 1913, Desmond Arthur was killed at RFC Montrose and is probably the first account of an apparition being witnessed on an airfield. Lesser known, perhaps, is the intriguing account of Lieutenant David McConnell who was seen on 7 December 1918 at RAF Scampton at the time he had just crashed his aircraft. The accounts of hauntings continued through the Second World War and indeed continue to occur to the present day, with recent personal communications to me from visitors to RAF Snaith, RAF Twinwood Farm, RAF Burtonwood, and RAF Scampton.

A question that I have often been asked, and one which I struggle to answer, is why are so many airfields haunted? To be sure, airfields during the wartime years have seen extreme emotions, and a common thread to the accounts is that the airmen felt that the airfield was home, where their friends were, and that was where they wanted to be – and who can blame them? But not all hauntings can be claimed to be by spirits, for there are recordings, crisis apparitions, and time slips to be considered and observed in the following pages.

One particular problem that I have uncovered with the data is the transient, almost ephemeral, nature of reports and accounts on the internet, which disappear overnight in some cases in a server crash or website deletion. I have made it my highest priority to record these accounts whenever I find them before they disappear for good. I myself have lost some accounts when a computer died, taking the files with it, five years ago.

Another problem with the gathered data is the almost unswerving belief in some that the Control Tower is naturally the most likely, or indeed the only, area that will be haunted on an airfield. This means that all the efforts of paranormal groups or interested individuals seem to be channelled to one particular place, which naturally creates a bias. To assume immediately that the place and time to be on a haunted airfield is the Control Tower and at night is a complete fallacy. Many, if not most, of the hauntings have occurred during the day and in all sorts of buildings, most especially it seems the hangars. It is truer to say, perhaps, that one has to be in the right place at the right time to see an apparition, or hear a sound, or experience a smell or even the definite presence of person or persons unseen. In Volume 3, I shall include an analysis of the reported phenomena and locations within an airfield to back my contention that the Control Tower is not the only nor the most haunted place on an airfield.

Some may have noted already my use of Control Tower in the text. The term for the building that controlled flying on the airfield was the Watch Office or Watch

Tower, but in modern parlance this is most often called the Control Tower, which is of course the USAAF term.

*Note on abbreviations:*
Ad., tech. & barr. – Administration, technical & barracks
Sat. airfield(s) – Satellite airfield(s)

*Note on airfield plans:*
All airfield plans face due north.

# Acknowledgements

Thanks are gratefully given to three people. Firstly, my wonderful girlfriend, Judith Walton, who has helped, supported, and encouraged me throughout, and without whom the plans for these volumes would not have been completed. Secondly, my mother, Patricia Huff, who has never lost faith that I had something like this in me, in spite of much evidence to the contrary. And thirdly, my late father, John David Huff, who sparked the interest that has ultimately resulted in these volumes.

As a special thank you I would like to acknowledge the immense contribution to the Haunted Airfields field made by Bruce Barrymore Halpenny and Jack Currie. I admit my great debt to both of these authors for their work. Gentlemen, thank you.

The *Ghost Stations* books by Mr Barrymore Halpenny remain seminal works in the field, and without them, later works such as this would have been impossible. His work has inspired many to go out and take an active interest in airfields and the airmen who served and died flying from them. Indeed, it is largely Bruce Barrymore's work that inspired me to start collating and preserving all the accounts that I could find. I urge all the readers of these volumes to read the *Ghost Stations* series and *Echoes in the Air* to gain even greater insights into the phenomena of haunted airfields than I have been able to accomplish within these pages.

I would also like to thank Jay Slater and Alan Sutton for their advice. Without them this research would probably never have made the transition from a website and a collection of files into a series of books.

And finally, I wish to thank everyone who has contacted me regarding accounts of the paranormal at former airfields. I am most indebted to you all. Of these, I would especially like to mention the following people: Thomas Ackroyd, Des Braban, Norman Brice, Jason John Cook, Sarah Darnell, John Dening, Harvey Ditchman, Damien Dyer, Sean Edwards, Andy Fazekas, Lee Hall, Glen and Sally Jolly, Rachel Keene, Jim Macan, Colin Pollard, Nigel Scullion, Kim Slater, Nick Smith, Suzanne Stafford, and Ron Street.

# List of Airfields by County

**Bedfordshire:** Henlow, Tempsford, Thurleigh, Twinwood Farm
**Berkshire:** Abingdon, Grove, Welford
**Buckinghamshire:** Halton, Turweston
**Cambridgeshire:** Bassingbourn, Bourn, Cambridge, Castle Camps, Duxford, Mepal, Oakington, Peterborough, Steeple Morden, Witchford, Wittering, Wratting Common
**Cornwall:** Davidstow Moor, St Merryn
**Devon:** Chivenor, Dunkeswell
**Dorset:** Warmwell
**Essex:** Bradwell Bay, Chipping Ongar, Debden, Earls Colne, Hornchurch, Little Walden, Matching, North Weald, Ridgewell, Rivenhall, Stansted Mountfitchet
**Gloucestershire:** Chedworth, Little Rissington, Stoke Orchard
**Hampshire:** Holmsley South, Lasham, Middle Wallop, Thruxton
**Hertfordshire:** Bovingdon, Hunsdon, Nuthampstead, Panshanger, Sawbridgeworth
**Huntingdonshire:** Alconbury, Graveley, Kimbolton, Little Staughton, Molesworth, Upwood, Warboys
**Kent:** Biggin Hill, Gravesend, Hawkinge, Lympne, Manston, West Malling
**Middlesex:** Hendon, Northolt
**Oxfordshire:** Bicester, Brize Norton, Culham, Enstone, Stanton Harcourt, Upper Heyford, Weston-on-the-Green
**Somerset:** Charmy Down, Whitchurch
**Surrey:** Croydon, Kenley, Redhill
**Sussex:** Appledram, Tangmere, Thorney Island
**Wiltshire:** Boscombe Down, Colerne, Larkhill, Lyneham, Netheravon, Upavon

# The Airfields

## Abingdon

Wessex Bombing Area
Central Area
No. 1 Group
No. 6 Group
No. 91 Group
No. 47 Group, Transport Command

| | |
|---|---|
| County: | Berkshire |
| Location: | 1 mile W of Abingdon |
| OS Ref.: | SU 475992 |
| Opened: | 01/09/1932 |
| Closed: | 31/07/1992 |
| Pundit code: | AB |
| Control Tower: | A. Watch Office with Met Section 5845/39 |
| | B. Watch Office, Vertical Split Control Type 2548c/55 |
| Condition: | A. Not known |
| | B. Disused, due for demolition |
| Runways: | Grass, then 2 concrete, tarmac, (190) 2,000 x 50 yards (270) |
| | 1,600 x 50 yards |
| Hardstandings: | 6 large loops, 24 pan type |
| Hangars: | C Type – 1, A Type – 4 |
| Ad., tech. & barr.: | Permanent, Expansion Period accommodation |
| Population: | RAF Officers – 186, OR – 1,254, WAAF Officers – 17, OR – 515 |
| Sat. airfield(s): | Stanton Harcourt |

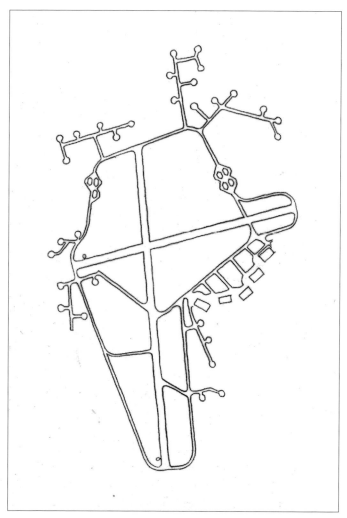

Abingdon

## History to 1946:

**1929**
Construction of the airfield began

**1932**
1 September: RAF Abingdon opened in the Wessex Bombing Area as a training
  station for Bomber Command
8 October: No. 40 Squadron arrived from Catfoss with Fairey Gordon bombers
3 November: Oxford University Air Squadron arrived from Upper Heyford

**1933**
November: Central Area took control of Abingdon

**1934**

1 June: No. 15 Squadron re-formed as a light bomber squadron equipped with Hawker Harts

**1935**

October: No. 40 Squadron re-equipped with Harts

**1936**

7 January: An RAF expansion phase saw more buildings completed on the camp and No. 104 Squadron re-formed from 'C' Flight of No. 40 Squadron

17 February: Part of 15 Squadron became the nucleus of No. 98 Squadron

February: No. 98 Squadron received Hawker Hinds

March: No. 40 Squadron received Hawker Hinds

August: Nos 98 & 104 Squadrons moved to Hucknall

**1937**

18 January: No. 15 Squadron parented No. 52 Squadron

February: No. 52 Squadron moved to RAF Upwood

3 May: No. 62 Squadron was formed from No. 40 Squadron

November: No. 802 FAA Squadron with Hawker Nimrods and Ospreys arrived on detachment

**1938**

January: No. 802 Squadron departed for HMS *Glorious*

3 March: No. 185 Squadron was re-formed from No. 40 Squadron

1 June: No. 106 Squadron formed from No. 15 Squadron

July: No. 15 Squadron was re-equipped with Battle IIs

7 July: Seven Battles arrived for 40 Squadron

1 September: Nos 106 & 18 Squadrons departed for Thornaby; Nos 15 & 40 Squadrons formed a Wing of the AASF; and No. 103 Squadron arrived to re-arm with Fairey Battles

**1939**

1 April: No. 103 Squadron moved to Benson

2 September: Nos 52 and 63 squadrons with Fairey Battles started to arrive from No. 4 AASF Group Pool

16 September: No. 166 Squadron swapped with No. 97 Squadron at Benson

3 November: Oxford UAS was disbanded

**1940**

January: No. 166 Squadron received Whitley Mk IIIs

8 April: Nos 166 & 97 Squadrons disbanded to form No. 10 OTU, within No. 6 Group, to train night bomber crews

21 July: No. 10 OTU first operated dropping leaflets

3 September: Abingdon's satellite at RAF Stanton Harcourt came into use for night flying, remaining under Abingdon's control until 15 January 1946

10 September: C Flight of 10 OTU was dispersed to Stanton Harcourt

8 October: Oxford UAS re-formed in 54 Group

24 October: Oxford UAS became functional and used a Tiger Moth based at Abingdon

## 1941

12 January: No. 1 BAT Flight formed at Abingdon with Whitleys and Ansons

February: 'C' Flight of 10 OTU disbanded and was replaced by 'A' Flight

12 March: A solitary raider dropped 16 bombs which damaged a Whitley and the bomb dump

21 March: 26 bombs fell, wrecking 7 offices; ceilings and windows were damaged in many others

23 July: No. 10 OTU began using Mount Farm

August: Lysander target tugs were added to the strength; further aircraft of that type arrived at the end of the year, being flown by 7 AACU

31 October: No. 1 BAT Flight became No. 1501 BAT Flight and Oxfords replaced the Whitleys

## 1942

11 April: No. 6 Group became No. 91 Group; a special Whitley flight of 10 OTU formed and was placed at St Eval for anti-U-boat patrols; 33 aircraft were modified to carry depth charges and ASV radar

30/31 May: The 1,000 bomber raid on Cologne – 21 Whitleys took off and all returned, one crash-landing at Manston

1/2 June: The 1,000 bomber raid on Essen – 22 Whitleys took off; Z6581 was shot down by a night fighter at Breedenbroek with all crew killed; all others returned safely

25/26 June: The 1,000 bomber raid on Bremen – 20 Whitleys took off; P4944 was lost near Hamburg; AD689 crashed at Lingen-Ems; BD201 was shot down by a night fighter at Werwershoof; P5004 ditched in the North Sea and the crew were rescued

4 August: The St Eval detachment began operational flying

## 1943

February and April: A few leaflet-dropping sorties were flown

April: Martinets replaced the Lysanders; Bullseyes and ASR sorties were flown; No. 91 Air Gunners Instructors' School opened with two Whitleys and two Martinets

18 April: No. 1501 BAT Flight moved to Stanton Harcourt

19 July: The St Eval detachment ceased Ops and returned to Abingdon

September: Nickel raids, the dropping of propaganda leaflets over German cities, began

**1944**

20 March: No. 10 OTU moved temporarily to Stanton Harcourt whilst two runways were laid at Abingdon; the unit establishment was temporarily reduced to three-quarter strength

16 November: No. 10 OTU returned from Stanton Harcourt with Wellington Xs, and daylight training resumed at Abingdon

21 December: No. 10 OTU became full size again upon absorbing the Polish Flight from No. 18 OTU

**1946**

10 September: No. 10 OTU disbanded

24 October: Abingdon was transferred to Transport Command

31 October: No. 525 Squadron arrived from Membury with Dakota IIIs

1 December: No. 525 Squadron renumbered No. 238 Squadron

16 December: No. 46 squadron arrived from Manston with Dakota IIIs

**Closure:**

In December 1992, RAF Abingdon was closed and handed over to the Army as Dalton Barracks.

**Current status:**

Dalton Barracks is used by the Royal Logistic Corps.

## Haunted RAF Abingdon

*Source: Keypublishing Aviation Forum*

Allegedly the pilot of a Beverley that crashed shortly after take-off in 1957 haunts the back runway. His apparition is said to walk along it to a dispersal close to the end of runway 08. The Beverley had developed a fault in one of its engines and was returning to base when it hit power lines at Sutton Wick, just short of the airfield.

# Alconbury

No. 3 Bomber Group
US Eighth Air Force

| | |
|---|---|
| County: | Huntingdonshire |
| Location: | 4 miles NW of Huntingdon |
| OS Ref.: | TL 295795 |
| Opened: | 17/05/1938 |
| Closed: | 15/04/95 |

| | |
|---|---|
| Pundit code: | AY |
| USAAF Station: | 120 |
| Control Tower: | A. Watch Office with Ops Room for Bomber Satellite Stations 7345/41; Observation Room added to pattern 13079/41 |
| | B. Watch Office for all Commands 343/43 |
| Condition: | A. Survived in 2001 |
| | B. Disused in 2003 |
| Runways: | 3 concrete, tarmac, extended in 1942 and again post-war, (180) 1,375 x 50 yards, (240) 1,240 x 50 yards, and (300) 1,110 x 50 yards; 1942 USAAF enlargement (240) 2,000 yards, (180) 1,400 yards, and (300) 1,400 yards |
| Hardstandings: | 30 pan type hardstandings, most leading off 5 long access tracks on the northern side of the airfield; (1942) USAF built additional hardstandings, all loops |
| Hangars: | A single T2 hangar was erected on the north-west side; a second T2 was sited adjacent to the hardstanding complex east of the threshold of runway 18 |
| Ad., tech. & barr.: | On the north-west side, accommodation was provided to the south-west side of the A14, around Alconbury House which had been requisitioned earlier |
| Sat. airfield(s): | Satellite to Upwood; satellite to Wyton |

## History to 1946:

### 1938
The Air Ministry acquired 150 acres of open meadowland north-west of Little Stukeley village as a satellite field for Upwood
May: No. 63 Squadron with Battles arrived from Upwood on a two-day training exercise; other squadrons were to follow over the next 15 months

### 1939
Soon after war was declared Alconbury became Wyton's satellite in No. 2 Group, with Nos 12, 40 & 139 Squadrons frequently deployed there

### 1940
14 April: No. 15 Squadron arrived from Wyton with Blenheim IVs
10 May: No. 15 Squadron flew its first operation as a part of a 33-strong Blenheim force attacking the German-occupied airfields of Waalhaven and Ypenburg near Rotterdam, all eight aircraft returning; a following Operation, to break the Albert Canal at Maastricht, saw 6 aircraft fail to return
15 May: The remnants of No. 15 Squadron moved back to Wyton, and Alconbury reverted to satellite status

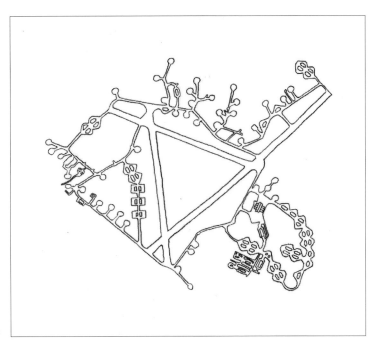

Alconbury

1 November: Wyton and Alconbury came under the control of No. 3 Group; Alconbury was then upgraded to bomber airfield status

## 1941
February: While construction was still in progress, No. 40 Squadron arrived from Wyton with Wellington 1c & IIs
October: Sixteen of No. 40 Squadron's Wellingtons were moved to Malta, one Flight remaining at Alconbury

## 1942
14 February: The Flight of No. 40 Squadron was formed into No. 156 Squadron
15 August: No. 156 Squadron was chosen to become one of the new Pathfinder Force units and was moved to Warboys and No. 8 Group; this marked the end of RAF Bomber Command's association with Alconbury, for earlier in the year the airfield had been included in the group area planned for the first USAAF 8th AF Wing with headquarters located at Brampton Grange
September: The 93rd Bomb Group arrived from Fort Myers Army Airfield with B-24 Liberators and was assigned to the 20th Combat Bombardment Wing of the 8th AF
9 October: The 93rd BG became operational when 24 B-24 s attacked locomotive manufacturing facilities at Lille; one B-24 failed to return and 5 crew were killed; subsequently the group operated primarily against submarine pens along the French coast and the Bay of Biscay

October: Runway lengthening commenced to make Alconbury up to Class A
   standard, the work being completed by the end of the year
6 December: Most of the 93rd BG was transferred to the Twelfth AF in North
   Africa to support the Operation Torch landings; the balance of the 93rd BG
   was moved to Hardwick

### 1943
15 April: The 95th BG arrived from Bovingdon with B-17s
May: The 92nd BG was re-formed as a combat unit
27 May: At approximately 20.30, ground personnel were arming B-17s in the
   dispersal area when a 500 lb bomb detonated, the explosion setting off several
   other bombs, and 18 men were killed, 21 injured, and four B-17s completely
   destroyed while eleven others were damaged
Late summer: Experiments with radar devices for bombing through cloud were
   carried out at Alconbury
September: The 92nd BG moved out and the 482nd Bomb Group arrived with
   Fortresses and Liberators to provide Pathfinder support with both H2S and H2X

### 1944
March: The 482nd Bomb Group was taken off regular operations and thereafter
   became an operational training and development unit for various radar
   devices

### 1945
26 November: Alconbury was handed back to the RAF and remained on care and
   maintenance status for 7½ years

**Closure:**
In 1995, the USAF withdrew from Alconbury.

**Current status:**
The airfield was sold to the British Airports Authority in 1997 for commercial
   development; the runway and hardened aircraft shelters were to be retained
   for ten years.

## Haunted RAF Alconbury

*Source: The Stars and Stripes website, 30 October 2005*
According to a story published in the *Cambridge Evening News* in 2005, children's
voices have been heard by base security personnel, most notably during the 1970s.
They are believed to be those of six children killed in a train crash near Abbots
Ripton in 1876.

*Source: ghostvillage.com, 9 June 2004*
In 1978, the writer of the piece was sent to RAF Alconbury in England for a 30-day temporary duty and to install a stabilator trim actuator on the first weekend.

Working on his own in the hangar on a Saturday evening it was deathly silent apart from the periodic sounds made when rummaging through the tool box. With the job done, and having put everything back into the tool box, he realised that all the exits to the hangar were closed and locked except for the front door. To get there meant turning off the hangar lights and walking from one end of the hangar to the other in the dark.

Slowly feeling his way along the wall in pitch darkness, he headed towards the hangar door. Two-thirds of the way across the hangar there came a distinct 'thunk' of the lighting relays kicking in, and the entire hangar lit up. There was no one else in the hangar, and shouting out to see who had turned the lights back on, he received no reply. Having turning the lights off again he crossed the hangar once more. This time the lights stayed off.

*Source: ghostvillage.com, 15 June 2004*
One of the commonly reported sightings at Alconbury was that of the 'Hardstand 70 Monster'. This account is related by the son of the NCO in charge of three men and their dogs in the early 1970s who were responsible for guarding the bunkers within a large fenced area.

One foggy night he received a radio call that there was an intruder within the perimeter, and that shots had been fired. He sped towards the location of the shooting and saw a figure in the fog. Stopping the truck, thinking it was one of his guards, he rolled down his window and was screamed at full in the face by what can only be described as a man-like, bipedal creature which in an instant ran off at an incredible speed.

The creature sped past another guard, who also fired upon it whilst his guard dogs were yelping and straining to flee in the opposite direction. The third guard and his dogs were running towards the scene when they turned the corner of a bunker only to be intercepted by the creature running at full speed. His dogs too struggled to flee, and the creature hit the taut leashes and tore them out of his grasp.

The guards all witnessed the creature making running bounds across the ground, before leaping over two tall and well-spaced barbed-wire fences in a single bound and disappeared into the surrounding woods.

The creature was described as hairy, approximately 5 feet 9 inches in height, and having intelligent, human-like eyes, a flat nose, and large ears. The teeth were large but not fanged. The lower face was rounded, the face was narrow around the eyes, but the head flared out again at the top. It had very muscular, frog-like thighs.

On the very same night that they encountered the hardstand monster the security guards also witnessed a floating apparition. On another occasion the NCO found himself surrounded by the disembodied voices of children.

*Source: ghostvillage.com, 13 November 2009*

People would report catching glimpses of figures in Second World War flight gear at the 'Rod & Gun' club, but always from a distance. Whenever anyone tried to approach, they would always manage to disappear around a corner or through a door. The club was supposedly the airfield's mortuary during the Second World War.

# Appledram

(No plan available)

No. 11 Group, Fighter Command

| | |
|---|---|
| County: | Sussex |
| Location: | 2½ miles SW of Chichester |
| OS Ref.: | SU 839018 |
| Opened: | June 1943 |
| Closed: | November 1944 |
| Pundit code: | AO |
| Watch Office: | ? |
| Condition: | ? |
| Runways: | Grass, Sommerfeld tracking |
| Hardstandings: | Nil; the aircraft were dispersed around the airfield and later on mats of Sommerfeld track |
| Hangars: | Extra-Over Blisters – 4; at first a single Blister, then 3 more of the same were constructed |
| Bomb stores: | The bomb dump was located near the 'Black Horse' pub |
| Ad., tech. & barr.: | Temporary buildings with a tented camp |
| Population: | Unknown |

## History to 1946:

### 1942

June: An expanse of grassland at Manor Farm, alongside the A286 and close to the Chichester Channel with good road access, was surveyed for a possible Advanced Landing Ground

10 December: Ministry of Agriculture objections were overruled and authority to requisition the land was granted

### 1943

February: An RAF Airfield Construction Unit arrived and removed obstacles such as hedges and laid two Sommerfeld track runways in the shape of a cross. This was completed within a matter of weeks and Appledram had the distinction of being one of the first batch of airfields constructed in this way. One Blister hangar was provided, and the accommodation was in tents. The main domestic site was located adjacent to the sharp bend in Appledram Lane. Some buildings were erected, but in the main tented accommodation was provided and field kitchens set up

May: The airfield, with spartan facilities, was complete

2 June: RAF Appledram opened with the arrival of Nos 175, 181 & 182 Squadrons with Typhoons and all personnel from Lasham as No. 124 Airfield within No. 2 Tactical Air Force. The aircraft were dispersed around the field and the personnel lived in tents. There were ongoing drainage problems at the landing ground, with the aircraft often bogged down after leaving the runway

12 June: The Typhoons began operations from Appledram with an attack on Abbeville airfield; operations against communications, installations, and airfields followed. There was only one serious accident during their stay

30 June: A USAAF B-17 made an emergency landing at Appledram; one of the crew was the actor Clark Gable

1 July: No. 175 Squadron moved to Lydd

2 July: Nos 181 & 182 Squadrons moved to New Romney; Appledram was reduced to standby status and underwent some development: the drainage problems were tackled and three EO Blister hangars and a number of Sommerfeld tracking dispersals were added. Living accommodation continued to be under canvas with the Officers' Mess located in a barn; temporary HQ buildings were set up near to Dell Quay

## 1944

3 April: No. 134 Airfield arrived from Mendlesham comprising Nos 310, 312 & 313 Czech squadrons with Spitfires as a part of 2 TAF. The Czechs supplemented their tents by taking over a few farm cottages. The squadrons were engaged in fighter sweeps, bomber escorts, and attacks on Noball sites

May: Three Czech pilots were killed in flying accidents at Appledram

May 31: Four pilots were lost when attacking targets in the St Malo area

6 June: The Appledram squadrons provided a part of the fighter umbrella with the Wing patrolling over the bridgehead without incident; a number of Fw 190s were engaged and five were destroyed. It is claimed that Appledram's Czech squadrons carried out more operational sorties on 6 June than any other unit

June: The squadrons flew fighter patrols and ground strafing as routine missions

22 June: With the increasing threat from V-l flying bombs Nos 310, 312 & 313 Squadrons moved to Tangmere for anti-Diver patrols

28 June: Nos 302, 308 & 317 Polish Squadrons No. 131 Wing arrived from Chailey with Spitfire IXs; they were engaged in dive-bombing forward German positions under Army direction

16 July: the Wing moved to Ford to prepare to move to the Continent, and Appledram was no longer required

**Closure:**

In November 1944, RAF Appledram was derequisitioned; the farm cottages were released a week later. In January 1945, two Flights of No. 5027 Works Squadron moved in to lift the Sommerfeld tracking used for the runways, remove the Blister hangars and restore the land for farming.

**Current status:**

Returned to agriculture. There is now virtually no trace of the airfield.

### Haunted RAF Appledram

*Source: Alan C. Wood,* Military Ghosts, *2010 (pp. 160-1)*

Alan Wood writes that a Mrs V. Watkins lived near to and worked in the fields by the former ALG of Appledram and reported that she, on occasion, felt a presence nearby. She would constantly look over her shoulder to see who was watching her but would always find that there was no one there.

One night she was awakened at 1 a.m. and claims to have witnessed the apparition of an airman wearing a Mae West lifejacket standing at the foot of her bed. She closed her eyes, undoubtedly wishing the figure gone, and upon reopening them saw that he had gone. At around the same time as the sighting, Mrs Watkins's husband had a brilliant white light enter his bedroom at which point he shouted out. Their daughter, in the next bedroom, also screamed at the same time. Alan Wood does not elaborate on the reasons why, but it is suspected that the airman also paid her a visit.

It is wondered whether the Watkins family lived in one of the farm cottages requisitioned for airfield accommodation during the brief service life of RAF Appledram.

# Bassingbourn

No. 2 Bomber Group
No. 3 Bomber Group
USAAF 8th Air Force

| | |
|---|---|
| County: | Cambridgeshire |
| Location: | 3 miles N of Royston |
| OS Ref.: | TL 330462 |
| Opened: | 03/38 |
| Closed: | 19/05/69 |
| Pundit code: | BS |
| USAAF Station: | 121 |

| Control Tower: | A. Pre-war Fort Type 207/36, modified with extra floor and extended tower |
| --- | --- |
| | B. Replaced post-war with Watch Office, Vertical Split Control Type 2548c/55, now demolished |
| Condition: | A. Tower preserved as a museum to the 91st Bomb Group |
| | B. Demolished in the 1990s |
| Runways: | Grass, 3 concrete and asphalt, 1,200 x 50 yards, (308) 930 x 50 yards and (350) 1,100 x 50 yards; 1942 extended to (254) 2,000 yards, (308) 1,400 yards, and (350) 1,400 yards |
| Perimeter track: | Additional perimeter track was added around the bomb store site, which was doubled in area, to reach the west end of the main runway |
| Hardstandings: | 35 pan type hardstands and 16 loop hardstands were constructed; 1942 4 dispersal areas were built |
| Hangars: | C Type – 4 erected in a semicircle at the south edge of the airfield |
| Ad., tech. & barr.: | Expansion Scheme permanent buildings. Bassingbourn was made one of the most attractive stations by the planting of hundreds of plum trees |
| Population: | USAAF Officers – 443, OR – 2,529 |
| Sat. airfield(s): | Steeple Morden |

In total, flying 340 missions, 197 B-17s failed to return to Bassingbourn, the highest heavy bomber loss in the USAAF

## History to 1946:

### 1937
April: Construction of the airfield began

### 1938
March: Bassingbourn opened into No. 2 Group and station personnel arrived from Uxbridge

2 May: No. 104 Squadron arrived from Hucknall and No. 108 Squadron arrived from Cranfield, both with Hinds

May: No. 104 squadron re-equipped with Blenheim Is

June: No. 108 squadron re-equipped with Blenheim Is

### 1939
Early in the year large brown nets were slung across the hangars, and camouflage painting followed when war was declared

17 September: No. 108 squadron moved to Bicester

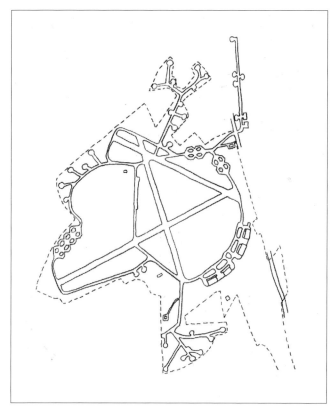

Bassingbourn

18 September: No. 104 squadron moved to Bicester

24 September: Bassingbourn was transferred to No. 3 Group; No. 215 Squadron
    arrived from Bramcote with Wellington 1s

**1940**

8 April: No. 215 Squadron became part of No. 11 OTU for navigational training

June: No. 11 OTU received Ansons

August: Bassingbourn had a single bomb dropped on the barrack block, killing 11
    and injuring 15

**1941**

January: Wellington Ics began replacing the older models

December: While runways were constructed, No. 11 OTU's aircraft moved to
    Tempsford

**1942**

24 April: No. 11 OTU started returning to Bassingbourn

30/31 May: The 1,000 bomber raid on Cologne – 20 Wellingtons of No. 11 OTU
    participated; R1065 was lost when taking off from Steeple Morden

1/2 June: The 1,000 bomber raid on Essen – Wellington DV767 taking off from Steeple Morden was lost

25/26 June: The 1,000 bomber raid on Bremen – Wellingtons R1078, X3213 & DV778 all taking off from Steeple Morden were lost

31 July: No. 11 OTU formed part of the 630 aircraft force that attacked Düsseldorf during Operation Grand National without loss

13/14 September: No. 11 OTU formed part of the 630 aircraft force that attacked Bremen; Wellingtons X3169 & X9744 taking off from Steeple Morden were lost

28 September: No. 11 OTU moved to Westcott

14 October: The 91st Bomb Group with B-17Fs arrived at Bassingbourn temporarily

10 October: The 91st BG moved to Kimbolton

13 October: Kimbolton was found unsuitable and the 91st BG returned to Bassingbourn whilst it was still under RAF control

## 1943

4 March: The 91st BG received a Distinguished Unit Citation for bombing marshalling yards at Hamm

April: Bassingbourn was handed over to USAAF 8th AF

20 April: The 94th flew a few missions from Bassingbourn

12 May: The 94th moved to Earls Colne

16 April: The 101st Provisional Combat Bomb Wing located its headquarters at Bassingbourn

7 November: The 91st began combat operations from Bassingbourn as one of the four 'pioneer' B-17 groups. The first eight months saw operations concentrated against German submarines, attacking U-boat pens in French ports or construction yards in Germany; secondary targets were Luftwaffe airfields, industrial targets, and marshalling yards

## 1944

11 January: The 91st BG successfully bombed its targets in spite of bad weather, inadequate fighter cover, and severe enemy attack, and was awarded a second Distinguished Unit Citation for the performance

June: The group contributed to the Battle of Normandy by bombing gun emplacements and troop concentrations near the beachhead area

24-25 July: Attacking enemy troop positions

August: The 91st BG bombed ahead of the front lines near Caen

December-January 1945: The 91st BG attacked communications during the Battle of the Bulge

## 1945

Spring: In support of Operation Varsity, striking airfields, bridges, and railways

25 April: The 91st Bomb Group ceased combat missions

June/July: The 91st BG withdrew from Bassingbourn and returned to the US
10 July: Bassingbourn was officially returned to the RAF to become one of the
main bases for long-range transport aircraft

**Closure:**
The barracks became the home of the Army Training Regiment Bassingbourn in
1993.

**Current status:**
Most of the original wartime buildings remain in Army use, including three of the
four C Type hangars, runways, perimeter track, Ops block, and pillboxes. In
1970, No. 2484 (Bassingbourn) Squadron Air Training Corps began using the
airfield.

## Haunted RAF Bassingbourn

*Source: Bruce Barrymore Halpenny,* Ghost Stations, *1986 (pp. 143-4)*
Peter Hyde whilst doing an After Flight service on a Canberra PR.3 in October
1968 called to another fitter, whom he believed to be in the rear cockpit, and to
whom he had been chatting away, to ask how long he would be. There was no one
in there.

Having heard other ground crew talking about the airman haunting the flight
line, Peter, having nothing better to do, jumped into the truck outside the office and
drove over there. As he approached the last pan he drove slowly round in a circle
and received two loud thumps on the side of the truck. Not stopping to investigate,
he raced back to the office, where the truck was found to be empty and no cause
for the bangs could be found.

The Airman at Bassingbourn has been seen by staff stationed there and numerous
people who have ventured onto the old runways. Alan Jones was an American who
served at Bassingbourn. He states that he saw an airman in American-style flying
gear walk across to a parked B-17 on the dispersal pan and around the back of the
tail section. Thinking it was one of his colleagues he called out, and walked towards
the aircraft following the airman, but there was no one around when he got there.

*Source: Army Rumour Service Forum, 28 November 2006*
There were two padres at Bassingbourn, one of whom had an experience whereby
on one winter's evening a chap entered and in an American voice asked for a chat.
He looked up to see an American airman in full flying kit in front of him – who
simply vanished. The other padre also spoke of seeing an airman sitting in the
chapel, who again vanished.

The medical centre had been the mortuary during the war and the staff refused
to go to the store in the dark. They all stated that it was freezing cold and doors

would close of their own accord. At least two of them believed they had seen ghosts of American airmen.

*Source: Keypublishing Aviation Forum,*
*1 February 2010*
A TA soldier of 100 Regiment RA whilst on dry firing exercises at Bassingbourn between 1993 and 1999 was told that the main gymnasium was supposed to be haunted, allegedly because of a suicide there.

*Source: Keypublishing Aviation Forum,*
*24 September 2010*
A witness had a trying time in an empty Second World War hangar. As he was trying to sleep there, he attested to hearing strange noises all night whilst on a Civil Contingency Reaction Force exercise. The attendees were to be sleeping in the hangar for the night, but for the first night there was just him. He set his sleeping bag up in one corner of the hangar, an Auster in another corner. The hangar doors were open.

A lot of noises started to be heard, more than the usual grunts and groans of a cooling down hangar. It sounded like something being worked on, with things being moved around, dropped, picked up, and scrapings. Getting up and walking down the hangar to the doors, he heard that the sounds were now coming from behind him inside the hangar. Being a hardy soul, he went back to his sleeping bag, put his earplugs in, and went to sleep.

*Source: Keypublishing Aviation Forum,*
*24 September 2010*
The Curator of the Bassingbourn Tower museum attests that it is haunted, for both he and his wife have heard strange noises in a supposedly empty hangar. His wife on several occasions, when working on her own in one of the offices attached to the hangar, has felt something brush past her

As he was relating his experiences, a loud clang was heard from inside the hangar. Unlocking the door of the otherwise sealed hangar, he went in and found nothing untoward. The sound he had heard was likened to that of a wrench or spanner being dropped from a height.

*Source: Keypublishing Aviation Forum,*
*4 January 2011*
A former Army recruit at Bassingbourn described hearing men going into the wash block at 5.30 a.m., hearing the taps running and voices chatting, but on investigation found that there was nobody there and the sinks were all dry and unused.

The tale generally related is of a returning B-17 crash-landing into the block during the Second World War.

# Bicester

Western Area
No. 3 Group
No. 1 Group
No. 6 Group
No. 7 Group
No. 92 Group
No. 70 Group

| | |
|---|---|
| County: | Oxfordshire |
| Location: | 1½ miles N of Bicester |
| OS Ref.: | SP 598245 |
| Opened: | 1917 |
| Closed: | 06/2004 |
| Pundit code: | BC |
| Control Tower: | Pre-war Fort Type 1959/34 (brick) |
| Condition: | In use |
| Runways: | Grass, NW-SE 1,200 yards, SW-NE 1,100 yards |
| Hardstandings: | 41 tarmac pans |
| Hangars: | A Type – 2, C Type – 2 |
| Ad., tech. & barr.: | Permanent to the NE of the airfield |
| Population: | RAF Officers – 172, OR – 1,639, WAAF Officers – 13, OR – 587 |
| Sat. airfield(s): | Weston-on-the-Green (RLG), Turweston (RLG), Finmere (RLG), Hinton-in-the-Hedges (RLG) |
| Decoy airfield(s): | Grendon Underwood Q/K |

## History to 1946:

The airfield, sited on the north-east side of Bicester, was a large grass area provided with various temporary buildings laid out in 1917 as part of the expansion of the Royal Flying Corps' training facilities.

### 1918

June: No. 118 Squadron arrived from Catterick as a Night Bomber Unit without aircraft; the squadron was destined to equip with the HP 0/400 bomber, but this never happened due to there being no further need for additional RFC squadrons of this type

November: No. 118 Squadron disbanded

1 October: No. 44 Training Depot Station arrived from Port Meadow with Avro 504s, Pups, and F2bs, but by this time there was little need for training and the unit was run down

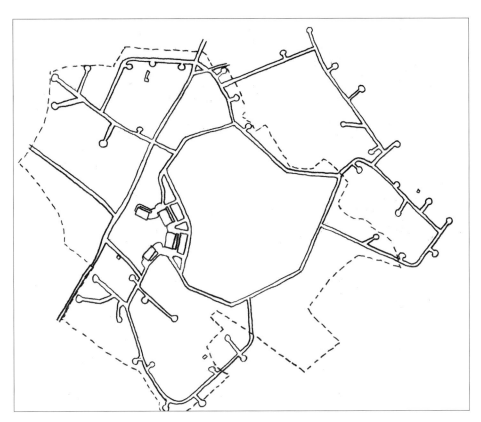

Bicester

## 1919

12 February: No. 2 Squadron, which had been reduced to a cadre at Genech, arrived at Bicester

August: No. 44 TDS was redesignated as No. 44 Training Squadron

8 September: No. 5 Squadron arrived from Hangelar

December: No. 44 TS was disbanded

## 1920

20 January: Nos 2 & 5 Squadrons disbanded

March: Bicester was closed

## 1925

The former airfield at Bicester was chosen as the location for an Expansion Period bomber station. Construction at the airfield was of the typical permanent buildings for technical and administration, which were placed within a pentagonal area, one hangar being on the south-west side and another on the south-east. The airfield surface remained a roughly oval, grass landing area

**1928**
January: RAF Bicester opened
10 January: No. 100 Squadron arrived from Spitalgate with Hawker Horsleys
14 April: No. 100 Squadron departed for Weston Zoyland
19 May: No. 100 Squadron returned

**1930**
November: No. 100 Squadron departed for Donibristle to become a Torpedo
    Bomber Squadron
November 5: No/ 33 Squadron arrived from Eastchurch with Hawker Harts

**1934**
27 November: No. 33 Squadron moved to Upper Heyford
1 December: No. 101 Squadron arrived from Andover with Sidestrands

**1935**
January: No. 101 Squadron received Overstrands

**1936**
1 April: Bicester was transferred to the Western Area
30 April: Bicester was transferred to No. 3 Group
17 August: Bicester was transferred to No. 1 Group
21 September: Bicester Station Headquarters formed
25 November: No. 48 Squadron re-formed from 'C' Flight of No. 101 Squadron
16 December: No. 48 Squadron moved to Manston

**1937**
11 January: No. 144 Squadron re-formed at Bicester from 'C' Flight of No. 101
    Squadron with 4 Overstrands but received Ansons by the end of the month
9 February: No. 144 Squadron moved to Hemswell
15 March: No. 90 Squadron formed at Bicester from 'A' Flight of No. 101 Squadron
    with Hinds
May: No. 90 Squadron converted to Blenheim 1s
16 August: No. 217 Squadron arrived from Tangmere with Anson 1s
11 September: No. 217 Squadron returned to Tangmere

**1938**
June: No. 101 Squadron received Blenheim 1s

**1939**
March: No. 90 Squadron received Blenheim IVs
April: No. 101 Squadron received Blenheim IVs
6 May: No. 101 Squadron moved to West Raynham

9 May: Nos 12 & 142 Squadrons arrived from Andover with Battles.

10 May: No. 90 Squadron moved to West Raynham

2 September: Nos 12 & 142 Squadrons departed for Berry-au-Bac

17 September: No. 108 Squadron arrived from Bassingbourn with 18 Blenheim Is and 6 Ansons; designated a No. 2 Group Training Squadron

18 September: No. 104 Squadron arrived from Bassingbourn with 18 Blenheim Is and 6 Ansons; designated a No. 6 Group Training Squadron

## 1940

8 April: Nos 104 & 108 Squadrons merge to form No. 13 OTU in No. 6 Group with 36 Blenheim Is and 12 Ansons

May: No. 13 OTU's establishment was 28 + 4 Blenheim IVs, 12 + 4 Blenheim Is & 12 + 4 Ansons

15 July: No. 13 OTU transferred to No. 7 Group

## 1941

August: No. 13 OTU's establishment was 48 Blenheims, 16 Ansons, and 2 Lysanders

1 September: No. 7 Group Communication Flight arrived from Wyton with Proctor Is

27 October: The Ferry Training Flight (FTF) formed, attached to No. 13 OTU, to train crews to ferry Blenheims overseas

## 1942

21 January: The FTF became No. 1442 Flight

11 May: No. 7 Group CF renamed as No. 92 Group CF

3 July: The Beam Approach Calibration Flight (BACF) arrived from Watchfield with Ansons, Masters, and Oxfords

1 August: No. 1442 Flight disbanded

14 September: No. 92 Group CF moved to Little Horwood

20 November: The BACF was redesignated as 1551 BACF

## 1943

April: Mitchells and Bostons were introduced

14 April : 1551 BACF disbanded into the Signals Development Unit at Hinton-in-the-Hedges but kept B & C Flights at Bicester.

1 June: No. 1655 Mosquito CU re-formed at the RLG of Finmere; No. 13 OTU establishment was 29 Blenheims, 10 Bostons, 9 Mitchells, 15 Mosquito IVs, 5 Mosquito (duals), 8 Oxfords, 6 Ansons, and 5 Martinets

1 July: No. 1655 Mosquito CU moved to Marham and Bomber Command; No. 13 OTU was transferred to No. 70 Group

28 August: The SDU had moved to Hinton-in-the-Hedges

1 November: No. 13 OTU was transferred to No. 9 Group and Mosquitos were reintroduced

**1944**
1 February: No. 420 Repair and Salvage Unit for No. 84 Group formed
19 February: No. 420 R&SU moved to Stapleford Tawney
April: The last of the Blenheims were phased out
15 September: No. 13 OTU was transferred to No. 12 Group
12 October: No. 13 OTU moved to Harwell and No. 2 Group
7 May: No. 34 Air Stores Park arrived from North Weald
2 September: No. 34 ASP moved to Mandeville

**1945**
1 January: No. 246 MU formed from the Fighter Command Forward Equipment
    Unit and remained until April 1948

**Closure:**
On 31 March 1976, RAF Bicester was placed under Abingdon on care and
    maintenance. Later it transferred to the Army and on 22 November 1978,
    it reopened as an RAF station. In June 2004, the RAF Gliding and Soaring
    Association moved to RAF Halton.

**Current status:**
The MoD still uses a part of the airfield for Army training. The main use of the site
    is now civilian gliding, being home to both the Windrushers Gliding Club and
    the Oxford University Gliding Club. In 2002, Cherwell District Council listed
    the area as a Conservation Area.

## Haunted RAF Bicester

Several instances of paranormal activity have been reported in the vicinity of the
Control Tower and runway 24. The threshold of runway 24 has several 'cold' areas
that cannot be explained. In addition, many visitors to the airfield have claimed
to have seen a young woman in wartime overalls entering the Tower, and when
investigated it was found to be locked up.

*Source: ghostfinderukforum.com,*
*22 February 2010*
Matt wrote that he was formerly a member of the MoD security at the airfield,
and only at the start of 2010 did they move out. When he worked there he
experienced footsteps which seemed to follow him around, and the sounds of
doors slamming which on investigation proved to be locked. On one occasion the
main gates unlocked and opened by themselves. This, as can be imagined, caused a
massive security search of the site but no one was found to account for the opening
gate.

*Source: Dark Knight Paranormal*

An investigation was conducted at the airfield by Dark Knight Paranormal, West Yorkshire Paranormal, and the Ridgeway Ghost Hunters in November 2011. It is said that from the outset paranormal activity was experienced.

# Biggin Hill

No. 11 Fighter Group
No. 46 Group, Transport Command
Reserve Command

| | |
|---|---|
| County: | Kent |
| Location: | 5 miles SE of Bromley |
| OS Ref.: | TQ 415606 |
| Opened: | 1917 |
| Closed: | 05/1992 |
| Pundit code: | BH |
| Control Tower: | A. Watch Office for Satellite Fighter Stations 7335/42 |
| | B. Watch Office 5223a/51 |
| Condition: | A. Demolished |
| | B. In use |
| Runways: | Grass field; asphalt. Grass field 710 yards E-W and 2,000 yards on the longest SW-NW axis; landings were also possible N-S (1,666 yards) and NE-SW (1,333 yards); 1939, runway (026) 1,670 x 50 yards, later two secondary runways (045) 1,000 x 50 yards and (108) 950 x 50 yards |
| Hardstandings: | 2 unique |
| Hangars: | SE – 19, Pens SE – 12 |
| Ad., tech. & barr.: | In 1929 an extensive building programme was begun whereby a new technical site was constructed on the northern perimeter, including hangars, workshops, barrack blocks, and administration offices. The Officers' Mess was a large house on the opposite side of the Bromley-Westerham road to the main camp. The station headquarters office at the south end of the RAF Biggin Hill West Camp site was built to a 1927 design. In 1938, sixteen married quarters and a radio receiving building were among the new additions |
| Population: | RAF Officers – 162, OR – 2,231, WAAF Officers – 14, OR – 737 |
| Sat. airfield(s): | Penshurst, Detling, Kenley, Redhill, Friston, Gravesend, Gatwick, Lympne, Hawkinge, West Malling |

*History to 1946:*

**1916**
February: Biggin Hill officially opened as an RFC Signals Unit

**1938**
Squadrons: 32, 79, No. 1 Anti-Aircraft Co-operation Unit
After the Munich crisis, buildings were camouflaged, air-raid shelters were dug
     and a large number of trees planted to camouflage the aerodrome

**1939**
Squadrons: 3, 32, 79, 229 (det) & 601

**1940**
Squadrons: 32, 42, 56 (det), 64, 66, 72, 74, 79, 92, 141 (det), 213 (det), 229 (det),
     242, 601, 610, No. 421 Flight, and No. 6 Radio Maintenance Unit
15 August: A formation of Bf 110s passed to the west of the airfield; one was
     brought down within sight of the aerodrome
18 August: The first attack on Biggin began at about 1.30 p.m., with most of the
     bombs falling on the adjacent golf course. Those that fell on the airfield caused
     only slight damage. Throughout the next two weeks, the aerodrome suffered
     almost daily air raids, the buildings of the station were put out of commission
     and the efficiency of the station was greatly reduced. All available men were
     fully occupied filling craters, clearing rubble, and keeping the aerodrome
     operational
30 August: A high level raid at midday cratered the landing area. At 6 p.m., 9 Ju
     88s dropped 16 HE bombs, six of which scored direct hits on the technical
     site. A No. 32 Squadron Hurricane, N2540, was destroyed on the ground and
     casualties were 39 killed and 26 wounded. Most of the buildings were destroyed
     or so badly damaged they were too unsafe to be used. The hangars in the North
     Camp, the transport yard stores, barrack stores, armoury, guardroom and
     meteorological office, the Station Institute, and other workshops were all hit.
     All power, gas and water mains were severed and the telephone lines running
     north were cut in three places. An air-raid shelter received a direct hit, killing
     many of those inside
31 August: Biggin was hit at 1 p.m. and at 5.30 p.m. Hangars in the South Camp
     were badly damaged together with the triple-bay hangar on the northern side.
     The Ops Room received a direct hit and communications to the Sector Ops
     Block were severed. The warrant officers' quarters were rendered unsafe,
     windows in the Officers' Mess broken, and the temporary telephone system
     was completely destroyed
1 September: More bombs dropped from a high level attack at 1.30 p.m., leaving
     Biggin capable of operating only a single squadron. Sections were dispersed

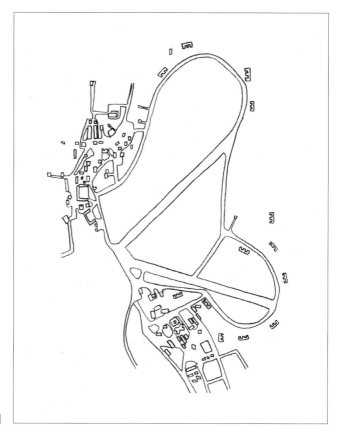

Biggin Hill

to Keston because of the danger from collapsing buildings. The main road through the camp was blocked by two large craters, and all services and communications were out of action

6 September: Another attack, with most of the bombs falling along the Westerham road

## 1941
Squadrons: 66, 74, 92, 124, 264, 287 (det), 401, 609 & 610

## 1942
Squadrons: 19, 72, 124, 133, 222, 287 (det), 340, 401, 602, 609 & 611

July: Biggin Hill's score of enemy aircraft destroyed had reached 900

August: American squadrons were based at the airfield; Nos 2 & 307 Pursuit Squadrons came for a month's experience

## 1943
Squadrons: 1, 41, 287 (det), 340, 341, 401, 411, 412, 485, 611 & No. 403 Repair and Salvage Unit

20 January: A low level raid gave ample time to scramble; 6 German aircraft were downed for no loss to the RAF

**1944**

Squadrons: 91, 154, 287 (det), 322, 345, 401, 411, 412 & No. 410 Repair and Salvage Unit

13 June: The first V-1 flying bombs were launched

June: The close proximity of Biggin Hill to London brought it within the defensive balloon barrage belt. The end of the station had to be evacuated to allow the balloon crews to take over. Six V-1s crashed inside the aerodrome boundary

October: Balloon Command moved out

**1945**

Squadrons: 154, 168, 322, 436 (det) & 314 (USAAF)

June: Biggin Hill was transferred to No. 46 Group

No. 168 (RCAF) Squadron and No. 314 (USAAF) Squadron operated with Dakotas

**1946**

Squadrons: 19, 436 (det), 600, 615 & London University Air Squadron

August: Biggin Hill was transferred to Reserve Command and Auxiliary Squadrons were the sole occupants

December: A fire broke out in the small St George's Chapel which, despite every effort, was totally gutted

**Closure:**

The Officer and Aircrew Selection Centre moved to Cranwell in May 1992, and this marked the end of active RAF involvement.

**Current status:**

London Biggin Hill Airport

## Haunted RAF Biggin Hill

Airmen dressed in Second World War flying kit have been seen walking in and out of the deserted buildings that were locked and bolted at the time. Others have been seen on the airfield and in the neighbourhood of the airfield, and there have been many accounts of a phantom aircraft heard in the area.

The experiences at St George's Chapel by Wing Commander (Retired) David Duval and other accounts from the Biggin Hill area are detailed in Bob Ogley's excellent book *Ghosts of Biggin Hill*.

*Source: Bob Ogley,* Ghosts of Biggin Hill
In about 1998, Wing Commander Alan Jones received a report from a sergeant who was in the Officers' Mess early in the morning checking one of the empty bedrooms, when he witnessed the apparition of an airman in flying kit sitting in a chair, who promptly disappeared.

*Source: Wood,* Military Ghosts, *2010 (p. 131)*
Wood writes that according to rumour, a lone Spitfire can sometimes be seen and heard over the airfield on a warm summer's evening. The aircraft does a victory roll and then disappears.

Wood also reports that the sounds of bombing have been heard on the airfield, and also the sound of an aircraft falling earthwards then crashing in an explosion. On runway 215 aircrew in Second World War flying gear have been seen walking. Lastly, in the Officers' Mess the apparition of a pilot officer in Second World War flying gear is said to stand on the staircase.

*Source: Haunted Airfields in Britain website (defunct)*
Mr Aldridge was an ex-officer who spent many years on the airfield while in the RAF and later as a civilian worker at the base. It had been reported to senior officers on at least three occasions at dusk that an officer had been seen entering the chapel in full flying kit, but on investigation no one was found inside. He decided to visit the chapel to say a few words for his brother who was killed in action. On this occasion, as he was kneeling down facing the front of the chapel, he heard the door open behind and someone enter. Footsteps approached and then followed a shuffling noise as if the person was taking a seat behind him. They then seemingly cleared their throat softly and started making a quiet intermittent humming sound. Turning around, he saw that there was no one there, and in some terror he fled the chapel. Three to four weeks later, as he was walking past the chapel's main entrance, someone shouted his name as if from inside the building, so he went inside to see who it was but again there was no one there.

*Source: Keypublishing Aviation Forum, 13 March 2004*
Martin wrote, 'I myself have a couple of times heard a Merlin but never seen anything. On one occasion when I heard it, it was winter and snowing.'

*Source: Keypublishing Aviation Forum, 26 February 2007*
A man working for a security company in the late 1980s or early 90s was on duty during an air show weekend and security for the event was tight. Nobody was allowed in a certain area. In the early hours of the morning he went outside for a cigarette and a short walk, and whilst walking was waved to by a man in a full flying suit of 1940s style. The figure approached him and said, 'Nice evening for flying,' and then walked straight past. Looking around immediately after the figure had passed him revealed that there was nobody there.

# Boscombe Down

No. 3 Group, Bomber Command
No. 16 Group, Coastal Command
No. 4 Group, Bomber Command

| | |
|---|---|
| County: | Wiltshire |
| Location: | 1½ miles E of Amesbury |
| OS Ref.: | SU 182398 |
| Opened: | 1926 |
| Closed: | N/A |
| Pundit code: | BD |
| Control Tower: | Watch Office for all Commands 12779/41 |
| Condition: | Unknown |
| Runways: | Grass, 1944-45 concrete, (240) 3,000 x 100 yards; grass, WNW-ESE 1,400 yards, SSE-NNW 1,400 yards |
| Hardstandings: | loop (BRC Fabric) – 14, pans (100 feet diameter) – 2, concrete square (150 x 150 feet) – 1 |
| Hangars: | Type A – 1, Type C – 1, Blisters – 12, GS Shed (204 x 173 feet) – 3, GS Shed (174 x 100 feet) – 1 |
| Ad., tech. & barr.: | Permanent Expansion Period style and content |
| Population: | RAF Officers – 111, OR – 2,529, WAAF Officers – 8, OR – 559 |
| Decoy airfield(s): | South Newton Q |

## History to 1946:

**1917**
Boscombe Down opened as a flying training unit
October: No. 6 Training Depot Station formed

**1920**
April: The airfield was deemed surplus to requirements and sold back to the
   original landowner

**1927**
The land was acquired again and work started on restoration of some of the old
   buildings, the construction of new buildings and work on the landing area to create a
   permanent station for two bomber squadrons as part of the Wessex Bombing Area

**1930**
1 September: The station reopened although it was not complete

A number of bomber squadrons were present at Boscombe Down during the
1930s

## 1935

16 September: No. 214 Squadron re-formed from a nucleus provided by 'B' Flight
of No. 9 Squadron, as a night bomber with Virginia Xs

16 September: No. 97 Squadron arrived from RAF Catfoss equipped with
Heyfords

15 October: Nos 9 & 214 Squadrons moved to Aldergrove

## 1936

Boscombe Down transferred to No. 3 Group

1 November: No. 78 Squadron re-formed with Heyfords from 'B' Flight of No. 10
Squadron; No. 166 Squadron re-formed with Heyfords from 'A' Flight of No.
97 Squadron

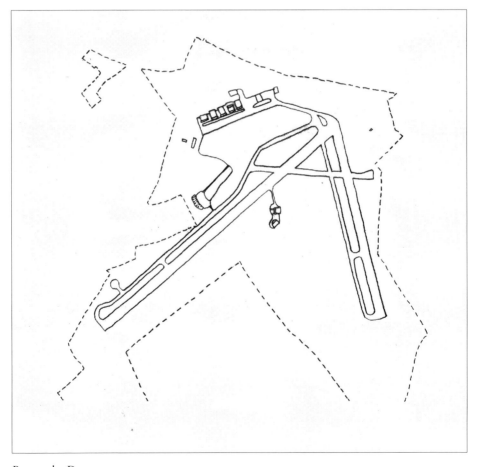

Boscombe Down

**1937**

Squadrons: 10, 51, 58, 78, 88, 97, 166, 217 & 224

February: Boscombe Down transferred to No. 16 Group Coastal Command

15 March: No. 217 Squadron re-formed in a General Reconnaissance role equipped with Ansons

8 August: No. 150 Squadron re-formed as a Light Bomber Unit with Battles

**1938**

Squadrons: 51, 58, 88, 150, 218 & the Special Duties Flight

1 July: Boscombe Down transferred to No. 4 Group

**1939**

Squadrons: 88, 150, 218, Aeroplane & Armament Experimental Establishment, No. 4 Group Experimental Flight, Blind Approach Training and Development Unit, and the Lysander Flight

August: Nos 88 & 150 Squadrons became No. 75 Wing with Boscombe Down as HQ

2 September: No. 75 Wing moved to Auberive-sur-Suippe

9 September: The Aeroplane & Armament Experimental Establishment arrived from RAF Martlesham Heath. The original two squadrons were subdivided: the Armament Testing Squadron gained small divisions dealing with navigation and radio, while the Performance Testing Squadron was divided into Flights, 'A' for fighters, 'B' for bombers, and 'C' for all multi-seat single-engine types including naval aircraft

18 September: The Blind Approach Training and Development Unit (BATDU) formed with a small number of Ansons

20 November: The Lysander Flight formed to undertake Special Duties Operations in France

**1940**

Squadrons: 35, 56, 109, 249, A&AEE, BATDU, Wireless Intelligence Development Unit, Handling Flight, Bomber Development Flight, and the High Altitude Flight

30 October: BATDU was renamed the Wireless Intelligence Development Unit

November 6: The Bomber Development Unit formed to undertake trials of new items of bombing equipment

November: The Handling Squadron was at Boscombe Down, staying until August 1942

5 November: No. 35 Squadron re-formed with Halifax Is

December: The High Altitude Flight arrived, staying until September 1944

10 December: The Wireless Intelligence Development Unit disbanded and re-formed as No. 109 Squadron

30 December: The High Altitude Flight was at Boscombe Down until September 1944

**1941**

Squadrons: 109, A&AEE, HF, BDF, HAF, Handling Squadron, Intensive Flying Development Unit, and the Aircraft Gun Mounting Establishment

11 June: The Handling Flight arrived at Boscombe as a detachment from the Central Flying School at Hullavington, with the duty of preparing handling notes for each type of aircraft in service

15 November: The Intensive Flying Development Unit was at Boscombe Down until June 1942

**1942**

Squadrons: 109, A&AEE, HAF, Handling Squadron, IFDU, AGME, Intensive Flying Development Flight, Intensive Flying Development Flight, and the Meteorological Research Flight

28 April: The Handling Flight gained squadron status

June: The Intensive Flying Development Flight formed at Boscombe Down

**1943**

Squadrons A&AEE, HAF, IFDU, MRF, Test Pilots' School

21 June: The Test Pilots' Training Flight became the Test Pilots' School within the A&AEE, to provide suitably trained pilots for testing duties in aeronautical research and development establishments within the service and the industry

28 August: The Handling Squadron joined the Empire Central Flying School at Hullavington

**1944**

Squadrons A&AEE, HAF, IFDU, MRF, TPS, and the Empire Test Pilots' School

28 July: The Test Pilots' School was renamed the Empire Test Pilots' School. The construction of the first runway commenced, but it was not completed until 1945

**1945**

Squadrons A&AEE, IFDU, ETPS, and the MRF

October: The Empire Test Pilots' School moved to Cranfield in No. 23 Group

**1946**

Squadrons A&AEE, IFDU, and the MRF

A civil aircraft test section was added to the strength at Boscombe Down, responsible to the Civil Aviation Authority for issuing Certificates of Airworthiness for transport aircraft

**Current status:**

Boscombe Down is an operational RAF station. In spite of all the buildings constructed in the 1930s, and the rebuild after the war, one of the original

1919 two-bay hangars still remains. Occupied by a variety of units over the years, it currently houses the Establishment archives.

**Museum:**
The RAF Boscombe Down museum at the airfield is accessible only by prior arrangement. Website: http://boscombedownaviationcollection.co.uk/index.htm

## Haunted RAF Boscombe Down

*Source: Alan C Wood,* Military Ghosts, *2010*
In the 1940s, Alan Wood was stationed at Netheravon, but one of his jobs was to drive to Boscombe Down and get the daily meteorological report. In 1947, during a chat at Boscombe, Alan was told that a ghost haunted Airmen's Billet 19. An airman in Billet 19 had asked to be taken up for a passenger ride and died when the aircraft crashed. In the night after this a friend of the airman was awakened by an icy cold hand gripping his neck. He jumped out of bed and saw a transparent bluish light and heard the dead airman's voice saying, 'I want my kit.' RAF accommodation H blocks were on the site of Billet 19 in the 1950s.

*Source: Bruce Barrymore Halpenny,* Ghost Stations, *1986 (p. 68)*
Barrymore Halpenny adds that the haunting continued until a body called the Psychic Research Unit was called in, and after an investigation advised that Hut 19 be emptied and sealed up for one year. Apparently the hut was reopened in September 1948.

*Source: unexplainable.net*
A pilot who was killed when his aircraft crashed into the sea has been heard walking about RAF Boscombe Down. The apparition is also claimed to leave wet footprints on the floor.

*Source: Keypublishing Aviation Forum, 16 September 2010*
The author states that she had a friend who had worked at Boscombe Down painting the stairs. One afternoon, receiving a strong feeling in one of the hangars, he had to get out quickly, but with only one more staircase to paint he thought he would put up with the feeling and get the job done. However, upon arriving there, he found that it appeared to have already been hurriedly painted.

# Bourn

No. 3 Bomber Group
No. 8 Bomber Group

| | |
|---|---|
| County: | Cambridgeshire |
| Location: | 6 miles W of Cambridge |
| OS Ref.: | TL 341595 |
| Opened: | 1941 |
| Closed: | 1948 |
| Pundit code: | AU |
| Control Tower: | Bomber Satellite Type Watch Office 15898/40, 15956/40 and 17821/40 |
| Condition: | Demolished |
| Runways: | (065) 1,430 x 50 yards, (007) 1,180 x 50 yards, and (168) 1,050 x 50 yards; 1942: (065) 1,960 yards, (007) 1,600 yards, and (168) 1,400 yards |
| Hardstandings: | 36 pan type aircraft standings had been put down during 1940-41. In 1942, when upgrade work was completed, only 27 of the original pan standings remained, although 9 loop types were added |
| Hangars: | T2 – 5, B1 – 1: A T2 hangar was located S of runway head 13 and a B1 nearby to the W. A second T2 stood north of Bourn Grange. In 1943, 3 T2 hangars were erected in the Grange Farm area to provide cover for Stirlings sent for repair and modification by a branch of Short Brothers |
| Bomb stores: | Located off the SE in Bucket Hill Plantation between runway heads 01 and 31 |
| Ad., tech. & barr.: | The technical site lay on the W side near Great Common Farm. Dispersed camp sites were situated to the W and S along Broad Way consisting of 6 domestic, 1 WAAF, and 2 communal blocks, and a sick quarters, the last being right beside Bourn Grange. Accommodation was in an assortment of huts, mainly Nissen, but some requisitioned buildings were used in the early days |
| Population: | RAF Officers – 185, OR – 1642, WAAF Officers – 4, OR – 230 |

Bomber Command lost 135 aircraft from Bourn: 19 Wellingtons, 32 Stirlings, 60 Lancasters and 24 Mosquitos.


## History to 1946:


### 1940

The site bordering the south side of the old A45 to St Neots was acquired for a satellite airfield for Oakington under No. 3 Group

Some four hundred acres of farmland between Bourn Grange in the south, Great Common Farm in the west and Highfield Farm in the east were eventually taken over for the airfield, which was not completed until the winter of 1941/42, although it is reported to have been used by Oakington during the summer of 1941.

## 1942
11 February: No. 101 Squadron arrive from Oakington with Wellingtons
11 August: No. 101 Squadron moved to Stradishall
13 August: No. 15 Squadron arrived from Wyton with Stirlings
15 August: Bourn became the headquarters airfield of the newly formed Pathfinder Force, and No. 15 Squadron's Stirlings set off on their first raid from the airfield

## 1943
The expanding No. 8 Group acquired Bourn
14 April: No. 15 Squadron was moved on to Mildenhall to make way for Pathfinder units
18 April: No. 97 Squadron arrived from Woodhall Spa and No. 5 Group with Lancasters

## 1944
23 March: No. 105 Squadron arrived from Marham with Mosquitos, when the airfield was scheduled to be upgraded to a very heavy bomber airfield
18 April: No. 97 Squadron moved to Coningsby to continue as a Pathfinder unit within No. 5 Group
28 October: No. 1696 (Bomber) Defence Training Flight arrived from Gransden Lodge with 12 Spitfires, 6 Hurricanes, and 1 Oxford
29 November: No. 1323 Automatic Gun Laying Turret Flight formed with Lancasters
18 December: No. 162 Squadron re-formed with a nucleus from No. 105 Squadron

## 1945
1 January: No. 1323 AGLT Flight departed for Warboys
2/3 May: The last Mosquito operation from Bourn was flown
28 June: No. 1696 (Bomber) Defence Training Flight departed for Warboys
29 June: No. 105 Squadron moved to Upwood
6 July: No. 162 Squadron moved to Blackbushe and Transport Command; thereafter Bourn was placed on care and maintenance and no further flying units were based there

**Closure:**
RAF Bourn was closed in 1948.

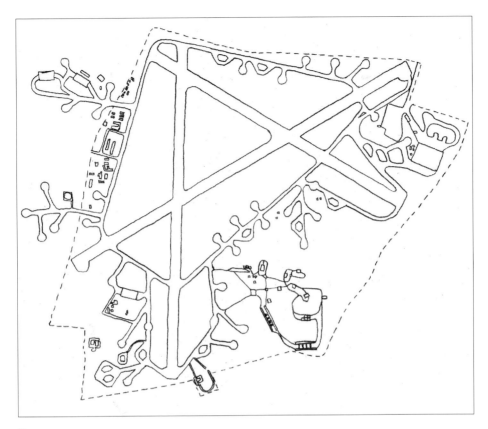

Bourn

**Current status:**

The airfield was returned to agriculture during the 1950s. A heliport was established close to the old Stirling hangars near the Cambridge road. The Highfield Farm area has now been developed into an industrial estate.

## Haunted RAF Bourn

*Source: Bruce Barrymore Halpenny,* Ghost Stations, *1986 (pp. 32-3)*

In June 1952, Helen Bevan and her friend Valerie Sager were hitch-hiking along the main A45 from Cambridge towards St Neots. It was warm, pleasant, and still as they passed the American War Cemetery at about 5 p.m., and they were engrossed in some gossip when Valerie said, 'What's that music?' At first Helen couldn't hear any music, but then caught the sound of a distant Big Band playing 'String of Pearls', which then gradually faded away. What puzzled them was exactly where the music was coming from, for they were in open countryside. There were no parked cars or lorries or houses which might have had a radio playing to account for the music. It was hard to tell the direction the music was coming from, but then it seemed to 'focus' in the area of some old Nissen huts. It was then that they realised that to their left was the remains of a disused airfield (Bourn), and they saw the runways, the distant Control Tower, and hangars. Then quite suddenly the music stopped and they heard men's voices singing, and laughter coming from the direction of the empty Nissen huts.

# Bovingdon

RAF No. 7 Bomber Group (Training)
USAAF 8th Air Force

| | |
|---|---|
| County: | Hertfordshire |
| Location: | 7 miles W of Watford |
| OS Ref.: | TL 005045 |
| Opened: | 15/06/1942 |
| Closed: | 1972 |
| Pundit code: | BV |
| USAAF Station: | 112 |
| Control Tower: | Watch Office with Met Section 518/40 (8936/40), with extended front and extra observation post on roof |
| Condition: | Demolished 2010 |
| Runways: | 3 concrete/tarmac, (220) 1,634 x 50 yards, (270) 1,433 x 50 yards, and (350) 1,300 x 50 yards |
| Hardstandings: | 36 loop and pan types |
| Hangars: | T2 – 4, between the E and SE runway heads and fronting the technical/administration area |
| Bomb stores: | NW of the airfield |
| Ad., tech. & barr.: | Between the E and SE runway heads; accommodation given as temporary |
| Population: | USAAF Officers – 635, OR – 2214 |

The 92nd lost 2 B-17 aircraft and crew, with 11 other casualties.

## *History to 1946:*

### 1941/42
A standard class airfield was constructed to the west of Bovingdon

### 1942
15 June: RAF Bovingdon opened and Bomber Command took up residence with aircraft of No. 7 Group for operational training

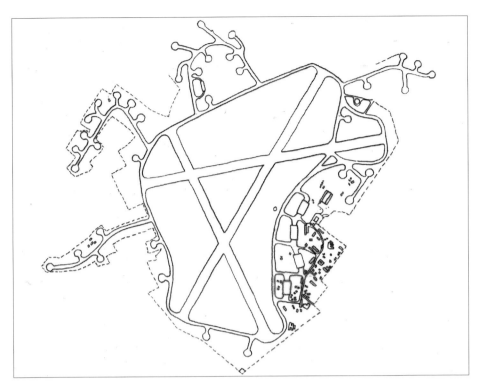

Bovingdon

August: the USAAC arrived at the airfield followed by the 92nd Bombardment Group from Florida

6 September: The 92nd BG flew a mission against the Avions Potez aircraft factory. One B-17 was last seen approaching the English coast but apparently left the formation with 5 enemy aircraft in pursuit; all the crew were killed

26 September: A diversion operation against Cherbourg

2 October: A diversion operation along the French coast

9 October: An operation against Lille and St Omer. One B-17E was last observed in flames over Holque; all the crew were killed and 7 other casualties in other aircraft resulted from the mission; 1 badly wounded airman baled out. There was also a mid-air crash of B-17s 19051 & 19021 at 24,000 feet above the coast of France. One made it back to base safely; the other made for the English coast, landing at Detling

21 October: An operation against Cherbourg airfield, but no bombs were dropped because of cloud cover

6 December: A diversion operation as 11 Combat Crew Replacement Centre (CCRC) was recalled while over base. The 92nd was withdrawn from combat and its B-17F bombers exchanged for the older B-17E bombers of the 97th BG. The 92nd then acted as an Operational Training Unit supplying combat crews to combat groups in the UK

### 1943

January: The 92nd BG moved to Alconbury. A number of B-17s and personnel from the 326th Bomb Squadron of the 92nd remained at Bovingdon to form the nucleus of 11 CCRU

28 April: Bovingdon was officially handed over to USAAF control as Station 112

May: The 326th was no longer under the operational control of the 92nd at Alconbury. Along with its training role, Bovingdon housed the 8th Air Force Headquarters and the Air Technical Section, both equipped with a variety of aircraft types

### 1944

September: 11 CCRU was disbanded and Bovingdon became the base for the European Air Transport Service for Americans returning to the US

### 1946

15 April: Bovingdon was returned to the RAF

**Closure:**

In 1969, all flying ceased at Bovingdon, and in 1976 all MoD property, except some married quarters, was sold off.

**Current status:**

HMP The Mount was built on the technical site and hangar area. The rest of the airfield is used for agriculture and landfill. The main runway and taxiways are still intact, though in a poor state of repair, and are used for markets and the occasional car rally.

## Haunted RAF Bovingdon

People walking their dogs in the area often report an invisible presence, and their animals howl and raise their hackles or run off. One of the odder phenomena at the airfield are the reports by several people of a strange mist that suddenly seems to appear, and, equally as suddenly, disappear. It is always described as being so dense that you cannot see through it.

*Source: Army Rumour Service Forum, 23 March 2007*

Sandhurst Block at Bovingdon is reputed to be haunted on the bottom floor, so much so that the duty sergeants wouldn't walk the corridors at night. The contributor adds a personal experience whilst he was rummaging in his locker, with both doors of his room open, and leaning on the left-hand side of the locker. For no discernible reason, the right-hand locker door slammed itself shut with violent force. As he writes, 'I physically jumped in the air and dived back. The other lad had shot up in his bed'.

*Source: Luton Paranormal Society*

Luton Paranormal Society conducted an investigation at the site of former RAF Bovingdon on 2 May 2008. During the course of the investigation, contacts with a medium were made and whispering was heard. Red lights and a yellow streak of light on the runway were seen at various times, and something amorphous, large, and white passed close to one of the investigators whilst on the runway area. The Bovingdon mist was seen on the runway, and investigators complained of the physical symptoms of headache and a pain in the ribs. Physical phenomena were also observed during the investigation: a dictaphone stopped recording, a walkie-talkie reset itself, trousers were tugged at, and a portable chair in a shoulder bag was pulled at. A pervading aura of sadness was also reported. The full report may be viewed on the Luton Paranormal website at www.lutonparanormal.com/reports.html.

*Source: Supernatural Shires website*

A strange, dense mist has been reported to appear on the runway seemingly from nowhere even on a clear summer's evening. This mist appeared to a colleague some years ago as he walked down the runway during the dead of night. He had gone there with other people who remained in the car at the time. The people who were in the car less than 20 feet from him also witnessed it and said the mist seemed to follow him, then he disappeared into it. The person caught in the mist turned around but could not see through it to the car; neither did he hear his friends in the car calling out to him. He walked back towards the car, and the mist disappeared as quickly as it had descended.

Another account of this mist occurred when two cars were travelling down the airfield some distance apart. The occupants of the car behind saw a mist in front of them appear from nowhere and seem to follow the car in front for a few moments before it disappeared.

The strong smell of what has been described as bubble or chewing gum has been reported by more than one person. The smell appears from nowhere on the airfield, lingers for a while, and then simply fades away.

The apparitions of uniformed airmen have been seen by people living in the area around the former airfield. They include the ghostly form of a person seen standing in the unused Control Tower. There are also a number of unexplained sounds heard at the airfield, including old aircraft engines, and Morse code.

# Bradwell Bay

No. 11 Group, Fighter Command

County:          Essex
Location:        6 miles NE of Southminster

| OS Ref.: | TM 005082 |
|---|---|
| Opened: | 1941 |
| Closed: | 01/12/45 |
| Pundit code: | RB |
| Control Tower: | Watch Office for Night Fighter Stations 12096/41 |
| Condition: | Converted into a house |
| Runways: | Concrete, tarmac – 3, (240) 1, 890 by 50 yards, (130) 1,400 by 50 yards, and (172) 1,000 by 50 yards |
| Hardstandings | TE – 12, Bomber pans – 3, TE protected pens – 24 |
| Hangars: | Bellman – 1, Blister – 12 |
| Ad., tech. & barr.: | Temporary accommodation |
| Population: | RAF Officers – 125, OR – 1,526, WAAF Officers – 7, OR – 445 |
| Sat. airfield(s): | Satellite of North Weald |

During the Second World War, 121 airmen lost their lives from this airfield.

## History to 1946:

Before the war an air-firing range existed on marshland known as Dengie Flats, which was used into the 1950s.

**1940**
A landing ground was created for refuelling purposes, but because of its strategic siting by the coast was developed as a grass-surfaced fighter satellite landing ground

**1941**
Squadron 23 (det)
February: Construction work began on Bradwell Bay and it became the only fighter airfield that was fitted with FIDO, a fog dispersal system to clear fog away from the runway by burning thousands of gallons of petrol
28 November: The station opened as an independent in Hornchurch Sector

**1942**
Squadrons: 23 (det), 264 (det) & 418
April: Bradwell Bay was declared operational
15 April: No. 418 (RCAF) Squadron arrived from Debden with Boston IIIs. Almost nightly the Bostons operated against airfields on the Continent, or against transport targets, and played a part during the 1,000 bomber raids

**1943**
Squadrons: 29, 56, 157, 198, 247, 418, 488 & 605

1 June: Bradwell Bay was transferred to the North Weald Sector

30 July: Eight crews of 141 Squadron from Wittering with Beaufighters flew a Serrate anti-radar operation from Bradwell Bay

August: No. 56 Squadron with Hawker Typhoon IBs arrived from Manston to mount attacks on shipping off the Dutch coast 31 August: A Halifax of 76 Squadron back from a raid belly-landed, having been badly shot up by fighters

12 December: Mosquito XII HK227 was shot down by Beaufighter V8619 of No. 68 Squadron from Coltishall

## 1944

Squadrons: 3, 64, 124, 125 (det), 126, 219, 278, 310, 312, 313, 488, 501, 605 & 611

30 August: Bradwell Bay received its first fighter Wing comprising Nos 64, 126 & 611 Spitfire Squadrons

31 August: The Bradwell Bay Wing went into action patrolling the Arras area and supporting a Bomber Command operation

December: The Bradwell Bay Wing disbanded

29 December: The Bradwell Bay Wing was re-formed from Nos 310, 312 & 313 Squadrons. Nos 310 & 131 Squadrons arrived from North Weald with Spitfire VIIs

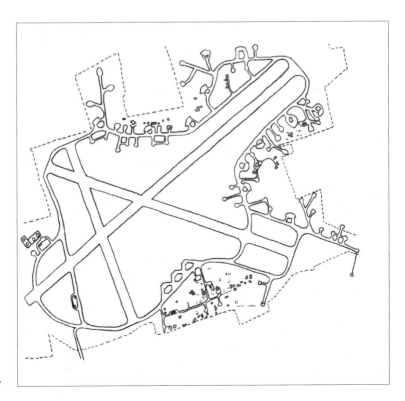

Bradwell Bay

**1945**

Squadrons: 13, 19, 25, 85, 124, 126, 151, 287, 309, 310, 312, 313, 456, 501, 2ATC & 2 APS

27 February: The Spitfire Wing departed for Manston

1 March: No. 151 Squadron arrived from Hunsdon with Mosquito NF Mk 30s to intercept V-1s and their carriers but soon switched to night bomber support

25 April: The last operations were flown from Bradwell Bay

17 May: No. 151 Squadron departed for Predannack

15 June: No. 456 Squadron disbanded

November: The main party of 2 APS staged through Bradwell Bay on posting from Hawkinge to Spilsby, their Masters and Martinets being the last aircraft to use the station

**Closure:**

Bradwell Bay closed on 1 December 1945.

**Current status:**

There is little to see of this one-time busy airfield. The Control Tower still exists as a private house and parts of the runway are still visible, along with a Bellman hangar and some Nissen huts.

## Haunted RAF Bradwell Bay

*Source: PPRuNe Ghostly Radio Transmissions, 28 May 2004*

Even on the brightest summer day there is an atmosphere at former RAF Bradwell Bay. Perhaps it could be put down to a psychological reason; as long as you know the history of the field you will feel it.

# Brize Norton

No. 29 Group, Training Command
No. 38 Group

| | |
|---|---|
| County: | Oxfordshire |
| Location: | 4 miles SW of Witney |
| OS Ref.: | SP 293058 |
| Opened: | 13/08/1937 |
| Closed: | N/A |
| Control Tower: | Unknown |
| Condition: | In use |

| Runways: | 2 concrete & wood chippings, (224) & (266) both 2,000 x 50 yards |
|---|---|
| Hardstandings: | 39 of various types |
| Hangars: | C Type – 5, Lamella – 6, Blister – 2 |
| Ad., tech. & barr.: | Permanent Expansion Period buildings to the N of the airfield |
| Population: | RAF Officers – 170, OR – 1,812, WAAF Officers – 8, OR – 340 |
| Sat. airfield(s): | Weston-on-the-Green, Akeman Street, Southrop, Hampstead Norris, Finmere |
| Decoy airfield(s): | Chimney Q |

## History to 1946:

### 1935
Construction of an airfield with five C Type hangars at Carterton began. To avoid confusion with Cardington, it was named Brize Norton

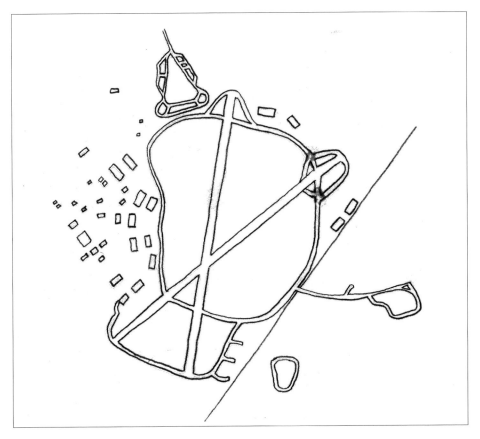

Brize Norton

**1937**

13 August: Brize Norton opened, even though incomplete

7 September: No. 2 FTS arrived from Digby with Harts, Audaxes, and Furies

**1938**

22 February: Airspeed Oxfords started arriving to replace the Harts, Audaxes, and Furies

10 October: No. 6 Maintenance Unit of 41 Group opened, using a group of buildings including Lamella hangars in the airfield's SE corner

**1939**

30 January: 6 MU received 2 Saro Cloud amphibians

March: No. 2 SFTS received 10 Harvard Is

June: Thirteen Harvard Is arrived

July: Two more Harvard Is arrived, with a further 13 in storage with 6 MU

August: No. 2 FTS establishment was 26 Harvards and 38 Oxfords

September: No. 101 Squadron from West Raynham dispersed Blenheims both at Brize and its satellite at Weston-on-the-Green

**1940**

11 June: Half of 15 SFTS moved from Middle Wallop which was needed for fighter squadrons while waiting for Kidlington to open

10 July: HQ 15 SFTS moved to Oldner House at Chipping Norton

28 July: A No. 2 SFTS Oxford was shot down over Akeman Street

16 August: Two Ju 88s attacked Brize Norton, dropping around 30 small HE bombs and a few incendiaries. Nos 1 and 3 hangars were destroyed and the roofs of a barrack block and the Institute building were severely damaged. One civilian was killed, and three civilians and 13 airmen injured. A total of 46 aircraft were written off by the attack. Following this the training aircraft were no longer hangared but dispersed at Akeman Street and Southrop

1 October: No. 15 SFTS departed for Kidlington

**1941**

1 November: No. 25 Blind Approach Training Flight formed in No. 23 Group with 6 + 2 Oxfords; it became No. 1525 Blind/Beam Approach Training Flight

November: The first Empire Air Training Scheme pilots arrived for acclimatisation flying. No. 6 MU acquired the use of 34 SLG at Woburn Park

**1942**

14 March: No. 2 SFTS was renamed 2(P)AFU

13 July: No. 1525 BAT departed and No. 2(P)AFU was disbanded

15 July: the Heavy Glider Conversion Unit arrived from Shrewton; Brize Norton became the training centre for Army glider pilots on Horsa gliders

21 October: Flying Training Command Instructors' School formed, a non-flying unit that taught instructional techniques

**1943**

8 February: 6 MU relinquished Woburn Park in favour of No. 28 SLG Barton Abbey and No. 22 SLG Barnsley Park

10 February: While Brize Norton's runways were resurfaced, flying was transferred to Grove

20 February: Brize Norton was operational once more

**1944**

1 March: The FTCIS moved to North Luffenham

2 March: The HGCU moved to North Luffenham, and Brize Norton transferred to 38 Group, Transport Command

14 March: No. 296 Squadron arrived from Hurn and No. 297 Squadron from Stoney Cross, both with Albemarles

20 March: Operational training commenced for the dropping of paratroops, towing and releasing gliders

4/5/6 June: Operation Tonga

6 June: Eighteen Albemarles from Nos 296 & 297 Squadrons participate in Operation Mallard

7/8 June: Three aircraft of No. 296 squadron flew in Operation Cooney Party

15 September: Nos 296 & 297 Squadrons were briefly at Manston before returning and converting to Stirling IVs

29 September: No. 296 Squadron moved to Earls Colne

30 September: No. 297 Squadron also moved to Earls Colne

15 October: The HGCU returned from North Luffenham with Whitleys and Horsas

16 October: The Flying Training Command Instructors' School returned from North Luffenham

20 October: The HGCU formed into No. 21 Heavy Glider Conversion Unit

**1945**

January: No. 21 HGCU receive Albemarles and, later in the year, Halifaxes

17 December: The FTCIS moved to Wittering

29 December: No. 21 HGCU moved to Elsham Wolds

29 December: The School of Flight Efficiency and Transport Command Development Unit arrived from Harwell and stayed until 1949; its principal task was the development of airborne delivery of mixed loads

**1946**

May: The Army Airborne Trials and Development Unit arrived

5 September: No. 297 Squadron arrived from Tarrant Rushton with Halifax IXs, staying until August 1947

**Current status:**

Brize Norton is an active RAF airfield.

## Haunted RAF Brize Norton

*Source: Bruce Barrymore Halpenny, Ghost Stations, 1986 (pp. 138-9)*

On 25 November 1941, Airmen Brice (an electrician) and Powell walked slowly from the guardroom towards the top hangar on 'A' site at RAF Brize Norton. By the time they reached the hangar side door it was about 7.20 a.m. They unlocked it and stepped inside and instantly sensed a feeling of 'oddness'. Both men saw what they likened to a beam of light, some four to six feet high, hovering over Boulton-Paul Defiant N3312. Within an estimated ten seconds Powell had found the main switch and turned it on. When the hangar lights came on, the apparition disappeared. Brice meanwhile was drawn towards Defiant N3312, and made an immediate investigation to see if anything was switched on inside the aircraft but found nothing amiss. There was nothing to explain their vision.

*Source: Keypublishing Aviation Forum, 7 March 2006*

At Brize, there were the alleged sightings of the ghost of a chiefy (flight sergeant) who, during the 1960s, would cycle up to the hangar site and keep a sneaky eye on his 'erks' to make sure they were working on the V bombers. Rumour had it that he was killed one foggy night by a car while he was cycling over to the hangar without his bicycle light on. His apparition has allegedly been seen several times since his death, and always at night.

*Source: E-Goat Forum, 20 September 2011*

Apparently one of Brize's VC10s is haunted by the ghost of a flight engineer who died in the aircraft during an Atlantic crossing. Rumours abound of the cabin lights being discovered on at night when no one was, or had been, working on the aircraft. When checked, the ground flight switch had been turned off. Nobody had ever been found in the VC10 to account for the lights.

# Cambridge

| | |
|---|---|
| County: | Cambridgeshire |
| Location: | 2 miles E of Cambridge |
| OS Ref.: | TL 486584 |
| Opened: | 1938 |
| Closed: | N/A |
| Pundit code: | CI |
| Control Tower: | Civil Tower |

| | |
|---|---|
| Condition: | In use |
| Runways: | Grass surface, NE-SW 1,400 yards, E-W 1,400 yards, N-S 1,300 yards, NW-SE 1,100 yards |
| Hardstandings: | Nil |
| Hangars: | On the N side of the airfield, Bellman – 1, civil (200 feet x 100 feet) – 1, (300 feet x 200 feet) – 1, (96 feet x 87 feet) – 1, MAP – 1, civil (160 feet x 150 feet) – 1, (195 feet x 95 feet) –1, Super Robin – 1 |
| Ad., tech. & barr.: | Unknown |
| Population: | Unknown |
| Sat. airfield(s): | Caxton Gibbet, Lords Bridge, Bottisham |

## History to 1946:

### 1929
An older airfield at Cambridge was established but this has completely disappeared under the Whitehill housing estate. Marshall's began using the airfield

### 1930s
With the RAF Expansion Scheme the present airfield at Teversham was acquired

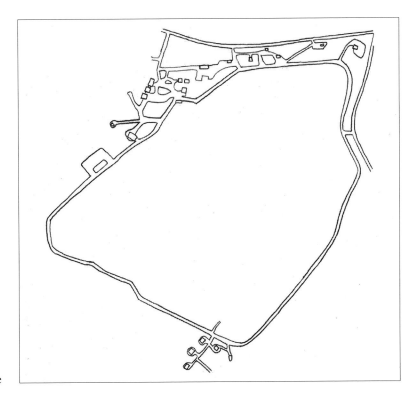

Cambridge

## 1937

Marshall's moved to Cambridge from a small airfield at what is now the Whitehill housing estate and conducted flying training using Tiger Moths. Marshall's handled a large number of training and operational types; the work included repairing and overhauling damaged and 'tired' aircraft. They were also engaged in the installation of modifications, such as the fitting of AI (radar) to Mosquito night fighters

## 1938

1 February: No. 22 Elementary and Refresher Flying Training School formed in No. 26 Group as a civil-run pilot training school, in this case Marshall's. It was equipped with a variety of Tiger Moths, Audaxes, Harts, and Hinds to provide initial flying training

8 October: Cambridge Airport was opened primarily as a flying training airfield operated by Marshall's. The Cambridge Aero Club and some private owners also had aircraft based here

## 1939

Squadrons: 22 ERFTS & 22 EFTS

1 February: No. 22 ERFTS transferred to No. 50 Group

3 September: The ERFTS was redesignated as No. 22 Elementary Flying Training School, though it remained under the control of Marshall's. It was soon raised to Class A status with 72 aircraft and 120 pupil pilots in four flights. Ultimately it became the largest EFTS in the UK, with 7 Flights and 126 aircraft

September: No. 3 Salvage Centre arrived and stayed until April 1948

## 1940

Squadrons: 2, 16, 26 (det), 239 (det), 268 (det), 22 EFTS, No. 4 Flying Instructors' School & Cambridge University Air Squadron

4 October: No. 54 Maintenance Unit formed from No. 3 Salvage Centre

8 October: Cambridge University Air Squadron reopened at Cambridge with the allocation of a single Tiger Moth at the EFTS

30 December: One German raider spent 20 minutes machine-gunning portions of the airfield. Bullet holes were found in three Tiger Moths, one Magister and one Oxford, none of which was rendered unserviceable

## 1941

Squadrons: 22 EFTS, No. 4 Flying Instructors School & CUAS

June: The airfield developed into a major CRO (Civilian Repair Organisation)

3 July: No. 4 Flying Instructors' School formed in No. 50 Group to train elementary training instructors

16 July: Ten bombs were dropped on the airfield but did no damage. A Tiger Moth was damaged whilst circuiting but crash-landed successfully

6 August: A raider asked for permission to land before dropping about 10 bombs
  on the airfield

24 August: Ten bombs were dropped on the airfield, causing 2 fatalities

**1942**
Squadrons: 22 EFTS & CUAS

**1943**
Squadrons: 22 EFTS & CUAS

30 April: No. 4 Flying Instructors' School was disbanded and 2 Flights of the EFTS
  took over that training role

**1944**
Squadrons: 22 EFTS & CUAS

January: The establishment of 22 EFTS was 108 Tiger Moths and 18 Austers, with
  assorted other types. Training had begun to reduce by late 1944

**1945**
Squadrons: 22 EFTS & CUAS

August: the school still had an establishment of 52 Tigers and 18 Austers with
  AOP pilot training a major part of the task

**1946**
Squadrons: 22 EFTS & CUAS

**Current status:**
Cambridge Airport.

## Haunted RAF Cambridge

David Curry wrote *The Men That Never Clocked Off* in June 2004, in which
he details an incredible number of paranormal occurrences and apparition
sightings. Anyone interested in the ghosts of Cambridge Airport should buy a copy
and spend time reading his first-hand accounts as they are well researched and
well written. David includes accounts from machine shops 1 & 2, hangar Nos
2, 3, 4, 10, 11, 12 & 13, the Civil Airport building, the canteen, and a host of
others.

Apparitions seen there have included a man in a suit, an RAF airman, an airman
in flying boots and Second World War flying gear, and a host of ordinary-looking
men and women who simply shouldn't – and more to the point – couldn't have
been there.

# Castle Camps

No. 11 Fighter Group

| | |
|---|---|
| County: | Cambridgeshire |
| Location: | 6 miles NE of Saffron Walden |
| OS Ref.: | TL 633420 |
| Opened: | 1940 |
| Closed: | 1946 |
| Control Tower: | ? |
| Condition: | Demolished |
| Runways: | 3 tarmac, (063) 1,950 x 50 yards, (317) 1,600 x 50 yards, and (100) 1,100 x 50 yards |
| Hardstandings: | 16 pan type |
| Hangars: | Bellman – 1, Blister – 8 |
| Ad., tech. & barr.: | Temporary to the SE of the airfield |
| Population: | RAF Officers – 68, OR – 1,110, WAAF Officers – 4, OR – 180 |
| Sat. airfield(s): | Satellite to Debden; satellite to North Weald |

*History to 1946:*

### 1939
September: Work began on a grass field with minimal facilities as a satellite to Debden

### 1940
23 May: No. 85 Squadron arrived at Debden with Hawker Hurricanes.

June: Castle Camps opened as Debden's satellite. At the satellite, the pilots had to sleep in tents at the dispersals and eat in a marquee set up in the woods

18 August: No. 111 Squadron rested at Castle Camps

19 August: No. 85 Squadron moved to Croydon

3 September: No. 85 Squadron arrived at Castle Camps

5 September: No. 85 Squadron moved to Church Fenton

5 September: No. 73 (RCAF) Squadron arrived with Hawker Hurricanes and was immediately put into action over the Thames Estuary. No. 73 Squadron lost one pilot, another was wounded, 3 Hurricanes were shot down and 3 damaged

7 September: No. 73 Squadron engaged Bf 110s in a heavy daylight raid on London and the Billericay area, claiming three destroyed

11 September: Nos 73 & 17 Squadrons engaged He 111s over the Isle of Sheppey

15 September: No. 73 Squadron intercepted a raid over Maidstone, claiming three Bf 109s. At 2.45 p.m. the squadron was scrambled again and 6 serviceable

Hurricanes engaged 100 German bombers over Maidstone, 3 of which were claimed as damaged

21 September: No. 73 Squadron was reinforced by 257 Squadron from Martlesham Heath

23 September: Nos 17, 73 & 257 Squadrons were 'bounced' over Kent; No. 73 Squadron lost 5 Hurricanes

13 November: No. 73 Squadron boarded HMS *Furious* and left for Takoradi in West Africa

## 1941
RAF Castle Camps was extended, better accommodation provided, and runways laid

13 December: No. 157 Squadron re-formed at Debden as a night fighter unit

17 December: No. 157 Squadron arrived at Castle Camps without aircraft

## 1942
January: No. 157 Squadron received its Mosquito night fighters

27 April: No. 157 Squadron began operational patrols against a Baedeker raid on Norwich

## 1943
14 March: No. 605 squadron arrived from Ford with Mosquitos

15 March: No. 157 Squadron moved to Bradwell Bay

15 June: No. 527 Radar Calibration Squadron was formed from various calibration flights at Castle Camps

3 September: No. 605 Squadron began Mahmoud sorties (operations on the flank of the bomber stream designed to intercept enemy night fighters)

October: No. 605 Squadron departed Castle Camps for Bradwell Bay

30 December: The Mosquito Mk XIIIs of 410 (RCAF) Squadron arrived from Hunsdon to guard the northern approaches to London

## 1944
28 February: No. 527 Radar Calibration Squadron moved to Snailwell

29 February: No. 91 Squadron arrived from Tangmere with Mk XII Spitfires and received the Mk XIV

6 March: No. 486 RNZAF Squadron arrived from Beaulieu with Typhoons

17 March: No. 91 Squadron departed for Drem

21 March: No. 486 Squadron departed for Ayr

29 March: No. 486 Squadron returned and received Tempest Mk Vs

29 April: No. 486 Squadron moved to Newchurch and No. 410 Squadron returned to Hunsdon

23 June: No. 68 Squadron arrived from Fairwood Common with Mosquitos

28 October: No. 68 Squadron departed for Coltishall

7 October: No. 151 Squadron arrived from Predannack with Mosquitos
27 October: No. 25 Squadron arrived from Coltishall with Mosquitos
19 November: No. 151 Squadron departed for Hunsdon

### 1945
27 January: No. 307 Polish Squadron arrived from Church Fenton
18 May: No. 307 Polish Squadron departed for Coltishall
27 June: No. 85 Squadron arrived from Swannington with Mosquito night fighters
9 October: No. 85 Squadron departed for West Malling

### 1946
January: No. 25 Squadron moved to Boxted

### Closure:
On 17 January 1946, the Station HQ left Castle Camps for Boxted and the station
was closed.

### Current status:
The main entrance was from the road leading beyond the village church, from
which the airfield site can be viewed, although apart from a handful of huts
there is nothing to see. Some of the airfield buildings are still in situ and being
used by local farms and industry.

## Haunted RAF Castle Camps

*Source: Keypublishing Aviation Forum, 10 April 2005*
Pete Truman wrote that there are few places more atmospheric than the north-east
corner of Castle Camps.

Not a lot of this place survives but if you go down to the church and along a
footpath, you will see that the end of the runway with its gullies still survives. If
you stand there you get a real feeling of the Mossies coming into the runways.

*Source: Keypublishing Aviation Forum, 1 November 2011*
Francis Gomme wrote about an experience he had as a boy in summer 1964 whilst
cycling from home near Ashdon to Castle Camps, very aware, as he states, of its
place in Mosquito history. Close to Wigmore Pond, they cycled up a Second World
War concrete roadway and headed north-east between the ruins of the various
brick buildings and shelters of the former airfield. As they cycled, avoiding the
potholes, they both stopped abruptly and looked at each other. Both were aware of
an odd, unaccountable, and constant whistling noise on a sunny day with no wind.
Was that sound from the Mosquitos' propellers? Their immediate reaction was to
turn around and cycle furiously away from the airfield.

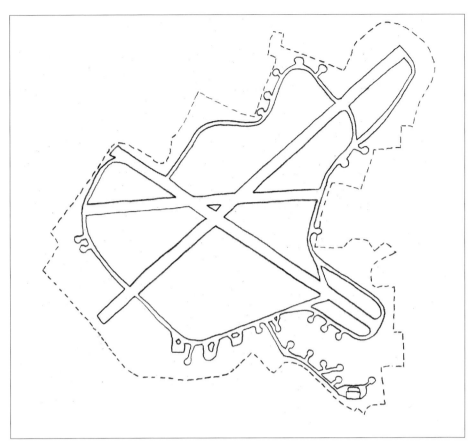

Castle Camps

# Charmy Down

No. 10 Group, Fighter Command
IXth USAAF
No. 23 Training Group
54 Group 1946

| | |
|---|---|
| County: | Somerset |
| Location: | 3 miles N of Bath |
| OS Ref.: | ST 764700 |
| Opened: | 11/1940 |
| Closed: | 10/1946 |
| Pundit code: | CH |
| USAAF Station: | 487 |
| Control Tower: | Watch Office for Night Fighter Stations FCW4514 |
| Condition: | Derelict |

| Runways: | Grass then 3 tarmac, (310) 1,450 x 50 yards, (250) 1,350 x 50 yards, and (012) 933 x 50 yards |
|---|---|
| Hardstandings: | 39 aircraft hardstandings (Willis & Holliss give a number of 45) |
| Hangars: | Bellman – 1, Blister – 12 |
| Ad., tech. & barr.: | Dispersed temporary accommodation to the NW; technical site at Holts Down Lane |
| Population: | USAAF Officers – 137, OR – 1,325 |
| Sat. airfield(s): | Satellite to RAF Colerne; satellite to RAF South Cerney |

## History to 1946:

### 1940

November: RAF Charmy Down opened as a satellite to Colerne and was used in the defence of Bristol and Bath. A detachment of No. 87 Squadron arrived from RAF Colerne with Hurricanes for night fighting duties

18 December: The accommodation at Charmy Down was completed and No. 87 Squadron arrived from RAF Colerne with Hurricane IIcs

### 1941

7 August: No. 87 Squadron exchanged with No. 125 Squadron at Colerne, which arrived with Defiant I night fighters. No. 263 Squadron arrived from Filton with Whirlwind 1s

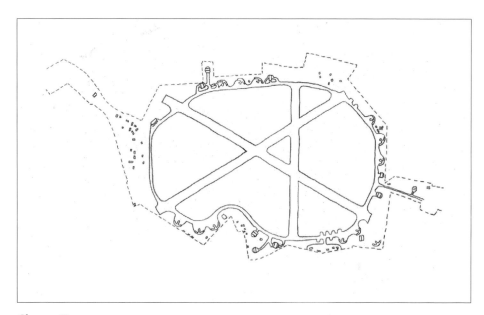

Charmy Down

20 September: No. 137 Squadron re-formed at Charmy Down from a nucleus provided by No. 263 Squadron

24 September: No. 125 Squadron departed for Fairwood Common

8 November: No. 137 Squadron moved to Coltishall

27 November: No. 417 (RCAF) Squadron formed at Charmy Down with Spitfire IIas

19 December: No. 263 Squadron departed for Warmwell

23 December: No. 263 Squadron returned to Charmy Down

**1942**

1 January: No. 87 Squadron returned to Charmy Down with 1454 Turbinlite Flight with their Havoc Is, Havoc IIs, and Boston IIIs from Colerne

26 January: No. 417 (RCAF) Squadron moved to Colerne

28 January: No. 263 Squadron departed for Colerne

24 March: The first patrol by a 1454 Flight Havoc and 87 Squadron Hurricane combination was flown

23 August: No. 234 Squadron arrived from Portreath with Spitfire IIas

30 August: No. 234 Squadron returned to Portreath

8 September: 1454 Flight became No. 533 Squadron

26 September: No. 245 Squadron arrived from Middle Wallop with Hurricane IIcs and received Typhoon Ibs

September: Nos 88 & 107 Squadrons from Wattisham and No. 2 Bomber Group briefly arrived for operations with No. 10 Group

2 November: No. 87 Squadron departed for Philippeville

30 November: No. 421 (RCAF) Squadron arrived from Angle with Spitfire Vs

4 December: No. 421 (RCAF) Squadron returned to Angle

**1943**

25 January: No. 533 Squadron was disbanded

29 January: No. 245 Squadron moved to Peterhead

February: The Fighter Leaders' School arrived from Chedworth

April and June: No. 88 Squadron from Swanton Morley was at Charmy Down practising tactics with the FLS

August: Charmy Down was provisionally allocated to the USAAF, and the FLS moved to Aston Down

**1944**

February: Charmy Down transferred to the IXth Air Force originally as a Troop Carrier Service Wing to support troop carrier units in South West England

March to May: Personnel of the 422nd, 423rd & 425th Night Fighter Squadrons arrived. The squadrons were to be equipped with the new Northrop P-61 Black Widow, but none of the P-61s were ever based at Charmy Down

7 March: The 422nd Night Fighter Squadron arrived

18 April: The 423rd NFS arrived

6 May: The 422nd NFS was sent to the RAF night fighter OTU at RAF Scorton

10 May: The 423rd NFS was assigned to the 10th Photo Group

12 May: The 423rd NFS was moved to Chalgrove

26 May: The 425th NFS arrived at Charmy Down

12 June: The 425th NFS departed to join the 422nd NFS at Scorton
September: The Troop Carrier Service Wing moved to RAF Kingston Bagpuize. Charmy Down was returned to the RAF and was allocated to 23 Training Group for advanced pilot training with Oxfords, as a satellite to South Cerney

**1945**

May: With the end of hostilities in Europe, No. 3 (P)AFU quickly withdrew from Charmy Down. The airfield reverted to care and maintenance under South Cerney control

**1946**

January: Charmy Down was transferred to 54 Group and 92 Gliding School. It was for a time used as a Personnel Resettlement Centre for Australian troops

**Closure:**

RAF Charmy Down was officially closed in October 1946.

**Current status:**

The hangars have been removed leaving only the Bellman on Holts Down Lane.

Most of the runways have been broken up but the perimeter track survives. The ATC tower on the north-western side of the field was renovated as a private house, but the remainder of the buildings, including the Control Tower, are derelict.

## Haunted RAF Charmy Down

*Source: Keypublishing Aviation Forum, 11 January 2010*

Just after Christmas 1988, three friends drove to former RAF Charmy Down to have a stroll across the old airfield on what was remembered as a misty, very quiet, cold afternoon. While they were on the perimeter track, facing RAF Colerne, all three witnessed an old-style parachute descending in the sky above. There were no accompanying sounds of an aircraft in the skies, and the weather conditions would have been unsuitable for parachuting. The vision was lost in the mist.

# Chedworth

No. 81 Training Group
No. 9 Training Group

| | |
|---|---|
| County: | Gloucestershire |
| Location: | 9 miles SE of Cheltenham |
| OS Ref.: | SP 042131 |
| Opened: | 04/1942 |
| Closed: | 1946 |
| Pundit code: | YW |
| Control Tower: | Fighter Satellite Watch Office 17658/40 |
| Condition: | Demolished |
| Runways: | 2 tarmac, 'Crossbow' airfield, (035) 1,400 x 50 yards and (115) 1,300 x 50 yards |
| Hardstandings: | 25 |
| Hangars: | Extra-Over Blister – 2 |
| Ad., tech. & barr.: | Temporary buildings to the NW of the airfield, some of them within Withington Woods |
| Population: | RAF Officers – 21, OR – 585, WAAF Officers – 1, OR – 65 |
| Sat. airfield(s): | Satellite to Aston Down |

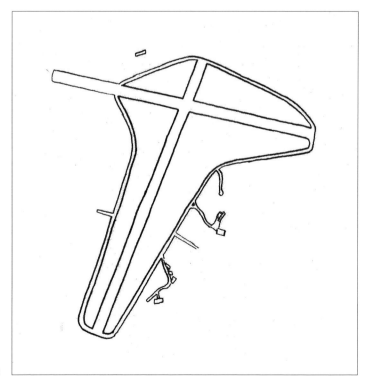

Chedworth

## History to 1946:

### 1942

April: Chedworth opened

25 August: No. 52 OTU detached to Chedworth permanently from Aston Down with Spitfires

December: Fighter Command's Banquet Scheme was put into effect. During their last three weeks in training pupils were to be formed into 552 Squadron and be available for operational scrambles, practice interceptions, GCI, and searchlight co-operation under the control of Colerne

### 1943

15 January: The Fighter Leaders' School was formed at Chedworth from half of the aircraft and personnel of No. 52 OTU. Pilots were given a three-week course in tactics, including 25 hours' flying

February: The Fighter Leaders' School moved to Charmy Down. Chedworth was used by the Oxfords of No. 3 (P)AFU at South Cerney, which was waterlogged, and then by aircraft of No. 6 (P)AFU from Little Rissington

October: Chedworth became a satellite to Honiley, and a combined 60/63 OTU air gunnery squadron arrived with ten Mosquito IIs and two Martinets

### 1944

25 January: 60/63 OTU returned to Honiley, and Chedworth was deserted

March: No. 3 (P)AFU returned for night flying when flying from South Cerney was deemed too dangerous due to aerial congestion

June: The 9th AF HQ Squadron and the 125th Liaison Squadron used the airfield for communications work

July: The 9th AF departed

14 July: No. 3 Tactical Exercise Unit with Mustangs moved into Aston Down

17 July: Chedworth became the satellite field for Aston Down, and 'C' Squadron was detached there

15 December: 55 OTU re-formed from 3 TEU at Aston Down for fighter-bomber training, with Chedworth remaining as its satellite

### 1945

The OTU had 120 aircraft, mainly Typhoons, divided between the parent and Chedworth

29 May: The end of hostilities in Europe brought an immediate end to Chedworth's role as a satellite airfield and it was placed on care and maintenance

3 December: Chedworth was transferred to the Admiralty, who used it for storage

**Closure:**

During the 1960s, the Central Flying School of RAF Little Rissington used Chedworth to practise forced landings, being joined later by a civilian gliding club.

Chedworth stopped being used during the 1970s, except for the occasional military exercise.

**Current status:**

The grass areas were returned to agriculture and the minor road from Chedworth village to Withington across the airfield was reopened. Some of the old RAF buildings have been reused.

## Haunted RAF Chedworth

*Source: Keypublishing Aviation Forum,*
*24 April 2008*

In the 1990s, a local scout troop would often hike to RAF Chedworth and meet up with the Chedworth scouts, whose scout hut was in the old station armoury, for spring camps.

Late one night, during a map and compass reading exercise, the scouts had to walk on a compass course across the airfield to a gate. As they passed where the two runways intersected, and were heading over the grass area towards the perimeter track, all three of them felt what can only be described as a 'wave' of energy come at them, pass right under their feet and right through them. The wave was so strong that it knocked them off their feet and left them confused for a while. Thinking it was possibly a minor earth tremor, they stated that 'it really did feel like something large and heavy moving quickly through the earth under us'. Arriving at the gate on the far side there were about twelve others already waiting. However, none of them had noticed anything untoward.

About six years after the above experience, a few of the now ex-scouts had a reunion and decided to go camping on the airfield. They rolled out their bedding on the runway, having collected all the scrap wood that was lying around to make a fire, as it was getting dark and sat around keeping warm and talking. At about 9 p.m., what was described as an enormous blast of air went right through them, blowing the kit around and almost extinguishing the fire. It lasted only for a second. It had been a still evening prior to the blast and returned to this state immediately afterwards. Many years after, someone commented that 'it was almost like downwash/prop-blast, and that we were actually camped on a runway'.

# Chipping Ongar

USAAF 8th
USAAF 9th
USSTAF Air Disarmament Command
USAAF 9th Troop Carrier Command

| | |
|---|---|
| County: | Essex |
| Location: | 2 miles NE of Chipping Ongar |
| OS Ref.: | TL 582055 |
| Opened: | 06/1943 |
| Closed: | 02/1959 |
| Pundit code: | JC |
| USAAF Station: | 162 |
| Control Tower: | Watch Office for all Commands 12779/41 with modified small front windows 15371/41 and rooftop VCR |
| Condition: | Demolished |
| Runways: | 3 concrete with wood chippings, (030) 2,000 x 50 yards, (090) 1,400 x 50 yards, and (150) 1,400 x 50 yards |
| Hardstandings: | 51 hardstandings, 48 standard loops, 2 large loops, and 1 pan |
| Hangars: | T2 – 2, one fronting the technical site, the other to the NNW of the airfield near Witney Green |
| Bomb stores: | Located on the NW side of the airfield, outside of the perimeter track, surrounded by large dirt mounds and concrete pens for storing the aerial bombs and other munitions required by the combat aircraft |
| Ad., tech. & barr.: | Situated to the E of the airfield, comprising largely of Nissen huts of various sizes. Various domestic accommodation sites were constructed dispersed away from the airfield, but within a mile or so of the technical support site, also using clusters of Maycrete or Nissen huts. The huts were either connected, set up end-to-end, or built singly and were made of prefabricated corrugated iron with a door and two small windows at the front and back |
| Population: | USAAF Officers – 443, OR – 2327 |

The 387th lost 10 aircraft while at Chipping Ongar; the 8061st Troop Carrier Group lost one C-47.

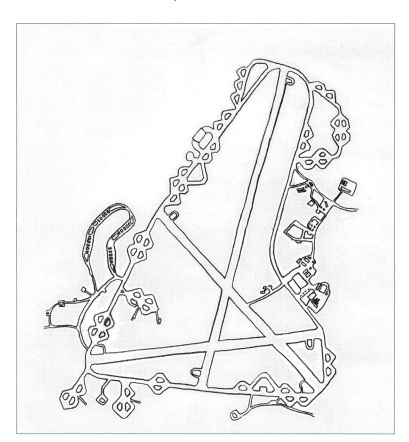

Chipping
Ongar

## History to 1946:

### 1942

One of 15 airfield sites in Essex in the Air Ministry A grouping, allocated to the
USAAF in August 1942. The most important facilities were completed by the
early spring of 1943. During airborne operations, tents would be pitched on
the interior grass regions of the airfield, or wherever space could be found to
accommodate the airborne forces for the short time they would be bivouacked
at the station prior to the operation

### 1943

June: The airfield was opened and was assigned station No. 162
25 June: Parts of the airfield were still under construction when the 387th
Bombardment Group arrived
15 August: The 387th Group concentrated its attacks on airfields during the first
months of operations
16 October: The 387th was transferred to 9th Air Force and made tactical strikes
on V-weapon sites in France

**1944**

21 July: The 387th Bomb Group moved to Stoney Cross. After the 387th had
vacated the station, only a USAAF station complement party remained and
control passed from 9th Air Force to the USSTAF

September: Chipping Ongar was used temporarily by IX Troop Carrier Command

**1945**

January: USSTAF relinquished the airfield

24 March: The C-47s of the 61st Troop Carrier Group briefly arrived to carry
paratroops of the British 6th Airborne Division to Wesel during Operation Varsity

18 April: Chipping Ongar was returned to RAF Bomber Command, but with
the departure of the Americans the airfield was never used again for military
flying

11 June: It was transferred to Technical Training Command and became a satellite
to Hornchurch. However, the airfield remained unoccupied

**1946**

25 April: RAF Chipping Ongar was handed over to the War Office, reverting
subsequently again to Technical Training Command as an inactive service
station parented by North Weald

**Closure:**

On 28 February 1959, RAF Chipping Ongar was closed, and with the end of
military control it quickly reverted to agricultural use.

**Current status:**

A section of the perimeter track and some loop dispersal hardstands are still intact,
connected to a small private landing strip converted from a straight section
of the wartime perimeter, aligned 04/22, and one small section of a secondary
full-width runway (09/27) on the south-east side. On the north-eastern side,
the Ops block, Norden Bombsight Store, and the base of the pilots' briefing
room are grouped together, and are in quite good condition.

## Haunted RAF Chipping Ongar

*Source: G503.com Forum, 14 October 2010*

At the beginning of October 2010, the contributor to the forum wrote that he was
walking the main runway at RAF Chipping Ongar, which is now a track between
cultivated fields. It was a slightly close autumn evening, unusually gloomy, with an
intense silence in the area. His dog had run on some distance ahead, and twice he
distinctly heard footsteps no more than 20 feet behind him. Both times he turned
around to look, but on each occasion there was nothing there but silence. He

claims that this really quite shook him up, and made the skin on the back of his neck prickle. There was a real atmosphere and an unusual, almost heavy, silence all the time that he was on the airfield. By the time he reached the peritrack it was almost dark, and although people claim that night terrors are usually responsible for feelings of a supernatural nature, the atmosphere noted above had completely passed.

# Chivenor

No. 19 Group

| | |
|---|---|
| County: | Devon |
| Location: | 5 miles W of Barnstaple |
| OS Ref.: | SS 492344 |
| Opened: | 01/10/1940 |
| Closed: | N/A |
| Pundit code: | CN |
| Control Tower: | Watch Office for all Commands |
| Condition: | Demolished in 1994 |
| Runways: | 3 concrete, (102) 2,000 x 50 yards, (242) 1,460 x 50 yards, and (162) 1,170 x 50 yards. The runways were slightly extended during 1944 |
| Hardstandings: | Spectacle – 45, 150-foot diameter pans – 5 |
| Hangars: | T2 – 4, Bellman – 4 |
| Ad., tech. & barr.: | Temporary buildings to the N of the airfield with extensive hutted accommodation |
| Population: | RAF Officers – 266, OR – 2,412, WAAF Officers – 2, OR – 331 |

## History to 1946:

### 1940
Squadrons: 252 & 3 (Coastal) OTU

May: Contractors moved on to the site of the old North Devon Airport and started work by laying three runways on fields just to the west of the original grass aerodrome

1 October: RAF Chivenor opened with No. 3 (C)OTU forming with Blenheims, Ansons, and Beauforts for training new Coastal crews

1 December: No. 252 Squadron arrived from Bircham Newton with Blenheim 1s

### 1941
Squadrons: 252, 272, 3 (Coastal) OTU & 5 OTU

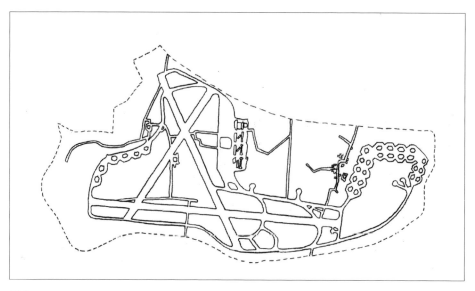

Chivenor

29 July: No. 3 OTU departed for Cranwell

1 August: No. 5 (C)OTU re-formed from the Beaufort section of No. 3 (C)OTU

26 November: A Ju 88 landed at Chivenor; the crew thought they had crossed the Channel and landed in France

### 1942

Squadrons: 51, 77, 172, 235, 547, 5 OTU & 1417 (Leigh Light Trials) Flight

18 March: No. 1417 Flight arrived with 16 Wellington VIIIs to work up on the new Leigh Light

April 4: No. 1417 Flight renumbered as No. 172 Squadron

June: 5 OTU departed and Chivenor transferred to 19 Group

16 July: No. 235 Squadron arrived from Docking with Beaufighters to take on the Ju 88s that were causing heavy losses over Biscay

### 1943

Squadrons: 59, 172, 235, 404, 407, 547 & 612

1 February: No. 59 Squadron arrived from Thorney Island with Fortress IIas

February: No. 172 Squadron received Wellington XIIs (Leigh Light) fitted with ASV Mk III which the U-boat receivers could not detect

22 February: U-665 was destroyed

March: No. 407 Squadron received Wellington XIIs

March: 12 sightings resulted in 7 attacks by No. 172 Squadron

### 1944

Squadrons: 14, 36, 172, 179, 304, 407, 612 & ASV Training Flight

5 May: 3041N caught two U-boats on the surface with searchlight and, despite heavy flak, one submarine was believed sunk

5 June: Coastal Command was given the task of helping to seal the Channel against U-boats, and a sustained 'maximum effort' was mounted by the Chivenor squadrons

18 June: Wellington 3041A sunk U-441 with six 250-lb depth charges

27 August: Wellington 1721B's port engine was hit by returned fire; as the depth charges were dropped, the starboard engine was hit and the Wellington was ditched. Fifteen hours after the ditching a 10 (RAAF) Squadron Sunderland landed in the open sea and picked up the three survivors

November: Nos 407 & 612 Squadrons were moved to St Eval when Chivenor's runways began to break up

## 1945

Squadrons: 14, 36, 254, 248, 407, 459, 517, 521 & ASV Training Flight

1 June: No. 14 Squadron disbanded and No. 254 Squadron arrived from North Coates with Mosquito XVIIIs

4 June: No. 407 Squadron disbanded

1 July: No. 248 Squadron arrived from Banff with Mosquito XVIIIs and with No. 254 to form a Strike Wing

## 1946

Squadrons: 26, 517, 521, 691 & Coastal Command Fighter Affiliation Training

1 April: No. 21 Aircrew Holding Unit was in sole occupation-and 6 years of association with Coastal Command was at an end

1 October: Chivenor was taken over by Fighter Command and No. 691 Squadron arrived with Spitfire XVIs, Oxfords, and Martinets for anti-aircraft co-operation work

**Current status:**
Operational airfield.

## *Haunted RAF Chivenor*

*Source: PPRuNe Archive, 9 March 2011*
Several sightings of a ghost have occurred recently in what is now the Sergeants' Mess but what was (*circa* 1980) built as the Officers' Mess.

*Source: PPRuNe Archive, 10 March 2011*
In the early 80s, those who lived in the old wooden huts at the Officers' Mess reported a ghost. They all heard someone 'clanking' down the corridor. Allegedly it was a dying Hunter pilot who hanged himself by the chain in the toilets. It broke under his weight. He crawled down the corridor to get help but died on the way.

# Colerne

No. 41 Transport Group
No. 10 Group
No. 41 Group

| | |
|---|---|
| County: | Wiltshire |
| Location: | 6 miles NE of Bath |
| OS Ref.: | TF 015023 |
| Opened: | 1940 |
| Closed: | N/A |
| Pundit code: | CQ |
| USAAF Station: | 353 |
| Control Tower: | A. Watch Office with Met Section 5845/39 (brick) |
| | B. Watch Office (Vertical Split Control Type) 2548c/55 |
| Condition: | A. Demolished 2002 |
| | B. In use for air traffic control |
| Runways: | 3 tarmac, (256) 1,200 x 50 yards, (196) 1, 950 x 50 yards, and (302) 1,150 x 50 yards; extended to 2,430, 2,040 and shortened to 1,050 yards |
| Hardstandings: | TE – 16, Fortress – 1 |
| Hangars: | J Type – 1, Blister – 1, K Type – 3, L Type – 5, Robins –6 |
| Ad., tech. & barr.: | Permanent Expansion Period to the N of the airfield |
| Population: | RAF Officers – 143, OR – 2912, WAAF – 24, OR – 261 |
| Sat. airfield(s): | Charmy Down |

## History to 1946:

### 1939
September: Colerne was one of the last Expansion Scheme airfields to be completed

### 1940
1 January: Colerne opened into No. 41 Group in a partially completed state
18 May: No. 39 MU was formed at Colerne as an aircraft storage unit
    September: No. 10 Group, Fighter Command Sector HQ at Colerne
28 November: No. 87 Squadron arrived from Exeter with night fighter Hurricane 1s
    November: Charmy Down opened as a satellite to Colerne
18 December: No. 87 Squadron departed for Charmy Down and Colerne was used for training new fighter squadrons

### 1941
Squadrons: 87, 316 & 600

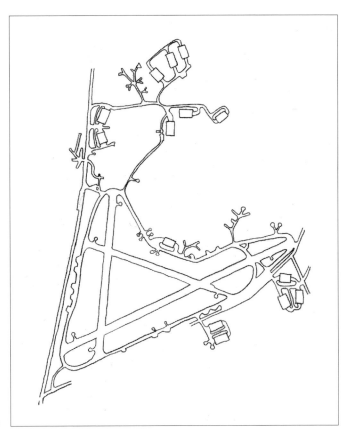

Colerne

A BOAC repair facility moved into Colerne in 1941 and used some of the new hangars to the north of the airfield

## 1942
Squadrons: 87, 184, 263 & 264

August: No. 218 MU changed from assembly to secret special installations

1 December: No. 184 Squadron formed at Colerne equipped with Hurricane IID tank-busters

December: No. 264 Squadron started day patrols over Biscay and occasional Rangers over France

## 1943
Squadrons: 151, 183, 184, 219, 264 & 27th FS 8th AF

30 April: No. 151 Squadron arrived from Wittering with Mosquito IIs to perform night intruder operations over France

12 September: The 27th Fighter Squadron arrived from High Ercall with P-38F Lightnings.

December: No. 151 Squadron converted to Mosquito XIIIs

### 1944

Squadrons: 410, 488, 604, 587 (det) & 286 AAC

20 May: No. 286 (Anti-Aircraft Co-operation) Squadron arrived with Oxfords, Hurricanes, and Martinets to provide a variety of training targets for Army gunners

23 May: A detachment from 587 Squadron at Westonzoyland arrived for the above duties

July: The Mosquitos of 147 Night Fighter Wing, Nos 604, 410 & 488 Squadrons, assembled at Colerne

### 1945

Squadrons: 74, 245, 504, 616 & 1335 Conversion Unit

8 March: No. 1335 (Meteor) CU formed at Colerne

May: No. 504 Squadron formed the first jet fighter Wing in the RAF

10 August: No. 504 Squadron renumbered as No. 245 Squadron

27 July: No. 1335 CU moved to Molesworth

### 1946

September: All fighter units left Colerne and it was transferred to No. 41 Group, Maintenance Command, with 39 and 218 MUs in residence. Apart from test flying and ferrying, the airfield was little used

### Closure:

On 31 March 1976, RAF Colerne was closed and transferred to the Army as Azimghur Barracks.

### Current status:

The airfield was initially retained on reserve. Recently, the MoD has been selling the land on the runway approaches, and it is presumably no longer considered as an emergency base.

## Haunted RAF Colerne

*Source: Peter Underwood,* Guide to Ghosts & Haunted Places, *1996 (pp. 154-6)*
In March 1995, Basil Wright was posted to the Royal Maritime Auxiliary Service HQ in Bath and was allocated a semi-detached house, No. 10, at former RAF Colerne. He was awoken just after midnight to the sounds of a lot of chattering and laughter. Assuming that a party must be going on next door, he eventually went back to sleep. In the morning he remembered that the houses on either side were empty, so he mentioned it to the Military Police. They told him that if he heard anything during the night it was probably their patrol checking the empty houses, as they had trouble with squatters.

One night, at about midnight, and having checked that the doors and windows were secured, he went to bed. But no sooner had he turned out the light when there was a lot of chattering and laughter. He realised this time that it was coming from the front room downstairs. Then he felt the bedclothes sharply pulled away from him, and the mattress sank as though someone had sat on the edge of the bed. He started praying fervently and the pressure on the bed eased and the voices and laughter faded.

He was giving a colleague a lift to the office a few months later, and discovered that the last Hastings aircraft on the station, whilst on circuits and bumps, had ploughed into the nearby woods and exploded, killing all the crew as it was taking off. On the evening before any flight, the crew would arrive at the pilot's house, which was No. 10.

*Source: PPRuNe Haunted Airfields, 27 October 2001*
One contributor mentioned that he heard ghostly aero engines over Colerne airfield.

# Croydon

No. 11 Group, Fighter Command

| | |
|---|---|
| County: | Surrey |
| Location: | 2½ miles SW of Croydon |
| OS Ref.: | TQ 306635 |
| Opened: | 01/1916 |
| Closed: | 30/09/1959 |
| Pundit code: | CO |
| Control Tower: | A. 1916-28, wooden air traffic control and customs building |
| | B. 1928, Croydon Airport terminal building and Control Tower |
| Condition: | A. Demolished in 1928 |
| | B. Terminal building and Control Tower now Croydon Airport Museum |
| Runways: | Grass airfield, NW-SE 1,300 yards, E-W 1,200 yards, NE-SW 1,100 yards |
| Hardstandings: | Twin engine – 22 |
| Hangars: | Extended-Over Blister – 4 |
| Ad., tech. & barr.: | Permanent and temporary buildings |
| Population: | RAF Officers – 83, OR – 576, WAAF Officers – 5 OR – 210 |

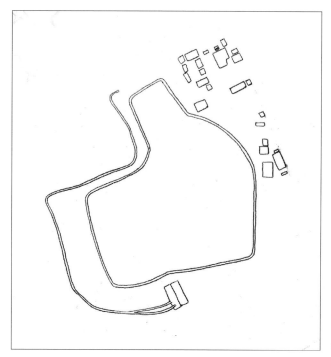

Croydon

## History to 1946:

**1916**

Beddington Aerodrome was opened, after a minimum amount of preparation, by the Royal Flying Corps as a reasonable landing field for Home Defence. Bessonneau hangars and tented accommodation were provided, with some buildings around New Barn Farm requisitioned. In addition to the operational squadrons, a number of training units were also based there

**1919**

The closure of No. 29 Training Squadron marked the end of this early phase of RAF occupation. The airfield was surplus to its requirements and handed over for civil use

**1920**

Beddington and Waddon airfields were merged to form Croydon Aerodrome
April: Croydon became London Airport and experienced a rapid expansion of commercial business

**1920s**

All evidence of the two former airfields was obliterated under considerable refurbishments to the site

**1924**
Imperial Airways was formed by the merger of a number of British companies

**1928**
Croydon was a purpose-built international airport with new buildings and an
   impressive terminal

**1939**
Squadrons: 3, 17, 92, 145 & 615
All civil aircraft were dispersed to other airfields and RAF fighters began to arrive

**1940**
Squadrons: 1 (RCAF), 3, 72, 85, 92, 111, 145, 501, 605, 607 & 11 Group AACF
15 August: In the space of 10 minutes Croydon received considerable damage.
   The armoury took a direct hit and the airfield was cratered. 'C' hangar used
   by Rollason Aircraft Services was hit by incendiary bombs and all the training
   aircraft stored inside were destroyed. 'D' hangar received blast damage and
   was raked by cannon fire. 'A' hangar escaped with only a few broken windows.
   The Officers' Mess was destroyed from the blast, killing 5 airmen from No.
   111 Squadron and an officer from No. 1 (RCAF) Squadron, together with 62
   civilians. A number of airmen, 2 civilian telephone operators, and 185 civilians
   were injured. No. 111 Squadron was temporarily diverted to Hawkinge while
   repairs to the airfield were carried out
18 August: Within 5 minutes, 11 HE and 8 delayed action bombs fell onto the
   airfield and around the boundary; there were no service casualties

**1941**
Squadrons: 1, 17, 287 & 605
Croydon was already becoming of secondary importance as the RAF went onto
   the offensive, and later in the year it was being used by Army Co-operation
   squadrons

**1942**
Squadrons: 287, 302, 317, 414 & 1 ADF

**1943**
Squadrons: 116, 285 (det), 287 & 1 ADF
Croydon was being used by support and transport units

**1944**
Squadrons: 116, 147, 285 (det), 287 & 1 ADF
5 September: No. 147 Squadron re-formed with Dakotas
13 November: RAF Transport Command started services from Croydon

**1945**

Squadrons: 147, 167, 271 (det), 435 (det) & 143 GS

After D-Day Transport Command used the airfield for flights to the Continent and it became home to No. 1 Aircraft Delivery Flight

**1946**

Squadrons: 147, 167, 435 (det) & 143 GS

31 August: The last scheduled Dakota service took place

13 September: No. 147 Squadron was disbanded

**Closure:**

In 1946, Croydon was relinquished by the RAF and commercial flights recommenced. Croydon aerodrome closed for good on 30 September 1959.

**Current status:**

Housing and industrial developments dominate. There is still a large grass area where the runways once were, and stretches of concrete survive. The Control Tower and the terminal building which houses the Croydon Airport Visitor Centre both survive. (Website: http://www.croydonairport.org.uk)

## Haunted RAF Croydon

There have been many sightings of RAF fighter pilots at former RAF Croydon. Airmen in flying gear seen walking about the estate and on the playing fields disappear if approached.

*Source: Bruce Barrymore Halpenny,* Ghost Stations, *1986 (pp. 72-4)*

Workmen in the late 60s and early 70s reported hearing singing. This has been ascribed, for no apparent reason, to the people killed in the bombing raid on the airport in 1940. There have been many other ghostly voices reported, some in the offices which were formerly the old terminal building and Control Tower.

A council workman, early one morning in late 1971, was moving rubbish on the Roundshaw Estate when he saw an airman on an old British motorcycle coming towards him. As the figure rode past, the workman saw he had no face. Local folklore has it that the faceless phantom motorcyclist was a Battle of Britain pilot who was killed when his fighter crashed at the end of the runway.

Bill Wood, on 30 September 1979, arrived at Croydon in a helicopter from Gatwick and landed at the rear of the terminal building. At just after 11 a.m., in a crowd standing next to his parents was a tall, thin and sandy-haired man, described as being in his 50s and wearing a blue blazer with RAF woven badge. He asked them to fill him in on what was happening and also enquired who was arriving in the helicopter. As the helicopter touched down, he said 'Cheerio' and made towards the helicopter and disappeared. Photographs taken of the event do not show the man in the blue blazer.

*Source: Alan C. Wood,* Military Ghosts, *2010 (pp. 135-6)*
Alan Wood reports that the site of the Second World War Officers' Mess has been the location for the sounds of men singing wartime songs. However, it is in one of the new houses on the airfield that he uncovered a very interesting account. In the late 1970s, a young couple moved into one of the houses. The man was a collector of militaria, and bought a Second World War German SS uniform on a tailor's dummy which he placed in the hallway. And that's when the trouble started.

In the bedroom, while dressing to go out, the woman saw a Second World War pilot dressed in an Irvin flying jacket and wearing suede flying boots and a leather flying helmet with goggles and oxygen mask. The ghostly pilot disappeared. The figure is said to have appeared three more times. The dummy with the SS uniform was found thrown across the hall.

On another occasion, when a couple were sleeping in the spare bedroom, when the man was using the toilet his wife felt the bedclothes being torn from the bed and flung across the bedroom floor. The local priest conducted an exorcism of the house, but it is not known if this was successful.

In addition, Wood writes that a Luftwaffe pilot in flying clothing has been seen in one of the old hangars; he is locally said to be a crew member of a German aircraft shot down over Croydon airfield.

*Source: D. W. Hauck,* The International Directory of Haunted Places, *2000 (p. 29)*
In the 1930s, a Dutch pilot was killed when his aircraft crashed whilst taking off in dense fog. It was alleged that his apparition warned pilots of approaching foggy conditions by appearing to them as they filed their flight plans in the Control Tower. Hauck continues that in the 1960s the pilot began appearing to the owners of a house on the Roundshaw Estate, which is built on the part of the airfield where the crash occurred. This was a celebrated case at the time and was investigated by the Society for Psychical Research.

Other apparitions at the former airfield include three nuns who were burned alive in a plane crash during a blizzard in January 1947, and a Second World War pilot riding a motorcycle who has been witnessed on Foresters Drive.

Passengers and staff at the former airport reported hearing singing coming from the location of a former perfume factory which was bombed in the Second World War with the loss of sixty workers. During raids the staff at the factory would sing to keep their spirits up.

# Culham (HMS *Hornbill*)

RN Receipt and Despatch Unit

| | |
|---|---|
| County: | Oxfordshire |
| Location: | 5 miles S of Oxford |
| OS Ref.: | SU 535958 |
| Opened: | 01/11/1944 |
| Closed: | 30/09/1953 |
| Pundit code: | CH |
| Control Tower: | Standard Naval 3-storey Watch Office, 3860/42 |
| Condition: | Demolished in the 1960s |
| Runways: | 3 concrete/tarmac, (240) 1,410 x 30 yards, (203) 1,400 x 30 yards, and (348) 1,200 x 30 yards |
| Hardstandings: | 16 |
| Hangars: | Equipping and servicing – 1, Storage – 20, Reserve servicing – 10 |
| Ad., tech. & barr.: | Temporary, Nissen huts |
| Population: | ? |
| Sat. airfield(s): | Beccles HMS *Hornbill II* |

## History to 1946:

The ground layout of RAF Culham was typical of many bomber stations, with three runways. However, it had a large number of hangars sited mostly around the perimeter. RAF Beccles was a temporary lodging area under Culham's administration and as such was called HMS *Hornbill II*.

### 1944
1 November: HMS *Hornbill* was commissioned by the Admiralty as an Aircraft Receipt and Despatch Unit. It attracted many types of aircraft for the RN Ferry Pool (later known as No. 1 Ferry Flight) based here. Culham's principal use was as a training centre for naval reservists located between London and Oxford

### Closure:
On 30 September 1953, HMS *Hornbill* was paid off and Culham was subsequently used as a storage facility.

### Current status:
In 1960, the airfield was transferred to the United Kingdom Atomic Energy Authority for use in nuclear and atomic research. The Joint European Torus

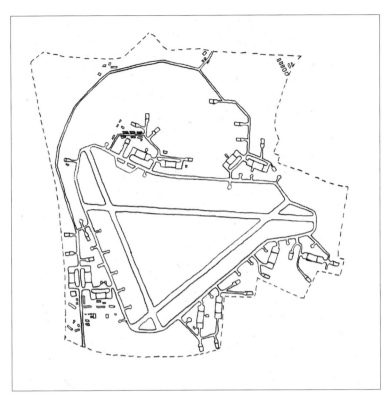

Culham (HMS
*Hornbill*)

(JET) high energy nuclear physics project is now based at Culham. Hangars of
the former airfield may be seen on its north-west side.

## Haunted RAF Culham

*Source: Bruce Barrymore Halpenny,* Ghost Stations, *1986 (pp. 140-1)*
Whilst at Culham in June of 1959, Brian Leigh, an officer in the ATC with nine
years' RAF service, was awakened one night by a violent thunderstorm. He opened
his eyes and lay looking at the glow of the stove reflecting on the roof of the Nissen
hut. The absurdity of this suddenly occurred to him, as it was high summer. The
glow he noticed seemed to get brighter; he sat upright in bed and turned to see
five naval types sitting round the stove, one of whom was an officer with two
gold rings on his cuff. Another he thought was possibly a Chief Petty Officer. The
figures – only a few feet away from his bed – were all in their No. 1 uniforms, and
all were bandaged on their arms or hands and heads. They did not look towards
him or even acknowledge his presence in the hut, and after what he estimated as
being some 30 seconds, realising that what he was seeing was not normal, he let
out a shout and they disappeared. He jumped out of bed and rushed towards the
stove, waking his fellows in the hut as he did so, and stood for a while looking at

it. When he eventually touched it, he realised that it was completely cold. Nobody got any sleep after that, and two of them later refused to sleep in that particular Nissen hut.

# Davidstow Moor

Coastal Command

| | |
|---|---|
| County: | Cornwall |
| Location: | 11 miles W of Launceston |
| OS Ref.: | SX 150850 |
| Opened: | 10/1942 |
| Closed: | 12/1945 |
| Pundit code: | DD |
| Control Tower: | Watch Office for all Commands 12779/41 with medium front windows to 343/43 |
| Condition: | Derelict |
| Runways: | 3 concrete, (304) 2,000 x 50 yards, (248) 1,400 x 50 yards, and (210) 1,400 x 50 yards |
| Hardstandings: | 50 x 130 feet-diameter concrete |
| Hangars: | T2 – 3 |
| Ad., tech. & barr.: | Temporary accommodation |
| Population: | RAF Officers – 298, OR – 2,500, WAAF Officers – 4, OR – 508 |

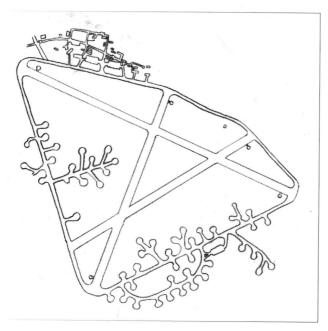

Davidstow Moor

## History to 1946:

The land was acquired in 1941 and with an extensive dispersal area was constructed in the first half of 1942.

### 1942
1 October: RAF Davidstow Moor opened before complete due to Operation Torch, when every airfield in the South West was in demand

9 November: Eighteen Liberators set off the following day to join B-17s in an attack on U-boat pens at St Nazaire in support of Torch

December: Two Henleys of No. 1603 Flight arrived from Cleave for target towing duties

### 1943
1 January: No. 53 Squadron arrived from Trinidad and re-equipped with Armstrong Whitworth Whitleys

27 January: No. 1603 Flight departed for Cleave

15 February: No. 53 Squadron departed for Docking

12 April: No. 612 Squadron arrived equipped with Vickers Wellingtons to fly anti-submarine patrols over the Channel and Biscay

17 May: Early in the morning 39 B-24s attacked Bordeaux pier and lock gates, and the Matford aero engine works

23 May: No. 612 Squadron departed for Chivenor

31 May: No. 547 Squadron arrived from Chivenor equipped with Vickers Wellingtons to fly anti-submarine patrols over Biscay

May: Control of the airfield was passed to No. 19 Group

7 June: No. 304 (Polish) Squadron arrived from Docking equipped with Mk XIII Wellingtons.

August: No. 547 Squadron started flare dropping during A/S patrols

25 October: No. 547 Squadron departed for Thorney Island

December: No. 281 Squadron on detachment arrived from Thornaby for ASR duties with Warwicks

13 December: No. 304 Squadron departed for Predannack and was replaced by a detachment of No. 280 Squadron with Warwicks

### 1944
8 January: Warwick 2801E, escorted by six Beaufighters, dropped a lifeboat to a Mosquito crew 95 miles SW of Brest

1 February: No. 282 Squadron re-formed to provide ASR cover of the Western Approaches

8 March: No. 269 Squadron moved to Lagens in the Azores

11 March: Nine Wellingtons of Nos 172, 304 & 612 Squadrons from Chivenor used Davidstow Moor to mount a concentrated anti-submarine patrol. No. 612 1R was lost, and 612 1C just made RAF Portreath, short of fuel

7 April: No. 524 Squadron re-formed with Wellington XIVs for patrols against E-
    boats along the French coast
10 May: No. 144 Squadron arrived from Wick with Bristol Beaufighters
12 May: The Wick Strike Wing (Nos 144 & 404 Squadron Beaufighters) arrived
    and joined No. 524 in working up for the anti-shipping role as 154 (GR)
    Wing
6 June: Nos 144 & 404 Squadrons attacked German ships off Belle Island; all were
    damaged and forced into Brest
July: The RAF Regiment began using Davidstow Moor as a training camp
1 July: 154 Wing moved to Strubby
August: Nos 404 & 236 Squadrons returned to take part in strikes on German
    naval forces
6 to 26 August: In a series of attacks, minesweepers, a floating dock, armed trawlers
    and 2 Sperrbrecher craft were destroyed or badly damaged
19 September: No. 282 Squadron departed for St Eval

### 1945
February: No. 281 Squadron moved to Tiree to provide ASR cover for Northern
    Ireland and Western Scotland
5 October: The RAF Regiment finally departed for North Witham

### Closure:
In December 1945, RAF Davidstow Moor was closed.

### Current status:
The site is currently used for agriculture and light aviation. More recently the
    Davidstow Airfield and Cornwall at War Museum have been set up to
    commemorate the work and people of RAF Davidstow Moor. It is located next
    to a creamery where 'Davidstow' and 'Cathedral City' cheeses are produced.

## Haunted RAF Davidstow Moor

*Source: Bruce Barrymore Halpenny,* Ghost Stations, *1986 (pp. 150-2)*
In July 1959, Prudence Pepper had just recovered from a lung infection, and to
convalesce she and her friend rented a small cottage on the edge of Bodmin Moor.
She claims to have heard noises coming from the nearby moor and decided to
investigate. Being a Despatch Rider in the London Fire Service during the Second
World War, Miss Pepper bought an old ex-Army motorbike, and in due course
found herself on Davidstow Moor airfield. At that time the runways were in pretty
good condition, but the Control Tower and other buildings were derelict. Two
roads had been built across the airfield and the southern part of the airfield had
been taken over by the Forestry Commission.

**RAF Davidstow Moor Control Tower**
Deserted and alone in an open expanse, the former Control Tower at Davidstow Moor is crumbling under the onslaught of the weather. The Cornish Paranormal Group (and others) have had interesting experiences within. It is located on the former airfield at OS TR 3354 6655. (*Courtesy of the Cornish Paranormal Group © Cornish Paranormal Group*)

On a Thursday night she again ventured to Davidstow Moor and made her way to the top of the old Control Tower to have a clear view of the two runways and settled down to wait. Just after 3.30 a.m., having dozed off for a couple of hours, she was awoken by the sounds of activity nearby and intermittent droning noises just as if aircraft were coming in to land. She recalls that the incident lasted for about six minutes, the planes seeming to overshoot with a swooshing sound and then crash at the end of the runway, for there were then flames in that direction followed by skidding noises, and a lot of voices and activity. This happened three of four times and then all was quiet once more. She spent the next half-hour wandering the runways looking for tracks, skid marks, or anything to account for what she had heard and seen, but found nothing.

On another night, Miss Pepper was returning home through the old airfield on her motorbike with a local poacher riding pillion. They were about halfway across when a Morris 8 of 1940 vintage was seen ahead of them, positioned at right angles to the road with all the doors wide open and the lights on. With torches they searched around but there was no trace of anyone. The next morning, Miss Pepper went out alone to the spot where they had seen the car, but there was no sign of it, no oil marks, no tyre marks, or any other sign of its ever having been there.

*Source: Keypublishing Aviation Forum, 26 January 2010*
Davidstow is extremely active regarding paranormal events and, so far, one group has experienced knocks, the sounds of something being dragged, footsteps, voices,

and whistles. On occasion, moving shadows and light anomalies were seen, and something sometimes messes with camera equipment and moves it around, even when the place is locked up. On the first visit, just as they had set up the cameras and were checking that they were all in position, all of the group witnessed a transparent figure walk past right in front of one of the cameras. Unfortunately, they had only just set up and were not yet recording.

*Source: The Cornish Paranormal Group, 24 July 2010*
At 9.30 p.m. they started the investigation in the derelict Control Tower, where two investigators felt a sudden chill, although this did not register on the thermometer. At one point, two investigators were located next to the stairs, one filming with a Mini DV camera, and the other taking a still photograph. They both heard a very clear woman's voice that seemed to come from right next to them and was captured on both of the audio recorders that were in different rooms, and also both Mini DVs. They left two audio recorders running in different rooms of the Control Tower while they went for a brief walk along the runway and then, because of the weather, returned to the Control Tower to listen to the audio recordings. They closed the investigation at 11.45 p.m. and as they were leaving, one of the investigators reported having a strange sensation on their right ear, akin to having their ear stroked, but like a mild electric shock.

A second investigation at Davidstow Moor produced some interesting audio results. Halfway through the investigation the team split up, three members remaining in the Control Tower and the rest exploring the airfield, runways, and other buildings on site. Following a request for a name, they received a reply which sounded very much like the name 'Eric'. On another recording there was the apparent sound of a Second World War propeller aircraft taking off from the airfield. The sound captured is very similar to that of a Bristol Beaufighter engine. Other auditory captures included three bangs that were heard by the investigators on the top floor, and again on the top floor a voice seemingly saying, 'Be quiet.' (Website: cornishparanormalgroup.org.uk)

The Davidstow Moor EVPs (Electronic Voice Phenomena) may be listened to at www.cornishparanormalgroup.org.uk/video_evp_29105974.html

# Debden

No. 11 Fighter Group
USAAF 8th AF

| | |
|---|---|
| County: | Essex |
| Location: | 2 miles SE of Saffron Walden |
| OS Ref.: | TL562351 |
| Opened: | 22/04/1937 |

| Closed: | 1975 |
|---|---|
| Pundit code: | DB |
| USAAF Station: | 156 |
| Control Tower: | 1937 Pre-war Fort Type Watch Office 1959/34 (brick), with later tower extension |
| Condition: | Demolished |
| Ops Room: | The Ops Room for the Debden Sector was moved away from the aerodrome after a raid on 31 August 1940 and a temporary hut was established in a disused chalk pit near Saffron Walden beside the A130 until Saffron Walden Grammar School was requisitioned for its use |
| Runways: | Grass, NE-SW 1,150 yards, E-W 1,200 yards, SE-NW 1,250 yards, and N-S 1,600 yards; 1940, 2 concrete runways and extensions to the taxiways, (280) 1,600 x 50 yards and (350) 1,300 x 50 yards; Mark II airfield lighting was installed |
| Hardstandings: | A mixture of steel mat and tarmac surfaces for 80 aircraft; additional 35-foot taxiways were constructed allowing aircraft to be dispersed in surrounding countryside. Some of the early tarmac hardstandings had earth and brick blast walls surrounding them for protection |
| Hangars: | C Type – 3, Bellman – 1, Blister – 11; 1938: 3 C Type hangars to accommodate three squadrons; 1940: a fourth hangar of the Bellman type was erected near the C Type hangars. During the early days of hostilities Blister hangars were added at various points around the airfield |
| Fuel stores: | Petrol storage totalled 72,000 gallons of aviation fuel |
| Ammunition stores: | A million rounds of small arms ammunition was in store available for immediate use |
| Ad., tech. & barr.: | On the E side of the airfield, comprising technical and administrative buildings and barracks, all brick-built in the mock-Georgian style of the Expansion Period. Accommodation was in permanent buildings adjoining the technical and administrative site, with a few new sites located in temporary buildings in the vicinity |
| Population: | USAAF Officers – 190, OR – 1,519 |
| Sat. airfield(s): | Castle Camps, Great Sampford |
| Decoy airfield(s): | Great Yeldham Q |

## History to 1946:

### 1935-39
The aerodrome was originally grass-surfaced

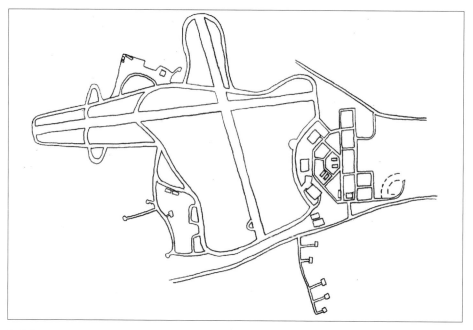

Debden

## 1937
22 May: No. 85 Squadron arrived from Lille/Seclin with Gladiators
7 June: No. 87 Squadron arrived from Tangmere with Gladiators
12 June: No. 73 Squadron arrived from Mildenhall with Gladiators

## 1938
Squadrons: 17, 87, 85 & 504

## 1939
Apart from a short spell within No. 12 Group, Debden was an 'F' sector station of
No. 11 Group, Fighter Command
May: Fighter sweeps were flown over Holland and Belgium, and French airfields
were used to cover the retreat of Allied troops

## 1940
The quiet period during the early months of the war provided the opportunity for
completion of buildings
Squadrons: 17, 25, 29, 73, 85, 111, 257, 264, 504 & 601
June: Castle Camps opened as Debden's satellite
During the Battle of Britain, the airfield was a sector station for No. 11 Group,
being occupied by 8 RAF fighter squadrons at different times
18 June: The first air raid sounded, although the first bombs were not dropped on
the airfield until seven days later

25 June: A German bomber using the returning No. 29 Squadron Blenheims' flare path as its marker dropped the first bombs on Debden

27 June: Debden became an all-Hurricane station

10 July: Debden suffered slight bomb damage from a Do 17 that dropped 22 small HE bombs, 5 of which landed near the married quarters breaking some windows

26 August: More than 100 HE bombs were dropped, scoring direct hits on the Sergeants' Mess, NAAFI, airmen's block, WAAF quarters, MT yard, equipment section, parade ground, and the landing area itself. One trench received a direct hit that killed 4 RAF personnel and a civilian. Electricity and water mains were damaged and several unexploded bombs remained buried in parts of the camp

31 August: Thirty Dorniers dropped about 100 HE and incendiary bombs, some falling on the N side of the landing ground. The sick quarters and a barrack block received direct hits and were badly damaged. The Sergeants' Mess, NAAFI, cookhouse, three wooden huts, a hangar, and a lock-up garage were also damaged. A civilian and an airman were killed and 12 RAF personnel were injured

**1941**

Squadrons: 52, 85, 264, 418 and 71, 121 & 133 Eagle Squadrons

14 February: A Heinkel He 111 landed and taxied to the Control Tower but took off before action could be taken

Additional hangars (a Bellman and 11 Blister type) were added to the S and W, plus further provision of hardstandings and revetments around the perimeter

**1942**

Squadrons: 65, 71 & 418

12 September: The three Spitfire-equipped Eagle Squadrons were turned over to the US authorities, becoming the 4th Fighter Group and renumbered as 334, 335 & 336 Squadrons

**1943**

January: 4th Fighter Group started to convert to P-47 Thunderbolts

**1944**

February: 4th Fighter Group converted to P-51 Mustangs

4 March: 4th Fighter Group led the 8th AF bombers on their first raid to Berlin

October: No. 616 Squadron RAF, the first RAF jet unit, had a detachment of Gloster Meteors at Debden to practise affiliation tactics with the 4th Fighter Group

**1945**

July: With the cessation of hostilities, the 4th Fighter Group was moved to Steeple Morden

5 September: Debden was returned to the RAF and became a unit of the Technical
   Training Commission as the Empire Radio School

**Closure:**
RAF Debden closed on 21 August 1975.

**Current status:**
The site is now known as Carver Barracks, Wimbish. Due to its post-war use, the
   airfield and technical site is almost completely intact

## Haunted RAF Debden

*A personal account*
Arriving early in 1976, I made my way to the hangar and the location of the Kirby
Cadet MK IIIs that we flew. I was alone in there, the first of the sprogs to arrive,
and as nowhere else was open I just sat and looked around. There were the usual
noises of a hangar – those clicks, groans, and creaks caused by the slightest of
winds. And then I got the most distinct impression that I wasn't alone in there, and
yet there was nobody around. I started to hear the unmistakable but seemingly
very distant tinkle and clatter of mechanics working, the occasional sound of a
dropped spanner. And then the next of my ATC companions roared in on his bike,
and the spell was broken.

   One lunchtime, I managed to have a look around one of the old buildings, and
there was a definite atmosphere, as though I had walked into a bar and everyone
had ceased their conversation and turned to look at me. Not that dreadful 'not
wanted' feeling that I had experienced elsewhere, but a 'who the hell are you?'
feeling.

*Source: Bruce Barrymore Halpenny, Ghost Stations V, 1991 (pp. 49-50)*
Steve Upton was at RAF Debden in 1973-74 training as a police dog handler. One
night he had just completed his round when a friend suddenly jumped up from
his bed screaming that an airman had just leaned over him. Upton states that he
saw no one there. Several others added that they had seen an airman on other
occasions wandering around the billet late at night. The next day Upton went to
the guardroom to find why someone was patrolling the billet in the middle of the
night. He was told that no one had.

*Source Army Rumour Service Forum, 16 March 2009*
At Wimbish Barracks, in the annexe out the back of the Officers' Mess above the
kitchen, one soldier was held down in bed and couldn't get up. Mentioning it to
another resident, described as a para, he also claimed to have had the same happen
that night. One of the Mess staff who had been there for years replied, 'Oh yes,

that would be the American pilot who shot himself in your bathroom. We see him all the time. Just ask him to leave you alone and he will!'

*Source: E-Goat, 14 June 2006*
Some boys of the soldiers stationed at Carver Barracks, whilst playing on the airfield at night, noticed some light coming from one of the old airfield bunkers. Curious to see who else might be on the airfield at this time of the night, five or six of them walked over to have a look. As they got closer they could hear voices, but by the time they arrived at the bunker there was no light and no voices.

Whilst playing football outside the gym on a Sunday, the boys became aware of noises coming from inside the building, which was locked up at the time. Reaching the main entrance they found it was indeed locked, as was the side entrance. Finally looking through the glass at the fire escape, they saw that nobody was inside but, to their amazement, a basketball was seen rolling across the floor.

*Source: E-Hangar, 4 May 2006*
Wade Meyers was told some interesting ghost stories during his visit to Debden, several of which were about a large 'ghost dog' climbing up on sleeping officers and pinning them to their beds before disappearing. On another occasion, a dog was barking furiously at the corner of the room in the Officers' Mess, then inexplicably whimpered and ran off to hide under a chair. In addition, late night workers in the Officers' Mess have sworn that they have seen figures walking up and down the large hallway.

# Dunkeswell

United States Navy

| | |
|---|---|
| County: | Devon |
| Location: | 5 miles NW of Honiton |
| OS Ref : | ST 132079 |
| Opened: | 07/1943 |
| Closed: | 02/1949 |
| Pundit code: | DW |
| USAAF Station: | 173 |
| Control Tower: | Watch Office for all Commands 12779/41 with medium front windows to 343/43 |
| Condition: | In use as Dunkeswell Airfield Museum |
| Runways: | 3 concrete/tarmac, (230) 2,000 x 50 yards, (360) 1,470 x 50 yards, and (270) 1,270 x 50 yards |
| Hardstandings: | 125-foot pan – 144, Spectacle – 6 |
| Hangars: | T2 – 5, US Navy Canvas – 2 |

Ad., tech. & barr.   Large dispersed temporary accommodation sites were to the SE
                    in wooded countryside
Population:          USN Officers & Men – 2,572

## History to 1946:

**1941-42**

Dunkeswell was built by Wimpey to a standard three-runway plan in the hills
  above Honiton, destined for use by No. 10 Fighter Group

**1942**

May: The airfield was transferred to 19 Group Coastal Command under
  whose direction it was provided with facilities to operate three squadrons.
  Unfortunately, it was not ready during the autumn of 1942, when the
  Command was stretched to the limit, and afterwards Coastal Command had
  no use for it

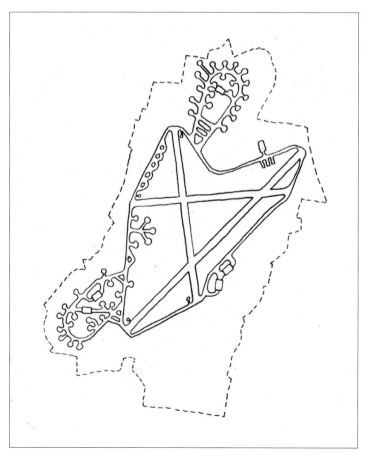

Dunkeswell

**1943**

July: Dunkeswell was turned over to the Americans, the RAF initially providing most of the ground personnel

21 August: The HQ of the US Navy's Fleet Air Wing 7 (FAW7) was established in Plymouth for Biscay operations

August: The 4th and 19th Squadrons of the 479 Bomb Group arrived from St Eval to fly anti-submarine missions over Biscay, using specialised B-24 Liberator bombers

September: The 4th and 19th Squadrons were replaced by VP 103, the first USN unit to complete training with the RAF; it was also equipped with Liberators

October: USAAF turned over the anti-submarine missions to the US Navy, and its Liberators were reassigned to Navy Patrol Bomber Squadron VPB-103, FAW7

**1943-44**

The winter was particularly severe and the US Navy Squadrons found it difficult to maintain operations, hampered by a shortage of ground staff and equipment

**1944**

March: Dunkeswell was handed over to FAW7, and all remaining RAF personnel were posted away

June: Intensive operations over the D-Day period resulted in many sightings by Dunkeswell aircraft, and the first operational U-boat use of the schnorkel tube was reported

22 June: Eight contacts and 4 attacks were claimed

July: A special air unit using PB4Y-Is converted into assault drones was formed to carry out attacks on V-1 and V-2 launching sites, codenamed Project Anvil

August: Six Seafires were supplied to the Americans. Retaining their British markings, they were fitted with American VHF R/T and used for air combat training for the patrol squadron crews

November: The Naval Squadrons moved to RAF Upottery while runway repairs were effected

**1945**

25 April: The crew of a VP 103 aircraft sighted a schnorkel and dropped one of the first homing torpedoes over 80 yards away

9 May: The crews of FAW7 were rewarded with the first surrender of a U-boat after the cessation of hostilities, when U-249 raised a black flag off the Isles of Scilly

June: The Liberators departed Dunkeswell for the US

11 July: The HQ of FAW7 moved from Plymouth to Dunkeswell, then back to the US at the end of the month

6 August: RAF Dunkeswell was transferred to No. 46 Group, Transport Command. No. 3 Overseas Aircraft Preparation Unit arrived from Llandow to become 16

Ferry Unit, absorbing 11 FU from Talbenny, for ferrying aircraft to the Middle East and for foreign air forces.

## 1946
16 March: 16 Ferry Unit disbanded

April: RAF Dunkeswell was placed on care and maintenance. However, the airfield does not seem to have totally closed to flying

7 May: A Lancaster III of 1 FU aborted take-off and finished up on its belly; it was scrapped on site

September: Dunkeswell became a sub-site of 265 MU RAF Grove, and then an equipment disposal depot for 267 MU until December 1948

### Closure:
In February 1949, the RAF withdrew from Dunkeswell and it became the base for the Devon & Somerset Gliding Club for a number of years, before they moved to the nearby North Hill site.

### Current status:
Part of the original technical site is used as a trading estate by a number of organisations, and two of the T2 hangars are in use for storage. It is a busy civilian airfield with a mix of light aircraft, microlights, and parachuting.

## Haunted RAF Dunkeswell

There are a number of accounts from Dunkeswell of Second World War aircrew being seen.

*Source: G503.com Forum, 14 October 2010*
Jeff Glasser wrote that before his retirement he had been one of the directors of a company that owned and operated Dunkeswell airfield. To keep costs down he and a friend would paint all the markings on the two remaining licensed runways, on summer evenings during the week, when it was fairly quiet. On one particular calm and pleasant evening, Jeff was painting the centre line markings for runway 23/05. His friend was working across the other side of the airfield and only just visible. Engrossed in the job, Jeff became aware of the sound of footsteps getting closer behind him, which he thought was his friend (who is known for practical jokes and having a wicked sense of humour) trying to creep up. At the point when Jeff thought his friend was right behind him, he turned and was about to shout something abusive but there was no one there. The footsteps veered away from him, becoming quieter and stopping after about 10-15 yards. Jeff admits that he seemed to be aware of the presence of a girl or young woman and, oddly, that she was aware of him and felt as surprised by him as he was by her. Calming down, he

continued with the painting of the runway and when his friend approached later he recounted the story. Jeff stated that he must have looked a bit spooked because normally his friend would have laughed.

A few months later, one of his drivers had a slight mishap with the rear of a car in traffic. His friend had a call from the old chap a few days later with a quote for repairs. During the conversation the man said that he knew of Dunkeswell from his days in the RAF, and asked if the ghost of the young girl still walked across the runway. Not long after this, someone who formerly had worked at the Met Office on the airfield came back for a visit, and told Jeff's friend that they would cut across the runways at the end of the day rather than go around the peritrack in the dark to get to the local pub. They did this until they had a similar experience to Jeff, after which they would always go the long way round.

# Duxford

No. 11 Group, Fighter Command
No. 12 Group, Fighter Command
USAAF 8th AF

| | |
|---|---|
| County: | Cambridgeshire |
| Location: | 8 miles S of Cambridge |
| OS Ref.: | TL 464558 |
| Opened: | 03/1918 |
| Closed: | 31/07/1961 |
| Pundit code: | DX |
| USAAF Station: | 357 |
| Control Tower: | A. 1917 Watch Office single-storey hut, replaced with later 1941 tower |
| | B. Observation post mounted on corner of hangar |
| | C. Watch Office for all Commands 12779/41 |
| Condition: | A. 1917 Watch Office now used for displays |
| | B. Removed post-war |
| | C. 12779/41 still in use for Flying Control (now has post-war VCR added) |
| Runways: | Grass, 1,600 yards x 2,000 yards. This allowed a 1,500-yard take-off run on the NE-SW and SE-NW diagonals, a 1,000 yard take-off from N-S, and a 1,400 yard take-off from E-W, although this approach was restricted by 40-foot-high trees at one end. In November 1944, US engineers had to lay down a 2,000-yard pierced steel planking runway on a NE-SW axis across the grass to extend the aerodrome at the E end. Duxford |

was closed in October 1949 for two years to have a single concrete runway laid

Hardstandings: Concrete – 26. In 1944, an additional 47 steel mat hardstandings were added

Hangars: 1917, 6 hangars (170 feet x 100 feet) and an aircraft repair shed; 1940s, Belfast Truss – 3 double and 1 single, Blister – 8

Ad., tech. & barr.: Permanent station buildings and married quarters were constructed N of the A505

Population: USAAF Officers – 190, OR – 1,519

Sat. airfield(s): Fowlmere

Decoy airfield(s): Horseheath Q/K, Great Eversden Q

During the Battle of Britain losses from Duxford were 25 aircraft and 9 pilots killed.

The 78th Fighter Group lost 264 aircraft.

## History to 1946:

### 1917

Both Duxford and Fowlmere were selected as sites for aerodromes

October: Construction started, both aerodromes being built to almost identical patterns each having 6 hangars, an aircraft repair shed, and a hutted camp for living and administration purposes

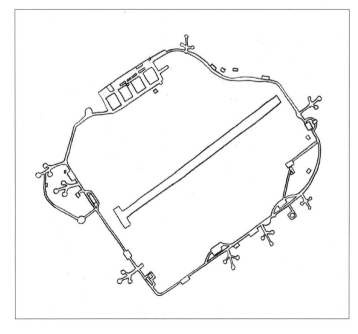

Duxford

**1920**
Duxford was selected as one of the RAF's first post-war training stations
May: Duxford opened as No. 2 Flying Training School

**1923**
April: Nos 19, 29 & 111 Fighter Squadrons were formed from Flights and
 personnel of the FTS equipped with Sopwith Snipes

**1924**
May: The FTS moved to RAF Digby and Duxford became a fighter station in No.
 6 Group

**1936**
July: No. 11 Group, Fighter Command formed; No. 66 Squadron formed at
 Duxford from No. 19 Squadron's 'C' Flight

**1937**
Duxford became part of 12 Group

**1938**
Cambridge University Air Squadron

**1939**
Squadrons: 64, 222, 611 & CUAS
5 October: No. 222 re-formed at Duxford as a shipping protection squadron
 equipped with Blenheim Is

**1940**
Squadrons: 19, 66, 222, 242, 258, 264, 310, 312 & Air Fighting Development
 Unit
11 May: No. 19 Squadron claimed a Ju 88
12 May: No. 264 Squadron's Defiants claimed a Ju 88 and an He 111 off the
 Dutch coast
10 July: No. 310 (Czechoslovak) Squadron formed with Hurricane 1s
29 August: No. 312 (Czechoslovak) Squadron formed with Hurricane Is
9 September: Duxford squadrons intercepted and turned back a large force of
 German bombers before they reached their target, claiming 20 destroyed for
 the loss of 4 Hurricanes and 2 pilots
15 September: The five-squadron wing took to the air three times against the
 continuous Luftwaffe attacks on London and claimed at least 42½ kills
21 September: No. 5 Radio Servicing Section formed and operated by No. 5 Radio
 Maintenance Unit
December: The Air Fighting Development Unit arrived from Northolt

**1941**

Squadrons: 56, 133, 310, 601, ADFU & No. 1426 (Enemy Aircraft Circus) Flight

**1942**

Squadrons: 56, 169, 181, 195, 266, 601 & 609, No. 1426 Flight & No. 1448 (Rota) Flight

October: The 8th USAAF 350th Fighter Group was activated at Duxford by special authority granted to 8th Air Force with a nucleus of P-39 Airacobra pilots. Initially the group received Airacobras and a few Spitfires

**1943**

Squadrons: 4, 124, 169, ADFU, No. 1426 Flight & USAAF

January–February: The air echelon of the 350th Fighter Group moved to Oujda in French Morocco

April: The 78th Fighter Group, 82nd, 83rd & 84th Squadrons, arrived from Goxhill and re-equipped with P-47Cs

15 June: RAF Duxford was officially handed over to the USAAF 8th AF and designated Station 357, with Mustangs of the 339th Fighter Group arriving

3 July: The USAAF 5th Air Defence Wing arrived from Norfolk Municipal Airport, Virginia, and was redesignated the 66th Fighter Wing

20 August: The 66th Fighter Wing was transferred to Sawston Hall near Cambridge

**1944**

December: The 78th FG converted to P-51 Mustangs

**1945**

October: The 78th FG returned to Camp Kilmer, New Jersey

1 December: Duxford was returned to the RAF

**1946**

April: No. 91 Squadron arrived from Ludham with Spitfire F.21s

1 September: No. 66 Squadron arrived from B.105 Twente with Spitfire XVIs

November: No. 91 Squadron moved to Debden

**Current status:**

Since 1991, the Imperial War Museum has been at Duxford.

## Haunted RAF Duxford

A presence has been felt in Hangar 3 and Hangar 5 at Duxford, and many have commented on the atmosphere at these locations and also the area between them and the Officers' Mess.

*Source: Keypublishing Aviation Forum, 13 March 2004*

Adam wrote that in 2003 a group of people stayed in the Control Tower at Duxford and reported numerous paranormal experiences during the night. He believes that a B-17 was seen crashing on the runway, but admits that he cannot attest to the accuracy of this as he was not present.

*Source: Keypublishing Aviation Forum, 15 March 2004*

Becka wrote that when working in the film vaults – the former airmen's quarters – doors suddenly opened or slammed shut and no one else had been in the building at the time. She has also felt a presence in the unrestored sections on the left and right of the Officers' Mess building, as well as noticing that the further away from the restored sections one gets, the more the presence is felt. She stated that it seemed as though a group of officers were sat round a fireplace with their beers and whiskies wondering what she was doing there.

*Source: Keypublishing Aviation Forum, 15 March 2004*

A man was at Hangar 5 early one morning before the doors had been unlocked. He let himself in and was working opposite the spray bay when he heard the door open and steps come towards him. When he came round the aircraft to see who had arrived, he found no one there.

Several radial-engined aircraft have been heard on approach during one of Duxford's Legends nights. The witnesses were staying on the north side and they ran up to the Bailey bridge to see what was landing. It seemed too late for normal flying, and indeed when they got to the bridge there were no aircraft to be found.

*Source: Keypublishing Aviation Forum, 24 May 2005*

Simon wrote about his experience at Duxford as a former employee. He was often one of the last daytime staff to leave the airfield, usually late in the evening and having to wait for a lift home. The workshop that had just been acquired was about 10 yards from the old base mortuary, and it was noticed that it would get incredibly eerie in the dark winter evenings. He also acknowledged hearing the slamming doors and footsteps in the hangars included above. At the time he assumed it was security staff checking on the buildings.

# Earls Colne

No. 3 Bomber Group
USAAF 8th AF
USAAF 9th AF
No. 38 Group

| | |
|---|---|
| County: | Essex |
| Location: | 3 miles W of Halstead |
| OS Ref.: | TL 848270 |
| Opened: | 08/1942 |
| Closed: | 03/1946 |
| Pundit code: | EC |
| USAAF Station: | 358 |
| Control Tower: | Watch Office for all Commands, 12779/41 with smaller front windows to 343/43 |
| Condition: | It was used as a house for at least 20 years (with two front windows bricked up and rooms divided) but then abandoned. In 2003, it was demolished |
| Runways: | 3 concrete/tarmac, (192) 2,000 x 50 yards, (250) 1,400 x 50 yards, and (302) 1,400 x 50 yards |
| Hardstandings: | Originally laid out with 36 pan type hardstandings but an additional 16 loop hardstandings were added after Earls Colne was allocated for USAAF use on 4 June 1942, one pan being eliminated in the process |
| Hangars: | 2 dispersed T2 hangars |
| Bomb stores: | On the SE of the airfield |
| Ad., tech. & barr.: | Technical site buildings, hangars, and accommodation were on seven dispersed domestic sites |
| Population: | RAF Officers – 208, OR – 1,805, WAAF Officers – 10, OR – 275 |

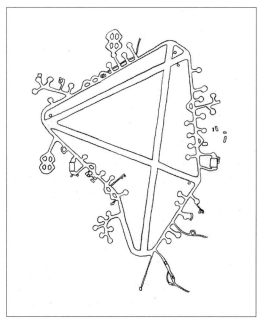

Earls Colne

## History to 1946:

### 1941
The airfield was built to the standard Class A bomber station plan

During construction, an American B-17F (41-24352) of the 301st Bomb Group from Chelveston made an emergency landing at the unfinished field

### 1942
August: Earls Colne was opened, and for the first year it was operated by No. 3 Group, Bomber Command. Apart from temporary use by F-5 Lightning photographic aircraft as a forward base, and emergency landings by a variety of types returning from operations, the site remained unused

### 1943
May: The airfield was allocated to USAAF

12 June: Earls Colne (along with nearby Marks Hall) served as headquarters for the 3rd Combat Bombardment Wing

12 June: The first American unit to use Earls Colne was the 94th Bombardment Group which arrived with the Boeing B-17 Flying Fortress from Bassingbourn

14 June: The 8th Air Force in a general reshuffle moved the B-17s into Suffolk and the group was moved to Bury St Edmunds in a general exchange of bases with B-26 Marauder groups. The 323rd Bombardment Group arrived from Horham with Martin B-26B/C Marauders

16 July: The 323rd commenced medium-altitude bombing missions against marshalling yards, airfields, industrial plants, military installations, and other targets in France, Belgium, and Holland

16 October : The 323rd was transferred to 9th Air Force. Tactical missions were flown against V-weapon sites along the coast of France

### 1944
20-25 February: During 'Big Week' the 323rd attacked airfields at Leeuwarden and Venlo in conjunction with the Allied campaign against the Luftwaffe and German aircraft industry

June: During the build up to D-Day, the 323rd bombed coastal defences, marshalling yards, and airfields in France

6 June: On D-Day, the 323rd bombed roads and coastal batteries

21 July: The 323rd was moved south to Beaulieu, a move designed to extend its range over western France

September: The airfield returned to RAF control and was passed to No. 38 Group operating Armstrong Whitworth Albemarles and Handley Page Halifaxes

30 September: Nos 296 & 297 Squadrons arrived from Brize Norton

**1945**
March: Nos 296 & 297 Squadrons participated in Operation Varsity

**1946**
23 January: No. 296 Squadron was disbanded
1 April: No. 297 squadron was moved to Tarrant Rushton, and Earls Colne was
    placed on care and maintenance status before being abandoned

**Closure:**
In 1955, Earls Colne was put up for public auction and much of the airfield was
    returned to agricultural use.

**Current status:**
Much of the airfield today is being used as a golf course. A flying club also operates
    from the old airfield, using a grass strip that runs along the line of the former
    SW-NE runway.

## Haunted RAF Earls Colne

*Source: Keypublishing Aviation Forum, 14 March 2004*
A contributor to the forum wrote, 'I believe Earls Colne has a haunted reputation,
with a number of stories about various sightings. A friend of mine has certainly seen
"something unexplainable" there and was somewhat shaken up by the experience.'

*Source: Keypublishing Aviation Forum, 29 August 2010*
The haunted jacket at the former Rebel Air Museum at Earls Colne had belonged
to Captain Jack Crane, a 322BG pilot killed during a mission on 17 May 1943. The
museum team had all felt a chill in the presence of the jacket, something the author
of the post had also experienced when passing its display cabinet. Apparently, a
medium was asked to try and find out more. She came up with the right name,
and said Jack had been upset by a romance with a girl he had met while stationed
at Andrews Field. I was told that some of the museum team, who would stay
overnight in the building, had had some very disturbing experiences there.

# Enstone

Bomber Command 21 OTU

| | |
|---|---|
| County: | Oxfordshire |
| Location: | 5 miles E of Chipping Norton |
| OS Ref.: | SP 390258 |

| | |
|---|---|
| Opened: | 09/1942 |
| Closed: | 1947 |
| Pundit code: | EN |
| Control Tower: | Watch Office for Bomber Stations and OTUs 13726/41 (shown with replacement windows) |
| Condition: | In use in 2001; upper floor windows and doors have been replaced with smaller double-glazed units |
| Runways: | 3 concrete/tarmac, (256) 2,000 x 50 yards, (329) 1,325 x 50 yards, and (195) 1,200 x 50 yards; extended to 2,225 and 2,000 yards |
| Hardstandings: | Heavy Bomber type – 27 |
| Hangars: | B1 – 1, T2 – 1 |
| Bomb stores: | To the E of the airfield; the present rally track was the former bomb dump and the 4x4 course runs around the old bomb hangars |
| Ad., tech. & barr.: | Temporary, to the SE of the airfield |
| Population: | RAF Officers – 72, OR – 711, WAAF Officers – 2, OR – 162 |
| Sat. airfield(s): | Satellite to Moreton-in-Marsh |

## History to 1946:

**1942**

15 September: RAF Enstone opened as a second satellite to 21 OTU based at Moreton-in-Marsh; however, it was not at first used

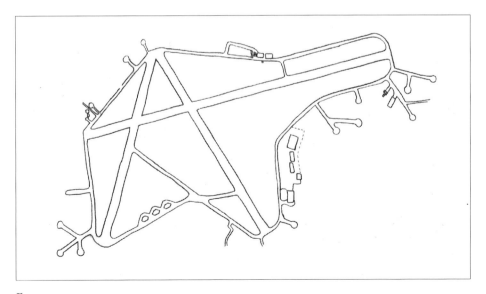

Enstone

**1943**

12 April: Enstone replaced Edgehill as the satellite to the parent airfield, the 466 personnel from Edgehill moving to Enstone

15 April: Wellington Z1142 swung off the runway on take-off, hit the windsock, and crashed in flames, killing three of the crew

30 April: No. 4241 AA Flight arrived at Enstone to provide guard duties for the station

17 May: 'X' Flight moved from Moreton to Enstone, with Lysanders and Martinets for target towing and Wellingtons for air gunnery

7 July: Wellington DV698 descending through cloud collided with Oxford LW783 underneath it; both aircraft and crews were lost

16 November: R1293 crashed at Enstone when its port engine cut on take-off, all the crew escaping with only slight injuries

17 November: DV918 from Enstone came down at Little Tew after overshooting the runway; 4 died

Late in 1943, the Wellington Mk Ics were phased out in favour of the Mk IIIs

**1944**

February-March: Wellington Xs replaced the Mk IIIs

22 February: No. 1682 (Bomber) Defence Training Flight arrived from Stanton Harcourt with 5 P-40 Tomahawks

24 February: No. 21 OUT's 'X' Flight departed for Moreton-in-Marsh

April: No. 1682 (B) DT Flight was equipped with Hurricanes

1 August: No. 1682 (B) DT Flight disbanded at Enstone and its Hurricanes were absorbed into No. 21 OTU

August: No. 21 OTU began using Honeybourne

16 September: LN771 was given the signal to take off just as Wellington LN429 was given permission to land. Only the WOp/AG from LN771 managed to escape as both aircraft caught fire

**1945**

9 April: Thirteen Lancasters from Bardney landed at Enstone along with a Halifax from North Creake

18 June: 'Cook's Tours' were arranged for the ground crews, and interest flights were made over Germany to show the results of Bomber Command's activities. Eight such tours left from Enstone

11 August: With the exception of a holding party, 21 OTU moved temporarily to Honeybourne so the runways at Enstone could be repaired

6 October: The Enstone detachment at Honeybourne returned, but within a month found out about the impending closure of the airfield

23 November: The last flights from Enstone took place and in the evening a farewell dance was held

24 November: All aircrew personnel left Enstone for Moreton, leaving only a
clearing-up party behind

**Closure:**
On 15 January 1946, the Marching Out parade took place and Enstone was closed
to flying. Official closure was on 17 January when RAF Enstone was handed
over to Maintenance Command.

**Current status:**
Part of the site is used as an industrial estate. An active gliding club, the Enstone
Eagles, uses the Tower and a good runway, at one time used for surface trials.
Microlights and light aircraft also use the airfield.

## Haunted RAF Enstone

The original Control Tower was used by the local gliding club where a presence
has been noted by many visitors. On another occasion when a boy was invited
by his father to one of the monthly summer barbecues held at the club, he saw
the hazy figure of an airman in what was described as 1940s dress, crossing the
peritrack behind the Oxfordshire Sports Flying club. He told his father, who
replied that this figure had also been seen by members of the flying club on earlier
occasions.

# Graveley

No. 3 Bomber Group
No. 8 Bomber Group

| | |
|---|---|
| County: | Huntingdonshire |
| Location: | 5 miles S of Huntingdon |
| OS Ref.: | TL 240630 |
| Opened: | 1942 |
| Closed: | 1968 |
| Pundit code: | GR |
| Control Tower: | Watch Office with Ops Room for Bomber Satellite Stations 7345/41, addition of Type B Observation Room 13079/41 and Control Room TD346 |
| Condition: | Converted into a house |
| Runways: | 3 concrete, (270) 1,600 x 50 yards, (330) 1,320 x 50 yards, and (210) 1,307 x 50 yards; extended (270) 2,000, (330) 1,420 yards, and (210) 1,407 yards |

Hardstandings:        36 pan type hardstandings distributed round the perimeter
                      track; during the runway extension work 3 pans were lost but
                      replaced by 3 loop standings

Hangars:              B1 – 1, T2 – 3 (2 T2 hangars on the technical site between
                      runway heads 15 and 21, and a T2 and the B1 in the SE corner
                      of the airfield between runway heads 27 and 33)

Bomb stores:          Located in open country to the SW

Ad., tech. & barr.:   A dispersed camp of temporary buildings lay to the N of the
                      airfield, consisting of sick quarters, a communal block, and 9
                      domestic buildings

Population:           RAF Officers – 159, OR – 2,141, WAAF Officers – 7, OR –
                      292

Sat. airfield(s):     Satellite of Tempsford

Bomber Command lost 150 aircraft in operations flown from this station: 83
        Halifaxes, 32 Lancasters, and 35 Mosquitos.

## History to 1946:

Graveley was a Class A airfield constructed as part of the Tempsford group for
Special Duties Units in No. 3 Group

**1942**
February-March: RAF Graveley was opened into No. 3 Bomber Group

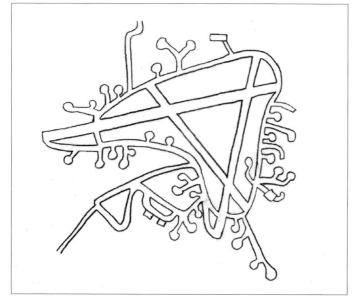

Graveley

March: No. 161 Squadron arrived from Newmarket with Lysanders and Wellingtons for Special Duties of dropping supplies and agents into occupied Europe

11 April: No. 161 Squadron moved to Tempsford and Graveley's runways were lengthened

August: Graveley was allocated to the Pathfinder Force of No. 8 Group, Bomber Command

15 August: No. 35 Squadron transferred into No. 8 Group and arrived from Linton-on-Ouse with Halifaxes

**1944**

1 January: No. 692 Squadron formed at Graveley to fly Mosquitos

**1945**

March: No. 35 Squadron exchanged its Halifaxes for Lancaster Is & IIIs

7 April: No. 35 Squadron's last mission before VE Day: 8 Lancasters marked an area at Rotterdam for dropping of food supplies to the Dutch

25 April: No. 35 Squadron's last operational mission: 8 Lancasters bombed gun batteries on the island of Wangerooge

2/3 May: No. 692 Squadron's last raid: 23 Mosquitos, operating in 2 separate waves of 12 & 11 aircraft, bombed Kiel

4 June: No. 692 Squadron moved to Gransden Lodge

8 June: No. 227 Squadron arrived from Strubby with Lancasters to prepare for the Far East as part of Tiger Force

5 September: No. 227 Squadron disbanded

10 September: No. 115 Squadron arrived from Witchford

**1946**

No. 35 Squadron took its Lancasters on a goodwill tour to the US

September: Nos 35 & 115 Squadrons were moved to Stradishall, with its permanent accommodation; Graveley was put on care and maintenance status and no more RAF units were based there. However, it was kept as a reserve airfield for the next 12 years, the main runway maintained in good condition and regularly used by training aircraft for circuits and bumps

**Closure:**

Graveley closed at the end of 1968.

**Current status:**

The site was reclaimed by Cotton Farm. The eastern end of the main runway still survived in the late 90s and a reduced perimeter track is used as a farm road. A number of Second World War buildings are still in existence. The Control Tower is a house and the fire tender shed still exists, as does the operations block.

**RAF Graveley Memorial**
The airfield closed in 1968 and was soon returned to agriculture; the Control Tower has been converted into a house and the runways have been broken up and removed. Little has been left on the ground to suggest that that an airfield once existed where there are now fields of crops growing. The memorial unveiled on 29 June 1991 lies beside Offord road at OS TL 5234 2654. (© *Chris Huff*)

## Haunted RAF Graveley

*Source: Bruce Barrymore Halpenny,* Ghost Stations, *1986 (p. 18)*
Bob Ballard was at Graveley on a late afternoon in November 1965. In the fading light, and just as a mist was descending over the old airfield, he found himself standing near the deserted and derelict airfield Control Tower. As he stood there he became aware of what he described as 'hustle and bustle' going on around him, and he then heard the clear sound of footsteps coming from inside the Control Tower. He thought he heard a door closing quietly in there too. Bob Ballard admitted that he made a hasty exit from the airfield.

# Gravesend

No. 11 Group, Fighter Command

County:          Kent
Location:         2 miles SE of Gravesend

| | |
|---|---|
| OS Ref.: | TQ 675720 |
| Opened: | 1932 |
| Closed: | 06/1956 |
| Control Tower: | Civil brick-built Watch Office, modified in 1942 by the addition of a third storey |
| Condition: | Demolished in 1965 |
| Runways: | Grass, N-S 275 yards, ENE-WSW 1,480 yards; 1942/1943, N-S increased to 1,420 yards and ENE-WSW increased to 1,800 yards and Sommerfeld steel tracking laid |
| Hardstandings: | Blenheim TE – 6, 36-foot diameter pan type – 30 |
| Hangars: | Blisters – 8, T1 – 1 |
| Fuel storage: | 32,000 gallons of aviation, 1,500 gallons of MT spirit, and 400 gallons of oil |
| Ad., tech. & barr.: | Temporary buildings |
| Population: | RAF Officers – 42, OR – 1,268, WAAF Officers – 6, OR – 212 |
| Sat. airfield(s): | Satellite to Biggin Hill |
| Decoy airfield(s): | Cliffe Marshes, Luddesdown QX |

## History to 1946

The airfield, covering 148 acres, was sited just south of Chalk village between the A226 and A2 roads.

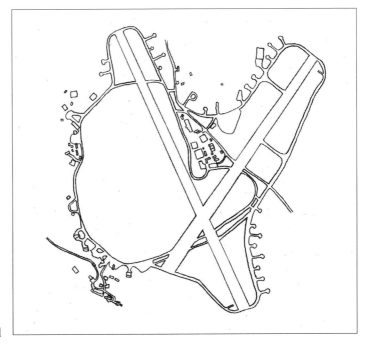

Gravesend

**1932**

June: The Gravesend Aviation Company was formed

12 October: Gravesend officially opened and in addition to charter services a flying school commenced

**1933**

July: The arrival of the RAF was heralded when three Hawker Audaxes and an Atlas used the airfield as a base during exercises

**1937**

October: Arrangements were made with the Air Ministry for Gravesend to become a training school under the rearmament programme. No. 20 Elementary and Reserve Flying Training School was formed

**1938**

Squadrons: 20 ERFTS

**1939**

Squadrons: 20 ERFTS

September: With the outbreak of the Second World War, No. 20 ERFTS closed and Gravesend airfield was requisitioned by the Air Ministry to become a satellite station of Biggin Hill

**1940**

Squadrons: 32, 66, 85, 141, 501, 604, 609, 610 & 1421 Flight

27 May: No. 610 Squadron arrived from Biggin Hill and took part in the Dunkirk evacuation

29 July: No. 501 Squadron engaged a large formation of Ju 87s and escorting Bf 109s, claiming 6 of the enemy shot down and 6 damaged

2 September: Enemy bombs fell on Gravesend aerodrome, injuring two soldiers

6 September: No. 501 Squadron members engaged a force of approximately 100 enemy aircraft over Ashford (Kent), losing 3 pilots

7 October: No. 421 Flight was formed at Gravesend to patrol the sky over the Channel to report any build-up of the Luftwaffe

**1941**

Squadrons: 72, 74, 85, 92, 141 & 264

**1942**

Squadrons: 65, 71, 72, 111, 124, 165, 232, 277, 350 & 401

December: No. 277 ASR Squadron arrived from Stapleford Tawney

**1943**
Squadrons: 2, 4, 19, 64, 65, 122, 132, 133, 174, 181, 193, 245, 247, 257, 266, 277, 284, 366 & 18 APC

**1944**
Squadrons: 19, 21, 65, 122, 277, 464, 487 & 501
17 April: Nos 21, 487 (RNZAF) & 464 (RAAF) Squadrons arrived from Hunsdon equipped with Mosquito VIs. These squadrons comprised No. 140 Wing in the 2nd Tactical Air Force
13 June: The first V-1 one fell on Swanscombe at 4.18 a.m.; soon the barrage of V-1s put an end to flying at Gravesend, as the airfield was directly in the line of fire
18 June: Nos 21, 487 & 464 Squadrons moved to Thorney Island

**1945**
Squadrons: 65

**1946**
Gravesend was placed on care and maintenance

**Closure:**
In March 1956, Essex Aero went into liquidation, Gravesend was closed to flying, and in June the Air Ministry relinquished control of the airfield.

**Current status:**
Today there is no longer any trace of the aerodrome, for much of the site is built up and is part of Riverview Park estate, two schools, playing fields and a sports centre having been constructed from 1958 onwards.

## Haunted RAF Gravesend

*Source: Bruce Barrymore Halpenny, Ghost Stations, 1986 (p. 21)*
In one of the houses on the Riverview Park estate the apparition of a German airman has allegedly been seen.

# Grove

91 Group, Bomber Command
USAAF 9th AF

| County: | Berkshire |
| --- | --- |
| Location: | 1 mile NW of Wantage |

| | |
|---|---|
| OS Ref.: | SU 389898 |
| Opened: | 10/1942 |
| Closed: | 1946 |
| USAAF Station: | 519 |
| Control Tower: | Watch Office for Night Fighter Stations 12096/41 |
| Condition: | Demolished in 1993 |
| Runways: | 3 concrete, (220) 2,000 x 50 yards, (340) 1,400 x 50 yards, and (270) 1,200 x 50 yards |
| Hardstandings: | 50 in total, 24 (originally 26) pan type and 26 loops |
| Hangars: | T2 – 6 |
| Bomb stores: | The ammunition dump was located outside the perimeter track surrounded by large earth mounds and concrete storage pens |
| Ad., tech. & barr.: | The ground support station was constructed largely of Nissen huts of various sizes. The technical site, connected to the ground station and airfield, consisted of 6 T2 maintenance hangars and large numbers of component maintenance shops. Various domestic accommodation sites were constructed dispersed away from the airfield but within a mile or so of the technical support site, also using clusters of Maycrete or Nissen huts |
| Population: | USAAF Officers – 214, OR – 3,188 |
| Sat. airfield(s): | Satellite to Brize Norton |

## History to 1946:

### 1941

May: Construction of the airfield commenced, with Grove originally intended for 91 Group, Bomber Command as a satellite to 15 OTU at Harwell

### 1942

October: RAF Grove opened as a very incomplete airfield

June: Grove was allocated to the USAAF for use as a transport base but was temporarily loaned back to the RAF when Brize Norton became a Glider Pilot Training Centre. Grove was used as a satellite to Brize Norton for advanced flying training; however, after just a short time the plan was abandoned due to the amount of glider activity in the area

1 November: Grove transferred to USAAF under the control of Bomber Command for transportation. At this time the airfield was for emergency use only and still not fully operational. Hangar No. 2 was under construction, and night landing and radio facilities were still incomplete

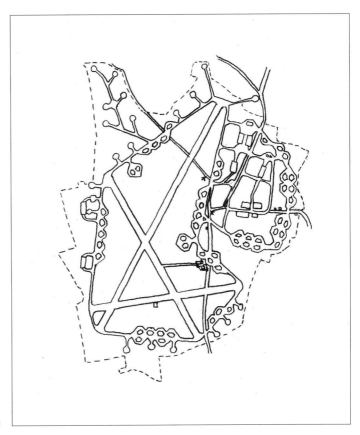

Grove

**1943**

January: Grove was returned to the RAF as an RLG for the Heavy Glider Conversion Unit from Brize Norton

27 April: Improved runway construction began

May: No. 15 (Pilot) Advanced Flying Unit arrived with Oxfords

Spring: Construction began on the West Technical Site and No. 2 Communal Site

June: Air Force Support Command took control of the airfield

July: The West Technical Site and No. 2 Communal Site construction was completed

27 July: The runways were completed

August: Grove became the home of the 3rd Tactical Air Depot and 31st Air Transport Group of the 9th AF, as a repair and maintenance base, at first for C-47 Douglas Dakotas, and later C-46 Commandos and Communication Flights

When the Tactical Air Depot Area was set up, Grove was used by the 3rd Tactical Air Depot of 9th Air Force Service Command

September: The RAF departed to allow the USAAF 9th Air Force to build up at Grove as part of the cross-Channel invasion of Europe

### 1944

The East Technical Site was built by the USAAF during 1944/45

September: The 31st Transport Group established a forward base at Querqueville early in the summer and moved its 92 C-47s there

2 September: The 1st Transport Group was established at Grove with a stated complement of 24 C-47s and 24 C-46s, although none of the latter were, as yet, in the UK

27 September: The 1st Transport Group moved to the 9th AFSC's depot at Creil

13 October: The 13th Photographic Reconnaissance Group of the 8th AF was stationed at Grove

December: The 31st Transport Group returned to Grove and remained until the end of the war

### 1945

June: The 31st Transport Group moved to Germany

15 October: The 36th Bombardment Squadron occupied part of the site until December 1945, using B-17s and B-24s flying occasional transport missions

23 November: The 13th Photographic Reconnaissance Group departed, to be briefly replaced by the 7th Photographic Reconnaissance and Magazine Group which then returned to the US

9 December: The 36th Bombardment Squadron departed for the US and Grove returned to the RAF, to be used for storage by No. 256 MU

### 1946

The airfield was placed on care and maintenance status and used for surplus aircraft disposal. In addition, No. 6 MU temporarily used the airfield to service captured German aircraft

### Closure:

In December 1958, RAF Grove was closed.

### Current status:

Today the area is used for agriculture, with the north-east part of the airfield under a large housing estate.

## Haunted RAF Grove

*Source: Bruce Barrymore Halpenny, Ghost Stations, 1986 (p. 77)*

In the late 1970s, the Metal Box Company took over some of the airfield buildings of No. 2 Communal Site for their research and development complex. Since their occupancy began, sightings have been reported in the area adjacent to the old wartime chapel, and the site of the Officers' Mess, of an apparition in full flying kit. This figure has only ever been seen late at night or in the early hours. A presence has also been noted in an area to the rear of the factory.

*Source: wantage.com/Museum*
Bill Fuller wrote a similar account of a ghostly figure clothed in flying gear and oxygen mask being seen in this area on several occasions.

Two theories were put forward to explain the apparition, the first being that he was possibly a fighter pilot who burnt to death when his aircraft crashed on landing at Grove airfield in 1945. The other theory is that it was a local man named Symons, from Wantage, who was one of a crew killed on 8 April 1945 when a Lancaster bomber crashed at Fyfield en route to Germany.

On the West Technical Site another apparition has been witnessed. A Mr Halliday worked shifts for the UK Atomic Energy Authority and was responsible for operating an irradiation plant in the old T2 hangar. At around 9pm on a summer evening in 1969, Mr. Halliday was working alone in the hangar when he was surprised to hear a group in conversation outside his office. On investigation he found the hangar still secure and empty. A similar incident occurred a few weeks later when the plant had broken down and everywhere was silent. Once these incidents had been reported, other employees came forward to relate similar experiences. It is believed that an American serviceman had hanged himself in the hangar during the war. (Website: wantage-museum.com/wp-content/uploads/2011/03/Grove-Airfield.pdf)

# Halton

Technical Training Command

| | |
|---|---|
| County: | Buckinghamshire |
| Location: | 4 miles SE of Aylesbury |
| OS Ref.: | SP 870112 |
| Opened: | 1917 |
| Closed: | N/A |
| Runways: | Grass, N-S 1,000 yards, NE-SW 620 yards, E-W 690 yards, and SE-NW 690 yards |
| Ad., tech. & barr.: | Permanent Expansion Period buildings |
| Population: | RAF Officers – 184, OR – 8,709, WAAF Officers – 134, OR – 1,841 |
| Decoy airfield(s): | Puttenham Q/QF |

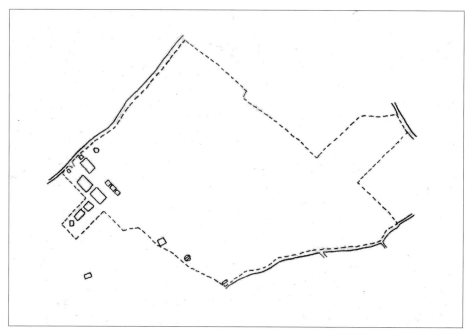

Halton

## History to 1946:

Halton is one of the oldest RAF stations, having been associated with military flying since 1912, and still plays an important part in the RAF.

### 1917
The Boys' Training Centre was formed in Halton Park

### 1919
An RAF hospital was established at Halton with limited medical and surgical facilities, together with the formation of the Hospital Orderlies Training Depot. This was a medical training establishment and school, and later the Institute of Hygiene and Medical Training

9 October: Opening of the Halton School of Technical Training (Boys)

November: Lord Trenchard's famous memorandum laid the foundations of Halton's apprentice scheme. He thought it impossible for the RAF's need for mechanics to be met merely by recruiting skilled men, and argued that the RAF must train its own mechanics. Alongside the camp was a grass airfield where old, worn out aircraft were flown in for technicians to be trained on

### 1922
January: The unit became No. 1 School of Technical Training, which title it retains

**1926**

August: Apprentices were learning mechanical trades trained at Halton; wireless training took place at Cranwell

**1927**

A larger hospital was opened by HRH Princess Mary, after whom the hospital was named

**1930s**

Building was proceeding apace at the station and by the outbreak of war there were four Wings of apprentices, each holding 1,000 boys under its own Commanding Officer and occupying a separate block of the camp. Competition to join was keen, and those desiring could proceed to Cranwell for permanent commissions

**1940**

A burns unit was established and became a leader in the field of plastic and maxillofacial surgery. By the middle of the war Princess Mary's Hospital held over 700 equipped beds

Wartime apprentice training was reduced. By the end of the war, 22,000 apprentices had passed out of Halton since 1920, and over 4,000 had become commissioned.

**Current status:**
Halton is the RAF's centre for recruit training and airmen's development training.

## Haunted RAF Halton

*Source: Luton Paranormal Society*
In the late 1960s, Halton was divided into two sections: the main camp and a separate hospital. A WRAF was living on the second floor of a block in what she described as a long and narrow room. One afternoon she was trying to get to sleep, whilst facing the wall against which her bed was placed. As she lay there she heard the door open and footsteps come towards her, and then felt someone was leaning over her as if looking to see if she was asleep. She turned round but there was no one there and she had not heard them leave.

There had been rumours of a strange dark shape that had been seen many times on the path from the hospital to the accommodation H blocks. One WRAF was walking from the hospital to the housing when about halfway along the narrow path she heard a strange unidentified sound. This was repeated several times over the next few minutes. Finally she looked around to see a tall, dark mass following her, at which point she ran as fast as she could without looking back.

*Source: E-Goat Forum, 1 March 2007*

The old IHMT training building was the burns and plastics ward during the Second World War; the ward opened onto a huge conservatory or balcony, onto which the beds would be pushed during the day to help the airmen get some fresh air. A foot patrol on guard duty to the building, which was a long way from the main camp, would sometimes find all the windows open. This would be a normal occurrence if it had not been a Saturday, and the fact that the balcony had been condemned, and that no one was supposed to go out there. This was called in over the radio and MPs arrived to secure the building. Another roving patrol, one hour later, reported all the windows open again. The MPs arrived and secured the building once more. After this happened a third time they refused to go into the building.

The building in question was used in the film *The Boys from Brazil*. It is alleged that the ghosts of the aircrew were not impressed by having Nazi uniforms around and made their displeasure known.

*Source: Keypublishing Aviation Forum, 5 February 2010*

In September 1977, two airmen heard voices and laughter when passing the Airmen's Mess. Inside were four airmen making merry. Dave, one of the two airmen passing by, told them to keep it down or they would attract the duty flight and get into trouble. The four airmen in the Mess looked a bit startled at Dave speaking, and then started to whisper to each other. Dave commented on the forum that they were wearing the old-style uniforms, and that he was going to ask them where they had got them from as he would like one. But as he started to speak to them again, they just vanished in front of him. Apparently several sightings of the group have been made over the years.

*Source: Keypublishing Aviation Forum, 17 February 2010*

In the building known as Harrier block there is a central staircase; on each landing you can either turn left or right and enter the dorms or walk forward into the toilets. On the top floor one dorm was used as a briefing room, the other had recruits in it. One night after evening briefing as the recruits were filing out of the briefing room, two of them turned round and saw the figure of someone darting behind a wardrobe in the dormitory. The senior man on the course went to find out who this was and to get him back into the group but there was no one to be found in the room.

One morning, someone was heard to leave the dormitory, followed by the sound of the heavy fire door shutting. Thinking it was someone wanting to grab the showers before the morning rush, nothing was particularly thought of it. A very short time after this the witnesses to the sound of the fire door closing walked into the showers and discovered that they were the only ones in there. They thought it was perhaps the training NCOs who had shut the door, but all three of them actually arrived together about 15 minutes later, so it couldn't have been them either. The closing of the door remains a mystery.

# Hawkinge

No. 22 Group
No. 3 Recruits Training Pool
No. 11 Group

| | |
|---|---|
| County: | Kent |
| Location: | 2 miles N of Folkestone |
| OS Ref.: | TR 211395 |
| Opened: | 1915 |
| Closed: | 1962 |
| Pundit code: | HA |
| Control Tower: | Watch Office Type A Timber Hutting |
| Condition: | Demolished |
| Runways: | Grass, NE-SW 1,100yards, E-W 1,100 yards, and N-S 900 yards; 1943, main runway extended and additional facilities provided |
| Hardstandings: | Twin engine – 9 |
| Hangars: | Blisters – 2, E-O Blisters – 4, GS sheds – 4; 1940, 3 double fighter pens on W boundary and 3 double fighter pens in Killing Wood; August 1941, 3 Extra-Over Blister hangars dispersed around the airfield |
| Ad., tech. & barr.: | Semi-permanent (some Nissen huts) to the NW of the airfield; 1931, station upgrade – two barrack blocks, an educational block, NAAFI, Officers' Mess, Sergeants' Mess, and married quarters were built |
| Population: | RAF Officers – 102, OR – 1,191, WAAF Officers – 1, OR – 202 |
| Sat. airfield(s): | Satellite to Biggin Hill |
| Decoy Airfield(s): | Wootton Q |

## History to 1946:

Hawkinge airfield first opened in 1915. It was taken over by the RAF Section of the Inter-Allied Commission of Control in 1920.

**1924**
April: No. 17 Squadron re-formed with Snipes
October: No. 56 Squadron received Grebes

**1933**
7 August: A Horsley of No. 504 Squadron returning from the bombing ranges lost power on approach and landed on top of No. 4 hangar. The crew scrambled

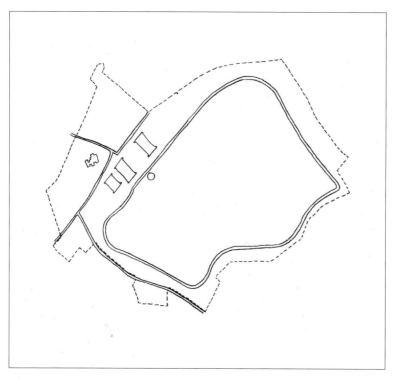

Hawkinge

clear but leaking fuel ignited and very quickly the hangar with 6 Blackburn Darts inside was destroyed

### 1939

22 August: No. 25 Squadron moved to Northolt as a night fighter unit
6 October: No. 2 Squadron moved to France
Hawkinge was transferred to No. 3 Recruits Training Pool but remained unused
December: No. 3 Squadron with Hurricanes arrived from Croydon

### 1940

Squadrons: 3, 16 AC, 17, 25, 79, 141, 604, No. 613 AAF, 421 Flight, and Lysander Flight
17 April: Hawkinge was used as a forward satellite field for Debden
May: German transmissions were picked up by the listening post, a linguist on the camp was found to translate, and soon a team of German-speaking WAAFs were maintaining a 24-hour watch. It was the beginning of the Y-Service
19 July: No. 141 Squadron with 12 Defiants arrived on rotation from West Malling. Ten Bf 109s dived on them and then a second *Staffel* attacked head-on. In less than a minute, 4 Defiants were shot down and another abandoned on fire. Only 2 survived the landing back at Hawkinge. No. 141 Squadron had been effectively destroyed in one engagement

12 August: Bombs cratered the airfield, the rest hitting the technical site. The end doors of No. 3 hangar collapsed, the main equipment store and 2 of the married quarters used for airmen's accommodation were destroyed, and a large workshop was set ablaze. Five were killed and another 7 badly wounded; 4 Hurricanes on the ground had been damaged

15 August: Eleven Stukas managed to destroy No. 5 (Handley Page) hangar, and a barrack block used by sergeant pilots was badly damaged. During the afternoon Do 17s raided the airfield but no significant damage was done

18 August: Six Do 17s, escorted by Bf 109s, came in low over the village and strafed the airfield but little damage was done

1 September: Five aircraft dropped 8 275-lb bombs. These hit the already wrecked No. 3 hangar and blew a small building nearby to bits. Some sections of the station were dispersed and work was started on a decoy Q site at Wootton

7 September: Bf 109s and 110s dropped 18 bombs that hit the Officers' Mess, No. 1 hangar and the SHQ. One soldier was killed, 12 station personnel injured, and 6 civilians killed in a direct hit on a village shelter

9 October: Six Bf 109s appeared over Hawkinge at midday but succeeded only in bombing the already abandoned buildings

## 1941
Squadrons: 41, 65, 91, 277 & Hawkinge ASR Flight

16 May: Marauding Bf 109s destroyed 2 shelters and the roof of No. 2 hangar, and damaged 2 Spitfires. One airman was killed and 5 more injured in the attack

## 1942
Squadrons: 91, 277, 415 & 616

15 June: Nos 41 & 65 Squadrons arrived for Rhubarbs and Rodeos over France

14 August: Nos 416 & 616 Squadrons arrived for Operation Jubilee

## 1943
Squadrons: 41, 91, 313, 322, 350 & 501

28 June: The Spitfire XII squadrons were formed into a bomber support Wing

9 July: A No. 460 Squadron Lancaster landed on two engines after a raid on Cologne. The pilot got it down on the N-S runway but only managed to stop the aircraft after it had demolished a Nissen hut

## 1944
Squadrons: 132, 277, 322, 350, 402, 501, 854 & 855

30 April: Departure of the fighter units from Hawkinge, leaving No. 277 ASR Squadron in residence

14 May: No. 157 Wing of No. 16 Group, Coastal Command moved to Hawkinge with 24 Grumman Avengers for Operation Channel Stop

5 June: A fully loaded Avenger of 855 Squadron crashed on take-off

3 July: No. 350 Squadron arrived for anti-Diver patrols and Ranger missions

9 July: No. 157 (GR) Wing moved to RAF Thorney Island

8 August: No. 402 Squadron arrived for anti-Diver patrols and Ranger missions

### 1945

5 January: A 388th BG B-17 appeared over Killing Wood during the afternoon, tore through a fence, hit a bank, and broke in two, killing 4 of the crew with only the pilot and tail gunner surviving

15 February: No. 277 Squadron disbanded at Hawkinge

October: The APS moved out and No. 278 Squadron detachment was disbanded

7 November: Hawkinge was reduced to care and maintenance.

### Closure:

RAF Hawkinge was closed on 8 December 1961.

### Current status:

The site has now been largely built over with housing. A small part is occupied by the Kent Battle of Britain Museum. (Website: www.kbobm.org)

**RAF Hawkinge**

The Battle of Britain Museum at former RAF Hawkinge with a replica Hurricane in the foreground. Not much of RAF Hawkinge survived the onslaught of modern development and the museum occupies a very small fragment of this once front-line airfield. The Operations Block and 'B' Flight Dispersal Hut are still extant and used for the museum's extensive displays. The museum is located off Aerodrome road at OS TR 2072 3952. (*Courtesy of Nick Smith © Nick Smith*)

## Haunted RAF Hawkinge

There have been many reports about a greyish hazy figure who appears to walk or stagger sideways as if wounded or, as some state, dragging a parachute.

Jim Macan wrote to me in 2009. After a visit around the museum, Jim collected his camera from the entrance, as photography is strictly not allowed in the museum for some reason, and asked, 'Do you have any ghosts here?' The man, strangely, was bordering on being angry and replied, 'I don't believe in any suchlike stories. Once a year I let the Society for Psychical Research from London in with their equipment to do tests. It takes them all day and they are usually dressed in black. There's a lot of history behind this airfield.' There was a long silence as he glared at Jim with a stare that was almost intimidating. 'Alright,' he continued; 'that hangar you saw last gives me a strong feeling that somebody is walking beside me when I'm locking up at night. But I know it's just because I'm tired, that's all.'

*Source: Bruce Barrymore Halpenny,* Ghost Stations, *1986 (pp. 112-3)*
On 14 August 1982, Clifford Dray had been to visit a friend in Hawkinge. At about 10.30 p.m., on his way home, he reached the gates to the Battle of Britain Museum where he heard the sound of an aircraft engine. At first he thought it might have been a generator but everything seemed to be closed and locked up, and he couldn't see any lights on anywhere. The engine noise seemingly revved higher, and sounded to him rather like that of an aeroplane taking off.

*Source: Bruce Barrymore Halpenny,* Ghost Stations, *1986 (pp. 112-3)*
One unnamed ex-WAAF commented that she had witnessed a phantom airman whilst at Hawkinge. He was dressed in flying kit, wearing a flying helmet, and possessing a sort of eerie glow. As she watched the figure, he just vanished in front of her.

*Source: Alan C. Wood.* Military Ghosts, *2010 (p. 131)*
Alan Wood asserts that in 1995 local people say they heard the distinctive sound of a V-1 flying bomb over the old wartime airfield.

*Source: East Kent Paranormal Investigation Group, 14 October 2008*
Manda wrote that during the course of a small investigation at Hawkinge, the group found the energies of a lot of airmen, picked up the sense of a large fire at the airfield, and in one or two places feelings of intense sadness. She also commented that she went to the Battle of Britain Museum in 2007, but had to leave the hangar because she was feeling very light-headed and sick.

*A personal account*
I have often been to the Battle of Britain Museum, located in buildings on what is all that remains of the former first-line defence airfield of RAF Hawkinge a couple

of miles on the hills above Folkestone in Kent. During my last visit in 2005, after I had finished looking at the aircraft exhibits in the Stuart-Buttle Hangar and the Dowding Memorial Hangar, with the mock-ups used in the film *Battle of Britain*, and the recovered remains from a number of crashed aircraft, I found myself in the Operations Block. This is now home to items gleaned from over 600 Battle of Britain aircraft, the majority of which were excavated by the museum's recovery team in the late 1960s and 70s, or donated by individuals since the foundation of the collection. I turned the artificially partitioned corner, noting its other-worldly atmosphere and definite chill as I did so, and made contact with a young man in RAF uniform. He was in his very early 20s, about 5 feet 10 inches tall, with short, Brylcreemed black hair combed into a side parting, a thin pencil moustache, and dark eyes. He wore the RAF No. 1 uniform with King's crown wing over the left breast pocket, and had a pilot officer's thin stripe at the wrist. Standing there casually with left hand in trouser pocket, his jacket rucked up and over the sleeve, he just looked at me and seemed as surprised as I was, then smiled at me. I asked, 'Why are you here?' and got an instantaneous reply. 'Oh, I pop in now and again.' And before I could think of a reply, he said simply, 'Oh well, cheerio,' then vanished.

*Source: Dover, Kent Archives*
'The Mayfly' pub was built to serve the new Hawkinge housing estate and has a Battle of Britain theme due to the estate being built on what was the landing area of the former airfield. The pub was featured in the *Kent Messenger* in April 2007, after paranormal activity had been experienced by staff members and was also captured on CCTV.

An investigation was conducted at the pub by Ghost Search UK on Saturday 23 June 2007. Whilst on site, the members of Ghost Search claim they made contact with three active spirits who had served in the WAAF, and also with a pilot who gave his name as Malcolm Smith. Smith said he crashed his plane as he left the airfield on a mission.

The investigation started in the main bar of the pub with a table tipping session. There was a general feeling throughout of 'Careless talk costs lives', and the information given was admitted to be a bit sparse. The investigation then moved into the kitchen and the first of the night's séances was held.

Adam was almost immediately aware of a male in his late twenties who had worked on the land; he had a problem with his breathing and he felt sick. Then Glen picked up on a woman called Mabel, about 5 feet 3 or 5 feet 4 inches tall and of a 'robust' build, who had worked in the NAAFI as a cook. Mabel said she was just passing and that she had some sad memories of the youngsters who had passed, and there was a feeling of sadness with her that was picked up by some of the group members. Adam then heard 'Incoming' called out and had the feeling that he should duck down for cover. Pete then noticed a man step forward who gave his name as Lance Corporal George Preston and stated that he was an air traffic controller (highly unlikely). He was described as thin with short black hair, about 5 feet 7 inches tall, aged 35, and had been burned to death. A guest of the group named Ashley kept seeing a reflection in a door with glass panels that moved behind him, but there was no one there. At one point in the investigation the pot wash turned itself on (this device requires someone to push the lever manually to let the water through). The entire group also heard an old-fashioned kettle whistle, although there was no kettle in the area.

The next phase of the investigation was conducted upstairs in the living room. They again formed into a circle and performed a séance. Pete saw a young boy, about 7 or 8 years old, looking very thin and pale and wearing a pair of grey flannel shorts that seemed too long for him, step into the room from behind Adam. He said his name was Edward but was always called Teddy. Pete told Chloe (another guest of the group) that Teddy was going to touch her. Chloe reported that she felt as if someone was holding her elbow. Teddy asked if it was alright to bring his dog in and then brought in a brown and white border collie. Then Teddy departed. Adam had a peculiar feeling in his arm as if something was moving under the skin, and Glen became aware of a male energy in the corner of the room; the male wouldn't step forward and talk to them. Steve wrote that in one of the bedrooms of the flat they encountered a woman in her fifties who was just passing through, and a male energy that brought with him a very depressive atmosphere, something that was felt by all the guests. Information was received that this was a sergeant in the Army, whose name was Charles. One of the guests and Pete smelt pipe tobacco associated with the presence.

# Hendon

26 Group
44 Group

| | |
|---|---|
| County: | Middlesex |
| Location: | 8 miles NW of St Paul's Cathedral, London |
| OS Ref.: | TQ 215905 |
| Opened: | 1909 |
| Closed: | 1957 |
| Pundit code: | ND |
| USAAF Station: | 575 |
| Control Tower: | A. Unique Grahame-White aircraft factory Watch Office built in 1911 |
| | B. Office for Duty Pilot, 2072/26 |
| Condition: | A. Demolished by the RAF Museum |
| | B. Office for Duty Pilot demolished in 1989 |
| Runways: | 3 concrete/tarmac, (339) 1,325 x 50 yards, (014) 1,020 x 50 yards, and (280) 1,000 x 50 yards |

Hardstandings:  Banjo type – 12
Hangars:        Steel Truss and Brick – 1, Belfast – 2, Grahame-White factory
Ad., tech. & barr.:  Permanent Expansion Period buildings to the SE of the airfield
Population:     RAF Officers – 80, OR – 1,157, WAAF Officers – 15, OR – 409

## History to 1946:

**1925**
The civil aerodrome at Hendon was sold to the RAF

**1930**
17 March: No. 604 Squadron formed

**1933**
July: No. 24 Squadron arrived from Northolt and would stay right through the
    war. The unit was involved with flying high-ranking officers, Ministers of State,
    and important civil servants around the country

**1936**
10 February: No. 611 Squadron formed

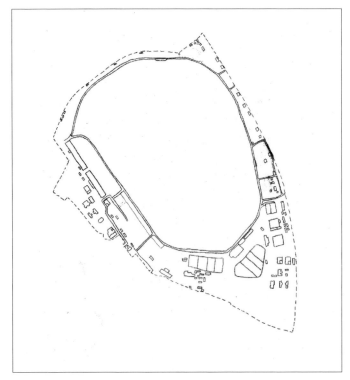

Hendon

**1937**

1 December: HQ No. 26 Group re-formed at Hendon within Training Command to control ERFTS units

**1939**

Squadrons: 24, 248, 600, 601, 604, The King's Flight, No. 50 Group Communications Flight & Blenheim Conversion Flight

During the war Hendon housed many fighter squadrons

3 February: No. 26 Group was renamed No. 50 (Reserve) Group and transferred to Reserve Command

11 September: Hendon became No. 21 Aircraft Park to 25 September

November: Became HQ No. 52 (Army Co-operation) Wing

**1940**

Squadrons: 24, 81, 248, 257, 504 BC Flight, No. 1 Radio Fitting Unit & No. 1 Camouflage Unit

7 October: No. 24 Squadron's hangar was destroyed by an oil bomb

11 November: A number of 250-lb bombs were dropped in the east camp, on the airfield, and in the west camp

**1941**

Squadrons: 24, 116, No. 1416 (Reconnaissance) Flight, No. 1 RFU, No. 1 CU & No. 1 Aircraft Delivery Flight

3 March: No. 1416 (Reconnaissance) Flight formed

August: No. 151 Wing at Hendon

9 September: No. 1416 Flight moved to Benson

**1942**

Squadrons: 24, 116, 510 & No. 1 AD Flight

15 October: No. 510 Squadron formed from 'A' Flight of No. 24 Squadron for communications flying

**1943**

Squadrons: 24, 510 & 512

18 June: No. 512 Squadron formed, equipped with Dakotas, and began training with airborne forces

**1944**

Squadrons: 24, 510, 512, 575, Metropolitan Communications Squadron, Transport Command Communication Flight, Allied Flight & No. 1316 Dutch Communication Flight

1 February: No. 575 Squadron formed, equipped with Dakotas, and began training with airborne forces

14 February: Nos 512 & 575 Squadrons moved to Broadwell

8 April: No. 510 Squadron was redesignated the Metropolitan Communications Squadron

30 June: A V-1 flying bomb hit a wing of Colindale Hospital, killing 4 airmen

3 August: A V-1 flying bomb exploded in front of a brick barrack block in the SE corner of the airfield; 5 huts were damaged beyond repair, 9 airmen killed, and 25 injured

7 July: Hendon was transferred to ACC No. 116 Wing, which moved in from Hendon Hall to No. 2 Mess at Hendon

23 July: Hendon became HQ No. 116 Wing

## 1945

Squadrons: 24, MC Squadron, TCC Flight, Allied Flight, No. 1316 Flight

1 January: Hendon ceased to be HQ No. 116 Wing

Autumn: All units except No. 24 Squadron, flying VIPs, had moved out

## 1946

Squadrons: 24, 601, 604, MC Squadron, TCC Flight, Allied Flight, No. 1316 Flight

25 February: No. 24 Squadron moved to Bassingbourn; with the departure of the resident unit, all flying ceased at Hendon

10 May: The Auxiliary Air Force was re-formed; Nos 601 & 604 Squadrons were re-formed

December: No. 601 Squadron commenced flying

**Closure:**

RAF Hendon closed in November 1957.

**Current status:**

The site of the airfield is now occupied by the Grahame Park housing estate, Hendon Police College, and the RAF Museum, which is situated on the south-east side of the site. (Website: www.rafmuseum.org.uk/london)

## Haunted RAF Hendon

During the construction of the museum, three building workers fell to their deaths through the glass roof.

*Source: Kevin Desmond,* Aviation Ghosts, *1988 (pp. 129-33)*

According to security officers at Hendon, a number of strange things have happened: men in overalls have been seen walking down the carpeted walkways; whistling, muffled talking, and music has been heard; and a strange and unaccountable movement has rocked items on display in the glass showcases. A pilot who was killed when his Avro 504K or B.E.2c crashed between the two original hangars is most often blamed for the various phenomena in the museum.

In 1940, a Spitfire of No. 604 Squadron overshot the runway and crashed into the corner of the E-shaped barrack block known as Building 46 (Vickers Block). In July 1972, a senior aircraftman at Hendon was returning home at 2 a.m. Turning off the light in the dormitory and climbing into his bunk, he was immediately aware of the smell of pipe smoke. Looking out of the window, he saw a man leaning against a tall beech tree and wearing the old-type flying jacket and boots, with a flying helmet slung across his right arm. In one of the old dispersal bays he saw the silhouette of what he thought was a Spitfire. He ventured outside to check, but everything was gone except the smell of pipe tobacco.

In the same barrack block, a corporal was up during the night to go to the lavatory. He turned on the light, opened the door, and saw a figure in flying gear with a polka-dot scarf, holding a flying helmet and just leaning against the corner of the main corridor wall, who then simply faded into the wall.

*Source: Bruce Barrymore Halpenny,* Ghost Stations II, *1990 (pp. 143-7)*
As two museum staff started to ascend the stairs at the far end of the building a rather posh accent said clearly, 'Hello there,' and then repeated it once more. A thorough search of the area was made but no one was found to account for the voice.

One night two cleaning ladies saw a man in overalls smiling down at them from the top of a scaffolding tower, at a time after all the workmen had gone home. They reported it to the warden who investigated the report but found no one there. A few days later the man in overalls was seen again on the same scaffolding.

One of the night security staff was walking past the Me 110 in the Battle of Britain Hall, when out of the corner of his eye he thought he saw a pair of boots walking along behind the aircraft. Turning on some more lights, he went upstairs to get a better view of the hall. Thinking an intruder had got in, he called for assistance and a thorough search was conducted, but nobody was found.

Bruce Barrymore Halpenny also records that seven members of a paranormal investigation group spent the night of 19/20 March 1988 at the museum. It seems that the investigators were free to wander and change positions whenever they felt like it – never a good strategy on an investigation. The team members were dispersed in pairs throughout the building whilst another member monitored the museum with his video camera. During the night the following incidents are said to have occurred:

At 9.30 p.m. Angie was standing near to a Hawker Hart biplane and felt as though she was struck firmly on the top of the head. The blow she described as being by a clenched, gloved fist.

At 10 p.m. Mark, while returning along the upper gallery, heard a loud bang as if something heavy had been thrown down. A thorough search revealed nothing.

At 4.02 a.m. an apparent cold spot accompanied by a tingling sensation in the fingers was reported by the Clarks.

At 4.20 a.m. Mark and the Clarks had entered the Bomber Command Wing, where they saw a vivid flash of blue light cross the wall beyond a Lancaster bomber. This was accompanied by the atmosphere in the building becoming noticeably colder. At the same time a microphone picked up what is described as the sound of something falling.

At 4.22 a.m. a metallic crash was heard by five members of the party. Mark, who had been strolling around the gallery, saw a stooping faceless human figure in black appear directly between a Typhoon and a Tempest aircraft. The figure glided across the kerb in the direction of a tubular maintenance gantry and disappeared. Shortly afterwards, Mark felt a light tap on the top of his head while he was near the centre stairs.

At 4.32 a.m. five members of the team heard a very loud groaning sound which appeared to come from the entrance area of the Aircraft Hall. No cause for this was established.

*Source: Peter Underwood,* Guide to Ghosts & Haunted Places, *1996 (p. 150)*
Reliable witnesses, including the directors of the museum, have heard distinct footsteps, the unmistakable sound of engine cowlings being lifted, and the throbbing sound of running motors at the museum.

*Source: Keypublishing Aviation Forum, 15 March 2004*
Melvyn Hiscock wrote that he took his father, who is very aware of the paranormal, on a visit to Hendon in the mid-1980s. As they walked past the bottom of the stairs that lead up to the first floor display level, he shuddered as if someone had poured ice down his neck. It is at that point an airman was said to have been killed when he ran his motorbike into a parked aircraft.

The Lancaster was also supposed to be haunted. His father said later that he felt a presence in the area. On a subsequent visit he said that the Lancaster man had gone from that spot and was now over by the 8th AF Memorial.

*Source: PPRuNe Aviation Ghosts, 12 January 2002*
The contributor's grandfather used to be a night watch security guard at Hendon museum, but had left the post because of the atmosphere at the place. One night, as he was passing through a section of the building where a tatty old British fighter was on static display, he claims to have seen an apparition. As he passed the Hurricane he casually shone his torch on the aircraft and did a double-take when, in the cockpit, there was a figure of a pilot in Second World War flying gear. He said that he thought it was a prank and shouted to the culprit to give himself up, but the apparition simply disappeared.

*Source: PPRuNe Ghostly Radio Transmissions, 30 May 2004*
Many years ago, the contributor was stationed at RAF Hendon. On the very first weekend that he was there, he and a mate were taking a short cut through the

Grahame-White hangar when they both broke into a sprint at exactly the same time and went for the door at the far end that led onto waste ground and the NAAFI. They had the sense of many eyes viewing them from the upper offices, which were covered in cobwebs. The feeling was one of complete and utter fear, so extreme that he states he still shivers thinking about it now. He never went in the hangar again, apart from to stand in the doorway to shout to one of the EPF guys in there.

A little over a year later, in Avro block, he spoke to a flight lieutenant who was looking for his dog. He assured the officer that if he saw it he would inform him immediately. Turning to go to his room, he turned around again to ask the officer where he could be found, only to discover that he was nowhere to be seen. Checking the immediate area, he found that there was no one there. Enquiries led him to believe this was a pilot who had crashed into the accommodation block in a Hurricane after evacuating from Dunkirk. He was killed, but his dog, which had been flying with him, survived. The crash damage could still be seen on the left side of the block at the time. The room where the aircraft had struck was described as always freezing cold.

# Henlow

Technical training
13 MU

| | |
|---|---|
| County: | Bedfordshire |
| Location: | 5 miles N of Hitchin |
| OS Ref.: | TL 165370 |
| Opened: | 10/05/18 |
| Closed: | N/A |
| Control Tower: | A. Original Watch Office building not known |
| | B. Unique Watch Office constructed from Hawker Hurricane wooden spares crates during the Second World War |
| | C. Single-storey portacabin Watch Office |
| Condition: | A. Demolished. |
| | B. Demolished, March 2006; Brooklands Museum attempted to rescue the building for preservation but unfortunately this proved impossible |
| | C. Operational in 2005 |
| Runways: | Grass, then 3 steel mat |
| Hardstandings: | 12 Chevron Type |
| Hangars: | T2 – 1, GS – 6, Bellman – 6, Blister – 7 |
| Ad., tech. & barr.: | 1935, new accommodation was erected in the NW corner of the station, and other huts between the road through the camp and Henlow village |

Population:        RAF Officers – 262, OR – 7,977, WAAF Officers – 18, OR
                   – 985
Sat. site(s):      Meppershall waterworks, Clifton (Beds)
Decoy airfield(s): Astwick QF

## History to 1946:

### 1918

April: Construction started of an Eastern Command repair depot
10 May: The first service personnel arrived from Farnborough to establish No. 5
    Eastern Area Aircraft Depot

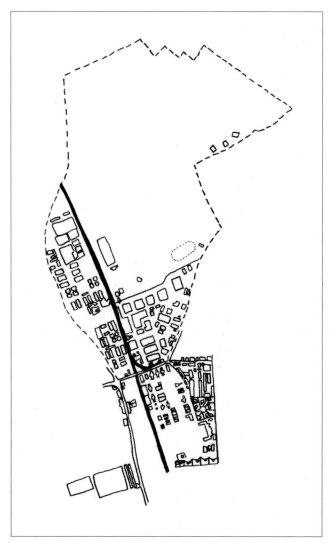

Henlow

**1920**

February: A further 161 acres were purchased for a flight test airfield

16 March: The station become the Inland Area Aircraft Depot

**1924**

April: The Officers' Engineering School arrived from Farnborough

**1925**

1 July: Nos 23 & 43 Squadrons re-formed with Snipes

September: The Parachute Test Section formed

**1926**

April: The squadrons begin to receive Gamecocks

4 April: Henlow became the Home Aircraft Depot

October: Northolt's PTS arrived and combined to form the Parachute Test Unit using Vimys

December: No. 43 Squadron moved to Tangmere

**1927**

February: No. 23 Squadron moved to Kenley, and Henlow transferred to 21 Group

**1930**

1 October: The R101 emerged from its Cardington hangar for its fatal flight

**1935**

August: The Home Aircraft Depot became an airframe riggers' school. No. 1 Wing trained machine tool operators and fitters; Nos 2 & 3, the flight riggers and flight mechanics

**1937**

January: Training of MT drivers and operatives began

15 March: No. 80 Squadron arrived from Kenley with Gauntlet IIs to receive Gladiator Is

9 June: No. 80 Squadron moved to Debden

July: An Initial Training Unit formed to introduce over 1,000 men to air force life, housed in tents

September: The ITU moved to Cardington, where huts had been erected

**1938**

Henlow had forsaken its repair role as the pupil population reached 5,000; the PTU remained

September: Two-thirds of the Training Wing moved to St Athan, and No. 2 Mobilisation Pool was formed to allow an increased repair role

October: The Home Aircraft Depot became 13 MU

**1939**

April: No. 1 Wing moved to Halton; No. 13 MU continued aircraft modification, manufacturing replacement parts, and handling armament tasks. Another task was unpacking, assembling, and testing Canadian-built Hurricanes

**1940**

Over 6,000 personnel were at Henlow, spread between 13 MU, 14 School of Technical Training, School of Aeronautical Engineering, Test Flying Section, and station staff

6 June: No. 13 School of Technical Training formed from No. 2 Electricians Wing

28 August: No. 13 SofTT renamed as No. 14 SofTT

26 September: A bomb fell between two hangars – 2 houses in Station Road, Lower Stondon, were demolished and 3 servicemen killed

**1941**

Whitleys replaced Virginias for parachute testing. No. 13 MU prepared for Operation Quick Force, where fitters served on aircraft carriers dismantling Hurricanes for shipment to Malta; the Hurricanes were then rebuilt for flying off the carrier's deck when it was about 300 miles west of Malta

**1943**

March: A Whitley IV was modified to enable it to snatch personnel from the ground by means of a long line. Throughout the war No. 13 MU remained at Henlow maintaining and modifying many aircraft, in particular Hurricanes, Mosquitos, and Typhoons

**1944**

No. 106 Gliding School was at Henlow, staying until 1 September 1955

28 August: No. 14 SofTT disbanded

**1945**

1 June: No. 14 STT (Polish) formed and stayed until 1 September 1948

**1946**

1 January: No. 43 Group Communications Flight formed and stayed until 28 June 1947

**Current status:**

Henlow is an active RAF station.

## Haunted RAF Henlow

*Source: Kevin Desmond,* Aviation Ghosts, *1998 (p. 127)*
Back in 1931 or 32, a friend of Desmond's had finished his RAF apprentice training and his first service posting was to the Home Aircraft Depot at Henlow. Part of his job was to patrol at night near the area known as the 'Pickle Factory'. This was a hangar full of engineless airframes held in storage. It was said at the time that airmen on guard duty at this location often heard a mysterious man's voice screaming with terror. The story was that not long before this, an airman had been carrying out a parachute jump but the parachute failed to open and he allegedly fell to his death, apparently screaming all the way down.

*Source: Alan C. Wood,* Military Ghosts, *2010 (pp. 132-3)*
Alan Wood writes that airmen at Henlow underwent parachute static line training, in which the parachute strop was attached to a static line in the aircraft and this opened the parachute. On one occasion, a parachute went into a 'Roman Candle' as a result of faulty packing, and the airman as he plummeted to the ground was screaming. He was, of course, killed when he hit the ground without his parachute opening. Airmen on night camp patrol after this event began to report hearing screams, as though the fatal jump was being replayed.

*Source: Keypublishing Aviation Forum, 1 April 2006*
Ollie Holmes wrote that he had often been at Henlow around dusk, walking back after retrieving a model aircraft, and was certain that he could hear Merlin engines. He also stated that he knew a few people who have experienced funny feelings inside one of the hangars.

*Source: Keypublishing Aviation Forum, 28 August 2007*
Stuart wrote that one night on guard duty at Henlow, he sat in a guard hut that looked down the main drag towards the old Belfast hangars. After some time he noticed that one of hangar's lights had just been switched on. As they had been off prior to this, a call was made to the guard commander. The RAF police went down to investigate, due to a series of previous problems with the building, and found it fully locked. On opening the door, they tried to send the dogs in to check it out but they refused. On another occasion, again at night, he was driving a forklift past the Sergeants' Office where he saw a figure wearing flying clothes standing next to the desk. The interesting part about this figure was that it seemed distorted and pastel in colour; it appeared to be almost in black and white. He found out later that the building was used for spares recovery from crashed aircraft.

# Holmsley South

No. 16 Group Coastal Command
No. 10 Group, Fighter Command
USAAF 9th AF
No. 116 Wing, Transport Command

| | |
|---|---|
| County: | Hampshire |
| Location: | 6 miles NE of Christchurch |
| OS Ref.: | NZ 215988 |
| Opened: | 09/1942 |
| Closed: | 1946 |
| Pundit code: | HM |
| USAAF Station: | 455 |
| Control Tower: | Watch Office for all Commands 12779/41 |
| Condition: | Demolished |
| Runways: | 3 concrete, (247) 1,970 x 50 yards, (302) 1,400 x 50 yards, and (058) 1,350 x 50 yards |
| Hardstandings: | 36 pans and 3 loop types connecting to an enclosing perimeter track, of a standard width of 50 feet |
| Hangars: | T2 – 5 |
| Ad., tech. & barr.: | Largely Nissen huts; various domestic accommodation sites were constructed dispersed away from the airfield but within a mile or so of the technical support site, also using clusters of Maycrete or Nissen huts |
| Population: | RAF Officers – 177, OR – 2,348, WAAF Officers – 10, OR – 328 |

## History to 1946:

During the late 1930s, the suitability of the land near Holmsley, west of the A35, had been noted

### 1942
1 September: RAF Holmsley South was opened to accommodate reinforcements for 19 Group during Operation Torch. None of the domestic sites were complete when RAF personnel began to arrive
25 October: Eight B-24Ds arrived from the 330th Squadron, 8th AF, seconded from Alconbury to 19 Group for anti-submarine work in the Bay of Biscay prior to Operation Torch
21 October: No. 547 Squadron was formed at Holmsley South and equipped with Wellington VIIIs for anti-shipping duties

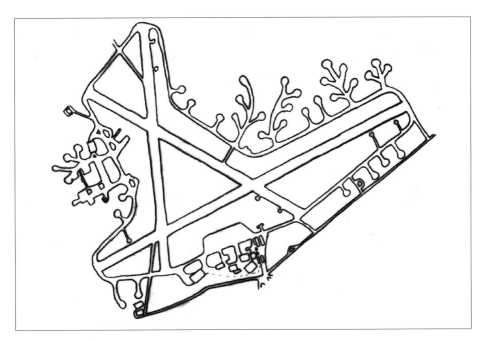

Holmsley South

28 October: The 330th Squadron commenced missions with a Biscay search
December: The 330th Squadron returned to Alconbury
2 December: No. 58 Squadron arrived from Stornoway and received Halifax IIs
10 December: No. 547 Squadron moved to Chivenor

### 1943

March: Holmsley South was used as a conversion base for Halifax squadrons
2 March: No. 502 Squadron arrived from St Eval for conversion to Halifax IIs
30 March: No. 502 Squadron returned to St Eval
May: No. 58 Squadron moved to St Eval; No. 295 Squadron arrived from
   Netheravon with Halifaxes to tow 36 Horsa gliders over Sicily
June: No. 502 Squadron arrived from St Eval for anti-submarine operations
July: No. 58 Squadron returned to Holmsley South for anti-submarine operations
August: In the space of nine days, No. 58 Squadron lost 3 Halifaxes in action and
   2 more in accidents
27 September: Halifax 58/B carrying the Station Commander on his first
   operational sortie with the squadron failed to return following attacking and
   sinking U-221. The Halifax was on fire and forced to ditch in the sea, but after
   11 days most of the crew were rescued
6 December: No. 58 Squadron moved to St Davids
10 December: No. 502 Squadron moved to St Davids
December: Holmsley South was transferred to No. 10 Group

**1944**

18 March: Nos 441, 442 & 443 (RCAF) Squadrons arrived from RAF Digby as 144 Wing received Spitfire IXs

27 March: No. 443 Squadron moved to Hutton Cranswick

1 April: Nos 441 & 442 Squadrons moved to Westhampnett; Nos 174, 175 & 245 Squadrons arrived from Westhampnett with rocket-equipped Typhoons

8 April: No. 418 Squadron arrived from Ford with Mosquito IIs and started intruder operations

25 April: No. 245 Squadron moved to Eastchurch

5-6 June: No. 121 Wing spent D-Day in direct support of troops on the beachhead. When the Army was established, they turned their attention to communications and harassing motor transport in the immediate rear of the front line

14 June: One of the crews of No. 418 Squadron reported the first V-1 sighted in flight, and together with 3 other Mosquito squadrons they concentrated on night anti-Diver patrols. During the first night operations, in 5 sorties, the squadrons accounted for 3 V-1s and a probable

19 June: No. 174 Squadron moved to B.2 Bazenville

20 June: No. 175 Squadron moved to B.3 Ste Croix

27 June: No. 245 Squadron moved to B.5 Camilly

14 July: No. 418 (RCAF) Squadron moved to Hurn

22 June: Nos 129, 306 & 315 Squadrons arrived from Coolham with Mustang IIIs for armed reconnaissance

24-27 June: Nos 129, 306 & 315 Squadrons moved to Ford

July: Holmsley South was assigned to USAAF as Station 455 for use by the 9th AF Bomber Command

24 July: The 394th Bomb Group arrived at Holmsley South from Boreham with Martin B-26 Marauders. The 394th started operations immediately

24-25 July: The 394th BG bombed in support of the St Lô breakout

7-9 August: The 394th received a Distinguished Unit Citation when it made a series of attacks against heavily defended targets: in the morning it destroyed 4 rail bridges at Nogent-sur-Seine; in the afternoon 34 B-26s devastated an ammunition dump south of Nantes

21 August: The 394th began to move to Tour-en-Bessin

October: Holmsley South was transferred to No. 116 Wing, Transport Command

December: No. 167 Squadron with Warwicks began services to the liberated parts of the Continent

December: No. 246 Squadron arrived from Lyneham and flew to the Middle and Far East using Liberators

**1945**

February: No. 246 Squadron absorbed the VIP Flight of the Metropolitan Communications Squadron at Northolt

27 March: No. 167 Squadron moved to Blackbushe

April: No. 246 Squadron received its first Douglas C-54 Skymasters

November: The last of the Halifaxes were retired and No. 246 Squadron was standardised with Avro Yorks

## 1946

15 October: No. 246 Squadron moved to Lyneham

**Closure:**

On 16 October 1946, all flying ceased at RAF Holmsley South. The airfield was placed on care and maintenance and was quickly closed and sold.

**Current status:**

Holmsley South has since stood derelict, and while a few odd parts of the runways and a few dispersal points remain, the vast majority of the concreted areas have been removed along with the buildings around the airfield. Some other areas have been planted with conifers by the Forestry Commission. Several public camping sites and a caravan park have been created on the former airfield.

## Haunted RAF Holmsley South

*Source: Richard McKenzie,* They Still Serve, *2008 (p. 104)*

At RAF Holmsley South there are reports of the sounds of aircraft taking off from this long-disused airfield. In addition, McKenzie states that the strains of 1940s music has been heard floating across the site.

# Hornchurch

No. 11 Group, Fighter Command

| | |
|---|---|
| County: | Essex |
| Location: | 2 miles SE of Romford |
| OS Ref.: | TQ 530845 |
| Opened: | 01/04/1928 |
| Closed: | 01/07/62 |
| Control Tower: | Watch Office for all Commands 12779/41 |
| Condition: | Demolished |
| Runways: | Grass, N-S 1,200 yards, NE-SW 1,130 yards, SE-NW 850 yards, and E-W 830 yards; extended in 1941 to N-S 1,600 yards, NE-SW 1,600 yards, and E-W 1,600 yards |
| Hardstandings: | Spitfire – 10, Blenheim – 2, pans – 7, 30-feet squares of Sommerfeld track – 2 |

Hangars:              A Type – 2, 9-bay C Type – 1
Ad., tech. & barr.:   Permanent Expansion Period buildings
Population:           RAF – Officers 192, OR – 882, WAAF – Officers 24, OR – 766
Sat. airfield(s):     North Weald Sector Station
Decoy airfield(s): Bulphan QK

## History to 1946:

### 1928

1 April: RAF Suttons Farm opened and No. 111 Squadron arrived from Duxford
   with Siskins

### 1929

January: Suttons Farm was renamed RAF Hornchurch

### 1930

15 January: No. 54 Squadron was re-formed as a Siskin-equipped fighter
   squadron

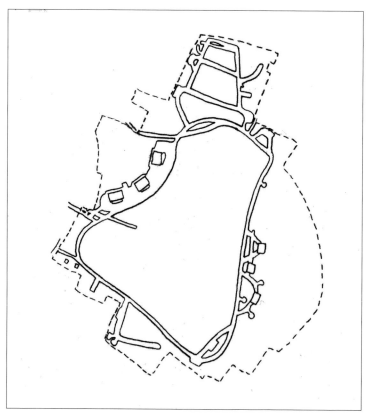

Hornchurch

**1936**
Squadrons: 54, 74 & 65
Hornchurch was to be a Sector HQ as a part of the newly formed No. 11 Group,
  Fighter Command

**1937**
Squadrons: 54, 74 & 65

**1939**
Squadrons: 54, 74 & 65
August: Orders were issued to camouflage all buildings
September: The Hornchurch Ops Room was manned continuously

**1940**
Squadrons: 41, 54, 65, 74, 222, 264, 266, 600 & 603
22 May: A Ju 88 was shot down over Flushing by No. 65 Squadron
During the battle of Britain Nos 41, 54, 65, 74, 222, 266 & 603 Spitfire Squadrons
  had a confirmed total of 122 victories, having lost 26 of their own aircraft
31 August: At 1.15 p.m., a large formation of German aircraft at 15,000 feet
  dropped up to 60 bombs in a line that stretched from the dispersal pens to
  the petrol dump and beyond into Elm Park. The grass surface, perimeter track
  dispersals, and barrack block windows all suffered but no other damage to
  buildings was caused, the aerodrome remaining serviceable. No. 54 Squadron
  was ordered to take off just as the first bombs were beginning to fall and 8
  machines safely cleared the ground. The remaining section had just become
  airborne as the bombs exploded. No. 603 Squadron claimed 14 enemy aircraft
  for the loss of only 1 pilot and 2 Spitfires lost.
9 September: The Ops Room suffered a near miss
20 September: Two land mines were dropped, one falling on the perimeter track in
  the SW corner just beyond the stop butts but failing to explode. The following
  day a naval demolition squad came to defuse the mine
15 October: The Ops Room was moved to Lambourne Hall, Romford

**1941**
Squadrons: 41, 54, 64, 313, 403, 411, 611 & 603
7 January: The Hornchurch Wing of Nos 41, 64 & 611 Spitfire Squadrons escorted
  a Circus formation of Blenheim bombers on a successful raid attacking
  Luftwaffe objectives in the Forêt de Guînes, without any loss whatsoever
19 August: During the course of a normal fighter sweep in which 6 German
  aircraft were destroyed, a Spitfire from Hornchurch dropped an artificial leg
  over France for Wing Commander D. R. S. Bader who had been shot down and
  captured

**1942**

Squadrons: 81, 132, 154, 313, 350, 340, 411 & 453

**1943**

Squadrons: 64, 66, 129, 132, 167, 222, 239, 350, 453 & 485

Throughout 1943 the RAF continued its attacks on occupied Europe. At the end of
the year, with the reduced threat of attack in the South East, the Hornchurch
Ops Room was stood down and the squadrons moved away. The Hornchurch
Wing had claimed 906 enemy aircraft destroyed, plus 440 probables for the
cost of 481 Allied pilots

**1944**

Squadrons: 66, 80, 129, 229, 274, 349, 485, 504 & 567

June: Hornchurch became a forward station of the North Weald Sector. It was also
the base for a repair unit engaged on restoring vital buildings in London

November: Hornchurch became a marshalling area handling personnel in transit
to and from the battle front

**1945**

Squadrons: 116 & 567

26 May: No. 116 Squadron disbanded at Hornchurch

June: Hornchurch was transferred to Technical Training Command

21 August: No. 567 Squadron moved to RAF Hawkinge

**Closure:**

RAF Hornchurch was placed on care and maintenance in 1947, closing in July
1962.

**Current status:**

It is now a housing estate, and the former Officers' Mess is now a medical centre
in Astra Close.

## Haunted RAF Hornchurch

*Source: Bruce Barrymore Halpenny,* Ghost Stations, *1986 (pp. 152-5)*

Ray Downs was posted to Hornchurch in April 1957 as an admin orderly. After a
few weeks he became a voluntary member of the crash crew attached to the Fire
Section and soon heard many stories that Hornchurch was haunted. One story
in particular was about an area of grass by the main hangar, where the police
dogs would not go, or only with great reluctance. It was locally said that an NCO
mechanic was killed when he walked into the propeller of an aircraft undergoing
an engine test.

One summer evening, while on duty, Downs decided to accompany the police dog handler on patrol. During their conversation Downs asked if there was any truth in the tale that the dogs would not go into certain areas on the airfield. The police dog handler said he wasn't sure but as they were approaching the area mentioned above, they would see what happened. As they neared the spot, the dog stopped and pulled the handler to the left, then to the right; its hackles were up and it was refusing to move. Only after great determination on the handler's part was the dog persuaded to cross the corner section. Downs notes that the police dogs were a pretty ferocious bunch and the dog on this particular evening was no exception.

Another incident that Downs recounts occurred when he was allocated to the Crew Selection Centre. This was located by the main entrance of the former Officers' Mess. On his first day he was informed that it was haunted by a fighter pilot who, having crashed, had crawled to the Mess and died there. The orderly responsible for the security of the building had to stay in reception until late evening by the telephone for incoming calls. He was also responsible for checking and, if necessary, locking all office doors, after which the keys would be returned to the guardroom. Downs recalled that in winter the place assumed what he described as an oppressive atmosphere and the orderlies agreed to share the duties so that two were always on duty. Previously it had been the duty of the orderly to sleep on a camp bed in the Reception Centre, remaining on call until office staff arrived in the morning. However, this was changed after an airman was discovered one night in a state of collapse on the steps of the guardroom, having run a quarter of a mile from the centre in bare feet and pyjamas. The result of the inquiry that followed stated that the airman was suddenly woken in the early hours of the morning by the lights flashing on and off, doors slamming, and footsteps running up and down the corridors.

On numerous occasions the station police would phone through to the Crew Selection Centre and inform them that a light had been left on in an office, even though the entire building had been checked before going off duty. Similarly, it was not uncommon to hear doors slam somewhere in the building, even though the orderly would have personally locked them earlier. Sometimes the orderlies would hear footsteps in the long corridors as they checked the building, as though someone was following them. The corridor was always empty at the time. At other times, while they were in the reception area, they would hear the sound of movement on the stairs, or of walking along the landing which continued on to the washrooms.

*Source: Bruce Barrymore Halpenny,* Ghost Stations, *1986 (p. 155)*
Some residents in the locality of the airfield after it closed in 1962 claim to have witnessed a pilot dressed in Second World War flying gear running towards the centre of the site. Others claim to have heard what was thought to be an aircraft engine.

*Source: Bruce Barrymore Halpenny,* Ghost Stations, *1986 (p. 155)*
Many people who live in the housing estate that covers the old airfield believe that it is still haunted. Mrs Kelvey, who lived in a flat in Heron Flight Avenue, noted that between 10 and 11 p.m. she would occasionally get a gust of wind going through the flat even when there was no wind at all.

*Source: Carmel King,* Haunted Essex, *2009 (pp. 33-4)*
Walkers in Hornchurch Country Park, and staff from the nearby hospital, have reported seeing the apparitions of men in Second World War RAF uniforms. They have also heard the faint sound of aircraft coming from the area that was once the airfield.

*Source:* Fate & Fortune *Magazine, February 2005*
Trudie and Des Lavender lived in an ex-MoD house with their 21-year-old daughter Molly. The house was built for RAF officers in 1952, when Hornchurch was an active airfield. All the family have witnessed unusual moans, groans, and footsteps. In September 2004, Des and Trudie heard what sounded like a metal cabinet being drawn across a carpeted floor in an upstairs bedroom. Molly, who was in that particular room at the time, felt her bed shake. On another occasion, Trudie heard very loud noises from the direction of the former airfield in the middle of the night, which she thought sounded like several old aeroplane engines running. On one occasion the family dog, Beautie, refused to go forward at a certain spot on the deserted airfield during a walk and tried to hide behind Trudie's legs.

On 18 September 2004, Chris and Jane McCarthy and Dave Coggins descended upon Hornchurch to evaluate what was happening there. They arranged for a midnight walk on the deserted site and as they walked onto the airfield all of them stopped, not knowing at the time that they were standing where the main landing strip had once been, experiencing the feeling of many entities around them. They then continued walking until they came to a crossroads, where again they all felt so many spirits around. These, they felt, were all young and had died around the same time, perhaps within a fortnight of each other. Whilst Jane was walking with Trudie, they suddenly experienced a whoosh of cold air, which went right through both of them. Jane felt the presence of a spirit and saw a Spitfire parked on the ground. Trudie saw the pilot and described him as young, around his twenties, with blond, curly hair. The name of Pearce or something similar was then received. The streets around the airfield are named after the Spitfire pilots, and one of them is called Pease Close. The full report may be viewed at:www.psychicinvestigations. net/html/psychic_investigations_4.html

# Hunsdon

No. 11 Group, Fighter Command

| | |
|---|---|
| County: | Hertfordshire |
| Location: | 2½ miles NW of Harlow |
| OS Ref.: | TL 426138 |
| Opened: | 05/1941 |
| Closed: | 1947 |
| Pundit code: | HD |
| Control Tower: | Watch Office for Night Fighter Stations 12096/49 & 10413/42 |
| Condition: | Demolished |
| Runways: | 2 asphalt, (270) 1,450 x 50 yards (later extended to the E to 1,750 yards) and (210) 1,250 x 50 yards (later extended to the S to 1,450 yards). Drem lighting and Angle of Approach indicator systems installed |
| Hardstandings: | Dispersals – 10, hardstandings – 18 |
| Hangars: | Blister – 16: Bellman – 1 |
| Ad., tech. & barr.: | Temporary buildings in 8 dispersed sites to the W of the airfield, mainly for accommodation. Bonningtons in Stanstead Road was used as the Officers' Mess |
| Population: | RAF Officers – 100, OR – 2,140, WAAF Officers – 8, OR – 454 |
| Sat. airfield(s): | Satellite to North Weald |
| Decoy airfield(s): | Braughing |

There were 124 airmen killed while on flying operations from Hunsdon; 26 aircraft were lost in local crashes.

## *History to 1946:*

### 1940
9 October: Work began on a fighter airfield to act as a satellite to RAF North Weald

### 1941
Squadrons: 3, 85, 242 (det), 287 (det), 1451 Flight & 1459 Flight
22 February: Hunsdon opened into No. 11 Group, Fighter Command
March: Completion of the runways and perimeter track
4 May: RAF Hunsdon opened for operational flying
8 May: A detachment of No. 242 Squadron arrived for operational night flying and training with Hurricanes

22 May: No. 1451 Turbinlite Havoc Flight formed at Hunsdon with Havoc IIs and Boston IIIs. A decoy airfield at Braughing had been in use for Hunsdon at this time but it had served little purpose

**1942**

Squadrons: 3, 85, 530, 605 (det), 1451 Flight & 1530 BAT Flight

1 July: No. 1530 Beam Approach Training Flight formed

2 September: No. 1451 Flight was renumbered as No. 530 Squadron and received Hurricane night fighters

23 November: No. 1530 BAT Flight moved to Wittering

**1943**

Squadrons: 3, 21, 85, 157, 410, 464, 487 & 530

25 January: No. 530 Squadron disbanded

**1944**

Squadrons: 21, 29, 151, 219, 264, 409, 410, 418, 441, 442, 464, 487 & 488

18 February: Nos 464 & 487 Squadrons, led by Group Captain Pickard in a very low-altitude raid, attacked Amiens prison as part of Operation Jericho. The Mosquitos of No. 21 Squadron acted as reserve and did not bomb. Pickard was killed when his aircraft was shot down near the target area by Fw 190s

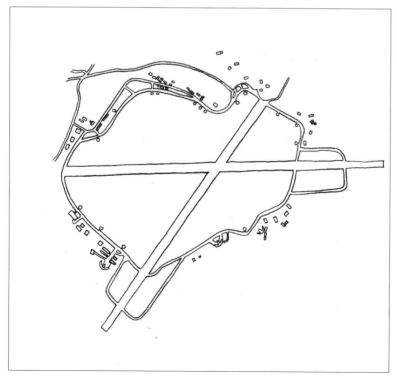

Hunsdon

14 June: Mosquito XIII, HK476, engaged and shot down a Ju 88 with a glider bomb attached to the top of the fuselage. Flight Lieutenant Dinsdale and Pilot Officer Dunn were the first RAF fighters of the Second World War to shoot down a Mistel

## 1945
Squadrons: 29, 151, 154, 285 (det), 287 (det), 501 & 611

22 February: No. 29 Squadron moved to Colerne, which marked the departure of all the Mosquito squadrons to advanced bases in England or France

31 March: No. 154 Squadron was disbanded

20 April: No. 501 Squadron was disbanded

23 April: No. 442 (RCAF) Squadron arrived at Hunsdon from B.88 Heesch with Mustang IVs for long-range bomber escort missions

29 April: No. 441 (RCAF) Squadron arrived from RAF Hawkinge with Mustang IIIs for long-range bomber escort missions

19 May: Hunsdon was placed on care and maintenance

## Closure:
On 21 July 1947, Hunsdon was finally abandoned by the RAF.

## Current status:
Hunsdon Microlight Club uses three grass runways situated in the north-east corner of the airfield. Only a few original buildings remain; one such is the Hunsdon Underground Battle Headquarters.

## Haunted RAF Hunsdon

The distinct feeling of not being alone on the airfield has been reported from Hunsdon on many occasions by many people. It is described as though someone unseen is walking with them.

*Source: Luton Paranormal Society*
The society carried out an investigation at Hunsdon on 5 August 2011 between 11.45 p.m. and midnight at a variety of locations around the former airfield. These locations included the landing area, the parachute store, the airfield memorial, a pillbox, and a hut. On the airfield the temperature felt as though it suddenly dropped, and one member reported that her hand felt warm as though someone was holding it. A flash of light was seen on the NNE runway. At the pillbox there were feelings of pain in the left ear and the collar bone, and a tightness in the throat. It seems to have been an uncomfortable place. Two flashes of red light and one flash of yellow light and a small red light on a tree were observed. In addition, a dark and indistinct figure was seen. At the airfield memorial there

were a variety of experiences, including one member feeling as though there was someone behind her. Another reported feeling a warm patch of air, a cold shiver on his right shoulder, and a pain like sciatica in his left leg. A huge orange ball of light was seen at one point in this area. In addition, there was a black dog-sized shadow that ran past the group, and three white or grey figures in a line. At the parachute store a number of lighting anomalies were observed. A bright flash of light was seen on the end of the farm building, and two small dots of pale blue light and a brief red dot on the ground in front of another investigator as well as a pale green light, interpreted as an aircraft's landing lights, a flash of light on the track, and a huge beam of light, rather like a searchlight. The dark shadow of a tall, slim man was also seen. A considerable amount of psychic communication was received during the investigation.
(Website: www.lutonparanormal.com/investigations/popups/2011_08_05.html)

# Kenley

No. 11 Group, Fighter Command
No. 46 Group, Transport Command

| | |
|---|---|
| County: | Surrey |
| Location: | 4 miles S of Croydon |
| OS Ref.: | ST 328580 |
| Opened: | 1917 |
| Closed: | 01/05/59 |
| Pundit code: | KE |
| Control Tower: | Small Watch Office built on side of GS Shed |
| Condition: | Demolished along with hangars after fire in 1978 |
| Runways: | Grass, then 2 concrete, (212) 1,200 x 50 yards and (312) 1,000 x 50 yards |
| Hardstandings: | 12 concrete triple pens off the perimeter track |
| Hangars: | 2-bay Belfast Truss – 7, Over Blister – 4, Extra-Over Blister – 4; 1939, 3 pairs of hangars were demolished to allow the runways and perimeter track to be laid |
| Ad., tech. & barr.: | Permanent Expansion Period buildings |
| Population: | RAF Officers – 142, OR – 480, no WAAF Officers, OR – 125 |
| Sat. airfield(s): | Croydon, Shoreham, Redhill |
| Decoy airfield(s): | Woldingham Q/QF, South Godstone Q, Walton Heath Q/QF, Farleigh Q/QF |

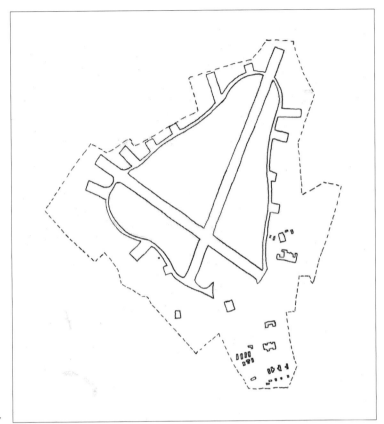

Kenley

## History to 1946:

**1917**
Kenley opened in the summer as No. 7 Aircraft Acceptance Park with 14 hangars

**1920s**
The airfield was selected for retention as a permanent RAF station and was partly reconstructed, although it appears to have continued as an active flying station and housed squadrons until September 1932

**1932**
September: Kenley closed for further construction work

**1934**
May: The SHQ arrived back at Kenley
10 May: No. 17 Squadron arrived from Upavon with Bulldog IIs
3 September: 'B' Flight of No. 17 Squadron was used to re-form No. 46 Squadron and was equipped with Gauntlet IIs

**1935**
October: No. 17 Squadron received Harts

**1936**
August: No. 17 Squadron received Gauntlet IIs
28 August: No. 3 Squadron arrived from Port Sudan with Bulldog IIs

**1937**
March: No. 3 Squadron received Gladiator Is
8 March: No. 80 Squadron re-formed with Gauntlets
15 March: No. 80 Squadron moved to Henlow
1 June: No. 615 AAC Squadron formed at Kenley with Audaxes
15 November: No. 41 Squadron moved to Digby

**1938**
March: No. 3 Squadron received Hurricane Is
29 August: No. 615 Squadron moved to Old Sarum
4 September: No. 615 Squadron returned from Old Sarum

**1939**
Squadrons: 3, 17, 600 & 615
2 May: No. 3 Squadron moved to Biggin Hill
23 May: No. 17 Squadron moved to North Weald
24 August: No. 56 ERFTS formed
August: The airfield was considerably extended, hangars and hardstandings were
    built and two concrete runways laid
September: With war declared, No. 56 ERFTS was closed

**1940**
Squadrons : 64, 66, 253, 501, 615 & 616
?-31 May: No. 61 Wing at Kenley
18 August: Equipment stores, 3 hangars, a Blenheim and 4 Hurricanes on the
    ground were destroyed and 4 other aircraft damaged; 9 were killed and 10
    injured, and all communications were cut
19 August: No. 616 Squadron arrived from Doncaster
4 September: No. 253 Squadron shot down 6 Bf 110s without loss
17 October: Nine aircraft on the ground were bombed
November: A night bombing attack resulted in 2 people being killed and
    damage to a hangar, living quarters, and offices. Low-level flights
    (Rhubarbs) commenced over France. These operations were not liked and
    presented serious hazards, hundreds of fighter pilots being lost on Rhubarb
    operations

## 1941
Squadrons: 1, 253, 258, 302, 485, 602 & 615

January: Circus operations were introduced (daylight escorts for Blenheim bombers to short-range targets in France)

September: The SHQ moved to Peterswood in Torwood Lane, Whyteleafe

## 1942
Squadrons: 111, 350, 402, 403, 412, 421, 452, 485, 602, 611 & 616

25 November: The Canadian Kenley Wing formed, with Ramrods forming the chief operations

## 1943
Squadrons: 66, 165, 400, 401, 402, 411, 412 & 421

4 June: HQ, No. 127 Airfield until 6 August

8 August: No. 165 Squadron arrived from Exeter to escort B-26s and B-17s over France

17 September: No. 165 Squadron moved to Church Stanton

## 1944
Squadrons: 401, 403, 416 & 421

17 April: HQ, No. 127 Airfield until 12 May

13 March: The last operation from Kenley, when Nos 403, 416 & 421 Squadrons escorted bombers to Namur in Belgium

16 April: No. 127 Wing, with the last three Canadian squadrons, moved to Tangmere; Kenley was thereafter administered by a holding party

June: Kenley was closed to flying as a result of the balloon barrage used as a counter to the German V-1s

28 June: A V-1 fell just south of the station, doing considerable damage to houses and the station cinema

## 1945
1 July: Kenley was transferred to No. 46 Group, Transport Command

## 1946
Squadrons: No. 61 Communications Flight

1 August: HQ, No. 61 Group Reserve was at Kenley, used as a store for captured German and Japanese equipment including V-1s and V-2s. Westminster Airways operated a passenger service from the aerodrome, sharing the only available hangar with No. 61 Group Communications Flight

## Closure:
RAF Kenley was closed on 1 May 1959.

**Current status:**

Kenley is thought to be the best preserved of all Second World War RAF fighter stations. The married quarters in the south-west corner have been redeveloped with modern housing.

## *Haunted RAF Kenley*

*Source: Bruce Barrymore Halpenny,*
Ghost Stations, *1986 (p. 21)*
Early one July evening, Bill Wood was at Kenley watching the gliders taking off and landing. Suddenly in the otherwise fairly silent and warm summer's evening he became aware of a distant hum above the sound of the gliders; it seemed to him remarkably like that of an air-raid siren's wail.

*Source: Alan C. Wood,* Military Ghosts, *2010 (p. 131)*
Alan Wood mentions that a Spitfire is seen to approach the airfield but on touchdown crashes, bursts into flames, and finally vanishes from sight.

# Kimbolton

USAAF 8th Air Force

| | |
|---|---|
| County: | Huntingdonshire |
| Location: | 8 miles W of Huntingdon |
| OS Ref.: | TL 102701 |
| Opened: | 1941 |
| Closed: | 1946 |
| Pundit code: | KI |
| USAAF Station: | 117 |
| Control Tower: | A. Watch Office with Ops Room for Bomber Satellite Stations 7345/41, 13079/41 |
| | B. Watch Office for all Commands 12779/41, small front windows to 15371/41 |
| Condition: | Both towers demolished 1977 |
| Runways: | 3 concrete/tarmac, (320) 1,340 x 50 yards (extended to 2,000 yards and later to 4,000 yards), (210) 1,400 x 50 yards, and (270) 1,400 x 50 yards |
| Hardstandings: | 30 loop type; increased in 1942 from 30 to 50 |
| Hangars: | T2 – 2 dispersed on the W and S sides of the airfield |
| Bomb stores & ammunition: | Sited beyond the S end of the runway near the A660 |

| Ad., tech. & barr.: | Temporary accommodation located between the S and SE runway ends |
| Population: | USAAF Officers – 421, OR – 2,473 |

The 379th flew 330 missions, lost 149 B-17s, and claimed 315 enemy aircraft.

## History to 1946:

### 1941

The airfield was originally built for RAF Bomber Command but then expanded to Class A airfield standards for use by American heavy bombers

November: Kimbolton opened into RAF Fighter Command but when the threat of German invasion subsided, the RAF decided it did not need many inland fighter bases and leased most of them to the USAAF

### 1942

September: The USAAF 8th AF 91st Bombardment Group arrived from Walla Walla AAF. The 91st was assigned to the 1st Combat Bombardment Wing of the 1st Bombardment Division and its squadrons were the 322nd, 323rd, 324th & 401st, all equipped with B-17s

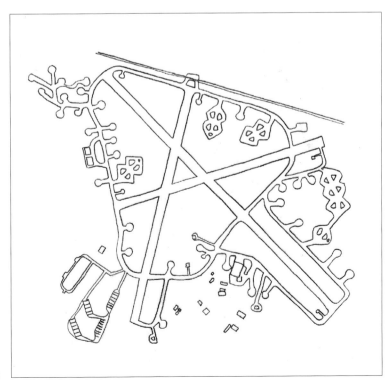

Kimbolton

14 October: The 91st BG transferred to Bassingbourn as the runways at Kimbolton were not sturdy enough for the B-17s

October: The 17th BG with B-26 Marauders arrived from Barksdale AAF. The operational squadrons were the 37th, 95th & 432nd. Originally intended for RAF Bassingbourn, the 17th BG used Kimbolton as a transitory airfield on its way to the North African campaign

November: The 17th BG began departing for Telergma in Algeria, and Kimbolton underwent an upgrade to its runways and hardstandings

## 1943

May: The 379th BG arrived from Sioux City and was assigned to the 41st Combat Bombardment Wing equipped with the B-17 Flying Fortress. Its operational squadrons were the 524th, 525th, 526th & 527th

19 May: The 379th BG began operations with 8th AF. It was to be primarily involved in bombing strategic targets such as factories, oil refineries, storage plants, submarine pens, airfields, and communications centres in Germany, France, Holland, Belgium, Poland, and Norway

## 1944

11 January: The 379th BG received a Distinguished Unit Citation for flying without fighter protection into central Germany to attack vital aircraft factories

The 379th BG received two Presidential Unit Citations for the period 28 May 1943 to 31 July 1944

June: The 379th BG bombed V-weapon sites, airfields, radar stations, and other installations before the Normandy invasion

6 June: The 379th BG bombed defended positions just ahead of the Allied landings and struck airfields, rail choke points, and gun emplacements during the campaign that followed

24-25 July: The 379th BG bombed enemy positions to assist ground troops at St Lô

December -January 1945: The 379th BG attacked German communications and fortifications during the Battle of the Bulge

## 1945

February-March: The 379th BG bombed bridges and viaducts in France and Germany to aid the Allied assault across the Rhine

25 April: The 379th BG flew its last combat mission

June: The 379th was transferred to Casablanca, and Kimbolton was returned to the RAF

## Closure:

In 1946, Kimbolton closed but was maintained in a standby status until 1960.

**Current status:**
The site is now used for agriculture and Bicton Industrial Park.

## Haunted RAF Kimbolton

Many people who have visited the airfield have commented that the place is a bit spooky and have experienced a cold sensation in the area where one of the former Control Towers stood.

*Source: Bruce Barrymore Halpenny,* Ghost Stations, *1986 (pp. 178-81)*
In August 1945, John Ainsworth was at Kimbolton soon after it had been transferred from the USAAF back to the RAF. It was, he states, a very bleak airfield, and this isolation led to one young airman's suicide. Ainsworth related an account of two airmen returning from supper in the Mess who saw the remains of a crashed B-17 bomber on the airfield. Inside the wreckage a number of American airmen were playing cards. They reported what they saw, but the report was apparently dismissed. The following evening, two more airmen walking back from supper claimed that they had also witnessed the Americans playing cards in a crashed B-17 bomber, the apparition lasting for some minutes before disappearing. Ainsworth records that on this occasion one of the airmen became mentally unstable and was subsequently admitted to the station sick quarters.

Following this, the RAF are said to have taken steps to counter the rumours circulating at the airfield. The next evening Ainsworth's No. 8 Flight was ordered On Parade and given orders that there were no ghosts present and that any more reports would be treated as a chargeable offence. Corporal Warwick, the NCO who administered the parade ground warnings, was himself admitted to station sick quarters the very next evening, after sighting the American airmen and B-17 bomber. At this, supper time was suddenly changed, and with nobody on the airfield at this late hour, the apparition was no longer reported.

In 1979, Ainsworth returned to Kimbolton and visited the 'White Horse' pub in the village seeking accommodation. In conversation with the landlord, the subject of Kimbolton ghosts came up. Ainsworth claims the landlord went white and asked if he meant the airman that walks from the airfield. He continued to relate that the ghost had gone and no longer existed. The RAF had arrived at the former airfield in late 1978, erected a green tarpaulin tented structure, and excavated the remains of a B-17 bomber. However, Barrymore Halpenny also relates the account from a courting couple in late 1981 who, as they were crossing the main runway on a fairly dark night, witnessed the apparition of a group of American airmen playing cards in what looked to be a crashed bomber. The incident was estimated to have been of two minutes' duration before it vanished, and was said to have been illuminated by a hazy, luminous glow.

# Larkhill

(No plan available)

| | |
|---|---|
| County: | Wiltshire |
| Location: | 2 miles NW of Amesbury |
| OS Ref.: | SU 1444437 |
| Opened: | 1937 |
| Closed: | 1942/3 |
| Runways: | Grass |
| Hangars: | BCAC |
| Ad., tech. & barr.: | Temporary huts |
| Population: | Unknown |

## *History to 1946:*

Larkhill is one of the oldest names in British aviation and also one of the most difficult airfields to locate. Several sites in the Salisbury Plain area have carried the name, and this has caused much confusion.

The first Larkhill, the pre-1914 aerodrome, is on Durrington Down and is marked by a small concrete plinth on which a brass plate states that this was the site of the first military airfield in Britain. This is a stretch of rough land south of the Packway, known locally as the Hill of the Larks.

**1909**
Horatio Barbe erected an airfield shed and was joined by G. B. Cockburn and
    Captain J. D. B. Fulton of the Royal Artillery

**1910**
The War Office offered free use of the area for flying and encouraged the
    development of the Bristol School of Aviation on the site. From here Captain
    Bertram Dickson, of the Air Battalion of the Royal Engineers, used a Bristol
    Boxkite to observe a mock battle

**1911**
No. 2 (Aeroplane) Company was formed and housed their aeroplanes in sheds on
    the Down, while the personnel lived at nearby Bulford Camp

**1912**
April: No. 2 Company became No. 3 Squadron when the Royal Flying Corps was
    formed; a new aerodrome was prepared for them at Netheravon. While based

at Larkhill, tents were provided for the men on the site of the present Packway church; the 'Bustard Inn' was used for the Officers' Mess

July: The first fatal air crash in the RFC occurred when Captain Eustace Loraine and his observer, Staff Sergeant R. H. V. Wilson, were killed when they crashed west of Stonehenge after flying out of Larkhill

August: Larkhill was the venue for the first Military Aircraft Trials

## 1914

June: After training 129 pupils at Larkhill, the Bristol School of Aviation closed and at the outbreak of war the aerodrome also closed. The site was soon covered with hundreds of corrugated iron huts for the army

## 1920s

Some aircraft taking part in the annual Army exercises were detached for field training to convenient stretches of Knighton Down, all of which were referred to as Larkhill. Nos 2, 4, 13 & 16 (Army Co-op) Squadrons all used the downs

## 1936

January: The main site became known as RAF Larkhill

## 1937

June: An Audax of No. 16 Squadron crashed on landing at Knighton Down

## 1940

2 June: 'D' Flight arrived at Larkhill, having recently returned from field trials in France using Taylorcraft light aircraft. 'D' Flight was accommodated in huts at the School of Artillery and started training pilots for No. 651 Squadron, which formed at RAF Old Sarum on 1 August

Air Observation Post units worked closely with Army units in artillery spotting and liaison. The AOP courses concentrated on precautionary landings, quick take-offs, and low-level flying to convert Army officers to operational flying after their basic flying training at EFTS units

## 1941

September: 'D' Flight became 1424 Flight

## 1942

October: 1424 Flight was involved in a demonstration of firepower on Salisbury Plain. By the end of the year a hangar had been constructed at the airfield

October: No. 1424 Flight was renamed as 43 OTU with 32 light aircraft on strength

November: 43 OTU moved to Old Sarum

**Closure:**

The airfield on Knighton Down was then relinquished by the RAF and returned to the War Office, but was little used as Austers could land on any cleared stretch of Salisbury Plain.

**Current status:**

Some of the original aeroplane sheds erected before World War 1 still exist at the southern end of Wood Road at Larkhill Army Camp. They are in use as barrack stores. The original BCAC hangar, near the corner of Wood Road and Fargo Road, is the oldest surviving military aerodrome building in the UK

## *Haunted RAF Larkhill*

*Source: Army Rumour Service Forum, 23 March 2005*

There was a hideous crash on what is now the paddock soon after inception at around 3 a.m. on a fogbound morning. People who live on the patch have consistently told of being suddenly woken for no earthly reason between 3 and 3.15 a.m.

# Lasham

No. 38 Wing, Army Co-operation Command
No. 83 Group
No. 10 Group, Fighter Command
No. 70 Group
No. 11 Group, Fighter Command

| | |
|---|---|
| County: | Hampshire |
| Location: | 6 miles SE of Basingstoke |
| OS Ref.: | SU 675435 |
| Opened: | 11/1942 |
| Closed: | 10/1948 |
| Pundit code: | LQ |
| Control Tower: | A. Watch Office for Fighter Satellite Stations |
| | B. Watch Office for Bomber Stations and OTUs 13726/41 |
| Condition: | Both demolished |
| Runways: | Concrete and wood chippings, (095) 1,900 x 50 yards, (063) 1,200 x 50 yards, and (175) 1,400 x 50 yards |
| Hardstandings: | 52 pan type hardstandings |
| Hangars: | T2 – 4 |
| Ad., tech. & barr.: | Temporary large technical area and dispersed accommodation sites to the SE of the airfield |

Population:            RAF Officers – 142, OR – 1,712, WAAF Officers – 10, OR
                       – 410
Sat. airfield(s):      Satellite to Blackbushe, Tangmere (sector)

## History to 1946:

### 1941

September: Farmland was requisitioned for an airfield intended as a satellite to the
    bomber OTU at Aldermaston. However, prior to opening, the OTU plans were
    cancelled

### 1942

9 November: Lasham was taken over by No. 38 Wing, Army Co-operation
    Command as No. 124 Airfield but remained unused for aircraft

### 1943

2 January: The airfield was bombed and strafed by a single Do 217
1 April: Z Group became No. 83 Group and No. 124 Airfield was put on a
    permanent basis using No. 2 Group personnel
3 May: No. 183 Squadron arrived from Gatwick with Typhoon 1b aircraft to join
    Nos 181 & 182 Squadrons to form a Typhoon Wing

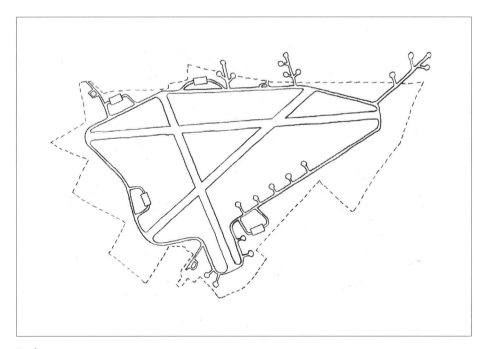

Lasham

1 June: Army Co-operation Command disbanded and Lasham was temporarily transferred to No. 10 Group, Fighter Command, and then to No. 70 Group

2 June: Nos 175, 181 & 182 Squadrons and all personnel at the airfield moved to Appledram ALG

28 August: Lasham transferred to No. 2 Group Tactical AF and the Foulsham SHQ staff transferred en bloc to provide admin services

30 August: No. 320 (Dutch) Squadron arrived from Attlebridge with Mitchell IIs

9 September: No. 320 Squadron made its first operational sorties from Lasham when 11 Mitchells attacking long-range guns at Boulogne. After this it was engaged upon raids on railway marshalling yards, airfields, and bridges

15 October: No. 613 Auxiliary Air Force Squadron arrived from Snailwell and converted to Mosquito VIs to become a day and night tactical strike unit

November: No. 320 Squadron began attacking Noball sites

## 1944

3 February: Nos 107, 305 & 613 Squadrons formed the Lasham Mosquito Wing under No. 138 Airfield HQ

15 March: No. 107 Squadron flew its first Mosquito mission on a Noball site

An American P-51 Mustang shot up a No. 107 Squadron Mosquito pilot who crash-landed on a south coast beach. Tracing his assailant by his code letters, he drove to his base and left him unconscious

5 June: 98 Mosquitos of Nos 138 (Lasham) & 140 (Gravesend) Wings bombed villages, roads, and rail junctions all over Normandy, causing chaos

6 June: The 2 Wings attacked anything that moved, this work continuing whenever the weather allowed

30 July: Group Captain L.W.C. Bower led 5 Mosquitos of No. 138 Wing in an attack on a château used as a rest centre for U-boat crews, killing 400 Germans

17 September: In support of Operation Market Garden, Nos 107 & 613 Squadrons were briefed for low-level attacks on individual houses in Arnhem, each aircraft dropping four 500-lb MC bombs. No. 107 Squadron lost two aircraft

October: The Mosquito Wing moved to Hartfordbridge

December: Spitfire and Typhoon squadrons began to bring their aircraft into Lasham for disposal

## 1945

15 January: Lasham transferred to No. 11 Group, Fighter Command to become a satellite to Blackbushe with No. 84 GSU as a lodger

August: No. 84 GSU was renamed the Group Disbandment Centre

24 October: No. 83 Group Disbandment Centre arrived from Dunsfold

## 1946

13 February: No. 49 MU arrived from Faygate

March: General Aircraft Ltd were given 2 T2 hangars and adjacent buildings to
   carry out Mosquito overhaul and conversion contracts. Flight trials on their
   tailless gliders also took place from Lasham

**Closure:**
RAF Lasham was closed on 26 October 1948.

**Current status:**
In January 1979, the Second World War Aircraft Preservation Society took over
   a former dispersal hut on the north-east corner of the airfield and now has
   a number of post-war machines on display. It is open on Sundays and Bank
   Holidays between 10.30 a.m. and 5 p.m. The airfield is now owned by Lasham
   Gliding Society and is also a base for a company maintaining Boeing airliners

## *Haunted RAF Lasham*

*Source: PPRuNe Aviation Ghosts, 21 October 2001*
At dusk one summer evening in the early 1990s, a contributor to the forum was
walking around the peritrack at Lasham. As he approached some woods he
experienced a real 'hairs on the back of the neck' feeling. He admits that he didn't
see anything, but also admits that he didn't hang around there either. Some time
later he was told about a pilot whose Mosquito crashed into those woods in 1944
and was killed there. His ghost has supposedly been seen many times there over the
years.

# Little Rissington

23 Group, Training Command
Central Flying School

| | |
|---|---|
| County: | Gloucestershire |
| Location: | 4 miles NE of Burford |
| OS Ref.: | SP 210188 |
| Opened: | 1938 |
| Closed: | 1994 |
| Pundit code: | LR |
| Control Tower: | Chief Flying Instructors Block, 5740/36 |
| Condition: | Demolished |
| Runways: | Grass strips, 3 concrete/tarmac, (050) 1,565 x 50 yards, (100) 1,150 x 50 yards, and (140) 1,050 x 50 yards. Later (050) was extended N (subsequently to become the main runway |

for instrument landings), and subsidiaries extended E and SE
respectively

Hangars:          Blister – 17, Bellman – 3, C Type – 2, AR5 – 1; MU site, Robin
                  – 8, E Type – 6, Super Robin – 3, D Type –2, C Type – 2

Ad., tech. & barr.: Permanent type to the SE of the airfield. Many buildings were
                  constructed from Cotswold stone and drystone walls were used
                  in place of standard military fencing. Extra land was added to
                  accommodate Sites A to E

Population:       RAF Officers – 151, OR – 1,166, WAAF Officers – 9, OR –
                  364

Sat. airfield(s): Chipping Norton, Windrush

## History to 1946:

### 1930s

During the build-up to the Second World War, the Air Ministry began constructing
major airfields across the UK in what was known as the Expansion Period;
Little Rissington was one of these airfields

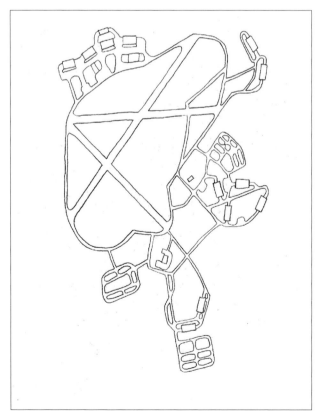

Little Rissington

**1938**

RAF Little Rissington officially opened, comprising the domestic site and a grass airfield

26 August: No. 6 Service Flying Training School arrived from Netheravon as the first flying unit with Audaxes, Furies, Harts, and Ansons

October: No. 8 Maintenance Unit (MU) was formed at the station, using the dispersed hangars for storage and repair of numerous aircraft

**1941**

October: No. 23 Blind Approach Training Flight formed with 6 + 2 Oxfords in No. 21 Group. It was renamed No. 1523 Beam Approach Training Flight

During the mid-1940s dispersal areas began openly storing aircraft that had arrived straight from the manufacturer. The level of security protection was stepped up during the war, including the station's own fighter force of several Spitfires. Later in the war, various satellite airfields were used to spread out the increased number of aircraft

**1942**

No. 8 Aircraft Storage Unit (ASU) renamed as No. 8 Maintenance Unit

1 April: No. 6 SFTS was redesignated No. 6 (P)AFU, providing final training for pilots who had completed basic training in the Commonwealth training schools

**1945**

17 December: No. 6 (P)AFU was renamed as No. 6 SFTS

**1946**

April: No. 6 Service Flying Training School moved to Ternhill

7 May: The RAF Central Flying School moved to Little Rissington, the airfield also becoming the home to the RAF's aerobatics teams which included the Red Pelicans and later the Red Arrows. The airfield was expanded during this period, and a new fire station and Control Tower were built

**Current status:**

In 2006, following a Defence Review, the planned disposal of Little Rissington was stopped and the immediate future of the aerodrome was secured. Several buildings also received some minor upgrades.

## Haunted RAF Little Rissington

*Source: PPRuNe Aviation History and Nostalgia, 11 January 2010*

A contributor commented that he had been informed that a ghostly airman in Second World War flying kit has been seen in one of the C Type hangars.

Source: Fortean Times Online, 2 September 2001
Justin Anstey wrote that a team of four from Cheltenham-based Circular Forum descended on RAF Little Rissington after receiving reports that the airfield was a hot spot for things that go bump in the night. There had apparently been a series of close encounters at the base in recent months, including sightings of ghostly airmen.

# Little Staughton

USAAF 8th Air Force
No. 8 Bomber Group

| | |
|---|---|
| County: | Huntingdonshire |
| Location: | 4 miles W of St Neots |
| OS Ref.: | TL 116615 |
| Opened: | 09/1942 |
| Closed: | 12/1945 |
| Pundit code: | LX |
| USAAF Station: | 127 |
| Control Tower: | Watch Office for Bomber Stations and OTUs 13726/41 |
| Condition: | Now used for storage and is a Grade 2 listed building |
| Runways: | 3 concrete, (250) 1,616 x 50 yards, (310) 1,156 x 50 yards, and (010) 1,020 x 50 yards. Before completion, (250) extended to 1,920 yards and (310) to 1,340 yards. USAF main runway was increased to 3,000 yards |
| Hardstandings: | 37 pan type; in May 1942, when the airfield was allocated to the USAAF, another 17 of the loop type were added (one cluster of loops lay across the road to Little Staughton village near Berrywood Farm) |
| Hangars: | T2 – 3, Robin – 8; 1 T2 hangar was positioned on the technical site between runway heads 25 and 31 near Moor Farm; a second T2 was located between runway heads 01 and 07; the third T2 was between 19 and 25 |
| Bomb stores: | Located to the S, between runway heads 01 and 31 |
| Ad., tech. & barr.: | The dispersed camp lay to the E of the airfield, comprising 6 domestic, 2 WAAF, 2 communal blocks, and a sick quarters site |
| Population: | RAF Officers – 151, OR – 1,166, WAAF Officers – 9, OR – 364 |

A total of 57 aircraft – 34 Lancasters and 23 Mosquitos – and crews were lost from this station. No. 582 Squadron flew a total of 165 raids, during which it lost 28 Lancasters

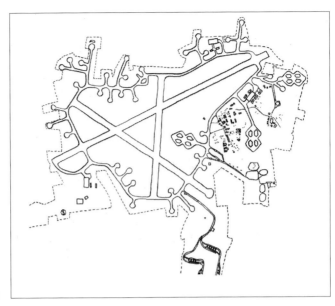

Little Staughton

## *History to 1946:*

### 1941-42

The airfield was built to Class A standard, necessitating the closure of a minor road across the north of the site

### 1942

September: The station was temporarily allocated to the USAAF as an advanced air depot

### 1943

January: Little Staughton was first occupied by the 8th Air Force

1 May: The station was officially transferred to the USAAF and used as the 2nd Advanced Air Depot for repair of B-17s of the 1st Bomb Wing. Additional work on the eastern side of the airfield was put in hand to develop an independent depot, but evidently the Americans felt the road communications to Little Staughton were poor and it was decided instead to build at Alconbury. At this time No. 8 Group RAF required more airfields in the area, so an exchange was arranged whereby Little Staughton would be returned to RAF control and the new airfield at Harrington allocated for USAAF use

### 1944

1 March: The RAF officially took over Little Staughton

1 April: 'C' Flight of No. 7 Squadron from Oakington and a detachment of No. 156 Squadron from Upwood arrived with Lancasters to form No. 582 Squadron

2 April: No. 109 Squadron with its Mosquitos arrived from Marham. These two squadrons were to be the only occupants of the station for the remainder of hostilities

9/10 April: No. 582 Squadron flew its first raid

23 December: A Victoria Cross was awarded posthumously to Squadron Leader Robert Palmer of No. 109 Squadron; while piloting a crippled No. 582 Squadron Lancaster, he perished after determinedly attacking the target

## 1945

23/24 February: A Victoria Cross was awarded posthumously to Captain Edwin Swales of No. 582 Squadron who lost his life in a gallant effort to save both his crew and aircraft

25 April: No. 582 Squadron flew its last operation

2/3 May: No. 109 Squadron flew its last sortie

September: Nos 582 & 109 Squadrons were disbanded at Little Staughton

## Closure:

Little Staughton was placed on care and maintenance, and agriculture returned to the land not covered with concrete. In the 1950s, it was one of a number turned over to the USAF for upgrading and the main runway was increased to 3,000 yards. Other work was also carried out to enable jet aircraft to use the base in an emergency.

## Current status:

In aviation use. Most of the original station buildings survive.

## *Haunted RAF Little Staughton*

*Source: Keypublishing Aviation Forum, 11 April 2005*

Steve Young wrote that while collecting one of the club aeroplanes from Little Staughton he had to gently manoeuvre it out from a packed bunch of aircraft in a fairly small space. At the time he thought it odd that all the aircraft were packed so tightly when there was quite a large open area about sixty yards away. When he mentioned it, he was told that apparently it is very rare that the boys at Staughton park anything on that particular spot, or indeed even go near it. The lads who work there try and avoid the place, especially at night. The story he heard involved a Mosquito that was being run up against the chocks on that particular spot during the Second World War. Unfortunately, it somehow jumped the chocks and killed an airman who was standing in front of it.

# Little Walden

USAAF 9th AF
USAAF 8th AF

| | |
|---|---|
| County: | Essex |
| Location: | 3 miles NNE of Saffron Walden |
| OS Ref.: | TL 558435 |
| Opened: | 1944 |
| Closed: | 1958 |
| Pundit code: | LL |
| USAAF Station: | 165 |
| Control Tower: | Watch Office for all Commands 12779/41, medium front windows to 343/43 |
| Condition: | Restored and in use as a house and office |
| Runways: | 3 concrete and wood chippings, (160) 1,900 x 50 yards, (100) 1,400 x 50 yards, and (40) 1,400 x 50 yards |
| Hardstandings: | Over 75 loop types |
| Perimeter track: | Concrete at standard 50-yard width |
| Hangars: | T2 –2; 1 to the N of the airfield and 1 fronting the technical site to the E of the site |
| Bomb stores: | An ammunition dump was located on the W side of the airfield, outside of the perimeter track, surrounded by large dirt mounds and concrete storage pens |
| Fuel stores: | Located to the S and N of the airfield |
| Ad., tech. & barr.: | Constructed largely of Nissen huts of various sizes, located on the SE side of the airfield. Accommodation sites were dispersed away from the airfield to the SE but within a mile or so of the technical support site, also using clusters of Maycrete or Nissen huts |
| Population: | USAAF Officers – 421, OR – 2,473 |

The 409th lost 10 aircraft flying from Little Walden

## *History to 1946:*

### 1942

During the summer, Little Walden Park and adjoining farms were selected for a Bomber Command airfield to be called Hadstock. However, by the time that construction began, the official name was changed to Little Walden

**1944**

9 March: RAF Little Walden opened and the 409th Bombardment Group USAAF
  9th Air Force arrived with A-20 Havoc and A-26 Invader light bombers. Over
  100 missions were flown by the group, attacking coastal defences, V-weapon
  sites, aerodromes, and other targets in France in preparation for the invasion
  of Normandy

July: The 409th aided the Allied offensive at Caen and the breakout at St Lô with
  attacks on enemy troops, flak positions, fortified villages, and supply dumps

10 September: The 409th Group moved to the ALG at A.48 Brétigny

26 September: Little Walden was transferred to the 8th Air Force and the 361st
  Fighter Group of the 65th Fighter Wing arrived from Bottisham. The 361st
  served primarily as B-17/B-24 escorts

September: The 361st supported the airborne attack on Holland

**1945**

February: The 361st deployed to Chièvres

March: The 493rd Bombardment Group arrived from Debach while repairs were
  carried out on their home runways

April: The 361st returned to Little Walden

20 April: Both groups flew their last combat missions

July: The 493rd Bombardment Group returned to Debach

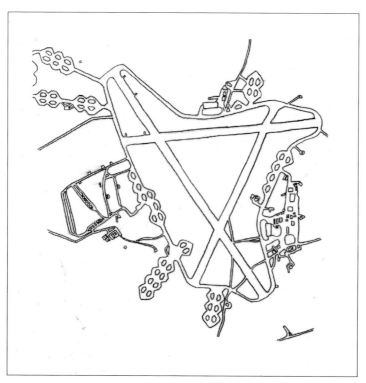

Little Walden

September: The 56th Fighter Group arrived from Boxted

October: The 56th FG moved to Camp Kilmer in the US

10 November: The 361st Fighter Group returned to Camp Kilmer, and Little Walden was returned to the RAF as a storage facility

**Closure:**

In May 1958, the airfield was finally declared surplus and sold, returning quickly to agricultural use.

**Current status:**

Very little remains of the former wartime airfield – only a few small concreted areas with agricultural buildings. Little Walden's tower has been converted to a house.

## Haunted RAF Little Walden

The airfield is not a place locals would perhaps venture to after dark, as it is said to be haunted by the ghost of a headless young airman. It is also alleged that the airman is that of a headless P-51 pilot who has been seen repeatedly by motorists on the road that crosses the site.

*Source: Keypublishing Aviation Forum, 14 March 2004*

The contributor wrote that he used to live in Saffron Walden just up the road from Little Walden/Hadstock, and it was common to hear tales of ghosts on the airfield. He and a friend went into the old Control Tower, which at that time was derelict and pitch dark. Everything was filthy and stunk, and the door slammed behind them for no known reason. Needless to say, they were petrified and ran for their pushbikes. Many years ago, riding past the airfield on a moped on his way home from work in the early hours of the morning, he always had the feeling of being watched and hoped that the little old bike didn't decide to pack up on him.

# Lympne

No. 1 Group, Bomber Command

No. 24 Group, Training Command

No. 22 Group, Fighter Command

RNAS

No. 11 Group, Fighter Command

| | |
|---|---|
| County: | Kent |
| Location: | 2½ miles W of Hythe |

| OS Ref.: | TR 110355 |
| --- | --- |
| Opened : | 1916 & 1936 |
| Closed: | 1920 & 1946 |
| Pundit code: | PY |
| Control Tower: | Watch Office for Fighter Satellite Stations 2658/42 |
| Condition: | Demolished |
| Runways: | Grass, NW-SE 1,400 yards, NNE-SSW 900 yards, and NNW-SSE 1,000 yards |
| Hardstandings: | SE type – 1 |
| Hangars: | Blister – 4 |
| Ad., tech. & barr.: | Temporary buildings to the W of the airfield |
| Population: | RAF Officers – 70, OR – 970, WAAF Officers – 3, OR – 90 |
| Sat. airfield(s): | Satellite of Biggin Hill |

## History to 1946:

### 1916

March: Lympne was chosen to be a night ELG for the Home Defence organisation. It became a 175-acre flying field with landing runs of up to 1,000 yards; a tented camp on the west edge of Lympne village was added to the main aerodrome site

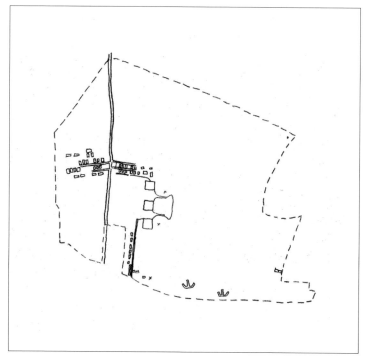

Lympne

October: Bessonneau hangars had been erected and technical buildings were starting to appear. Lympne Castle had become the Officers' Mess and the airmen's tents were being replaced by wooden huts, erected on allotment gardens to the south of the road

## 1920

December: Lympne was declared surplus to RAF requirements but survived as a customs airport with a wireless station and a 30-mile aerial lighthouse. It became a reporting point and an ELG for aircraft on the London-Paris air route

## 1936

Squadrons: 21 & 34

28 October: Lympne became a temporary No. 1 Group station

3 November: Nos 21 & 34 Squadrons arrived from Abbotsinch with Hawker Hinds and an SHQ was formed. The remaining Belfast Truss hangars were used and temporary living accommodation was provided for the personnel

## 1937

Squadrons: 21 & 34

## 1938

Squadrons: 21 & 34

11 July: No. 34 Squadron departed for Upper Heyford

15 August: No. 21 Squadron departed for Eastchurch

1 October: Lympne was reduced to care and maintenance

17 October: Lympne reopened as the School of Clerks and Accounting in No. 24 Group, Training Command

## 1939

24 May: Lympne transferred to Fighter Command

1 July: Lympne transferred to the Navy and was commissioned as HMS *Buzzard*, Skuas and 3 Roes disembarking from HMS *Ark Royal* the following week

September: The squadron with 9 Skuas re-embarked to HMS *Ark Royal*. Lympne was recommissioned as *Daedalus II*

## 1940

Squadrons: 2, 16, 18, 26, 53 & 59

May: Many Lysander and Blenheim aircraft of the AASF retreated across the Channel and arrived at Lympne before dispersing. Nos 16 & 26 Squadrons remained at Lympne, which became one of the 'back violet' bases after communications in France broke down

26/27 May: No. 26 Squadron took part in drops of water and ammunition to the garrison at Calais

May: The Air Mechanics School was moved to Newcastle-under-Lyme

23 May: Lympne transferred to No. 11 Group as a forward satellite airfield of Biggin Hill

3 July: Bombs fell on Lympne without doing very much damage

12 August: Fifteen Do 17s dropped 141 bombs on the airfield. The three GS hangars received direct hits, as did the SHQ, the Cinque Ports clubhouse, and many accommodation huts. An airman was killed and 2 badly injured; repair work was hindered by delayed action bombs. Another raid later in the day dropped a further 240 bombs, nearly a third of which fell outside the perimeter. Additional damage was done and the airfield surface was badly cratered. Lympne was out of action

13 August: More bombs were dropped

15 August: About 40 Ju 87s made for Lympne and bombed the airfield, cutting electricity and water supplies; the sick quarters received a direct hit and the airfield was littered with fragmentation bombs

September: Lympne took no active part in the Battle of Britain apart from an emergency landing field role


## 1941

Construction work commenced to upgrade Lympne


## 1942

Squadrons: 65, 72, 91, 130, 133 & 401

August: Operation Jubilee saw Nos 133 & 401 (RCAF) Squadrons moved in from Biggin Hill


## 1943

Squadrons: 1, 91, 137, 245(det) & 609

Lympne was further upgraded so that prolonged operations by a 2-squadron Wing could be mounted

15 March: No. 1 Squadron arrived from Biggin Hill with Typhoon Ib aircraft tasked with intercepting the Fw 190 nuisance raids


## 1944

Squadrons: 33, 41, 74, 127, 137, 165, 86, 310, 312, 313, 350, 504, 567(det) & 610

5 April: No. 186 Squadron was renumbered as No. 130 Squadron

17 May: No. 33 Squadron with Spitfire IXcs and No. 74 Squadron with Spitfire LFIXes arrived from North Weald to join No. 127 Squadron as a Spitfire IX Wing for sweeps and bomber escorts over France

5 June: The Spitfire IX Wing escorted gliders and then transferred to beachhead patrols. Thereafter No. 74 Squadron was diverted to anti-Diver V-1 interception, and the whole Wing dive-bombed Noball sites

July: Nos 1, 41 & 165 Squadrons begin anti-Diver operations

5 December: No. 41 Squadron departed for Continental airfields and with the departure of the Spitfire Wing to Europe, Lympne reverted to its ELG role

## 1945
Squadrons: 451, 453, 567 (det) & 598 (det)
22 May: Lympne ATC was withdrawn and the airfield reduced to care and maintenance

## Closure:
On 1 January 1946, Lympne was transferred for civil use.

## Current status:
The site is now an industrial estate. Concrete bases of the old hangars are still extant, together with a single Blister, the 1942-style Control Tower, and a few huts near Bellevue. Port Lympne, the wartime Officers' Mess, is now part of Howletts Wild Animal Park.

## Haunted RAF Lympne

*Source: Kent History Forum website*
A contributor to the forum wrote that a friend of theirs used to work at Nusteel, a factory built on the old airfield, where he stated that the blasting shed was haunted. At night it was alleged that one could hear banging and other unaccountable strange noises.

# Lyneham

No. 41 Group
No. 23 Group
No. 116 Wing
No. 2 Group

| | |
|---|---|
| County: | Wiltshire |
| Location: | 3¾ miles SW of Royal Wootton Bassett |
| OS Ref.: | SU 004788 |
| Opened: | 18 May 1940 |
| Closed: | 2012 |
| Pundit code: | LM |
| Control Tower: | A. Unknown |
| | B. Vertical Split Control Type 2548/55 with a two-storey extension to the W side |

| Condition: | A. ? |
| | B. In use |
| Runways: | Grass; in 1941, 3 concrete runways were laid (252) 2,000 x 50 yards, (356) 2,000 x 50 yards, and (135) 1,600 x 50 yards |
| Hardstandings: | 32 pans, diamond – 1, concrete apron for 80 aircraft |
| Hangars: | 14: a central group of 4 hangars and domestic buildings, and 4 other groups of hangars dispersed around the main site |
| Ad., tech. & barr.: | Living accommodation was in huts, some on the main site and others in 5 groups dispersed around the perimeter of the aerodrome. The WAAF accommodation and Mess Hall were in Lyneham village, E of the main camp, where Pound Close and St Michael's Court now stand |
| Population: | RAF Officers – 290, OR – 2,450, WAAF Officers – 11, OR – 292 |
| Sat. airfield(s): | Townsend SLG, Everleigh |

## History to 1946:

**1937**
The area was surveyed for a possible airfield

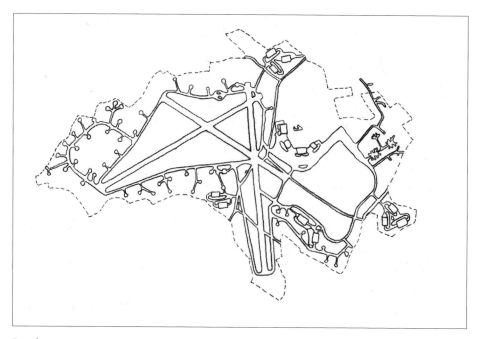

Lyneham

**1939**
The moated manor house of Lyneham Court and Cranley Farm were demolished
   to make way for a new RAF aircraft storage unit

**1940**
18 May: The station opened as No. 33 Maintenance Unit with no ceremony, and
   very few people. By the end of the month the first 2 aircraft had arrived: a Tiger
   Moth and an Albacore
19 September: A raider dropped an incendiary and 2 HE bombs and made a strafing
   run, killing 5 civilian workmen and destroying the east end of the hangar they
   were building
By the end of the year there were 422 civilians, 18 officers (including the first 2
   WAAFs), and 181 other ranks on the station

**1940-1941**
Construction of the airfield and runways continued

**1941**
The station was transferred to No. 23 Group, Flying Training Command
16 August: No. 14 FTS arrived from Cranfield with Oxfords for advanced training
   on twin-engine aircraft

**1942**
19 January: No. 14 FTS moved to Ossington
14 February: Lyneham transferred to No. 44 Group, Ferry Command
April: No. 1425 Communications Flight arrived from Honeybourne with converted
   Liberators on shuttle services to the Mediterranean area, carrying passengers
   and freight outbound and returning ferry crews inbound
September: Townsend SLG was relinquished for Everleigh
October: No. 1425 Communications Flight was redesignated No. 511 Squadron,
   adding Armstrong Whitworth Albemarles
1 November: Nos 1442, 1444 & 1445 Flights amalgamated to form No. 301 Ferry
   Training Unit

**1943**
March: BOAC took over a hangar for its Liberators. They remained at Lyneham
   until 1945. No. 33 MU was now increasingly holding Spitfires and Seafires,
   with stocks of other types reducing. It also had responsible for the completion of
   General Aviation Hamilcar gliders. These were the only Allied gliders capable of
   carrying a light tank and used on D-Day and for the Rhine crossing. Most
   of those built at Lyneham were towed out by Halifax tugs to North Luffenham
March: Transport Command was formed with Lyneham as its main base in the
   south. It acted as the clearance airfield for planning, diplomatic clearance,

customs, and briefing purposes for transport aircraft from other stations flying abroad

## 1944

16 February: No. 525 Squadron arrived from Weston Zoyland with Warwicks, flying via Gibraltar to Tunisia and other destinations in North Africa

16 March: No. 301 FTU moved to Pershore

July: No. 511 Squadron had Dakotas withdrawn; 'A' Flight operated Yorks, and 'B' Flight Liberators

11 October: No. 246 Squadron re-formed from the Liberator Flight of 511 Squadron to fly long-range trips to India and the Far East

1 December: No. 246 Squadron moved to Holmsley South

## 1945

April: BOAC departed for Hurn

The war ended with Lyneham home to the Maintenance Unit and 2 Transport squadrons

15 July: No. 525 Squadron moved to Membury

October: No. 1359 Flight, operating PAMPA reconnaissance flights using Mosquito PR XVIs, arrived from Holmsley South

## 1946

May: No. 1359 Flight was disbanded

By late 1946, the MU held nearly 750 aircraft, the great majority of them Spitfires

**Current status:**

On 4 July 2003, it was announced that Lyneham would be surplus to Strike Command needs by 2012.

## Haunted RAF Lyneham

*Source: Alan C. Wood, Military Ghosts, 2010 (p. 124)*
Whilst Alan Wood was on night duty as runway controller at Lyneham, a ground mechanic tyre-checker was killed by stepping backwards into the arc of the revolving port inner propeller of a Hastings at the end of the main runway by the airfield control caravan.

*Source: Keypublishing Aviation Forum, 8 February 2010*
Whilst stationed at Lyneham, a couple of mechanics were detailed to fix a problem with an aircraft on Bay 4, which was adjacent to the J1 hangar. Later, the corporal sent one of his colleagues to see how they were getting on, as he wanted to run the engine before the midnight running deadline. As he approached, he asked who the

officer was that they had been talking to, and where he had gone. The two hadn't a clue what he was talking about. He explained that there had been an officer standing on the ground looking up at them, and the officer's gestures suggested that he was talking. He was assured that the two mechanics had seen no one other than him on his arrival at the aircraft. They later found out that the bay was apparently haunted by an RAF officer. The follow-up was that whoever saw this apparition, it was said, would suffer a misfortune. The colleague who saw the officer apparently suffered a broken arm a couple of days later.

*Source: Keypublishing Aviation Forum, 7 June 2012*
One forum member was stationed at RAF Lyneham and who worked nights for about four years recalled that there was plenty of 'odd stuff' that occurred in the C2 hangar over the far side of the airfield. People would be seen in the hangar and yet there was no way that they could have gained entrance; similarly, figures were sometimes seen in the Hercules aircraft, checking the airframe or simply disappearing through doors within the hangar. The odd thing about this was that these doors, which would invariably squeal loudly when moved, would make no sound when these figures went through them.

He recalled that on one occasion, when he was showing a former girlfriend around the hangar and aircraft within it, she saw one such figure inside a Hercules but didn't mention it at first as she thought it was meant to be there. At the end of the tour of the hangar as they were leaving, they witnessed another figure in the corner of the hangar entering the office. This had one of the squeaky doors, which again did not sound as he entered. As it was the forum member's office at the time, he shouted a challenge to the figure but received no answer and found there was no one there. Quickly making for the exit, they then witnessed the hangar lights flicker on and off without being first turned on. They were the only people in there at the time, and no one else could have entered as the hangar was secured and he had the keys. The figures that were seen were mostly dressed in blue clothing/overalls, which stood out because it was current RAF issue to have green overalls when working on aircraft. Airmen were never allowed on or in the aircraft in the standard RAF blue uniform due to a risk of damage from items carried in the pockets.

Another of the airmen working there, Jason, thought he saw our contributor walk into the wash room behind him and enter one of the toilet cubicles. Jason at the time was washing some foreign body out of his eye and called out, wanting a hand with the eyewash bottle. Receiving no reply and no one emerging from the toilet, after swearing a lot, he kicked the toilet doors open one by one (SAS style) only to find there was no one there.

On another occasion, they had a WAAF corporal in charge of the crew one night, and whilst they were working on the under-cart bay in a Hercules, she was inside the main cargo hold of the same aircraft. After about 15 minutes she came out and started chatting to them until it was time for tea break, something which was most unusual for her. Over tea she told them that she thought one of the lads had brushed past behind her in the aircraft, but on looking around she saw no one there. At the time she passed it off as a bit of air breezing past her, but when she felt the same thing brush past the nape of her neck a minute later she freaked out and had left the aircraft.

# Manston

No. 11 Fighter Group

| | |
|---|---|
| County: | Kent |
| Location: | 2¾ miles W of Ramsgate |
| OS Ref.: | TR 332559 |
| Opened: | 05/1916 |
| Closed: | 31/03/1999 |
| Control Tower: | A. Night Fighter Watch Office 12096/41 with additions |
| | B. Modern Tower |
| Condition: | A. Use unknown |
| | B. In use |
| Runways: | Up to 1941 the grass-surfaced aerodrome had three landing lanes, (278) 1,600 x 200 yards, (233) 1,900 x 200 yards, and (159) 1,100 x 200 yards. In 1943, construction started on a 3,000-yard concrete/tarmac crash runway 250 yards wide |
| Hardstandings: | SE type – 26 |
| Hangars: | Callender –2 (1916), Blister – 7 |
| Bomb stores: | In 1941, munitions storage existed for 40 tons of bombs and 5 million rounds of small arms ammunition |
| Fuel stores: | Petrol storage of 44,000 gallons of aviation fuel and 3,600 gallons MT was provided for refuelling by trailer (1941) |
| Ad., tech. & barr. | To the N of the airfield in permanent and semi-permanent buildings |
| Population: | RAF Officers – 150, OR – 3,409, WAAF Officers – 7, OR – 143 |
| Sat. airfield(s): | Satellite to North Weald Sector Station |
| Decoy airfield(s): | Monkton Farleigh Q, Ash Level Q |

## History to 1946:

The airfield that was to become RAF Manston resulted from the problems experienced by anti-Zeppelin patrols at Detling and Westgate in 1915. The RNAS looked about for a safer NLG and settled on a large field of 650 acres beside the A253 near Ramsgate.

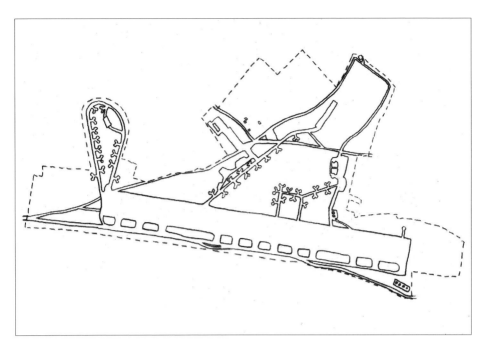

Manston

### 1916

September: The station was virtually complete, with 1 small and 8 large aircraft sheds, two MT sheds, and 3 large workshops (apart from the underground hangars which were never finished and demolished in 1924)

### 1917

It was decided that Manston would become a permanent station and work started on schools buildings, workshops, and additional aircraft sheds

### 1919

October: There was a refurbishment of the accommodation at Manston

### 1924

Construction work began on the married quarters in Manston Court Road

### 1936

The personnel strength of the station rose rapidly; new huts were erected and other buildings were converted into billets. However, the accommodation was still inadequate

### 1938

During the Munich crisis, 700 men had to live in tents

**1939**
Squadrons: 3, 48, 79, 235, 253, 600, No. 3 School of Technical Training, School of Air Navigation & No. 1 General Reconnaissance Unit

**1940**
Squadrons: 32, 56, 79, 235, 253, 600, 604, Nos 1 & 3 General Reconnaissance Units
22–28 May: Manston was HQ for No. 50 Wing
June: The first German HE and incendiary bombs were dropped on Manston, near the explosive store, but no damage was done
12 August: At 12.50 p.m. Manston was attacked and bombed at low altitude by 15 Bf 110s and some Heinkels. Two of the hangars were damaged, workshops were destroyed, and a civilian clerk was killed. The station was pitted with about 100 bomb-craters and was unserviceable until the next day. The raids continued, with the damage to the station mounting
15 August: Four hangars were damaged and one large crater was made in the centre of the aerodrome
20 August: Hangars in the East Camp were damaged and 7 men were killed. The landing area was covered with craters and unexploded bombs, with buildings and aircraft burning fiercely
24 August: Communications were cut and the station was completely isolated
Between September and December only minor raids occurred at the airfield, causing little damage. Manston was already serving in another capacity – that of an ELG for crippled aircraft returning from combat and bombing missions. The aerodrome at the time was comparatively limited for landings of larger aircraft, some without flaps or brakes, and many aircraft overshot

**1941**
Squadrons: 26, 32, 74, 92, 222, 601 & 607

**1942**
Squadrons: 23, 32, 56, 137, 158, 174, 242, 331, 332, 403, 607 & 609

**1943**
Squadrons: 3, 56, 137, 164, 184, 263, 415, 609, 611 & No. 1401 (Meteorological) Flight
April: Manston served as the base for the 'bouncing bomb' experiments taking place at Reculver
June: Construction began on a 3,000-yard long and 250-yard wide concrete/tarmac crash runway, together with an aircraft dispersal loop over 2,000 yards long leading off the western end, and 12 crash bays off the southern edge of the new runway. The work was to include the installation of lighting and drainage

**1944**

Squadrons: 1, 3, 26, 63, 80, 91, 118, 119, 124, 137, 143, 183, 193, 197, 229, 257, 266, 274, 406, 415, 501, 504, 605, 609, 616 & No. 1401 Flight

22 April-19 September: Manston was HQ for No. 155 (General Reconnaissance) Wing

By 1944, with the tally of emergency landings at Manston now reaching 779, it was appreciated that medical facilities must likewise be increased. The casualty centre was converted to a 60-bed hospital with provision for 35 more casualties at Westgate

**1945**

Squadrons: 1, 29, 56, 91, 124, 130, 175, 222, 263, 310, 311, 312, 313, 406, 451, 504, 567, 616, No. 1401 Flight, SCR & 584 Training Unit

27-28 February: Manston was HQ for No. 134 Wing

Manston, unlike so many other airfields, avoided post-war closure because of its strategically important location

**1946**

Squadrons: 3, 4, 16, 33, 46, 77, 130, 305 & 567

18 February-24 July: Manston was No. 91 (Forward) Staging Post

15 September: Manston housed the Transport Command Examining Unit

**Closure:**

On 31 March 1999, RAF Manston closed and the site became a civilian airport called London Manston

**Museums:**

The RAF Manston History Museum (Website: www.rafmanston.co.uk)

The Spitfire & Hurricane Memorial Museum (Website: www.spitfiremuseum.org.uk)

The Manston Fire Museum (within the MoD Defence Fire Service Central Training Establishment site) (Website: www.manstonfiremuseum.com/mfm_home.html)

## Haunted RAF Manston

*Source: Bruce Barrymore Halpenny, Ghost Stations, 1986 (pp. 123-4)*

Sergeant David Petrie arrived at RAF Manston in April 1944 and was put in charge of a crash crew section. At about 11 a.m. in the immediate post D-Day period, Manston received information that a crippled bomber was approaching from across the Channel. Soon an Avro Lancaster with a damaged port undercarriage crash-landed on Manston's wide runway, skidding and finally catching in wire netting, with its starboard wing high in the air. The crew made a hurried escape

**RAF Manston History Museum**
The museum is a fascinating place documenting the long history of RAF Manston from its origins during the First World War to its current use as Kent International Airport. It has numerous displays chronicling the airfield's history together with a number of aircraft and, as can be seen in the photograph, a V1 Flying Bomb on static display outside. A radar hut and the runway are in the background of the photograph. It is located off the B2190 at OS TQ 6745 5500. (© *Chris Huff*)

**RAF Manston Control Tower**
RAF Manston's surviving wartime Control Tower was a Watch Office for Night Fighter stations type 12096/41 with additions and modern cladding over the exterior. It is located on the airfield at OS TR 3354 6655. (© *Chris Huff*)

and in so doing, the pilot left the engines running. Sergeant Petrie boarded the Lancaster to switch the engines off, but upon entering the aircraft he met a civilian, who was wearing what he described as a brown pin-stripe suit. The civilian told Petrie to get out quick because of the risk of fire. David Petrie states that the next thing that happened was that the man leaned across him, switched the engines off, and seemingly left the aircraft. After making sure that everything was safe, Petrie made his way out as quickly as possible, and enquired of an RAF sergeant near the door if he could tell him where the civilian in the brown pin-stripe suit had gone. He was told that no civilians were allowed on Manston airfield.

*Source: PPRuNe website, 27 May 2004*
An account describes a young airman who is said to haunt RAF Manston. The apparition has been seen walking through the old debriefing huts by several reliable witnesses, including people unfamiliar with RAF Manston's history. He would walk through the room and disappear through the wall at the end where there used to be an adjoining hut that was destroyed at some point during the war.

*Source: Personal communication, 19 March 2011*
Phil Crowe wrote to me detailing an account of paranormal happenings at Manston while he was a fireman on the crash line at Manston in the 1970s. One January night the power failed all over the camp so the crew turned in for the night, leaving Phil to clear up with the help of a 'Glim' lamp, as he was on kitchen duty. After a few minutes, he was aware of being watched, and turning around, saw the outline of a person – but not a solid form. Being young, Phil made a hasty retreat through the vehicle bay to the bunk room. In the corner of the vehicle bay, a large bell marked '1941', the type they used for scramble, was making an eerie sound like that of a wet finger on a wine glass. Next shift, Phil consulted a crew member that he knew wouldn't take the 'mick' and found that he knew of this haunting, telling the story of a Mosquito that crashed into a snow drift in the Second World War, whose long-dead pilot walks back to the dispersal via the corner of the fire station, which was not built until the 1950s. There were other stories of crew members being woken in the night, and that 'no one sleeps in the last bunk'.

# Matching

USAAF 9th AF 1944
No. 38 Training Group

| | |
|---|---|
| County: | Essex |
| Location: | 5 miles E of Harlow |
| OS Ref.: | TL 550120 |
| Opened: | 12/1943 |

Closed:                10/1945
Pundit code:           MC
USAAF Station:         166
Control Tower:         Watch Office for all Commands 12779/41, front windows
                       reduced to small size 15371/41
Condition:             Radar test station; an extra door has been added and many
                       windows bricked up
Runways:               3 concrete and wood chippings, (210) 2,000 x 50 yards, (270)
                       1,400 x 50 yards, and (320) 1,400 x 50 yards
Hardstanding:          50 loop hardstands connecting to an enclosing perimeter track
Hangars:               T2 –2, on the technical site
Bomb stores:           The ammunition dump was located on the S side of the airfield,
                       outside the perimeter track, surrounded by large earthen
                       mounds and concrete pens for storing the aerial bombs and
                       other munitions required by the combat aircraft
Ad., tech. & barr.:    Temporary Maycrete or Nissen huts were located on the SE side
                       of the airfield. Various accommodation sites were constructed,
                       dispersed away from the airfield to the E
Population:            USAAF Officers – 417, OR – 2,241

The 391st Bomb Group lost 20 B-26s in operations from Matching.


## History to 1946:


### 1942

August: Construction began by the 834th and 840th Engineer Battalions USAAF
    and was due to be completed by spring 1943, but this was delayed due to the
    necessity of woodland clearance


### 1943

December: Matching Green airfield opened as USAAF Station AAF-166


### 1944

26 January: The 572nd, 573rd, 557th & 575th Squadrons of the 391st
    Bombardment Group arrived at Matching from the US with Martin B-26
    Marauders
15 February: The 391st Bombardment Group flew its first mission
During the ensuing weeks the 391st Group flew 150 more missions and bombed
    targets such as airfields, marshalling yards, bridges, and V-weapon sites in
    France and the Low Countries to help prepare for the invasion of Normandy
July: The 391st Group launched attacks on fuel dumps and troop concentrations
    in support of Allied forces during the breakout at St Lô, and continued to fly

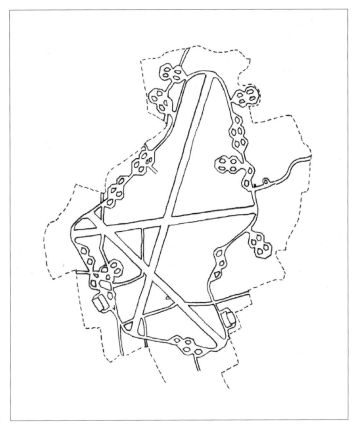

Matching

strikes on transportation and communications to block the enemy's retreat to the east

19 September: The 391st Group were moved to ALG A.73 Roye/Amy. Douglas C-47 Skytrains of IX Troop Carrier Command were detached to Matching later in 1944 for exercises with British paratroops

## 1945

25 February: Matching was transferred to No. 38 Training Group and the Operational and Refresher Training Unit moved here from Hampstead Norris with Stirlings then re-equipped with Halifaxes

April: No. 1677 Target Towing Flight arrived with Martinets from Shepherds Grove

October: No. 1677 Target Towing Flight disbanded

## 1946

RAF Matching was closed and sold to private owners. With the facility released from military control, it was rapidly returned to agricultural use and the concrete removed for road hardcore

**Current status:**

The remains of the airfield are used for agriculture. Part of the main runway is now used as a public road; another surviving portion was used for heavy goods vehicle instruction. Many sections of the perimeter track are now given over to agriculture.

The Control Tower still stands and many Nissen huts and corrugated-roofed buildings in the former technical site are used for small industrial units and storage.

## Haunted RAF Matching

### A personal account

Many years ago (some time in the early 1970s), I was taken out by my father into the Essex countryside and ended up at an old airfield. I do remember that it was late summer and that dusk was approaching, but it was still warm and quite light, insects were buzzing and birds were singing. Then the atmosphere completely changed from a pleasant summer walk in the fields to something far more melancholy. The place had suddenly got a lot colder, as though something was going to happen, but nothing did. There was just an expectant feeling, coupled with the hairs standing up on the back of my neck, and a general feeling of sadness. This lasted for about 20 minutes, when it was time to jump back in the car and head home. I remember chatting to my dad in the car about the change that had happened on the airfield, but all he said was, 'Yes, old RAF airfields often do that,' so I took it for a normal occurrence at the time.

### Source: Keypublishing Aviation Forum, 21 October 2010

Harvey Ditchman wrote that he was once a cab driver in Great Dunmow (not far from Matching) and had to drop off some customers in Matching Green village. As he turned into the approach to the airfield, he felt that he knew the site and knew where everything was, even though he had never been there before. After dropping off the customers, he drove back across the airfield and found a place to stop. After a few minutes there he felt as if he was being watched and felt the urge to leave. He has only ever been back during the day.

# Mepal

No. 3 Bomber Group

| | |
|---|---|
| County: | Cambridgeshire |
| Location: | 6 miles W of Ely |
| OS Ref.: | TL 445796 |

| | |
|---|---|
| Opened: | 06/1943 |
| Closed: | 07/1963 |
| Pundit code: | MP |
| Control Tower: | Watch Office for all Commands 12779/41, medium front windows to 343/43 |
| Condition: | Demolished in 1988 |
| Runways: | 3 concrete/tarmac, (260) 2,000 x 50 yards, (230) 1,400 x 50 yards, and (320) 1,400 x 50 yards |
| Hardstandings: | 36 loop types |
| Hangars: | B1 – 1, T2 – 2; a T2 and the B1 were positioned on the technical site between runway heads 26 and 32, the Bl being to the N, with the other T2 on the N side of the airfield between runway heads 23 and 26 |
| Bomb stores: | Located to NW, between 08 and 14 |
| Ad., tech. & barr.: | The 11 dispersed sites were all to the E of the airfield around Witcham and consisted of 2 Mess, 1 communal, and 8 domestic blocks |
| Population: | RAF Officers – 87, OR – 1,040, WAAF Officers – 9, OR – 187 |

No. 75 (New Zealand) Squadron lost 43 Stirlings and 47 Lancasters, in addition 8 Lancasters were lost in crashes.

## History to 1946:

Mepal airfield was built to Class A specification as one of the two satellite stations for the Waterbeach cluster. The site, on a 20-foot rise out of the Cambridgeshire fens, was confined by the New and Old Bedford Rivers to the west, the village of Sutton to the south, Mepal to the north, and Witcham due east. As the A142 between Mepal and Sutton ran across the middle of the site, it was closed off and diverted to run on the road through Witcham.

### 1942
July: Construction of the airfield began on a £810,000 contract

### 1943
June: RAF Mepal was officially opened and No. 75 (NZ) Squadron, the first Commonwealth squadron to be formed in Bomber Command, arrived with Stirlings from Newmarket Heath

3 July: No. 75 Squadron commenced operations. It was to remain in residence, seeing out the war from Mepal. No other squadron was based there during this period. No. 75 Squadron maintained three flights, their complements often totalling more than 30 aircraft

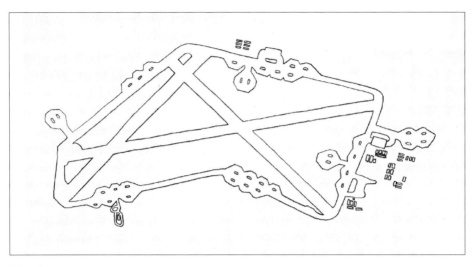

Mepal

**1944**

March: No. 75 Squadron received Lancasters to replace the Stirlings

**1945**

July: No. 75 Squadron moved to Spilsby to make way for the assembly and
    training of Tiger Force, the RAF bomber contingent scheduled to move to the
    NE Pacific for operations against Japan

21 July: No. 44 Squadron arrived from Spilsby with Lancaster IIIs

24 July: No. 7 Squadron arrived from Oakington with Lancaster IIIs

25 August: No. 44 Squadron moved to Mildenhall

28 September: No. 49 Squadron arrived from Syerston with Lancaster IIIs

**1946**

July: Nos 7 & 49 Squadrons moved to Upwood. The contraction of the RAF during
    the first year of peace provided several stations with better accommodation
    than the
tin huts at Mepal and the airfield remained empty of active units for 12 years

**Closure:**

In July 1963, the Thor missiles stationed at the airfield were considered obsolete
    and were removed. Mepal was quickly closed and sold for commercial and
    agricultural use.

**Current status:**

The site is now used for agriculture and industry. Little of the airfield remains
    apart from odd lengths of perimeter track used as farm roads.

## Haunted RAF Mepal

*Source: Richard McKenzie,* They Still Serve, *2008 (p. 113)*
In November 1960, an RAF policeman patrolling the airfield in fog came face to face with a Second World War RAF pilot in full flying gear. The figure abruptly dissolved into the fog in front of him. He apparently tried to report the sighting but was told not to bother as it had been seen before. Another account from the airfield involved hearing the sound of an aircraft flying low as if to land, though no aircraft were visible at the time.

# Middle Wallop

No. 10 Fighter Group
No. 11 Fighter Group
USAAF 9th AF

| | |
|---|---|
| County: | Hampshire |
| Location: | 6 miles SW of Andover |
| OS Ref.: | SU 303385 |
| Opened: | 1940 |
| Closed: | 1957 |
| Control Tower: | Watch Office with Met Section 2328/39, with post-war VCR to 5871c/55 |
| Condition: | Army Air Corps Air Traffic Control |
| Runways: | Grass with maximum run of 1,400 yards; extended to 1,900 yards in 1941. Sommerfeld track steel mat runways were laid in 1942 |
| Hangars: | C Type – 5, Blister – 16 |
| Ad., tech. & barr.: | Permanent accommodation, with a large hutted camp on the other side of the A343. Officers were originally billeted in Andover |
| Population: | RAF Officers – 93, OR – 1,860, WAAF Officers – 17, OR – 284 |
| Sat. airfield(s): | Beaulieu, Christchurch, Chilbolton, Ibsley, Warmwell |
| Decoy airfield(s): | Houghton Q |

## History to 1946:

### 1940

Squadrons: 32, 56, 93, 236, 234, 238, 501, 601, 609, 604, No. 15 Flying Training School & No. 420 Flight

18 April: Middle Wallop was planned as a standard bomber station with facilities for 2 squadrons

20 April: The HQ and half of 15 SFTS arrived from Lossiemouth to a partially completed No. 10 Group station

11 June: No. 15 SFTS moved to Brize Norton and Middle Wallop reverted to No. 11 Group

20 June: No. 1 (RCAF) Squadron formed at Middle Wallop with Hurricanes

11 July: No. 609 Squadron claimed a Bf 110 off Portland Bill

14 August: Three He 111s bombed 609's hangar and offices, killing 3 civilians and 3 airmen while attempting to shut the hangar door; 3 Blenheims and a number of Spitfires were destroyed. Two aircraft of 609 managed to take off during the raid and shot down an He 111

15 August: Twelve Ju 88s dropped twelve 1,000-kg bombs, which missed the main camp but damaged 2 hangars and 5 aircraft and destroyed one. Nos 609 & 234 Squadrons claimed a Ju 88 and 4 Bf 110s destroyed

September: No. 420 Flight was formed at Middle Wallop with Harrows to test a system of laying an aerial minefield codenamed Mutton

26 October: No. 420 Flight flew its first operation flight, it proving difficult to position the parachute mines accurately in front of the approaching aircraft

7 December: No. 420 Flight became No. 93 Squadron with Harrows, Wellington Ics, and Havoc Is

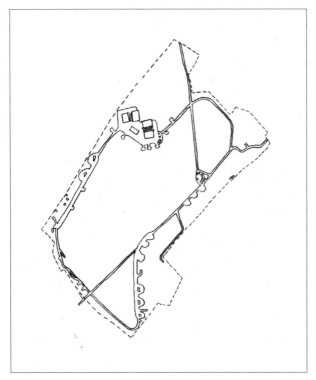

Middle Wallop

**1941**

Squadrons: 32, 93, 238, 245, Fighter Experimental Establishment & No. 1458 (Fighter) Flight

13 March: A German bomber was destroyed by the aerial mines of No. 93 Squadron

7 July: Middle Wallop was bombed by the Luftwaffe at night, losing 4 of No. 604 Squadron's Beaufighters

24 November: No. 93 Squadron became No. 1458 Turbinlite Flight with Havoc Is and Boston IIIs

**1942**

Squadrons: 245, 400, 406, 537, 501, 504, 604 & No. 1458 Flight

2 September: No. 1458 Turbinlite Flight became No. 537 Squadron

27 December: No. 400 (RCAF) Squadron arrived to conduct Rhubarbs over France

30 December: No. 504 Squadron moved to Ibsley

**1943**

Squadrons: 16, 19, 151, 164, 169, 182, 247, 400, 406, 414, 456 & 537

1 February: No. 414 Squadron arrived to conduct Rhubarbs and Populars over Northern France and the Channel

August: 9th AF USAAF Fighter Command HQ moved to Middle Wallop

**1944**

Squadrons: 125, 418 & No. 371 Repair and Salvage Unit

4 January: 19th Air Support Command formed at Middle Wallop

10 January: The station was formally transferred to the USAAF

January: Nos 12 & 107 Squadrons became operational, taking photographs of the French coastline in readiness for D-Day

April: The 15th & 109th Squadrons arrived

2 July: Middle Wallop transferred back to the RAF and No. 10 Group control

31 July: No. 125 Squadron arrived from Hurn with Mosquitos for anti-V-1 operations

18 October: No. 125 Squadron moved to Coltishall

**1945**

Squadrons: No. 371 Repair and Salvage Unit & No. 1 Aircraft Delivery Flight

16 February: Middle Wallop was transferred to the Royal Navy, becoming HMS *Flycatcher*

**1946**

Squadrons: 63, 164, 165 & No. 62 Group Communications Flight

10 April: Middle Wallop returned to the RAF and Fighter Command

June: No. 164 Squadron arrived and converted to Spitfires

31 August: No. 164 Squadron was renumbered as No. 63 Squadron

**Closure:**
The airfield was transferred to the Army Air Corps in 1957.

**Current status:**
The site remains as an Army Air Corps airfield and is the location of the Museum of Army Flying. (Website: www.armyflying.com)

## Haunted RAF Middle Wallop

*Source: paranormaltours.com*
The Museum of Army Flying has been the location for a number of unexplained occurrences since its opening in 1984. Phantom footsteps have been heard and unexplained shadows have been witnessed when no one has been in the area. A small boy has been seen sat in one of the display helicopters, and the apparition of a woman standing on the mezzanine floor has also been observed. Another female apparition, who allegedly was killed during a raid on the airfield during the Second World War, is said to have been seen both in the building and on airfield.

# Molesworth

USAAF 8th AF
No. 11 Fighter Group

| | |
|---|---|
| County: | Huntingdonshire |
| Location: | 10 miles NW of Huntingdon |
| OS Ref.: | TL 008775 |
| Opened: | 15/05/1941 |
| Closed: | N/A |
| Pundit code: | MX |
| USAAF Station: | 107 |
| Control Tower: | A. Watch Office with Met Section 518/40. |
| | B. Post-war temporary USAF Tower, 1954-58 |
| | C. Later USAF multi-storey Tower, not used for air traffic control |
| Condition: | A. Demolished during USAF rebuilding, 1951-54 |
| | B. Demolished |
| | C. Not known |
| Runways: | 3 concrete/tarmac, (191) 2,000 x 50 yards, (255) 1,400 x 50yards, and (09) 1,400 x 50 yards |
| Hardstandings: | 36, then later 50, loop types |
| Hangars: | T2 – 2 |

Ad., tech. & barr.: Temporary accommodation
Population:        USAAF Officers – 443, OR – 2,529
Decoy airfield(s):  Graffham Q


During its 364 missions the 303rd BG lost 165 bombers missing, with 817 of its men killed in action and another 754 becoming prisoners of war. It dropped 24,918 tons of bombs, claimed 379 enemy aircraft shot down, with a further 92 probables and 174 damaged.


## History to 1946:


### 1940
May: A flat area of farmland west of the village of Old Weston was requisitioned for the construction of a bomber airfield. Construction, including the removal of field boundaries, destroying farm buildings and closing a number of roads, commenced in the autumn

### 1941
22 July: Molesworth was due to open in No. 2 Group but this was delayed
5 September: RAF Molesworth opened for use by heavy bomber squadrons
15 November: No. 460 RAAF Squadron formed, from 'C' Flight of 458 Squadron at Holme-on-Spalding Moor, with Wellington IVs

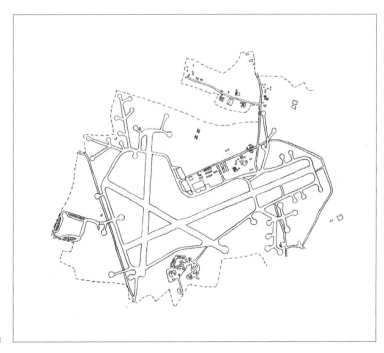

Molesworth

## 1942

1 January: No. 460 Squadron moved to Breighton

2 January: No. 159 Squadron re-formed at Molesworth without aircraft

12 February: The cadre of No. 159 Squadron departed for the Middle East

20 April: Molesworth was passed to the USAAF and further construction took place to bring it up to USAAF specification for heavy 4-engine bombers. The main runway was lengthened to 2,000 yards and the number of hardstandings increased.

13 March: No. 5 Flying Training School with 13 Blenheims from Ternhill used Molesworth as an RLG

16 April: No. 5 FTS found Molesworth unserviceable and departed

9 June: The 15th Bombardment Squadron arrived from Grafton Underwood with Douglas Boston IIIs which they had received from No. 226 Squadron and started a few weeks of familiarisation training with the new aircraft

June: Elements of the 5th Photographic Squadron arrived

4 July: Six American crews from the 15th Bomb Squadron joined with six RAF crews from Swanton Morley for a low-level attack on Luftwaffe airfields in the Netherlands, thus becoming the first USAAF unit to bomb targets in Europe. The raid had been specifically ordered by General Henry H. Arnold and approved by President Roosevelt. Arnold believed that 4 July would be an ideal day for the USAAF to open its strategic bombing campaign. Two of the 15th BS's planes did not return from the mission, along with one No. 226 Squadron aircraft

5 September: The 15th BS received Douglas A-20 Havocs

10 September: The 5th Photographic Squadron departed Molesworth

11 September: The 15th BS moved to Podington

12 September: The 303rd Bombardment Group 'Hell's Angels' began arriving from Biggs AAF, Texas, with B-17s, under the command of Colonel James H. Wallace. They were to spend their entire operational service at Molesworth. It was comprised of the 358th, 359th, 360th & 427th Bombardment Squadrons

16 September: Molesworth served as HQ for the 41st Combat Bombardment Wing of the 1st Bomb Division

17 November: The 358th BS flew the first mission for the group. Initially missions were conducted against targets such as aerodromes, railways, and submarine pens in France. By the end of the war, the 303rd Bombardment Group had flown more missions than any other B-17 group in the 8th AF

## 1943

27 January: The 303rd took part in the first penetration into Germany by heavy bombers of the 8th AF by striking the U-boat yard at Wilhelmshaven. After this they bombed ball-bearing plants at Schweinfurt, shipbuilding yards at Bremen, a synthetic rubber plant at Hüls, an aircraft engine factory at Hamburg, industrial areas of Frankfurt, an aerodrome at Villacoublay, and a marshalling yard at Le Mans

**1944**

11 January: The 303rd received a Distinguished Unit Citation when, in spite of continuous attacks by enemy fighters in weather that prevented effective fighter cover from reaching the group, it successfully bombed an aircraft assembly plant at Oschersleben

5/6 June: The 303rd bombed gun emplacements and bridges in the Pas-de-Calais area during the invasion of Normandy

July: The 303rd bombed enemy troops to support the breakout at St Lô

December-January: The 303rd bombed airfields, oil depots, and other targets during the Battle of the Bulge

**1945**

March: The 303rd bombed military installations in the Wesel area to aid the Allied assault across the Rhine

25 April: The last operational mission for the 303rd involved an attack on an armament works in Pilsen

31 May: The 303rd BG departed for Casablanca in French Morocco

1 July: Molesworth was handed back to the RAF

16 July: No. 441 (RCAF) Squadron arrived from Hunsdon with Mustang IIIs

17 July: No. 442 (RCAF) Squadron arrived from Digby with Mustang IVs

27 July: No. 1335 Meteor Conversion Unit arrived from Colerne to provide operational training for pilots of No. 11 Group

15 July: No. 124 Squadron arrived from Hutton Cranswick to convert to Meteors

7 August: Nos 441 & 442 Squadrons disbanded

18 June: The HQ of the 41st Combat Bombardment Wing of the 1st Bomb Division departed Molesworth

7 September: No. 19 Squadron arrived from Bradwell Bay to receive Spitfire XVIs

2 October: No. 124 Squadron operational with Meteors

5 October: No. 124 Squadron moved to Bentwaters

23 October: No. 222 Squadron arrived from Tangmere with Tempests to convert to Meteors

9 November: No. 129 Squadron arrived from Gardermoen, Oslo

3 December: No. 129 Squadron moved to Hutton Cranswick

11 December: No. 222 Squadron moved to Exeter

**1946**

12 February: No. 234 Squadron arrived from Hawkinge to convert to Meteors

28 March: No. 234 Squadron moved to Boxted

22 June: No. 19 Squadron moved to Wittering

15 August: No. 1335 CU was renamed as No. 226 CU

5 September: No. 54 Squadron arrived from Odiham

30 September: No. 54 Squadron returned to Odiham

**Closure:**
In October 1946, with the decision taken to close Molesworth, the No. 226 CU departed to Bentwaters. However, the station reopened in 1951, and after runway extensions, it was used by the USAF between 1954 and 1957 as a transport base.

**Current status:**
It is now a non-flying airfield under the control of the United States Air Forces in Europe.

## Haunted RAF Molesworth

*The Molesworth Pilot, 5 September 2010*
Tom Mendell wrote that from 1962 to 1964, while his father was stationed at Alconbury, Molesworth was a satellite base to Alconbury. Tom worked weekends on the Molesworth airbase at the Community Club as a glass washer/bar stocker and played pool with the GIs at the old Service Club that was run by some British ladies. During summers and on weekends when not away at the high school at Lakenheath he and his friends would roam all over Molesworth airbase including the defunct flight line. There was a rumour that one of the Quonset huts was haunted – it was alleged that one could hear people playing craps/dice, but no one was ever found there to explain the sounds.

# Netheravon

No. 38 Group
No. 10 Group, Fighter Command

| | |
|---|---|
| County: | Wiltshire |
| Location: | 6 miles N of Amesbury |
| OS Ref.: | SU 165490 |
| Opened: | 06/1913 |
| Closed: | 07/1963 (RAF) |
| Pundit code: | NE |
| Control Tower: | 1. Watch Office for All RAF Commands 12779/41 ? |
| | 2. Modern Control Tower. |
| Condition: | 1. Demolished. |
| | 2. In use. |
| Runways: | Grass, E-W 2,000 yards, SE-NW 1,500 yards, and NE-SW 1,400 yards |
| Hardstandings: | Nil |

| Hangars: | Flight Sheds – 3, Type A (250 feet x 120 feet) – 2, Cathedral – 2, Bessonneau – 1 |
|---|---|
| Ad., tech. & barr.: | |
| Population: | RAF Officers – 142, OR – 1,202, WAAF Officers – 10, OR – 375 |
| Sat. airfield(s): | Boscombe Down, High Post RLG, Shrewton RLG, Chilbolton |

## History to 1946:

**1912**

Netheravon airfield was laid out as an upper camp comprising landing ground, aircraft sheds, and operational buildings; and a lower camp with domestic and training facilities

**1913**

14 June: RFC Netheravon opened and No. 4 Squadron arrived from Larkhill

16 June: No. 3 Squadron arrived from Farnborough. Both squadrons were engaged in experimental aircraft co-operation roles such as aerial photography. Netheravon was quickly selected to become a major training airfield

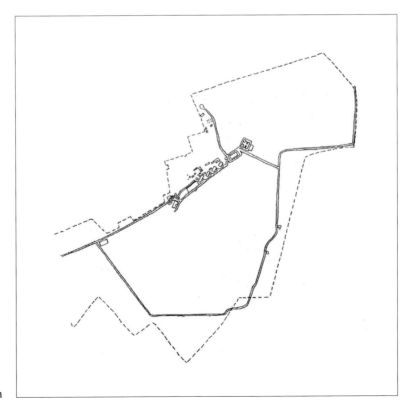

Netheravon

**1918**

1 April: With 2 or more training squadrons being amalgamated into Training Depot Stations, Nos 8 & 12 TDS formed at Netheravon

**1919**

15 May: No. 8 TDS was renamed as No. 8 Training Squadron to train new pilots; No. 12 TDS was disbanded

29 July: No. 8 Training Squadron was renamed as the Netheravon Flying School

23 December: The Netheravon Flying School became No. 1 Flying Training School in No. 7 Group and trained RAF and naval pilots, with a satellite airfield at Boscombe Down

**1931**

1 February: No. 1 Flying Training School disbanded

**1935**

1 April: No. 6 Flying Training School re-formed at Netheravon to provide advanced training for qualified pilots by introducing them to service types and teaching formation flying and air-firing

**1938**

26 August: No. 6 FTS moved to Little Rissington, and No. 1 FTS arrived from Leuchars equipped with Harts

**1939**

August: No. 1 FTS establishment was 32 Harts and 32 Harvards

1 September: No. 1 FTS was given the modified title of No. 1 Service Flying Training School and was the only SFTS handling exclusively FAA training, with RLGs at High Post and Shrewton

**1941**

1 January: No. 1 SFTS had an establishment of 54 Harts/Masters and 54 Battles

26-30 September: No. 239 Squadron was briefly at Netheravon for training exercises with its Lysanders

**1942**

19 January: No. 38 Wing re-formed in Army Co-operation Command

22 January: No. 297 Squadron formed at Netheravon from the Parachute Exercise Squadron with Whitleys for parachute training

1 February: No. 296 Squadron arrived from Ringway for a few days with 2 Hotspur gliders and 5 Hectors

7 March: No. 1 SFTS disbanded as Netheravon was required for use by No. 38 Wing

5 June: No. 297 Squadron moved to Hurn

3 August: No. 295 Squadron formed at Netheravon as an airborne forces unit equipped with Whitleys

12 August: The Glider Pilot Exercise Unit formed at Netheravon in No. 38 Group from 'B' Flight of No. 296 Squadron to provide periodical refresher and flying practice facilities for pilots of the Army Glider Pilot Regiment. It had satellite airfields at Shrewton and Chilbolton, and an establishment of 12 Hectors, 24 Hotspurs, and 10 Tiger Moths

### 1943

8 January: The GPEU moved to Chilbolton

February: No. 295 Squadron received a few Halifaxes

1 May: No. 295 Squadron temporarily moved to Holmsley South

1 June: No. 38 Wing transferred to No. 10 Group, Fighter Command and was redesignated as No. 38 (Airborne Division) Wing

6 May: The Heavy Glider Maintenance Unit arrived from Hurn to maintain, repair, and modify all heavy gliders attached to the 3 tug squadrons in No. 38 Wing

14 October: The GPEU moved to Thruxton

1 December: The Airborne Forces Tactical Development Unit arrived from Tarrant Rushton and was redesignated the Air Transport Tactical Development Unit

### 1944

1 March: No. 1677 Target Towing Flight formed at Netheravon with 3 Martinets

16 August: No. 1 Heavy Glider Servicing Unit formed from No. 1 Heavy Glider Maintenance Unit and No. 235 MU in No. 38 Group at Netheravon with an establishment of 840 Horsas and 80 Hamilcars

12 October: No. 1677 (TT) Flight moved to Rivenhall

### 1945

31 August: The ATTDU was redesignated as the Transport Command Development Unit

20 September: The TCDU moved to Harwell

4 November: The School of Air Transport formed at Netheravon

### 1946

March: The SoAT disbanded

3 October: No. 187 Squadron arrived from Membury with Dakotas for transport flights to the Continent

1 December: No. 187 Squadron was renumbered as No. 53 Squadron; No. 53 Squadron re-formed at Netheravon with Dakotas

31 December: The HGSU disbanded

**Closure:**
In July 1963, the RAF departed from Netheravon, which for a number of years
was used as a transit camp.

**Current status:**
The site is now Airfield Camp Netheravon.

## Haunted RAF Netheravon

*Source: Alan C. Wood,* Military Ghosts, *2010 (pp. 133-4)*
Alan Wood was posted to RAF Netheravon in the 1940s, and allocated a barrack
with ten other airmen in one of the wooden huts immediately on the edge of the
airfield. One night, he awoke for no reason and saw in the dim light a dark figure
dressed in First World War flying clothing standing at the bottom of his bed. Alan
sat up and stared at the figure, which did not move. He then started swearing at
the figure, which then moved and faded away. With his outburst, Alan had woken
the entire billet and was sworn at in turn when he told them that he had seen a
ghost.

*Source: Keypublishing Aviation Forum, 15 January 2007*
A contributor wrote that some years ago, when he was working in the Met Section
at Netheravon, a cleaner on one occasion mentioned that she didn't like going
into the 656 Squadron hangar on her own. When asked why, she replied that
once when she was walking across the hangar, pulling her vacuum cleaner behind
her, she happened to turn around. Standing in the middle of the hangar were a
couple of well-dressed officers having a conversation, wearing old-fashioned long
leather coats of the First World War era. The day outside had changed from dull
and wet to bright and sunny. Having looked down and back up again, everything
returned to normal: the two figures were gone and the weather was back to
normal.

One evening, in the accommodation called the lines, which was once part of the
original Officers' Mess, he was on his bed watching TV when he felt something
cold pass straight through him. It disappeared as quickly as it arrived and he never
felt it again.

*Source: Keypublishing Aviation Forum, 20 November 2006*
Another forum contributor wrote about the former Officers' Mess at Netheravon
House, which some 18 months previously his brother bought one half of, intending
to renovate as a family house. When his sister-in-law started hearing about the
ghost stories associated with it, he was forced to sell up.

The Officers' Mess had long been the location for unaccountable slamming of
doors and of baths being filled when there was no one around.

# North Weald

No. 11 Fighter Group

| | |
|---|---|
| County: | Essex |
| Location: | 2 miles NE of Epping |
| OS Ref.: | TL 488044 |
| Opened: | 1916 |
| Closed: | 1964 |
| Pundit code: | NQ |
| Control Tower: | A. 1916-1940 air traffic control building(s) not known |
| | B. Watch Office for Fighter Satellite Stations 17658/40 with rooftop observation room 658/42 |
| | C. Watch Office 5223a/51 |
| Condition: | A. & B. Demolished |
| | C. Derelict |
| Runways: | 1927, North Weald still retained a grass surface; 1939, 2 paved runways, (314) 1,600 x 50 yards and (027) 1,400 x 50 yards |
| Hardstandings: | SE type – 11, TE – 2, 21 pans |
| Perimeter track: | 1939, a perimeter track was also laid on the W side of the airfield |
| Hangars: | Type A – 2, T2 – 2, Blister – 12 |
| Ad., tech. & barr.: | Permanent |
| Population: | RAF Officers – 156, OR – 2,999, WAAF Officers – 36, OR – 189 |
| Sat. airfield(s): | Hunsdon, Stapleford Tawney |
| Decoy airfield(s): | Nazeing Q |

## History to 1946:

**1916**

Early in the year an aerodrome was constructed on a requisitioned site west of the village of North Weald Bassett

**1919**

With the end of hostilities, the airfield lay dormant for several years

**1926**

Reconstruction began

**1940**

Squadrons: 25, 46, 56, 111, 151, 249, 257 & 604

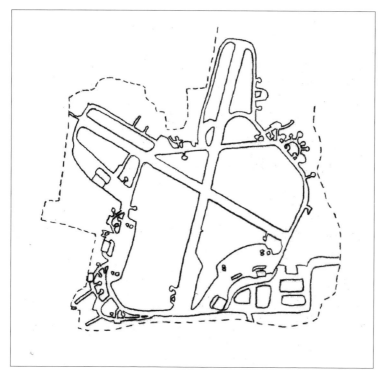

North Weald

24 August: About 200 bombs fell on or around the airfield, severely damaging the officers' and airmen's married quarters. Nine members of the Essex Regiment, in a shelter that received a direct hit, were killed and 10 other personnel injured

31 August: 200-plus aircraft approached, but nearing the coast they split into groups, one of which headed for North Weald. No. 56 Squadron put up 12 Hurricanes but before they could attack the Dorniers they were bounced by the escorting Bf 109s and 110s, losing 4 of their number almost immediately. This brought the total to 11 aircraft lost in 5 days of hard fighting. The squadron was almost wiped out

2 September: More than 200 bombs hit the aerodrome area, killing 2 and injuring 37. The hangars were hit and gutted by fire; the MT yard was badly damaged and many vehicles set alight, various other buildings on the airfield also receiving damage

29 October: When a group of Bf 109s strafed and bombed the airfield, a great deal of damage was caused by about forty-five 100-kg bombs. No. 249 Squadron was taking off when the raiders struck. The first 3 Hurricanes had just become airborne when a 100-kg bomb exploded below and to the right of them. Sergeant A .G. Girdwood's Hurricane took the full blast, blowing him past the other 2 aircraft. His Hurricane hit the ground and burst into flames; the pilot was burned to death

November: For the next few weeks the North Weald fighters were engaged on
coastal patrols

December: No. 249 Squadron commenced flying Rhubarbs over France

## 1941
Squadrons: 56, 71, 111, 121, 242, 249 & 403
All units were actively engaged on fighter sweeps over the Continent

## 1942
Squadrons: 121, 222, 242, 331 & 332

## 1945
1 July: The airfield was transferred to No. 46 Group, Transport Command and
Nos 301 & 304 Squadrons with Wellingtons and Warwicks arrived

September: Both squadrons moved to Chedburgh, leaving North Weald without
any flying units

October: From 1945 to September 1948 the station was used as No. 9 Personnel
Despatch Centre and various selection boards were also established there

**Closure:**
In January 1966, North Weald was transferred to the Army Department.

**Current status:**
The M11 motorway cuts across the western edge of the airfield.

## Haunted RAF North Weald

*Source: Bruce Barrymore Halpenny,* Ghost Stations, *1986 (pp. 59-60)*
In 1946, Bernard Hughes was stationed at North Weald and remembers that the
WAAFs were scared to go anywhere near the Ops Room, let alone go into it. One
night in 1949, Flight Lieutenant John Attrill was night Duty Officer. At about 12.30
a.m. there was a slight sound, so he quietly opened the door. On hearing the sound
of dragging footsteps, a crash, then a heavy bump, he rushed down the corridor
and unlocked the door to find the telephone off the hook and dangling on its cord
to the floor, but there was no one around to account for the noises.

*Source: Bruce Barrymore Halpenny,* Ghost Stations, *1988 (pp. 122-8)*
Epping Forest District Council purchased hangars and some of the other buildings
in 1979, and the airfield museum was established soon after. In September 1985,
at about 6.30 p.m. when Mike Bailey was crossing to Hangar 1, in the dusk he
saw an airman standing. The figure vanished as he watched. Two nights later, at
about the same time, he was again going into Hangar 1 and saw the same airman

and two WAAFs with a further two airmen behind them. They were all dressed in uniforms of the 1940s and all, he thought, looking very unhappy.

In 1990, an investigation was carried out in the WAAF accommodation block (now demolished) and an old air-raid shelter, in which a tape recorder picked up unidentifiable interference. In the WAAF block the tape recorded the sound of a door slamming. When the investigators were upstairs, one of them got an overpowering smell of what he thought was after-shave lotion. Then two members got a localised strong scent of perfume which they seemingly walked through but had vanished when they tried to locate it again. While they were walking around, they heard yet another door slam shut; again this was recorded by one of the tape recorders.

A former cleaner at the aerodrome, in the period when they were getting the place ready for the Army to arrive, commented that the buildings were always locked when they entered and left, and so apart from the cleaners themselves, no one could have been in the buildings. While working in a room on the lower floor two cleaners heard loud banging, with the noise of furniture being moved about upstairs, and were naturally quite worried. One of them rushed upstairs only to find no one there. The same thing occurred to the same two cleaners just two days afterwards. This time when they rushed upstairs to find out what was going on, they found that all the windows had been opened.

*Source: Jack Currie,* Echoes in the Air, *1998 (pp. 64-70)*
In the early 1970s, North Weald was the setting for some of the scenes for the film *Battle of Britain*. The directors decided to install field telephones so that when they needed an actor, a technician or an extra it was easy to contact them from a distance. This however was only a partial success, for as often as not, the extension required was found to be engaged. When the film-maker drove to the location he would invariably find that the receiver had been taken off the field telephone.

*Source: Ken Llewelyn,* Flight into the Ages, *1991 (p. 103)*
Corporal Roderick Broomhead was in an accommodation block which was known on the station as ghost block 101. A part of this building suffered damage when bombed during the Second World War. Broomhead swapped the room after he found that a window had been opened and a light switched on after he had locked the door. The next occupant of the room was Lance Corporal Steve Lovatt, who opened the door one night and a heavy blanket that had been folded under a solid case spread out like a parachute and fell on him. The window was closed at the time and there were no draughts to account for this.

*Source: RAF News, 17 November 1995*
On 3 September 1940, three Blenheims returning to North Weald had been mistaken for Junkers 88s and shot down by Hurricanes. Among those killed was a Pilot Officer Hogg. D. G. Williams wrote that in the summer of 1975 he returned

to North Weald where he had been stationed in 1940. Getting out of his car, he attempted to close the door but it seemed as though someone was holding on to it. He was immediately aware of a shadowy figure surrounded by mist. The mist cleared and Williams clearly saw Pilot Officer Hogg holding a flying helmet in his hand. Williams wrote that as he watched, the mist reappeared and Hogg vanished, as did the mist.

Gerald Betts was posted to North Weald early in 1954. He asserted that a WAAF's ghost was said to haunt the barrack block. At sometime in either 1953 or 1956, as one of the electrical mechanics was walking along the top floor corridor, he heard footsteps walking on the concrete floor behind him. When the mechanic moved to the side of the corridor to let the individual, whom he believed was a female, pass him, he found there was no one there. The electrical mechanic came into the room that Betts was in and recounted his experience, whereupon Betts told him of the haunting of the building by a ghostly WAAF. Betts asserted that the information shook him up a bit.

*Source: Keypublishing Aviation Forum, 10 April 2005*
A contributor wrote that one of his dad's friends had reported seeing a figure in a Second World War flight suit crossing the motorway that runs next to North Weald.

*Source: Keypublishing Aviation Forum, 15 December 2009*
Around 1980, the Control Tower at North Weald, which was used as a bar for the gliding club, had a distinctly eerie atmosphere which everyone noticed, but nothing specific was seen or heard.

# Northolt

No. 11 Group, Fighter Command

| | |
|---|---|
| County: | Middlesex |
| Location: | 3 miles E of Uxbridge |
| OS Ref.: | TQ 098850 |
| Opened: | 1915 |
| Closed: | N/A |
| Control Tower: | Watch Office for all Commands 343/43 |
| Condition: | Demolished |
| Runways: | Grass, tarmac, Sommerfeld tracking, (260) 1,800 x 50 yards, (308) 1,700 x 50 yards, and (205) 980 x 50 yards |
| Hardstandings: | Twin engine – 2, single engine – 30 |
| Hangars: | A1 (Belfast Truss) – 1, C1 – 2 |
| Ad., tech. & barr.: | Permanent Expansion Period buildings to the N of the airfield |

Population:          RAF Officers – 145, OR – 1,608, WAAF Officers – 14, OR
                     – 509
Sat. airfield(s):    Heston
Decoy airfield(s):   Barnet Q/K

## History to 1946:

### 1915

An airfield of 283 acres with 6 flight sheds and a twin hangar, plus workshops and
  long wooden barrack huts was constructed
1 March: Northolt opened and No. 4 Reserve Aeroplane Squadron arrived from
  Farnborough. Soon a line of hangars had been completed on the north side
  which made it impossible for aircraft to taxi from the hangars to the landing
  area, so the middle of the aerodrome was covered with clinker

### 1919

June: The South-Eastern Communications Flight arrived, which was a refresher
  course for officers
Northolt was licensed as a joint RAF/civil flying field and the Central Aircraft
  Company moved in to operate a flying school and a charter organisation as
  well as manufacturing aircraft

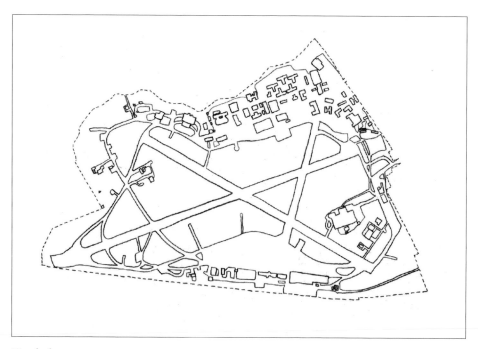

Northolt

**1940**

Squadrons: 1, 25, 65, 92, 111, 229, 253, 257, 302, 303, 306, 600, 601, 604, 609
& 615

The airfield was camouflaged

2 August: No. 303 Polish Squadron formed with Hurricanes

11 October: No. 303 Polish Squadron moved to Leconfield

**1941**

Squadrons: 1, 303, 306, 308, 315, 316 & 601

June: All units based at Northolt were Polish Spitfire squadrons and, with the odd
exception, were to remain so until April 1944. They flew Rhubarbs, Ramrods,
and Circuses. With two Polish squadrons at Heston, they operated as a Polish
Wing and were the first to fly as a Wing over Germany

**1942**

Squadrons: 303, 306, 308, 315, 316, 317, 515, Defiant Flight & Sub Stratosphere
Flight

August: The Sub Stratosphere Flight formed, equipped with specially modified
Spitfire IXs in an attempt to combat the high-flying Ju 86 bombers at altitudes
over 40,000 feet

1 October: No. 515 Squadron formed, with Defiants for radar jamming duties,
and moved to Heston

**1943**

Squadrons: 124, 302, 303, 306, 308, 316, 317 & Sub Stratosphere Flight

July: The Sub Stratosphere Flight was incorporated into No. 124 Squadron

November: The Northolt squadrons became part of the 2nd Tactical Air Force to
give close support and air cover. Northolt was designated No. 131 Airfield

**1944**

Squadrons: 16, 69, 140, 271, 302, 308 & 317

March: The Transport Command Communication Flight was raised to squadron
status and became known as the Air Defence of Great Britain Communications
Squadron

April: The N-S runway was closed so that it could be used as additional parking
space, and the main NE-SW runway was extended

1 April: Nos 302, 308 & 317 Squadrons moved to Deanland in preparation for
D-Day, bringing to an end Northolt's days as a fighter station

8 April: No. 34 Photo Reconnaissance Wing arrived and was camped out on the
west end of the airfield, completely divorced from all station facilities

30 July: A V-1 exploded on the south side of the airfield, causing little damage

September: No. 34 Photo Reconnaissance Wing moved to Balleroy

November: New night lighting was installed

## 1945

Squadrons: 271 & FCC Squadron

A new NW-SE runway of pierced steel planking was laid and the NE-SW runway was resurfaced. Work also started on an aircraft parking apron, and passenger and freight buildings on the south side of the aerodrome

February: Dakotas of No. 271 Squadron were based at Northolt to operate a scheduled passenger service to Brussels

## 1946

Squadrons: FCC Squadron, No. 85 Group Communications Flight & No. 11 Group Communications Flight

4 February: Northolt became officially a civil airport on loan from the Air Ministry to the Ministry of Civil Aviation while the former RAF airfield at Heathrow was reconstructed

**Current status:**

RAF Northolt is the only airfield in use during the Battle of Britain that is still operated by the RAF.

## Haunted RAF Northolt

An airman in a Second World War uniform has been witnessed walking along the E-W runway. The old stables are also allegedly haunted by airmen.

*Source: Bruce Barrymore Halpenny,* Ghost Stations VI, *1994 (pp. 80-1)*

Many members of the Air Training Corps have claimed to have seen the apparition of a pilot sitting in a deck chair reading a newspaper by what would have been the Second World War dispersal area. When approached, the apparition slowly disappears.

*Source: E-Goat Forum, 8 March 2008*

A few people have reported seeing a Second World War pilot in full flying kit in the accommodation blocks. He is believed to be a member of No. 303 Squadron who crashed his Spitfire either into the building or a spot of land where one of the barrack blocks are now. There are tales of him sitting on people's beds and looking in lockers. Allegedly, if you talk to him he wanders off.

*Source: E-Goat Forum, 21 September 2011*

Whilst at Northolt, rumours abounded that the Aeronautical Information Documents Unit was being continually found unlocked, despite being locked up earlier. Northolt was built on some of the plague pits from London, and this was credited at the time as being the cause of the problem.

*Source: PPRuNe Airfield Ghosts, 31 January 2006*
Some years back, the author of the piece worked at the Saddle Club of RAF Northolt, which was located on the station. The horses would spook violently at a spot past the green gates when being led back to their fields alongside the A40. They would gallop away from a certain area around that field and huddle in the corner. One atmospheric night, the wind howling, the horses were about to be put into the paddock when a rather oddly dressed female figure walked across it. There was nowhere for the figure to go except the genuine entrance, unless a hole had been cut through the fence. As the horses entered the paddock, the figure was seen to move slightly, but after turning away briefly to close the gate it was gone. When the police arrived, they found no sign of an intruder, no hole in the fence, and no footprints in the mud.

*Source: castleofspirits/stories/rafnortholt*
Having joined the RAF in 1985, Mark Webster's first operational posting was to Northolt. In 1986, having bought a TV and video recorder after the Christmas break, a boys' night in was organised, watching movies and drinking. They locked the only door to the room, drew the curtains, and settled in for a relaxing night. As they started watching the second film, all seated in a semi-circle around the TV, they heard the locker doors begin to open slowly. When the doors were fully open, the next locker started to do the same, both doors opening very slowly. Somebody unseen was moving round the room, deliberately opening the doors to everyone's lockers only four feet away from them. As they sat there transfixed, the doors that had been opened first suddenly closed with a bang, just as if somebody had shut them in anger, the force of the doors being slammed rocking the lockers violently. Then the next locker did the same, and so on down the line. As the last locker doors slammed shut, one of them rushed for the main light switch. Everything stopped. All the windows were still shut, and the door to the room was still locked and bolted.

In the summer of 1986, when returning from a day's work, Mark entered the barrack block at about 7.30 p.m. As he walked up to the first set of double doors he saw through the glass of the second set of double doors somebody coming down the stairs, wearing the old RAF flying uniform. The figure was around 5 feet 8 inches tall, with old-pattern Second World War leather flying boots, Hairy Mary blue trousers, an old worn brown leather flying jacket, and was carrying a leather flying helmet in his right hand. His left hand was holding on to the hand rail. Mark could see from the look on his face that he too had been seen through the glass, as the figure smiled and began to raise his hand in a gesture of a friendly greeting. Mark opened the second set of double doors, and was about to ask him if there was a fancy dress party at the NAAFI that he had not heard about, but the figure was gone. It was simply not possible – the man had been more than halfway down the double set of stairs when they saw each other, and there was no time for him to get up or down them without being seen. He had simply vanished on the stairs.

# Nuthampstead

USAAF 8th AF

| | |
|---|---|
| County: | Hertfordshire |
| Location: | 5 miles SE of Royston |
| OS Ref.: | TL 420346 |
| Opened: | 05/43 |
| Closed: | 10/54 |
| Pundit code: | NT |
| USAAF Station: | 131 |
| Control Tower: | Watch Office for all Commands 12779/41, small front windows to 15371/41 |
| Condition: | Demolished |
| Runways: | 3 concrete/tarmac, (230) 2,000 x 50 yards, (350) 1,400 x 50 yards, and (290) 1,400 x 50 yards; extended to 2,430, 2,015 and 2,200 yards |
| Hardstandings: | Concrete Spectacle type – 50 |
| Hangars: | T2 –2, both fronting the technical site to the W of the airfield |
| Bomb stores: | Located in woodland to the S of the airfield |
| Fuel stores: | E of the airfield and slightly NW of the technical site |
| Ammo dump: | SE of the airfield in woodland |
| Ad., tech. & barr.: | In and around Nuthampstead village; mostly Nissen huts. The 17th-century 'Woodman Inn' served as the Officers' Mess of the 398th |
| Population: | USAAF Officers – 421, OR – 2,473 |

The 55th FG lost 12 aircraft while at Nuthampstead; the 398th Bomb Group flew 195 combat missions, losing 58 B-17C Flying Fortresses.

## *History to 1946:*

### 1942
Construction of this heavy bomber airfield was begun by the 814th and 630th Engineer Battalions of the US Army for the USAAAF 8th Air Force

### 1943
May: RAF Nuthampstead opened into the 8th USAAF

14 September: The 55th Fighter Group arrived from the US as a part of the 67th Fighter Wing

15 October: The 55th FG's Lockheed P-38H Lightnings began operations

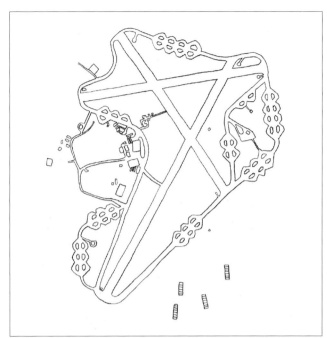

Nuthampstead

## 1944

February: The 55th FG provided cover for missions against aircraft plants during 'Big Week'

19 February: The station was raided by 8 to 10 enemy aircraft, dropping large numbers of small bombs

3 March: The 55th FG became the first Allied fighters to reach Berlin on an escort mission

16 April: The 55th FG moved to Wormingford

22 April: The 398th Bombardment Group arrived from Rapid City AAF, South Dakota, with Boeing B-17Gs

6 May: The 398th BG flew its first combat mission and from then on flew primarily against strategic objectives in Germany, attacking targets such as factories in Berlin, warehouses in Munich, marshalling yards in Saarbrüchen, shipping facilities in Kiel, oil refineries in Merseburg, and aircraft plants in Münster

June: The 398th BG attacked coastal defences and enemy troops on the Cherbourg peninsula during the invasion of Normandy

September: The 398th BG attacked gun positions near Eindhoven

December: The 398th BG raided power stations, railways, and bridges during the Battle of the Bulge

## 1945

14 February: A formation of 38 aircraft from this group mistakenly bombed Prague

March: The 398th BG flew missions attacking airfields to aid the Allied assault across the Rhine

25 April: The 398th BG flew its last combat mission

June: The 398th BG returned to the US

10 July: With the departure of the 398th BG, Nuthampstead was transferred to RAF Maintenance Command and the airfield was used for ordnance storage

**Closure:**

RAF Nuthampstead was closed on 1 March 1959.

**Current status:**

The north-east end of the main runway has been converted to a grass landing strip for small crop-spraying aircraft. Many of the former airfield technical site buildings are in use by private companies.

## Haunted RAF Nuthampstead

*Source: Luton Paranormal Society*

In 1984, Adam Gurney along with an old school friend decided to visit Nuthampstead, which was then deserted with only a few remaining buildings and

**RAF Nuthampstead Memorial**

The impressive 398th Bomb Group Memorial at Nuthampstead was dedicated on 21 September 1982. It commemorates the USAAF servicemen of the 600th, 601st, 602nd & 603rd squadrons of the 398th who lost their lives between 6 May 1944 and 25 April 1945. The memorial is located beside the former Airfield and to the side of the Woodman Inn at OS TL 4118 3454. (© *Chris Huff*)

a section of runway. Just after dusk they drove onto the runway. Twenty minutes later, Adam suddenly felt compelled to look into his rear-view mirror. He was surprised to see a ghostly horse and rider bearing down on the car at full gallop. Adam nudged his friend, who looked round at the figure then quickly locked his door. He drove off as fast as he could, but realising he couldn't go fast enough due to the potholes, Adam drove around a clump of trees on the runway and turned off his car's engine and lights. When the figure did not appear, he drove back onto the runway only to find that the horse and rider had vanished.

*Source: Keypublishing Aviation Forum*
Harvey Ditchman wrote about his experience at Nuthampstead in 1986. For many years, his ATC squadron held their annual fly-in at Nuthampstead. They had an advisory air traffic control in place, and on the Saturday morning it was Harvey's turn on the radio. He finished his stint and was preparing for the afternoon orienteering exercise around the station. After the Second World War, a bomb disposal team was called in to clear the whole site, including the wooded areas. The map-reading exercise took them into one of these areas, which had concrete roads situated within them, and they were told on no account to leave the roadways, just in case. Wandering through the area, they saw a Nissen hut and decided to have a look around, and as they left, a 1940s-style Big Band started playing as if on a radio. Needless to say, they left rather quickly. Apparently in B Hangar the 398th Bomb Group used to hold dances, and Glenn Miller had visited the station prior to his disappearance.

*Source: Flak News*
Vic Jenkins wrote that he was one of the maintenance party of about thirty RAF personnel at Nuthampstead in late June of 1945, at the time of the handover of the airfield from the USAAF to the Royal Air Force. Whilst on guard duty the topic invariably moved onto ghosts and one member admitted that he had seen a figure dressed in full flying gear in the mortuary on numerous occasions. Others finally admitted they felt a strange presence when they entered the building. Not long after this, Vic was on patrol checking out B Hangar. Although he had a torch, it was very dark inside. Suddenly there was the very faint sound of 1940s Big Band music. Frozen to the spot by the sound, he listened again and just as quickly as it had started, it stopped and all was deathly quiet again. Some of the other airmen with him told of hearing talking and laughing coming from the deserted squadron huts that straddled the road to the back gate and hospital.

# Oakington

No. 2 Bomber Group
No. 3 Bomber Group

No. 8 Bomber Group
Transport Command

| County: | Cambridgeshire |
|---|---|
| Location: | 5 miles NW of Cambridge |
| OS Ref.: | TL 412654 |
| Opened: | 1940 |
| Closed: | 1999 |
| Pundit code: | OA |
| Control Tower: | Watch Office with Met Section 5845/39 (brick) with 5871c/55 VCR |
| Condition: | Demolished |
| Runways: | Grass, then 3 concrete/tarmac, (230) 1,700 x 50 yards, (190) 1,300 x 50 yards, and (280) 1,400 x 50 yards; 1942, (230) extended to 2,000 yards at its 23 end and (190) to 1,526 yards at its NE end, necessitating the closure of the B1050 road |
| Hardstandings: | In 1940, a perimeter track and at least 26 pans and 6 square hardstandings were laid, 2 of the former being lost when two T2 hangars were erected. In 1941, 30 pan type hardstandings were provided. A reworking in 1942 of the perimeter track to meet the extensions resulted in some loss of hardstandings, these being reduced to 28, to which 8 loops were added |
| Hangars: | B1 – 1, J Type – 2, T2 – 2. The original plan called for a crescent of C Type hangars on the technical site but 2 J Type were erected instead. In 1940, 2 T2 hangars were erected on the NW side of the technical area, and a B1 hangar on the NW side of the airfield near Longstanton village |
| Bomb stores: | Located off to the N |
| Ad., tech. & barr.: | Temporary buildings were dispersed around the village of Longstanton adjacent to the camp site at the NW side of the landing ground. The domestic accommodation was enlarged in 1942 |
| Population: | RAF Officers – 181, OR – 1,480, WAAF Officers –12, OR – 357 |
| Decoy airfield(s): | Rampton Q, Boxworth Q |

Total operational losses of bombers flying from the airfield amounted to 258 aircraft: 113 Stirlings, 93 Lancasters, 36 Mosquitos, and 16 Wellingtons.

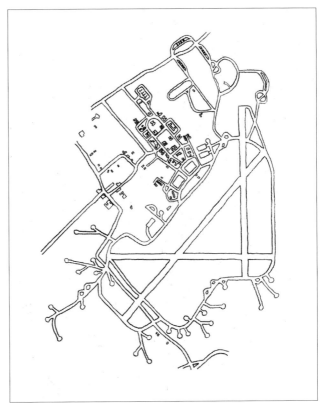

Oakington

## History to 1946:

### 1939

Construction of an airfield began on meadowland 5 miles north-west of the centre of Cambridge

### 1940

July: RAF Oakington opened into No. 2 Group for No. 218 Squadron returning from France, re-equipping with Blenheims

19 August: No. 218 Squadron recommenced operations

September: Oakington transferred to No. 3 Group

29 October: No. 7 Squadron arrived from Leeming with Stirling Is

16 November: No. 3 Photographic Reconnaissance Unit formed with 6 Spitfires for daytime flights and 2 Wellington Mk Is for night flights. Due to poor surface conditions during winter months, the unit often operated from Alconbury

### 1941

10/11 February: No. 7 Squadron made its first bombing attack on oil storage tanks at Rotterdam

April: No. 7 Squadron bombed Berlin

28 April: No. 7 Squadron flew a daylight raid on Emden

16 June: No. 3 PRU amalgamated with No. 1 PRU

1 July: No. 101 Squadron arrived from West Raynham with Wellington Is

21 July: The PRU moved to Benson

## 1942

February: No. 101 Squadron received Wellington IIIs

11 February: No. 101 Squadron moved to the new satellite at Bourn

May: No. 7 Squadron Stirlings undertook mine laying missions

May-June: The 1,000-bomber raids on Cologne, Essen, and Bremen

August: No. 7 Squadron was assigned to the Pathfinder Force

## 1943

8 January: The Pathfinder Force became No. 8 (Pathfinder Force) Group

May: Lancasters began to replace the Stirlings of No. 7 Squadron

17/18 August: Seventeen of the squadron's Lancasters took part in the raid on Peenemünde

November: No. 627 Squadron was formed at Oakington with Mosquitos

24/25 November: No. 627 Squadron became operational

## 1944

15 April: No. 627 Squadron moved to Woodhall Spa in No. 5 Group

24 April: No. 571 Squadron arrived from Downham Market with Mosquito B.XVIs tasked with bombing German industrial centres, particularly Berlin, with 4,000-lb 'cookie' bombs

30 November: No. 571 Squadron, as part of a force of 39 Mosquitos, attacked a synthetic oil plant at Meiderich outside Duisburg with no losses

## 1945

25 April: No. 7 Squadron flew its last operational mission in the Second World War when 10 Lancasters as part of a force of 482 aircraft bombed gun batteries on the island of Wangerooge

26/27 April: No. 571 Squadron flew its last operational mission when 11 Mosquitos bombed Grossenbrode airfield without loss

7 May: Seven Lancasters of No. 7 Squadron marked 2 areas for supply-dropping to the Dutch at The Hague

20 June: No. 571 Squadron moved to Warboys

July: Oakington was transferred to Transport Command

24 July: No. 7 Squadron moved to Mepal

1 August: No. 206 Squadron arrived at Oakington from Leuchars with Liberator VIs for long-range troop transport to the Far East

14 August: No. 86 Squadron arrived from Tain with Liberator VIs for long-range troop transport to the Far East

## 1946
25 April: Nos 86 & 206 Squadrons disbanded; this was followed by the arrival of a succession of transport squadrons, RAF Oakington contracting in size

**Closure:**
In October 1974, Oakington was closed and the land transferred to the Army as a barracks for the Royal Anglian Regiment.

**Current status:**
The runways have now been removed for hardcore, but the perimeter track remains.
In 2000, the station domestic area was leased to the Home Office and converted to an Immigration Reception Centre. Since 2007, plans have been developed to build Northstowe, a new town of 9,500 houses, on the site.

## Haunted RAF Oakington

*Source: Fighter Control Forum, 2 January 2011*
Paul wrote that many years ago he had served with 657 Squadron Army Air Corps based at Oakington Barracks as a driver. One night in 1984 he was the Duty Driver, night flying had just finished, and all the aircraft were away. He was sent to lock up the Tower, where on several previous occasions he had experienced the hair on the back of his neck rise and a discomfort in his stomach. Starting at the top, he worked his way down the building, checking that all the rooms were empty and locked. The building was empty and no one had entered, and yet as he reached the ground floor he heard footsteps on the linoleum of the floor above. He called out to see who was there but got no answer. Feeling very uncomfortable, he decided to vacate the building quickly. He told the Duty NCO when he arrived back at the office, who said that he was not going over there and just entered it in the duty log. The next day, Paul was quizzed about the report by the CO.

# Panshanger

No. 50 Group Flying Training

| | |
|---|---|
| County: | Hertfordshire |
| Location: | 2½ miles W of Hertford |
| OS Ref.: | TL 278128 |

| | |
|---|---|
| Opened: | 1941 |
| Closed: | 1953 |
| Pundit code: | PG |
| Control Tower: | Type unknown possibly unique |
| Condition: | Demolished |
| Runways: | Grass, N-S 1,000 yards, NE-EW 1,033 yards, E-W 1,166 yards, and NW-SE 1,033 yards |
| Hangars: | Blisters – 7, Double Extra-Over – 2, Extra-Over – 2, Triple Standard – 1, Double Standard – 1, Standard – 1 |
| Ad., tech. & barr.: | Temporary buildings |
| Population: | RAF Officers – none, OR – 43 |
| Sat. airfield(s): | RLG for Hatfield |
| Decoy airfield(s): | Decoy for Hatfield |

## History to 1946:

Situated between Welwyn Garden City and Hertford, this airfield was originally known as Holywell Hyde and used as a landing ground for the Hatfield-based No. 1 Elementary and Reserve Flying Training School.

### 1940

Panshanger became a decoy airfield for the de Havilland aircraft factory at Hatfield, a large dummy factory being constructed on the site. This decoy aerodrome, equipped with hangars and facilities made by film set experts, was complete

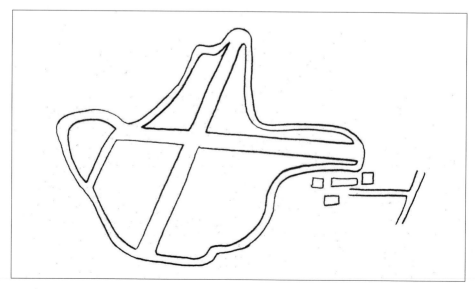

Panshanger

with dummy aircraft, cars, smoking chimneys, and deliberate blackout leaks. It was so successful that many British pilots landed at Panshanger by mistake

## 1941
16 June: The airfield was brought back into use as an RLG as Holywell Hyde for No. 1 Elementary Flying Training School at Hatfield with Tiger Moths

## 1942
7 September: No. 1 EFTS moved to Holywell Hyde. The main task of the school – grading prospective pilots – continued right until the end of the war when the EFTS reverted to its role of training reserve pilots. Aircraft repair and maintenance were carried out on site but there is nothing in the EFTS Ops Book to suggest that these operations were undertaken anywhere but in the buildings provided

## 1943
11 March: Recorded in the Ops Book, Sergeant N. C. Powell of No. 14 OTU crashed at 1.15 a.m. while trying to land Wellington Ic ZI154-P on the short flare path at Holywell Hyde
23 June: Two enemy HE bombs fell 100 yards outside the southern boundary
13 September: Holywell Hyde was renamed RAF Panshanger

## 1944
18 February: Out of 1,200 incendiary devices dropped in a raid, 700 landed on the airfield

## Closure:
On 31 March 1953, No. 1 Reserve Flying School disbanded. Since that time the airfield has been used by private aircraft.

## Current status:
A number of the original buildings are still present and form part of the East Herts Flying Club which currently operates from the site. Housing has also encroached on parts of the airfield.

## Haunted RAF Panshanger

There are a number of accounts of a female apparition haunting a decoy air-raid shelter at Panshanger. The paranormal database records that this woman is believed to have committed infanticide in the area, although this is undoubtedly local folklore to explain a haunting.

*Source: Keypublishing Aviation Forum, 19 January 2010*

Boys playing around a bomb-proof guard post at Panshanger would dare each other to enter the building, as it had a completely different and sinister atmosphere to the shelter further along the peritrack. On more than one occasion they saw a figure darting towards the entrance of the guard post as they entered the peritrack from the Black Fan Road entrance, only to find the guard post empty and with no sign of anyone in the immediate location.

The same contributor, in a post on 20 January 2010, added that on another occasion six boys were playing war games in an area of woodland that had been cleared behind the T5 hangar but had overgrown with bracken and ferns over time. One boy came bursting out of the undergrowth saying that he had seen a man wearing light brown overalls, watching from the open ground just to the side of the hangar. This figure then disappeared. The boys looked around but found no sign of the man. At the time two technicians were working on an aircraft in the hangar and when asked about a man in overalls, they replied that they had both been present in the hangar for at least half an hour and neither of them wore light brown overalls.

*Source: Luton Paranormal Society, 16 March 2012*

An account of an investigation at Henry Wood, Panshanger:

When Sarah arrived and got out of her car, she felt like someone had walked up the concrete drive from the gate area towards the road; this happened twice. She also heard rustles in the undergrowth but no animal could be seen. As a second team of investigators arrived, Marion received the communication 'Steward helped me.' While walking around the wood in a general reconnaissance, she saw a pale lilac shadow of a child, thought to be a little girl, which shimmered as it stepped part way out from behind a tree as if having a look to see who was there. Later, Marion received the communications, 'Chocks away, Sally', 'Michael', 'Donald came' and, just before the end of the session, 'He broke my little girl.' When asked who, she was told, 'That vile man who made off with her; she was so lovely.' Slightly later, Marion heard footsteps to her right and Steph heard what sounded like wind chimes and then someone whistling a slow tune coming from the derelict building on the airfield. Bill saw a flash of pale blue light on a building, and Marion could hear clanking noises to her right coming from the airfield.

# Peterborough

No. 21 Group
No. 50 Group

| | |
|---|---|
| County: | Cambridgeshire |
| Location: | 2 miles NW of the city |

| | |
|---|---|
| OS Ref.: | TF 174005 |
| Opened: | 02/08/1932 |
| Closed: | 1948 |
| Pundit code: | PH |
| Control Tower: | Unknown Watch Office |
| Condition: | Demolished |
| Runways: | Grass, NNW-SSW 1,200 yards, NE-SW 1,020 yards, ENE-WSW 780 yards, and SSE-NNW 780 yards |
| Hardstandings: | 3 loop types |
| Hangars: | An aircraft shed, Bellman hangars, and Blister hangars |
| Ad., tech. & barr.: | Permanent Expansion Period architecture with wooden huts, each housing one NCO and 24 airmen, in addition to extra housing for officers and instructors |
| Population: | RAF Officers – 98, OR – 742, WAAF Officers – 5, OR – 210 |
| Sat. airfield(s): | Sibson, Kings Cliffe, Sutton Bridge |

## History to 1946:

**1930**

Marshall's Flying School Ltd for civilian flying was set up on the family farm located within the site of future RAF Peterborough

Peterborough

**1931**

29 September: The Air Ministry agreed to take over 12 acres of land

**1932**

2 August: Westwood Airfield or Westwood Farm aerodrome (as it was then named) was opened

**1932**

February: The Hawker Audax squadron arrived as an operational unit

**1935**

2 December: No. 7 Service Flying Training School formed at Peterborough in No. 21 Group with a total establishment of 22 officers and 390 other ranks

**1936**

6 January: The first course for No. 7 SFTS

1 March: The Advanced Training Squadron formed. Students undertook a three month flying course, spending another three months studying applied flying, weapons training, formation flying, and tactics

**1938**

September: More technical facilities were constructed and machine gun stop-butts built

**1939**

17 January: Airspeed Oxfords, the first monoplane trainers at Peterborough, arrived. The course was extended from 16 to 20 weeks' duration

March: Oxford L9689 crashed into a hangar

September: At the outbreak of war, the flying course was reduced to 4 months' duration

October: No. 7 SFTS switched to single-engine aircraft courses and the Oxfords departed

**1940**

January: Fairey Battles arrived and No. 7 SFTS was ordered to hold 12 Harts in readiness for bombing duty within Operation Banquet Light, where every available aircraft was to be used in a last-ditch effort to repel an expected German invasion. Instructors were told to 'take every opportunity to carry out practice bombing'

7 July: RAF Sibson was used as an RLG for night flying training

29 August: The first echelon left to join No. 31 SFTS in Canada

20 December: Peterborough was transferred to No. 50 Group and No. 13 EFTS arrived from White Waltham with Tiger Moths

**1941**

1 June: No. 13 EFTS disbanded to form Nos 21 & 25 (P)EFTS. No. 25 (Polish) EFTS formed in 21 Group at Peterborough with Tiger Moths

15 July: No. 17 EFTS arrived from North Luffenham with Tiger Moths

16 July: No. 25 EFTS departed for Hucknall

**1942**

1 June: No. 17 EFTS disbanded at Peterborough and No. 7 (Pilots) Advanced Flying Unit formed with Miles Master Is and IIs. This refresher school expanded fast and was soon able to place two Flights permanently at the satellite at Sibson

**1943**

April: No. 7 (P)AFU had up to 130 Masters (mainly Mk IIs) and 4 Ansons; the pupil population was similarly increased from 90 to 211 pilots

25 June: Night flying commenced at Kings Cliffe

July: Kings Cliffe was required for operational flying and was relinquished

**1944**

June: Sutton Bridge was used as a satellite for night flying

8 August: Sutton Bridge became a satellite to Peterborough, leaving Sibson largely unused

September: The opening of a new No. 7 (P)AFU and a new SFTS, with the arrival of 22 Oxfords

21 December: No. 7 SFTS re-formed from No. 7 (P)AFU at Peterborough

**1945**

May: Harvards and Spitfire IIs replaced the Masters. Night flying was being undertaken at Wittering

June: AZ497, the last Miles Master, was retired

**1946**

4-16 April: No. 7 SFTS departed for Kirton to be absorbed into No. 5 SFTS

**Closure:**

No. 259 Maintenance Unit stayed for two years before the airfield was placed under care and maintenance.

**Current status:**

A Bellman hangar was taken from Peterborough in the 1960s for use at Sibson. In October 1993, a plaque was unveiled in the old Officers' Mess, now used by Cambridgeshire County Council. By 2008, the airfield had almost disappeared under housing development, although some of the old permanent blocks have survived and are still used for various purposes.

## Haunted RAF Peterborough

*Source: peterborough.gov.uk*
A serious crash in 1936, when four men were killed, is generally blamed for the paranormal events at former RAF Peterborough. Witnesses have reported the sounds of phantom aircraft passing overhead when nothing was seen in the sky, A number of Second World War pilots have been seen wandering the area that is now the Westwood housing estate. In addition, ghostly footsteps have allegedly been heard at the locations of former buildings from the RAF period.

*Source: Keypublishing Aviation Forum*
There are said to have been a lot of ghostly goings-on at the now-closed Freemans warehouse, which was built partly on the old Westwood airfield.

*Source: Keypublishing Aviation Forum*
In the mid-1990s at Highlees School, which had started a Living History project for 9- and 10-year-old pupils, one sunny summer lunchtime a group of children ran back into school reporting that a man carrying a parachute over his shoulder had just walked across their playing field. The teachers went to investigate but saw nothing.

An airman in a white suit has been seen in the Saville Road area a number of times over the years. Much has been made by certain sceptical local people of the fact that the reported uniform was not described as the standard RAF blue. This is unwarranted, as the training school undertook instruction to RN Fleet Air Arm and French air forces as well as RAF units, so there were a variety of colours and shades of uniforms present.

# Redhill

No. 11 Group, Fighter Command
No. 55 Group

| | |
|---|---|
| County: | Surrey |
| Location: | 2 miles SE of Redhill |
| OS Ref.: | TQ 298476 |
| Opened: | 07/1937 |
| Closed: | 1947 |
| Pundit code: | RE |
| Control Tower: | Unknown Watch Office |
| Condition: | Demolished |
| Runways: | Grass, steel matting, (087) 1,567 yards and (019) 1,057 yards |
| Hardstandings: | 12 pan type, 12 Blenheim |

Hangars:              Civil – 9, Blister – 8
Ad., tech. & barr.:  Temporary, with permanent civilian buildings
Population:         RAF Officers – 30, OR – 333
Sat. airfield(s):     Satellite to Kenley; satellite to Biggin Hill

## History to 1946:

**1937**
1 July: No. 15 EFTS formed with Magisters and Harts

**1938**
February: No. 15 ERFTS transferred to No. 26 Group

**1939**
1 February: No. 15 ERFTS transferred to No. 50 Group
3 September: No. 15 ERFTS was redesignated as No. 15 Elementary Flying
    Training School with Magister trainers

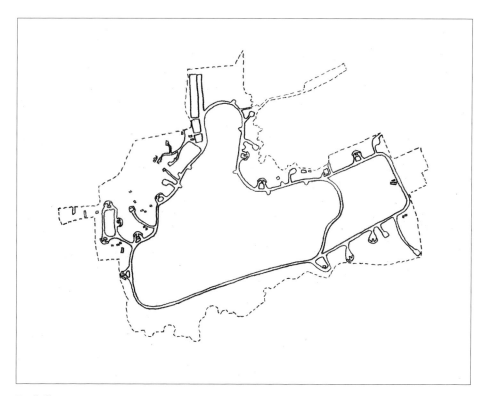

Redhill

**1940**

Squadrons: 219, 600, No. 15 EFTS, Polish Grading and Testing Flight

March: An RLG at Penshurst was used

June: No. 15 EFTS moved to Kingstown, and Redhill and its buildings were requisitioned for use

2 June: No. 16 (AC) Squadron arrived from Lympne

29 June: No. 16 (AC) Squadron moved to Cambridge

9 June: HQ, No. 50 (Army Co-operation) Wing until 6 August

12 September: No. 600 Squadron arrives from Hornchurch with Blenheims

**1941**

Squadrons: 1, 16, 258, 452 & 485

From May 1941 to January 1944, numerous fighter squadrons were based at Redhill, most with Spitfires

**1942**

Squadrons: 303, 308, 310, 312, 340, 350, 402, 412, 416, 452, 457 & 602

19 August: Nos 350, 611, 303, 310 & 312 Squadrons arrived for Operation Jubilee

**1943**

Squadrons: 66, 131, 231, 400, 401, 411, 412, 414, 421, 504, No. 83 Group Communication Flight & No. 1 Casualty Air Evacuation Unit

4 July: HQ, No. 17 Wing until 6 August

1 August: HQ, No. 39 Wing until 10 August

14 October: HQ, No. 39 Wing until 1 April 1944

**1944**

Squadrons: 116, 231, 400, No. 84 Group Communication Flight/Squadron, No. 1310 Transport Flight & No. 1 Aircraft Delivery Flight

14 July: No. 970 (Balloon) Squadron formed

27 August: No. 970 (Balloon) Squadron disbanded and No. 950 (Balloon) Squadron formed

17 October: No. 1 Aircraft Delivery Unit arrived from Gatwick

**1945**

Squadrons: 116, 287 & No. 1 ADF

16 January: No. 1 ADF moved to Middle Wallop

20 January: No. 287 (Anti-Aircraft Co-operation) Squadron arrived from Gatwick with Oxfords, Spitfires, and Tempests

2 May: No. 116 Squadron departed for Hornchurch

3 May: No. 287 Squadron departed for Hornchurch

By the end of the war, the RAF had largely withdrawn from Redhill and the airfield was used to store armaments

**Closure:**
Redhill returned to civilian use in 1947.

**Current status:**
The site is currently Redhill Aerodrome.

## Haunted RAF Redhill

*Source: wingsmuseum.co.uk*

One of the volunteers at the Wings Museum, when it was located in Redhill's Hangar 9 before it moved to Balcombe in Sussex, was working late in a back room of the hangar with the main door firmly locked. He heard the door to the main museum area open and then close again. Walking towards the door, expecting to see a museum volunteer, there was no one there, but as he approached the door he could hear what sounded like movement in the corridor. Just as he reached another door it suddenly closed in front of him – a firm, deliberate action. Again hearing what he thought was the sound of movement, he opened the door, went through, and looked around the corner to see who was there, but again there was no one. On checking the front door to the hangar it was found to be firmly locked.

Another volunteer at the museum, whilst working on a computer, heard footsteps approach along the corridor which led up to the office he was in, which then stopped directly outside the door. Getting up to see who was there, he found no one. This happened twice more while he was working in the office; each time on investigating there was no one there and, as before, the front door was locked and no other people were in the building.

One early evening, one of the founders of the museum was drying his hands in the toilet when a tap in plain sight suddenly turned itself on.

# Ridgewell

No. 3 Bomber Group
USAAF 8th AF

| | |
|---|---|
| County: | Essex |
| Location: | 7½ miles NW of Halstead |
| OS Ref.: | TL 756416 |
| Opened: | 1942 |
| Closed: | 1957 |
| Pundit code: | RD |
| USAAF Station: | 167 |

| Control Tower: | Watch Office for all Commands 12779/41, with medium size lower front windows 343/43 |
| Condition: | Demolished in the 1970s |
| Runways: | 3 concrete and wood chippings; 1942, (280) 2,000 x 50 yards, and the subsidiaries (240) 1,400 x 50 yards and (340) 1,400 x 50 yards |
| Hangars: | T2 – 2, one on the technical site between runway heads 06 and 34, the other between runway heads 10 and 16 |
| Hardstandings: | 36 pans; in 1943, the hardstandings were increased to 45 pans plus 5 loops |
| Bomb stores: | Located off the N side of the airfield between runway heads 16 and 24 |
| Ad., tech. & barr.: | Nine dispersed domestic sites to the S of the airfield towards the A604, with two communal sites and sick quarters also in this area |
| Population: | USAAF Officers – 421, OR – 2,473 |
| Sat. airfield(s): | Satellite to Stradishall |

No. 90 Squadron lost 27 Stirlings and crews: 24 during operations and 3 in non-operational accidents; the 381st Bomb Group flew 296 missions and lost 131 B-17s.

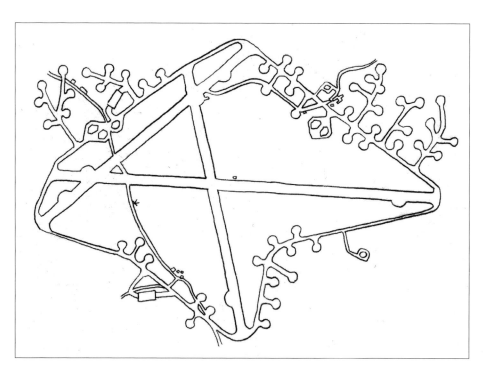

Ridgewell

## History to 1946:

Ridgewell was a wartime construction to Class A standard close to the A604 and west of the village of the same name on the edge of the Stour valley. Two country roads across the airfield site were closed prior to construction.

### 1942

29 December: Ridgewell was temporarily assigned to No. 3 Group for No. 90 Squadron which arrived from Bottesford with Stirlings before the airfield had been fully completed

### 1943

8/9 January: No. 90 Squadron flew its first operation from Ridgewell

March: No. 90 Squadron received Stirling IIIs

31 May: No. 90 Squadron moved to No. 3 Group's new airfield at West Wickham, and Ridgewell was handed over to the USAAF 8th AF

30 June: The 381st BG arrived from Pueblo AAB in Colorado with B-17s. The squadrons were the 532nd, 533rd, 534th & 535th. The group operated chiefly against strategic objectives on the Continent. Specific targets included an aircraft assembly plant at Vélizy-Villacoublay, an airdrome at Amiens, locks at St Nazaire, an aircraft engine factory at Le Mans, nitrate works in Norway, aircraft plants in Brussels, industrial areas of Münster, U-boat yards at Kiel, marshalling yards at Offenburg, aircraft factories at Kassel, aircraft assembly plants at Leipzig, oil refineries at Gelsenkirchen, and ball-bearing works at Schweinfurt

8 October: The 381st BG received a Distinguished Unit Citation for its performance when bombing shipyards at Bremen amid persistent enemy fighter attacks and heavy flak

### 1944

11 January: The 381st BG received a second DUC for similar action during a mission against aircraft factories in central Germany

20-25 February: The B-17s of the 381st BG took part in the intensive campaign against enemy aircraft factories during 'Big Week'

June: The 381st BG supported the Normandy invasion by bombing bridges and airfields near the beachhead, attacking enemy positions in advance of ground forces at St Lô in July 1944

September: The 381st BG was involved in the airborne assault on Holland

December-January 1945: The 381st BG bombed airfields and communications near the battle zone during the Battle of the Bulge

**1945**

March: The 381st BG operated during the Allied crossing of the Rhine and then turned to missions against communications and transportation in the final push through Germany

June: The 381st BG returned to Sioux Falls AAF, Dakota

15 July: The USAAF handed the station back to the RAF and it was used to store surplus wartime bombs

**Closure:**

On 31 March 1957, Ridgewell was closed, sold, and rapidly returned to agriculture.

The USAF retained the old aircraft hangars, which were used by units from nearby Wethersfield and Alconbury for storage until both bases were closed in the early 1990s.

**Current status:**

The site is now used for agriculture and gliding, and includes a small museum located in the airfield's former hospital and run by the Ridgewell Airfield Commemorative Association. (Website: www.381st.com)

## Haunted RAF Ridgewell

*Source: Carmel King,* Haunted Essex, *2009 (p. 33)*

After Ridgewell closed, people began to report ghostly lights across the expanse of the disused airfield. They also reported hearing men shouting, the distinct revving of engines, and the sound of screeching tyres on tarmac as if a Second World War bomber was landing. Very occasionally, people have reported hearing the sound of crashing aircraft, as though they are making a forced landing. The apparitions of aircrew have also reportedly been seen on the old airfield.

*Source: Keypublishing Aviation Forum, 23 April 2008*

A couple went over to RAF Ridgewell a couple of years back, and while the man went to have a look around the old WAAF accommodation near to the Haverhill road his wife stayed behind. Suddenly she heard what sounded like a large group of aircraft passing overhead and looked up to see what they were, but although it was a clear day there was nothing there. She was really surprised at the sound because it was like a group of large four-engine heavy aircraft. When her husband returned a short time later, his wife asked him if he had also heard it, but he hadn't.

*Source: WW2 Talk.com, 17 September 2010*

After the war, the HQ building on the airfield was used as offices for a plastics factory that worked around the clock. Two of the night workers used to swear blind that they would, on a fairly regular basis, see two American airmen walk up from the road, into the offices, and out through the wall at the other end of the corridor. Nobody would believe them until someone else had to fill in on one of the night shifts and saw the exact same thing. The factory is long gone and houses were built on the site in about the late 1990s.

The Nissen hut that houses the Ridgewell Airfield Commemorative Association museum was previously used as a workshop and then for storage. The chap who was there always used to find his tools moved around and one day, hunting for a particular spanner, he eventually found it on a window sill. It was completely covered in dust, and when he picked it up he saw its perfect outline on the dusty window sill, as if it had been lying there for years. Apparently he left and never went back. Since the building has become a museum, it has been noticed that there is a presence, not hostile nor cold, but warm and friendly. (Website:http://www.381st.com/)

# Rivenhall

USAAF 8th
USAAF 9th
No. 38 Group, Transport Command

| | |
|---|---|
| County: | Essex |
| Location: | 2 miles N of Rivenhall |
| OS Ref.: | TL 820206 |
| Opened: | 1943 |
| Closed: | 1945 |
| Pundit code: | RL |
| USAAF Station: | 168 |
| Control Tower: | Watch Office for all Commands 12779/41 with small front windows 15371/41 |
| Condition: | Demolished in the 1960s |
| Runways: | 3 concrete/tarmac, (100) 2,000 x 50 yards, (060) 1,400 x 50 yards, and (170) 1,400 x 50 yards |
| Hardstandings: | 51 loops |
| Hangars: | Blister – 1, T2 – 2 |
| Bomb stores: | Located on the N side of the airfield, outside the perimeter track, surrounded by large dirt mounds |
| Ad., tech. & barr.: | Nissen huts of various sizes, mostly on the S side of the airfield; dispersed accommodation to the SE |
| Population: | RAF Officers – 421, OR – 2,479 |

The 363rd flew 20 missions, with 16 aircraft missing; the 397th undertook 86 missions, with a total of 16 B-26s missing in action.

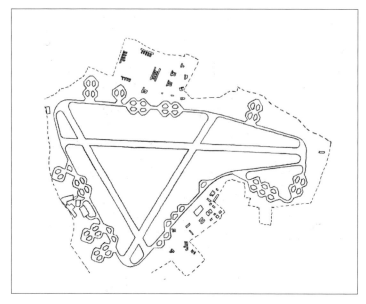

Rivenhall

## History to 1946:

### 1944

22 January: Rivenhall opened with the arrival of the 382nd Squadron of the 363rd
Fighter Group from Keevil with the new P-51B Mustang

24 January: The 382nd Squadron received Mustangs and began training. Many of
the Mustangs had already seen service with the 354th FG at Boxted

February: The 380th & 381st Squadrons of the 363rd Fighter Group arrived.

22 February: Bad weather caused the 363rd FG's first combat mission to be
abandoned

24 February: Twenty-four P-51s took off from Rivenhall for Belgium on bomber
support duties

4 March: While supporting a raid over Germany, the group was surprised by the
Luftwaffe and 11 Mustangs failed to return. The 363rd continued to provide
escort cover but also undertook fighter-bomber work. On two occasions, the
Mustangs involved broke up while attempting to pull out of a dive, which led
to a questioning of the technique employed

12 April: The 363rd moved to Staplehurst, with the HQ moving 2 days later

15 April: The 397th Bomb Group arrived from Gosfield. Over the next few days,
more than 60 bare metal B-26s were to be seen at Rivenhall

20 April: The 397th Squadrons undertook their first combat mission, an attack
on a Pas-de-Calais V-1 site. Whilst at Rivenhall, the 397th flew 86 bombing
missions: 32 were attacks on bridges; the others were on enemy airfields, rail
junctions, fuel and ammunition stores, V-weapon sites, and other locations in
France and the Low Countries

5 August: The 397th moved to Hurn to give the Marauders a better radius of
action with the breakout of the Allied forces from the Normandy beachhead.
This marked the end of the USAAF use of the airfield, and RAF No. 38 Group,
Transport Command took control

10 October: Martinets of No. 1677 Target Towing Flight arrived

11 October: No. 295 Squadron arrived from Harwell with Stirlings to start
operations of supply drops to Norwegian, Dutch, and Danish resistance forces

28 December: No. 1677 Target Towing Flight departed

## 1945

February: No. 295 Squadron undertook tactical bombing in support of the 1st
Army Group

24 March: No. 295 Squadron towed 60 Horsa gliders from Rivenhall as part of
Operation Varsity

April: No. 570 Squadron, another Stirling squadron, arrived and joined No. 295 in
night operations in support of resistance forces in occupied countries

26 April: Seven Stirlings took part in Operation Tablejam 343 and were assigned
to different targets in Denmark. The defences were reputed to be severe and
the instructions were to 'go in low'; 4 aircraft were lost

10 May: The squadrons of No. 38 Group were engaged in Operation Doomsday
– the airlifting of troops for occupation duties in Norway

December: Parts of No. 295 Squadron left the station for Shepherds Grove

### Closure:

In January 1946, both squadrons completed the move to Shepherds Grove;
Rivenhall was declared surplus to requirements and placed on a care and
maintenance basis.

### Current status:

Currently there are plans to demolish everything remaining at Rivenhall and build
an incinerator and waste site.

## Haunted RAF Rivenhall

*Source: Keypublishing Aviation Forum, 9 April 2005*
A contributor wrote that a former munitions unit airman said that the place was
so haunted, especially the Tower, he was pleased when he eventually left.

*Source: Keypublishing Aviation Forum, 14 March 2011*
Jim C. wrote that about four years ago, having a free afternoon to himself, he
thought he would have a nose round a Second World War airfield in Essex. At
Rivenhall he came across the Ops Block, and a few attached Nissen huts hidden

in woods, and began wandering through them. All the time he was there he had a feeling of being watched, but put that down to the airfield enthusiast's expectation of seeing a shotgun-wielding farmer with a 'git orf my land!' greeting. On another occasion with a colleague, after looking inside a flight office (on a different part of the airfield), they were standing outside when both heard an audible sigh from inside the hut. They left the scene quite sharpish after that.

*Source: Rachel Keene website*
On 5 March 2005, Rachel Keene, a respected medium, conducted an investigation of the remaining bunker and Nissen huts at Rivenhall. On arrival she immediately received the impression that explosions had occurred on or near the runways during the war, and saw wooden aircraft (probably glider) fuselages lying in the fields around. A number of names were received during the visit: 'Flight Lieutenant Peterson' and 'Fox', 'Peter' and 'John'. 'John' gave the number 363, the impression he was of a rank like a squadron leader and that he wasn't English. Eventually Rachel received his surname as 'Ulricson'. Considering that this was the home of the 363rd FG (which she was unaware of beforehand), this was spot-on information.

Inside the bunker there was a sad and depressed male presence standing at one side of the room, who felt responsible for a great loss of crew and that March was a significant date. Slightly later a 'cheeky young man' of about 18 or 19 who gave the name 'David' made contact. In one Nissen hut she felt a push backward and two hands grabbed each of her mid-upper arms, as if she was being stopped by two guards. Inside there was the impression of a large board with maps, and a man with a baton pointing out areas on the maps to a room full of men. The dread and anticipation felt like it was residual energy from the room of men – they were being briefed on what to expect and that they possibly wouldn't be coming back this time. This is such a good description of a pre-flight briefing, even to the reference to the MPs at the door. The dread would, I am sure, have been a genuine emotion when a forthcoming mission was announced during the war years. There was also a strong presence in the hut of a moustached man in a senior officer's uniform, constantly pacing and chain-smoking.
(Website: http://rachelkeene.co.uk/rivenhall.html)

# St Merryn

Royal Naval Air Station

| | |
|---|---|
| County: | Cornwall |
| Location: | 3 miles SW of Padstow |
| OS Ref.: | SW 888715 |
| Opened: | 10/37 |
| Closed: | 10/01/56 |

| | |
|---|---|
| Pundit code: | MGF |
| Control Tower: | A. Pre-war civil Watch Office |
| | B. 1944, 4-storey Naval-type Watch Office |
| Condition: | A. Derelict |
| | B. Not known |
| Runways: | 4 tarmac, (014) 1,000 x 30 yards, (056) 1,000 x 50 yards, (105) 1,030 x 30 yards, and (147) 1,270 x 30 yards |
| Hardstandings: | 7 tarmac |
| Hangars: | 185 x 105 feet – 1, 60 x 84 feet – 12, 60 x 70 feet – 18, Pentad – 2, Teesside S – 4 and Mains – 13 |
| Ad., tech. & barr.: | Temporary buildings to the NE of the airfield. Hotels at Padstow, St Merryn, and Harlyn were requisitioned for accommodation |
| Population: | RN Officers – 220, OR – 870, WRNS Officers – 8, OR – 231 |

## History to 1946:

**1937**

A small aerodrome was developed on a site at Treginegar under the direction of W. Rhodes Moorhouse

October: A large hangar had been built and the 52-acre field was being promoted as Cornwall's first civil airfield, although it was little used

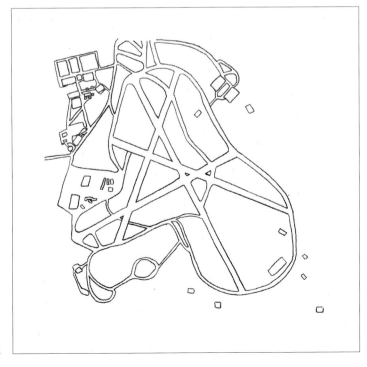

St Merryn

**1939**

The St Merryn site was surveyed by the Admiralty

December: The original airfield and adjoining fields were acquired and work commenced on St Merryn Naval Air Station. Contracts were signed for the laying of 4 1,000-yard runways, the diversion of roads, and the erection of 4 hangars

**1940**

April: The first aircraft landed at St Merryn – a Shark from Roborough which mistook St Merryn for St Eval

10 August: The airfield was commissioned as HMS *Vulture*. Accommodation was in local requisitioned hotels and the sick bay was established at Woodlands, Treator, near Padstow

No. 792 Squadron was formed with Roes and Skuas as an air target-towing unit, and No. 774 Squadron arrived from Evanton with Swordfish and Roes to provide telegraphist air gunner training. These 2 units were the main occupants of St Merryn until late 1943, but a series of front-line squadrons spent short periods for work-up training

3 October: A Bf 110 caused slight damage to the airfield

9 October: The airfield was bombed by 2 Do 215s

14 October: He 111s machine-gunned the camp

11 November: An He 111 made a low-level attack, badly damaging 2 hangars and injuring 2 people

**1941**

Fighter units appeared early in the year.

15 January: No. 809 Squadron formed at St Merryn, equipped with Fairey Fulmars

19 January: No. 80 Squadron arrived from Hatston, intended for dive bombing attacks on shipping in the Channel and daylight assault on the *Scharnhorst* and *Gneisenau*, while these ships lay in the port of Brest

April: A Luftwaffe low-level attack caused some damage

5 May: Six bombers dropped HE bombs and incendiaries, damaging 22 aircraft and injuring 2 ratings

**1942**

October: No. 748 Squadron formed to operate as a Fighter Pool for Seafire pilots

**1943**

The airfield was virtually rebuilt to accommodate the School of Air Combat

September: The School of Air Combat opened and No. 736 Squadron arrived from Yeovilton as the flying element, initially with Seafires and Masters

## 1944

Yet another rebuilding programme was under way

August: A new ATC tower was nearing completion, and two T2 hangars were among the many new structures

December: The School of Air Combat was renamed School of Naval Air Warfare and No. 719 Squadron was disbanded

## 1945

April: The rebuilding programme was largely complete but, as on so many other airfields, it was never fully utilised

September: Nos 725 & 748 Squadrons arrived but neither stayed for long, leaving No. 736 Squadron as sole occupant

## 1946

July: Nos 741 & 736 Squadrons equipped with Seafires

## Closure:

St Merryn finally closed as a naval base on 10 January 1956. The Parachute Centre moved in during May 1979 and applied for planning permission for the use of an airstrip and buildings at St Merryn for its Cessna 182; after some delay this was granted.

## Current status:

Part of the old airfield is fenced off for flying and a large number of buildings are in use for farming purposes. Some of the Second World War buildings are owned by a plant hire firm and the bases of dismantled hangars are used by a caravan site.

## *Haunted RNAS St Merryn*

*Source: Bruce Barrymore Halpenny,* Ghost Stations, *1988 (p. 157)*

Squadron Leader Colin Pomeroy served as a flight commander at RAF St Mawgan from 1978 to 1980, living in one of five ex-Royal Navy Officers' quarters at the old RNAS St Merryn. He became friendly with the members of the Padstow/Trevose Head Lifeboat crew, and on one of his visits the conversation turned to St Merryn and the allegedly haunted holiday hut. Apparently, a cleaner was working in one of the huts on the old airfield when she felt a presence and an urge to look around at the bed which was just behind her. She turned to see a pilot wearing a fur-lined leather jacket and similar-style knee-length boots sitting on the bed with a leather flying helmet in his hand. She refused to work in that hut again.

# Sawbridgeworth

Army Co-operation Command
Maintenance Command 1944

| | |
|---|---|
| County: | Hertfordshire |
| Location: | 3 miles SW of Bishop's Stortford |
| OS Ref.: | TL 464178 |
| Opened: | 1940 |
| Closed: | 03/47 |
| Control Tower: | Watch Office for all Commands 343/43, located near Shingle Hall |
| Condition: | Demolished |
| Runways: | Grass, Sommerfeld tracking with a coir matting underlay. Due to the high water table, the wet matting soaked into the grass, turning into a marsh for several weeks in the winter; (306) 1,700 x 50 yards, (244) 1,400 x 50 yards, and (188) 1,350 x 50 yards |
| Hardstandings: | 13 Blenheim type pens and 15 pans |
| Hangars: | T2 – 1, Blister – 16; the T2 was erected on the Shingle Hall site, with the Blister hangars situated around the perimeter track |
| Ad., tech. & barr.: | Great Hyde Hall was requisitioned as the HQ and 6 dispersed accommodation sites were built along Parsonage Lane. Medical buildings were constructed at Parsonage Farm, and fuel stores, a generator, and a grocery store were at Blounts Farm |
| Population: | RAF Officers – 69, OR – 927, WAAF Officers – 4, OR – 130 |

## History to 1946:

### 1937

An ALG originally named Mathams Wood was established on a 430-acre site to the north of the Much Hadham road near Mathams Wood

### 1940

19 May: No. 2 Army Co-operation Squadron with Westland Lysanders under Commanding Officer Geddes retreated from Boulogne

20 May: No. 2 AC Squadron landed at Lympne and Bekesbourne to participate in the defence of Calais with supply drops to beleaguered forces

8 June: No. 2 AC Squadron arrived at Hatfield and Cambridge, with a detachment at Mathams Wood ALG

September: No. 2 AC Squadron was re-equipped with Lysander IIIs and conducted trials with Defiant Is and Battles for photographic, spotting, and message dropping flights

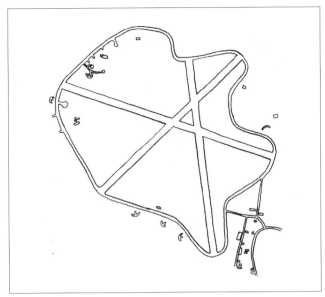

Sawbridgeworth

24 October: No. 2 AC Squadron was based at Sawbridgeworth and began Special Operations sorties to occupied France

**1941**

19 July: No. 2 AC Squadron moved to Firbeck

10 August: No. 2 AC Squadron returned from Weston Zoyland and received Tomahawk I, IIA & IIB aircraft

5 December: No. 2 AC Squadron moved to Martlesham Heath, returning 2 days later

**1942**

April: No. 2 AC Squadron received Mustang Is

15 June: A detachment of No. 268 Squadron arrived with Mustang Is

7 December: No. 182 Squadron arrived from Martlesham Heath with Typhoon Ia & Ib aircraft

**1943**

30 January: No. 182 Squadron returned to Martlesham Heath

31 January: No. 2 Squadron moved to Bottisham

27 March: No. 2 Squadron returned from Fowlmere

16 July: No. 2 Squadron moved to Gravesend

12 November: No. 63 Squadron arrived from Thruxton with Mustang Is

November: Nos 170 & 168 Squadrons arrived from Thruxton with Mustang Is

30 November: Nos 63 & 168 Squadrons exchanged with Nos 2 & 4 AC Squadrons at North Weald

December: The beginning of the month saw torrential rain and the airfield was declared unserviceable. All operations were cancelled

3 December: The final operations with the Mustang were flown off the Dutch coast and No. 4 Squadron was stood down. Pilots were then sent on Mosquito conversion courses, others proceeding to Photo Reconnaissance courses at the PRU

## 1944

January: No. 4 Squadron moved to Aston Down

15 January: No. 170 Squadron was disbanded

February: No. 4 Squadron returned from Aston Down, with 'B' Flight forced to operate its Mosquitos from Hunsdon due to the runway conditions

22 February: No. 2 Squadron moved to North Weald

29 February: No. 2 Squadron returned to Sawbridgeworth

11 March: No. 2 Squadron moved to Dundonald

24 March: No. 2 Squadron returned to Sawbridgeworth

1 April: No. 126 Squadron arrived from Grottaglie in Italy with Spitfire IXs and received Spitfire IXbs

4 April: No. 2 Squadron moved to Gatwick

April: No. 80 Squadron arrived from Naples with Spitfire IXs

5 May: No. 80 Squadron departed for Hornchurch

22 May: No. 126 Squadron moved to Culmhead

June: No. 4 Squadron moved to France

10 November: All flying ceased from Sawbridgeworth

**Closure:**
RAF Sawbridgeworth was closed in March 1947.

**Current status:**
Most of the perimeter track and many buildings survive, in use as industrial units.

## Haunted RAF Sawbridgeworth

The airfield is reputed to be the haunt of the apparition of an American airman who sits at the side of a nearby road as if waiting for a lift. Many locals have claimed to have seen the airman; one was reported as saying that if he didn't see him at least once a week while on the way to work, then he would start wondering where he had got to.

*Source: Keypublishing Aviation Forum, 14 March 2004*
Denis wrote that several well-respected local people have stopped and watched the figure rise from a sitting position and simply melt away before their eyes. He was allegedly the pilot of a P-47 with the 335th FS in 1944 that developed engine trouble and crashed whilst trying to land at Sawbridgeworth airfield.

**RAF Sawbridgeworth Memorial**
The RAF Sawbridgeworth memorial was dedicated and unveiled on Sunday May 14th 2006 at the former entrance to the airfield. The Guardhouse and Fire Party House, with the Fire Tender Shed are still in existence behind it. It is to be found at the entrance to the Shingle Hall farm estate located at OS TL 4705 1716. (© *Chris Huff*)

*Source: Keypublishing Aviation Forum, 10 April 2005*
Pete Truman wrote that the taxi track at Sawbridgeworth is an atmospheric place.

*Source: Luton Paranormal Society*
Towards the end of 1988 or in the early part of 1989, Stephen Day saw the figure of a man dressed in an American uniform as he traversed the site of the former airfield. He reported that the figure was visible for a few minutes before it slowly vanished.

# Stansted Mountfitchet

USAAF 8th AF
USAAF 9th AF
2nd Tactical Air Depot

| | |
|---|---|
| County: | Essex |
| Location: | 3 miles NE of Bishop's Stortford |
| OS Ref.: | TL 538228 |

| | |
|---|---|
| Opened: | 07/08/1943 |
| Closed: | 10/47 (RAF closure) |
| Pundit code: | KT |
| USAAF Station: | 169 |
| Control Tower: | Watch Office for all Commands 12779/41 |
| Condition: | Demolished in February 2008 |
| Runways: | 3 concrete, wood chippings, (243) 2,000 x 50 yards, (190) 1,400 x 50 yards, and (134) 1,400 x 50 yards |
| Hardstandings: | 48 loops and 2 pans; an additional 24 aircraft standings and more T2 hangars and workshops were later to be clustered on the E side of the airfield at Takeley |
| Hangars: | T2 – 4 |
| Ad., tech. & barr.: | Temporary accommodation in extended Nissen huts |
| Population: | USAAF Officers – 417, OR – 2,241 |

The 344th Bomb Group flew more than 100 missions and lost 26 aircraft in combat.

## History to 1946:

**1942**

4 July: The 817th US Engineering Air Battalion arrived to build the 1,919-acre airfield

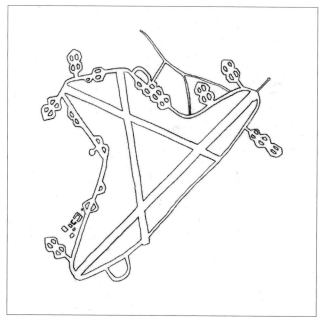

Stansted Mountfitchet

August: Construction of a Class A airfield was started by the 817th Engineer Battalion, and the station was allocated to the 8th Air Force

## 1943

Spring: The 817th Engineer Battalion was sent to North Africa and replaced by the 825th & 850th Engineer Battalions

7 August: Stansted was opened and the 30th Air Depot Group arrived

October: The station was selected to serve as an advanced air depot for the other A grouping bases

16 October: Stansted was officially transferred to the 9th Air Force

## 1944

8 February: The 344th Bombardment Group arrived with B-26 Marauders

29 February: The 344th BG flew its first mission from Stansted

6 March: The 344th BG began operations attacking airfields, missile sites, marshalling yards, submarine shelters, coastal defences, and other targets in German-occupied France, Belgium, and the Netherlands

May: The 344th BG began operations against vital bridges in France in preparation for the Normandy invasion

6 June: The 344th BG was selected to lead the IX Bomber Command formations on D-Day. The mission was flown at low altitude; a B-26 was lost

24-26 July: The 344th BG received a Distinguished Unit Citation for a 3-day action against troop concentrations, supply dumps, a bridge, and a railway viaduct

30 September: The 344th BG flew its last mission from Stansted and moved to Cormeilles-en-Vexin. This left the 30th Air Depot Group alone

## 1945

12 August: The USAAF withdrew from the depot area and the station was taken over by No. 263 Maintenance Unit for storage

## 1946

March: One of the domestic sites at Stansted was used to house German prisoners of war

14 December: Civilian aircraft began using the airfield and it became the base for London Aero Motor Services (LAMS), which bought six surplus Halifax VIIIs from the RAF to conduct a charter cargo service, particularly for perishables. Halifaxes were costly to operate, cargo capacity was limited, and LAMS ceased trading

## Closure:

In October 1947, No. 263 MU moved to Hitcham and RAF Stansted Mountfitchet was closed.

**Current status:**

The site is now London Stansted International Airport. A number of the old
dispersals remain on the western technical site, now devoted to a business
aviation centre. Air traffic is still co-ordinated from the original Control
Tower.

## Haunted RAF Stansted Mountfitchet

*Source: Personal communication, 2011*

Colin Pollard wrote that a few years ago he worked at Stansted, employed as a
security officer by a company which had the contract to provide security cover for
some of the more remote locations on the airport. One of these was Hangar 4, built
by the Americans during the Second World War and later modified in the 60s and 70s.
It was on a quiet Sunday morning in June at about 1:30 a.m. and having completed
a circuit of the deserted building ensuring that all windows and doors were shut and
locked, Colin was making tea when he heard a series of footsteps in the corridor
above. At first he tried to convince himself that it was just his imagination but he
then heard the unmistakable sound of one of the office doors shutting. Grabbing his
keys and torch, he started to climb the stairs very slowly. The corridor was empty and
all the doors from it were locked. He then went back to the security office, locked
the door, and made himself a very strong cup of sweet tea and didn't move from the
office until his relief arrived at about 6:45 a.m. Colin asked him if he had ever heard
or seen anything strange during his time working at the hangar at night, and without
hesitation he said, 'Footsteps in the corridor, on several occasions.' Other people who
had worked in Hangar 4 over the previous few years said that they had experienced
strange noises during the early hours which had sounded like footsteps and/or doors
closing when the building was known to be empty and locked.

Colin also related some of his friend Terry's experiences at the former airfield.
Part of the duties of his team was the cleaning of Hangar 4. One evening, when
they had just finished cleaning the empty building and Terry was giving the office
keys back to the security guard, as they were talking they heard footsteps above
them in the main corridor on the first floor which ran almost the complete length
of the hangar. In addition, an engineer working at the hangar late on a December
night had seen the apparition of a man without legs sitting on a chair and laughing
in the office block.

The sighting of a man in 1940s dress (wearing an overcoat and a bowler hat
and holding a briefcase) standing just outside the hangar on the taxiway came
from two different persons. One a BAA employee, and the other a tanker driver,
who was delivering 'red' diesel to a storage tank located at the hangar in the early
afternoon in June.

Colin also discovered that he had been employed to replace a security guard
who had witnessed something strange in the early hours of one morning that had

resulted in him locking himself in a small storage room and refusing to come out until the morning. He refused to go back to the building and always refused to talk about what he had witnessed, eventually leaving the company.

From a cleaner who started work in the early morning came the sighting of a woman in what appeared to be Welsh national dress, muttering to herself whilst walking beside the office block. In another account from Terry, there was an old building close to the caravan site that later was on part of the airfield near to the runway. The building had been used as some sort of Mess by the Americans and was haunted by the crew of a plane that never returned from a raid.

Finally, during the construction of the Diamond Hangar, built in the late 1980s, a worker who was installing a window on the top floor fell to his death. His apparition has evidently been seen on numerous occasions by different people within the building.

# Stanton Harcourt

No. 4 Group, Bomber Command

| | |
|---|---|
| County: | Oxfordshire |
| Location: | 5 miles W of Oxford |
| OS Ref.: | SP 410040 |
| Opened: | 1940 |
| Closed: | 1946 |
| Control Tower: | Watch Office for all Commands 343/43 |
| Condition: | Demolished |
| Runways: | 3 runways placed far apart, (056) 1,600 x 50 yards, (177) 1,100 x 50 yards, and (117) 1,100 x 50 yards |
| Hardstandings: | 27 Heavy Bomber type on E and W sides |
| Hangars: | T2 – 1 (1941), B1 – 1 (1943) to the N of the airfield |
| Bomb stores: | Armaments were stored in the SE of the airfield |
| Ad., tech. & barr.: | Temporary buildings; the main technical and support area was on the NE corner, and the communal sites were just outside the airfield boundary in dispersal sites N of the village |
| Population: | RAF Officers – 49, OR – 673, WAAF Officers – 3, OR – 98 |
| Sat. airfield(s): | Satellite to Abingdon |

## History to 1946:

### 1940

23 May: Land at Stanton Harcourt was requisitioned for the construction of a satellite airfield for use by Abingdon

16 August: Stanton Harcourt was attacked by 3 enemy bombers whilst still under construction; 5 construction workers were killed outright and another 4 died of their wounds later. As a result anti-aircraft defences were installed at developing airfields

3 September: No. 10 OTU at Abingdon commenced night flying here. No. 10 OTU was a Whitley unit to train crews for No. 4 Group and it retained the Whitley long after most other units had re-equipped with the Wellington

10 September: 'C' Flight of No. 10 OTU with Whitleys arrived to concentrate on night flying training

**1941**

February: A shortage of aircraft caused the Flight to disband; 'A' Flight, converting crews to Whitley flying, replaced it

May-June: The station contributed aircraft to the 1,000-bomber raids, for which a detachment of No. 10 OTU at Lossiemouth were deployed. (No. 10 OTU losses on the raids are detailed in the account for the parent station of Abingdon)

July: Halifaxes of Nos 35 & 76 Squadrons attacked the *Scharnhorst* in La Pallice from Stanton Harcourt

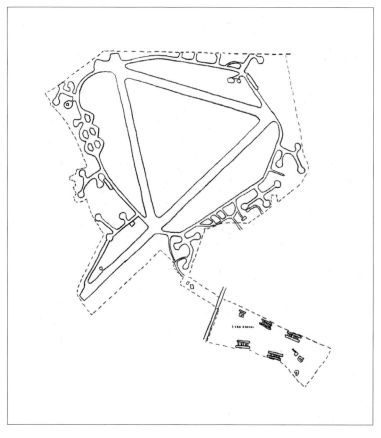

Stanton
Harcourt

## 1942
Training with Whitley Vs continued throughout the period

## 1943
February: A reorganisation of No. 10 OTU meant that 'A' and 'B' Conversion Flights were stationed at Stanton Harcourt, where gunnery trainers joined them

18 April: No. 1501 Beam Approach Training Flight arrived from Abingdon with a small number of Oxfords. No. 1661 Defence Training Flight, also from Abingdon, spent a few months with its Hurricanes and Tomahawks to provide fighter affiliation

November: No. 1501 Flight disbanded and the training was absorbed into the OTU role

## 1944
February: No. 1661 Defence Training Flight moved to Enstone

20 March: No. 10 OUT's HQ arrived and all flying was switched to Stanton Harcourt while two runways were laid at Abingdon

May: No. 10 OTU was reduced to three-quarter strength primarily because of the limited facilities

For two months the airfield hosted the newly formed No. 1341 Special Duties Flight, a special unit formed for signals and radio countermeasures work, to develop equipment and techniques

July: Wellington Xs began to replace Whitley Vs

October: The last Whitley Vs were replaced

16 November: No. 10. OTU HQ moved back to Abingdon, and Stanton Harcourt reverted to its satellite status

## 1945
Summer: All flying ceased from Stanton Harcourt

## Closure:
RAF Stanton Harcourt closed on 15 January 1946.

## Current status:
Parts of the airfield have become gravel extraction quarries. Some of the original buildings remain, including a turret trainer and crew room. The hangars have been converted into office and industrial units.

## *Haunted RAF Stanton Harcourt*

*Source: Bruce Barrymore Halpenny,* Ghost Stations, *1988 (pp. 170-1)*
Stan Galloway was posted to Stanton Harcourt in 1942 as an instructor with No. 10

OTU. In the late 1970s, he returned to look around his former RAF posting, but as he drove down the entrance road to the perimeter track all he could see was the gradual conversion of the airfield into a quarry. When he got to the old Control Tower, he got out of the car and entered the building, which he thought was in good condition at the time. Stan made his way upstairs and out onto the balcony and then, after a short time, came down and went out to his car. He was just about to get in when a farm worker shouted to ask what he was doing on the old airfield. Apologising for trespassing, Stan explained that he had been stationed at Stanton Harcourt during the war, and during the course of their conversation was told that the Control Tower was haunted by a young Flying Officer who had been killed in a flying accident. Apparently no one in the village would go into the building.

# Steeple Morden

No. 11 OTU
USAAF 8th AF

| | |
|---|---|
| County: | Cambridge |
| Location: | 3½ miles W of Royston |
| OS Ref.: | TL 300420 |
| Opened: | 1940 |
| Closed: | 1946 |
| Pundit code: | KR |
| USAAF Station: | 122 |
| Control Tower: | Watch Office for Bomber Satellite and OTUs 13726/41 |
| Condition: | Demolished |
| Runways: | 3 concrete and wood chippings, (056) 1,600 x 50 yards, (177) 1,100 x 50 yards, and (117) 1,075 x 50 yards |
| Hardstandings: | 55 concrete pan type |
| Hangars: | T2 – 1, Blister – 9; the T2 hangar was located to the end of the NW runway, close to Litlington Road; 7 of the Blister hangars were dispersed around the airfield |
| Ad., tech. & barr.: | The technical site was located on the N of the airfield, close to Litlington Road, with the dispersed living sites to the NE |
| Population: | RAF Officers – 30, OR – 575, WAAF Officers – 3, OR – 98 |
| Sat. airfield(s): | Satellite to Bassingbourn |

The 385th lost 175 aircraft in action.

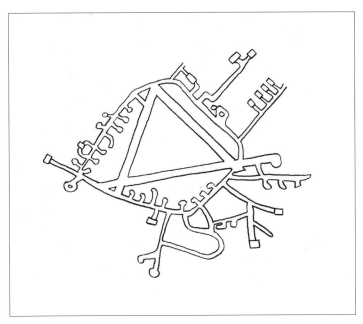

Steeple Morden

## History to 1946:

Steeple Morden was a somewhat strange choice of location for an airfield as it lay on slightly sloping ground with rising ground beyond.

### 1940
Steeple Morden was a grass satellite dispersal airfield of RAF Bassingbourn and No. 6 Group, and was used by No. 11 OUT's Wellingtons to train night bomber crews

### 1941
15 February: A Ju 88 landed at the airfield, its undercarriage collapsing as soon as it touched the grass. All 4 crew were captured

### 1942
30/31 May: Aircraft of No. 11 OTU participated in the 1,000-bomber raid on Cologne. Wellington B1065 E-JZ was lost, with all crew interned as prisoners of war

1/2 June: Aircraft of No. 11 OTU participated in the 1,000-bomber raid on Essen. Wellington DV767 UP-J was lost, with only 1 survivor interned as a prisoner of war

25/26 June: Aircraft of No. 11 OTU participated in the 1,000-bomber raid on Bremen. Wellingtons R1078 TX-Q, X3213 KJ-L, and DV778 KJ-A were lost, with only 2 survivors taken prisoner

September: The parent station of Bassingbourn was allocated for the USAAF 8th
   AF

16 October: Steeple Morden was first used by the USAAF 8th Air Force 3rd
   Photographic Reconnaissance Group which arrived from Membury. The 3rd
   consisted of the 5th, 12th, 13th, 14th, 15th & 23rd Squadrons

10 December: 3rd Photographic Reconnaissance Group departed for La Sénia,
   Algeria, as part of Operation Torch

## 1943

Steeple Morden was earmarked as an 8th Air Force fighter base and assigned USAAF
   designation Station 122. The airfield was then upgraded and expanded

9 July: The 354th, 357th & 358th Squadrons of the 355th Fighter Group arrived
   as part of the 65th Fighter Wing of the 8th AF

14 September: The 355th FG flew its first combat mission, a fighter sweep over
   France

## 1944

April: The 355th FG converted from P-47s to P-51s

5 April: The group successfully bombed and strafed German airfields in snow, a
   mission for which it was awarded a Distinguished Unit Citation

6 June: The group provided fighter cover for Allied forces landing in Normandy
   and afterwards hit transportation facilities to cut enemy supply lines

July: The 355th FG attacked fuel dumps, locomotives, and other targets in support
   of ground forces during the breakout at St Lô

## 1945

25 April: The 355th FG flew its last combat mission

3 July: The group transferred to Gablingen

July: The 4th FG arrived from Debden

1 November: Steeple Morden was returned to the RAF

4-10 November: The 4th FG returned to the US

## Closure:

On 1 September 1946, Steeple Morden was closed down and abandoned.

## Current status:

The former airfield is virtually unrecognisable today. A few single-width concrete
   farm roads, remnants of the perimeter track and runways, are all that remains.

**RAF Steeple Morden Memorial**
This is an impressive memorial to all the units based at Steeple Morden during the Second World War. The Control Tower was demolished and the stone block in front of the memorial is all that remains of it. The three huts behind the memorial were part of the technical site of the airfield. The memorial is located at the former entrance to Steeple Morden Airfield beside Littlington Road at OS TL 5300 2424. (© *Chris Huff*)

## Haunted RAF Steeple Morden

*Source: Mysterymag.com*
Jamie wrote that he had been working for a telecoms company in Milton Keynes over the Christmas/New Year period. The weather had been very foggy and frosty, making driving hazardous. Whilst alone in the office he received a phone call from another engineer asking if he could drive to Cambridge to meet him and drop off some parts that he urgently needed to repair a machine, something Jamie was a little reluctant to do, owing to the weather. On the way back from Cambridge he saw road signs for Steeple Morden, which he knew was a Second World War airfield, and thought it would be interesting to take a look at the memorial at the former main gate. A few minutes later when he arrived at the memorial, the airfield was completely covered in a thick blanket of fog, with visibility estimated to be a maximum of 50 to 60 feet, and hoar frost everywhere. Opening the gate and walking up to the memorial, he was struck by how very quiet it was. And then he remembers hearing American voices, talking quite loudly, and the occasional laugh, as he stood at the memorial staring into the fog, trying to hear exactly what was being said. Even though the voices were distinct, the words could not be understood. At this point a car drove past on the road, the voices immediately ceased, and all was silent again.

# Stoke Orchard

No. 50 Training Group

| | |
|---|---|
| Opened: | 09/1941 |
| Closed: | 01/1945 |
| County: | Gloucestershire |
| Location: | 3 miles NW of Cheltenham |
| OS Ref.: | SO 928275 |
| Pundit code: | SZ |
| Control Tower: | Unknown Watch Office |
| Condition: | Demolished |
| Runways: | Grass, N-S 1,090 yards, NE-SW 1,160 yards, E-W 1,160 yards, and NW-SE 1,125 yards |
| Hangars: | Bellman – 4, Double Blister – 7, Treble Blister – 1 (Michael Bowyer's *Action Stations 6* adds another Double, plus 4 Single Blisters) |
| Fuel stores: | 12,000 gallons, MT fuel 5,000 gallons, oil 3,500 gallons |
| Ad., tech. & barr.: | Temporary buildings |
| Population: | RAF Officers – 46, OR – 598, WAAF Officers – 4, OR – 197 |
| Sat. airfield(s): | Northleach |

## History to 1946:

Stoke Orchard was an RAF station originally intended as an RLG and was definitely an unusual airfield. The SE corner had the Bellman hangars and rows of assorted huts each accommodating an NCO and 57 other ranks, 16 sergeants or 8 officers. The Sergeants' Mess could accommodate 122 RAF sergeants and 5 WAAFs, and the Officers' Mess 50 RAF and 5 WAAF officers. Workshops, stores, SHQ, and MT Section were in temporary brick buildings. An ROC bunker was constructed along the E part of the perimeter track between the road and the railway.

### 1941
July: No. 10 EFTS based at RAF Weston-super-Mare moved to Stoke Orchard as it had more extensive accommodation, although the camp was still incomplete
September: RAF Stoke Orchard opened under No. 50 Group
23 September: The first of No. 10 EFTS's Tiger Moths arrived
27 September: No. 38 Course arrived and the strength had increased to 54 Tiger Moths. The School was rapidly increased in capacity with additional aircraft and the training commitment considerably enlarged. As accommodation in the district was difficult to find, it was necessary to house civilians as well as service personnel on the camp

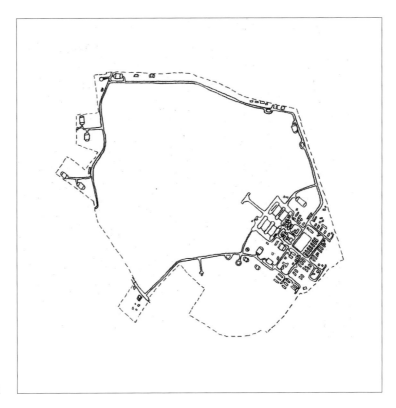

Stoke Orchard

## 1942

19 June: Stoke Orchard was informed by FTC that the imminent EFTS closure would be followed by the formation of a new No. 3 Glider Training School, which would absorb some personnel

21 July: No. 10 EFTS closed and No. 3 Glider Training School was formed, with Hotspur IIs arriving over subsequent days. For towing, the unit equipped with Master II GTs. Airfield surface conditions and intense flying caused detachments of the GTS to operate from Northleach RLG as it was intended to have three flights operating from Stoke Orchard. Northleach was only meant to be temporary but it was decided to have one day and one night glider flight, plus a few navigation and instructor flights based at Stoke Orchard and keep Northleach on for a second day flight. Detachments were also based at Aldermaston and Wanborough

## Closure:

On 11 January 1945, No. 3 Glider Training School left for Exeter, and Stoke Orchard was consigned to care and maintenance until closure later in the year. It became home to a Ministry for Aircraft Production shadow factory run by the Gloster Aircraft Company at Brockworth. There were two large buildings: one for production and one flight shed.

**Current status:**

The site became the Coal Research Establishment of the National Coal Board following the war. Today the airfield has been largely returned to agriculture, although various wartime buildings survive.

## Haunted RAF Stoke Orchard

*Source: Keypublishing Airfield Forum, 2 January 2010*

The contributor's grandparents lived on the airfield in the former airmen's accommodation, which they found to be a very spooky place. On one occasion when they were entering the place, an icy blast shot out the door and they felt as if something had passed through them. Their dog, a Labrador called Blackie, ran off and refused to enter the house.

# Tangmere

No. 11 Fighter Group

| | |
|---|---|
| County: | Sussex |
| Location: | 3 miles E of Chichester |
| OS Ref.: | SU 913061 |
| Opened: | 1918 |
| Closed: | 1970 |
| Pundit code: | RN |
| Control Tower: | A. 1918-27, air traffic control building(s) not known |
| | B. 1927 Watch Office 1597/27, unique to Tangmere |
| | C. 1941 Watch Office for Night Fighter Stations 12096/41 |
| Condition: | A. Demolished |
| | B. Demolished |
| | C. Derelict in 2007 |
| Runways: | 2 concrete, (255) 2,000 x 50 yards and (170) 1,600 x 50 yards |
| Hardstandings: | Single-Engine – 14 |
| Hangars: | T2 – 1, Bessonneau – 2, Extra-Over –6, Over Blister – 10 |
| Ad., tech. & barr.: | Permanent Expansion Period buildings to the N of the airfield |
| Population: | RAF Officers – 225, OR – 3398, WAAF Officers – 17, OR – 748 |
| Sat. airfield(s): | Blackbushe, Ford, Odiham, Lasham, Westhampnett |
| Decoy airfield(s): | Colworth Q, Gumber Q/K |

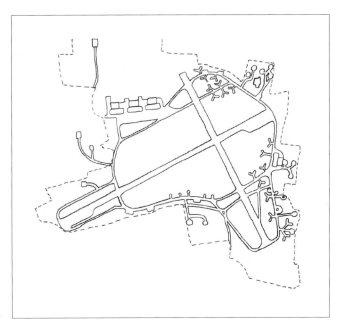

Tangmere

## History to 1946:

**1917**
The aerodrome was founded for use by the Royal Flying Corps as a training base

**1918**
It was turned over to the American Air Force as a training ground
November: The airfield was mothballed

**1925**
The airfield reopened to serve the Fleet Air Arm

**1930s**
The Expansion Period saw an upgrading of Tangmere

**1939**
Squadrons: 1, 43, 92, 217, 601, 605 & 607
The airfield was enlarged, Tangmere's only hotel and some houses being demolished in the process. The RAF commandeered the majority of houses in the centre of the village, with only 6-8 families being allowed to stay

**1940**
Squadrons: 1, 17, 43, 65, 145, 213, 219, 238, 601, 605 & Fighter Interception Unit

By now the villagers had mainly been evacuated and extensive ranges of RAF buildings had sprung up. Tangmere was a Fighter Command station with a Sector Ops Room and a number of satellite airfields

16 August: 100 Stukas caused damage to hangars, buildings, and the airfield surface, as well as killing 13 people and destroying more than 10 aircraft

### 1941
Squadrons: 65, 145, 219, 616 & 1455 (Fighter) Flight

### 1942
Squadrons: 1, 43, 66, 118, 124, 131, 141, 165, 219, 412, 486, 501, 534, 616 & 1455 (Fighter) Flight

Winter: Airfield facilities were improved with asphalt runways and 16 Blister hangars

August: The Ibsley Wing's 3 squadrons operated from Tangmere for Operation Jubilee

### 1943
Squadrons: 91, 129, 165, 183, 197, 302, 486 & 534

### 1944
Squadrons: 26, 74, 91, 33, 127, 130, 183, 197, 198, 229, 257, 266, 310, 312, 313, 329, 331, 332, 340, 341, 349, 401, 403, 411, 412, 416, 421, 485, 486, 609 & Central Fighter Establishment

August: With the operational squadrons gone, Tangmere was suddenly very quiet

### 1945
Squadrons: 74, 85, 340, Central Fighter Establishment, Day Fighter Leaders' School, Enemy Aircraft Flight, No. 161 Gliding School, Fighter Interception Development Squadron & Night Fighter Training Squadron

January: The CFE arrived

A number of T2 hangars were constructed on the airfield

### 1946
Squadrons: 1, 74, 85, 222, 587, No. 161 Gliding School & High Speed Flight

September: A world air speed record of 616 mph (991 kph) was set by Group Captain Donaldson in a Gloster Meteor

**Closure:**

Tangmere closed on 16 October 1970, as a single Spitfire flew over the airfield while the RAF ensign was hauled down.

**Current status:**

Most of the site is now given over to agriculture, but includes the Tangmere Military Aviation Museum. (Website: www.tangmere-museum.org.uk)

## Haunted RAF Tangmere

A number of visitors to the Battle of Britain Hall have reported being aware of presences; sometimes these feelings have been so intense that they have fled. Dogs have refused to enter the building.

*Source: Personal communication*
Sarah Darnell, editor for the Ghost Club, wrote saying that a friend of hers knows the couple who own the farm at Tangmere airfield. In one of their pepper greenhouses, one of their employees saw a solid-looking airman who completely ignored her when she tried to speak to him, and then completely freaked her out when he disappeared in front of her! She immediately left her job and refused to come back.

*Source: Personal communication*
John Dening wrote to say that in April 1985, he and two friends spent an evening in the museum building with tape recorders. Apart from a strange, cold sensation up the legs on two occasions, and a rather creepy atmosphere, the evening was paranormally free and the recorders did not pick up any anomalous noises.

**The derelict Control Tower at RAF Tangmere**
Since 1979 the runways at Tangmere have been removed and the airfield has been transformed to arable land. The Airfield Nurseries have built huge glasshouses on part of the site and housing has spread around the airfield. Many of the RAF buildings have been demolished. The officers' houses were retained as homes and three large hangars, the Control Tower and one of the 'H Block' accommodation buildings remain. The Control Tower forms part of the farm but is derelict and boarded up. (*Courtesy of Norman Brice © Norman Brice*)

*Source: Bruce Barrymore Halpenny, Ghost Stations II, 1990 (pp. 56-9)*
During renovation work on Tangmere Museum many of the workmen reported
hearing footsteps. There are a few accounts of the apparition of a man in RAF
uniform who would stare at the witness and then just vanish. In one such report,
the volunteer worker alone in the building went into a kitchen to make tea. While
there, he heard someone walking about in the hall outside. As he was expecting
another volunteer he called out, 'I'm in the kitchen.' Turning round, he saw a man
in RAF uniform pass the open doorway. His colleague arrived some ten minutes
later and when they searched the building, found it was empty.

*Source: Bruce Barrymore Halpenny, Ghost Stations V, 1991 (pp. 134-6)*
Harry Jury was posted to RAF Tangmere between 1952 and 1957, where he did
many duties as night guard commander. He recalled that on numerous occasions
many of the lads reported seeing a ghostly lady in grey floating around the PBX
Signals No. 1 Squadron and Electrical Section which is now Tangmere Museum.
Many airmen refused to work that section, so new arrivals were given the
assignment, some coming back white with fear. There is also an account of one
airman running out of the building, after messing himself, having seen a blurred
vision of a WAAF.

*Source: Martin Caidin, Ghosts of the Air, 1994 (pp. 145-50)*
In 1985, Jim Gray visited the museum, which he described as a dark, dreary,
gloomy place full of ghosts. He relates the tale of some workmen who were building
displays at night in order to get things ready for reopening. Two of the men heard
a bumping sound and, knowing that nobody should be around but themselves,
suspected someone might be trying to break in. As they started down the hall
they saw a three-foot length of four-by-two bouncing towards them. Thinking it
was a practical joke, one of them said aloud, 'All right, chaps, enough is enough!'
whereupon the piece of wood fell to the floor and lay inert. On another occasion,
after one workmen had placed his hammer on the floor, he looked back to pick it
up and it was gone. It was later found on a nearby table.

In 1978, Len Jepps was chairman of the parish council. The old NAAFI was
the village's community centre, and a party of visitors from West Germany were
being entertained in the bar in the evening. One of the Germans asked Len about
model kits with the swastika on that he had seen on sale in the town, mentioning
the ban on the symbol in Germany. Len pointed out that the war was over, and
the ill feeling had been for the Nazis. As he said this, his glass of beer took off
from the table alongside and hit him in the chest, and when one of the German
ladies put her sherry glass down in the middle of a group of glasses on the nearby
table it began to rock, fell over, and then proceeded to wangle its way between the
other glasses until it fell off the table. At this point the German guests thought it
advisable to leave.

Villagers regularly walk their dogs around the perimeter track and along the runway. Many of them, in the late evening, had the feeling that coming in from behind them was an aircraft, an Avro Lancaster, which all agreed was in trouble. A Lancaster had come into Tangmere and blown up on touch down.

One winter during the mid-1990s, a man in his late twenties and a young woman were at the airfield museum undertaking carpentry work. The young woman had arrived at the museum first and, on opening the main door, saw a man in a grey uniform standing to the left of the entrance, who simply faded away. She said nothing about this sighting. A few days later the young man was working by the top fire door in the Battle of Britain Hall when he looked over his shoulder and saw a tall figure in grey. He asked the man what he wanted, whereupon the figure faded away. Working alone late one winter night in the closed period, Bob Shears, a carpentry volunteer, had just gone to the woodpile and cut himself a piece of two-by-two and left the cut-off piece at the pile. Back at his job, he heard the sound of wood hitting concrete and looked up just as the two-foot piece of wood that he had just cut off was bouncing down the hall like a pogo stick.

Grant Davis and Bernard Hammond were working on the central partition that runs lengthwise down the hall using the empty shop counter as a bench. They put the pencil down on the counter, but on turning back to pick it up to mark the wood again, they found the pencil missing. Grant Davis then announced loudly to the hall at large, 'Oh, come on, fellows! Stop messing us about; we've got work to do,' whereupon the pencil reappeared on the counter.

*Source: PPRuNe Aviation History and Nostalgia, 12 January 2010*
A volunteer at Tangmere wrote that the staff know well that the museum is haunted, a cold spot in the museum being commented on by many. One museum visitor once questioned the staff about it, and was directed on a long route past such a spot. At exactly the right place, he stopped and said, 'It's here, isn't it?' One evening, two colleagues were closing down the place. One went to turn off some breakers towards the end of a hangar and saw someone, partially obscured by a Hunter aircraft, walking to the cold spot mentioned above. Thinking at the time that it was his colleague, he was soon disabused of this when his colleague turned up behind him very shortly afterwards. A quick investigation, just in case they had missed a visitor, confirmed that they were alone.

One visitor experienced someone looking like a technician walk straight past him in a corridor that was the old radio workshops. He turned round to see the corridor empty. There are other persistent reports of an RAF officer seen at the site of the old main gate. This area is no longer used and not marked.

*Source: Paranormal Pondering*
One day, a woman was out on the airfield with her dog; the wind was howling and everything seemed really strange. The dog started barking and with hackles raised, head down, teeth bared, refused to come when called. Then, striding across the grass and coming right towards her, were three airmen wearing Second World War

uniforms; one had a flying hat on and goggles on his head. The one in the middle looked in his late thirties, whilst the other two were in no more than their mid-twenties. Suddenly, the airfield changed – there were other airmen around, vehicles driving about, and so much noise and planes everywhere. The three airmen, still walking quickly and talking to each other, seemed to be looking right through her, and she tried to restrain the dog by his collar because they were getting so close. Then they started merging into a grey, hazy mist until there was just one left, standing still, about 30 feet away, looking directly at her. And then he was gone.

*Source: GhostHaunted.com, 15 January 2005*
Samantha Stenning wrote that she arrived at the airfield at around 3:30 p.m. and met with Teresa and Sue who had arrived almost an hour earlier. The museum was closed. As they were all making their way back towards the Tower, Sue felt as though she had been touched on her head. When Samantha walked around the side of the Tower she connected with an energy of a woman, in uniform, leaning against the railing at the top of the Tower, looking away from the runway. After a meal in the 'Douglas Bader' pub they returned to a now-dark airfield. One member connected with the name 'Michael' and for some reason 'Dunfermline'.

*Source: Sussex Paranormal Research & Investigations Team*
An investigation was conducted on 9 October 2004, with seventeen members of the group. Footsteps were heard on the runway prior to the investigation beginning, and one member saw a figure at the spot where the footsteps had been heard. It is possible that the same figure was seen later by another member in a different group. At one point, a bright white light was seen moving quickly towards the hangar, and there were a number of physical sensations including anxiety, nervousness, and a sick feeling.

*Source: Spook Central, 4 May 2012*
Ron Street wrote that he went to Tangmere at the end of September 2008 with his wife to investigate the airfield. He states that it was about 11.30 p.m. when they got out of the car and stood on the cold and damp airfield. Suddenly they heard the drone of a Spitfire's Merlin engine – the engine was not from a modern aircraft and was clearly a piston engine – flying overhead. Looking up, Ron saw no sign of an aircraft in the sky. It seemed to start from the museum end of the airfield, heading towards the other end, past the old Control Tower. This was the only occasion that he heard the sound above Tangmere, but he says that he will remember the sound for years to come. One photo he took while at the old Control Tower showed the bottom half of a pair of legs standing on the balcony above. Ron noted that they were the only (living) people there that night, and there was no way to climb up to that level on the outside.

# Tempsford

No. 3 Bomber Group

| | |
|---|---|
| County: | Bedfordshire |
| Location: | 4½ miles S of St Neots |
| OS Ref.: | TL 188525 |
| Opened: | December 1941 |
| Closed: | 1947 |
| Pundit code: | TQ |
| Control Tower: | Watch Office with Met Section 518/40 & 3446/42 |
| Condition: | Demolished |
| Runways: | 3 concrete, (190) 1,200 x 50 yards, (250) 1,580 x 50 yards, and (310) 1,333 x 50 yards; 1942, (190) and (250) were extended on their northern ends to comprise overall lengths of 1,610 and 2,000 yards respectively |
| Hardstandings: | 36 pan type round the perimeter track; in 1942, the number was raised to 50, and, in 1943, 3 were lost and replaced by 3 loop standings elsewhere on the airfield |
| Hangars: | T2 – 6, B1 – 1, Blister – 4; in 1942, 4 T2s were built on the technical site, while a B1 was erected near Bigginwood Spinney not far from the Everton crossing gates on the LNER main line. Two more T2s were added in 1943 on the E side of the technical site, south of runway head 31. Blister hangars were put up on 4 of the pan standings to provide shelter for Lysanders |
| Bomb stores: | Located on the N side between runway heads 19 and 25, close to Woodbury Lodge Farm and Woodbury Low Farm |
| Ad., tech. & barr.: | The technical site lay to the S between runway heads 01 and 31. In 1943, 7 domestic and 2 communal blocks and the sick quarters were dispersed in fields mostly on the S side of the Tempsford-Everton road. The combined WAAF communal and domestic site was located in Everton village |
| Population: | RAF Officers – 262, OR – 1,555, WAAF Officers – 10, OR – 265 |
| Sat. airfield(s): | Satellite to Bassingbourn |

A total of 126 aircraft failed to return or were lost in crashes: 16 Whitleys, 80 Halifaxes, 18 Stirlings, 4 Hudsons, 5 Lysanders, 2 Lancasters, and 1 Liberator.

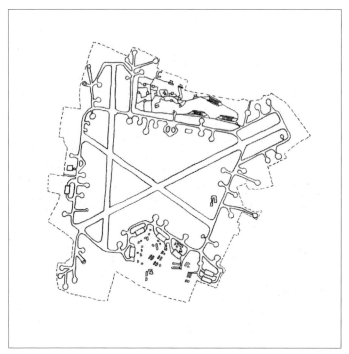

Tempsford

## History to 1946:

### 1941

December: Although the station was far from complete, Wellingtons from No. 11 OTU at Bassingbourn commenced using the runways while work was in progress on those at the home station. Tempsford had been selected as a base for the special duty units, which mostly operated under No. 3 Group

### 1942

January: No. 109 Squadron arrived with Wellingtons engaged in experiments with new radio equipment. They were soon joined by the Wellingtons of No. 1418 Flight also engaged in radio developments, although both units were soon to move to other airfields

March: No. 138 Squadron arrived, flying Whitleys, Halifaxes, and Lysanders, joined the following month by No. 161 Squadron with Whitleys and Lysanders, both units tasked with the air support of the Special Operations Executive (SOE). Tempsford had now become the main centre for this most secret of activities: the dispatch of agents and material aid to resistance forces in occupied countries

### 1943

Whitleys were gradually withdrawn from the Tempsford squadrons and replaced by Halifaxes, although several other types, principally Stirlings, Albermarles,

Liberators, Hudsons, and Havocs, were employed during the 39 months the station supported SOE activities. Operations with Lysanders were flown mostly from forward airfields to reduce the range

### 1943/44
During the winter over 40 aircraft were often present at Tempsford, but by the following year activity had dropped off to a point where the work could be handled by a single squadron

### 1945
March: No. 138 Squadron was transferred to Tuddenham for bombing operations, being rebuilt with Lancaster crews and aircraft. At this time, No. 3 Group relinquished control of No. 161 to No. 38 Group, Transport Command

June: No. 161 Squadron was disbanded. Tempsford then became a base and modification centre for the Liberators employed by Transport Command. This lasted for a year, after which the airfield passed to Maintenance Command

**Closure:**
In 1947, the RAF closed Tempsford and the hangars and land were quickly sold.

**Current status:**
The majority of the airfield concrete was removed for hardcore apart from strips used as farm access roads. All the T2 hangars were removed, but the solitary B1 still survives.

## Haunted RAF Tempsford

*Source: Bruce Barrymore Halpenny,* Ghost Stations, *1986 (p. 80)*
A presence is claimed to be often felt in the area of the barn, which manifests as an involuntary shudder coupled with a freezing cold atmosphere. One unnamed person said he felt as if he was being watched after he had looked around in the drizzle and stood wet and alone in the barn. He commented that he suddenly felt cold and experienced a shudder, noting that it was as if an aeroplane was taking off. Another unnamed person suggested that the area by the ruins of Gibraltar Farm and in the grounds of Hazells Hall both have presences that chill and produce a shuddering response.

# Thorney Island

No. 16 Group Coastal Command
No. 7 (Training) Group

| | |
|---|---|
| County: | Sussex |
| Location: | 6 miles SW of Chichester |
| OS Ref.: | SU 762025 |
| Opened: | 03/02/1938 |
| Closed: | 31/03/1971 |
| Pundit code: | TC |
| Control Tower: | Vertical Split Control Type Watch Office 2548c/55 |
| Condition: | Demolished |
| Runways: | 3 concrete/tarmac, (099) 2,100 x 50 yards, (350) 1,400 x 50 yards, and (043) 1,400 x 50 yards |
| Hardstandings: | 42 pan type, 120 feet wide |
| Hangars: | C Type hangars – 6 in pairs, Extra-Over Blister – 17 |
| Ad., tech. & barr.: | Standard permanent Expansion Period administrative, technical, and accommodation buildings |
| Population: | RAF Officers – 330, OR – 3,406, WAAF Officers – 19, OR – 489 |
| Decoy airfield(s): | West Wittering Q/K |

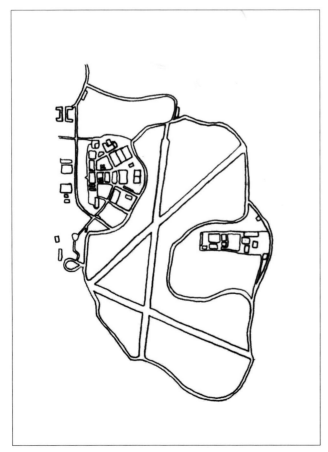

Thorney Island

## *History to 1946:*

Located on a large oval island, RAF Thorney Island was one of Coastal Command's airfields, planned to be capable of holding three or four squadrons.

### 1938
3 February: The airfield opened into No. 16 Group Coastal Command, with two Vildebeeste torpedo bomber squadrons

April: Thorney Island was transferred to No. 7 (Training) Group

4 April: No. 1 School of General Reconnaissance formed

November: The airfield was transferred to No. 16 Group for anti-shipping strikes, coastal patrols, and anti-submarine warfare

### 1939
Squadrons: 22, 42, 48, No. 1 Coastal Artillery Co-operation Unit & School of General Reconnaissance

### 1940
Squadrons: 22, 42, 48, 53, 59, 235, 236, 248, 431 Flight, No. 1 CAU Unit & SoGR

26 April: No. 1 SoGR moved to Guernsey and for the remainder of the war Thorney Island was used by a variety of Coastal Command squadrons

August: Bombing of the airfield began

18 August: Stukas damaged two hangars and various other buildings, as well as destroying a number of aircraft. Blenheims arrived to combat the raids

### 1941
Squadrons: 22, 53, 59, 217, 280, 404, 407 & 415

Thorney Island's squadrons continued to attack shipping, ports, and other land targets as well as undertaking ASR duties

October: No. 16 Group Armament Practice Camp

November: Renamed No. 2 ATC

### 1942
Squadrons: 59, 86, 129, 130, 131, 143, 217, 233, 280, 407, 415, 489 & 612

Three surfaced runways were laid with extended perimeter tracks leading to large circular dispersals to the N and W; 17 E-O hangars were also constructed

July-August: Spitfire squadrons operated from the airfield throughout the Dieppe raid period

### 1943
Squadrons: 53, 59, 86, 280, 415, 547, No. 83 Group Communications Squadron & No. 2 ATC (to 16 June 1943)

**1944**

Squadrons: 21, 164, 183, 193, 198, 464, 487, 547, 609 & No. 83 Group Support
Unit

The airfield was virtually emptied of Coastal Command units and became a 2nd
Tactical Air Force base with Typhoon squadrons attacking radar sites and
barracks up to D-Day, and afterwards roaming Normandy attacking road/rail
transport and supporting ground troops

1 April-12 May: HQ, No. 123 Airfield

6 April-12 May: HQ, No. 136 Airfield

9 April-12 May: No. 20 Wing

12 May-17 June: HQ, No. 123 Wing; HQ, No. 136 Wing

12 May-12 July: No. 20 Sector

18 June: HQ, No. 140 Wing arrived with its three Mosquito squadrons to support
most major ground operations and special pinpoint raids

**1945**

Squadrons: 21, 278, 464, 487, Coastal Command Fighter Circus, Air-Sea
Development Unit, Engine Control Instruction Flight & Survival and Rescue
School

6 February: HQ, No. 140 Wing departed, Thorney Island reverting to Coastal
Command which based its main Strike Wing there

**1946**

Squadrons: 36, 42, 248, 254, ASDU, SARS & No. 1 Torpedo Training Unit

May: Mosquito units arrived to convert to Brigands

15 December: The Torpedo Training Unit arrived from Tain

**Closure:**

RAF Thorney Island was closed on 31 March 1976.

**Current status:**

The site is now a Royal Artillery barracks.

## Haunted RAF Thorney Island

*Source: Fighter Control Forum, 12 November 2010*

Pete Hemsley wrote that he had a strange encounter in a hangar at the old Thorney
Island airfield. His brother was stationed there in about 2004. when all the hangars
were in good condition but still had various strafing holes in the doors and walls.
After being out on a drive around the airfield, they arrived back at the hangar
(which in the past housed Catalinas), to try out the javelin shoulder-mounted SAM
simulators. After hearing various noises from the old officers' rooms directly above,

they locked the simulation room and walked out below the officers' rooms only to see what appeared to be a US officer walking past the window of one of the offices. They both ran out of the building.

# Thruxton

| | |
|---|---|
| County: | Hampshire |
| Location: | 5 miles W of Andover |
| OS Ref.: | SU 200457 |
| Opened: | 1941 |
| Closed: | 1946 |
| Pundit code: | TX |
| USAAF Station: | 407 |
| Control Tower: | Watch Office for Bomber Stations and OTUs 13726/41 |
| Condition: | In use |
| Runways: | 3 concrete and wood chippings, (260) 1,400 x 50 yards, (310) 1,150 x 50 yards, and (200) 1,000 x 50 yards |
| Hardstandings: | 1941, 24 pans 125 feet wide & 6 double pans. Marsden matting and concrete reinforcements were laid to increase hardstandings to 51 |
| Hangars: | T2 – 1, Blister – 9, Bessonneau – 1 |
| Bomb stores: | Located on the SE side of the airfield, outside the perimeter track, surrounded by earth mounds and concrete storage pens |
| Ad., tech. & barr.: | Temporary dispersed station buildings, largely Nissen huts of various sizes to the S of the airfield. Various dispersed temporary domestic accommodation sites were constructed within a mile or so of the technical support site |
| Population: | RAF Officers – 56, OR – 1,068 |
| Sat. airfield(s): | ELG & Satellite to Andover |

The 366th Fighter Group lost 27 P-47s on missions flown from Thruxton.

## History to 1946:

### 1940
Thruxton Down was an ELG for RAF Andover. It was then scheduled for development as an airfield for Army Co-operation Command as a satellite to Andover

### 1941
22 June: The runways were tested by Blenheims of No. 2 School of Army Co-operation, the concrete surface proving too rough and resulting in 3 tyre bursts.

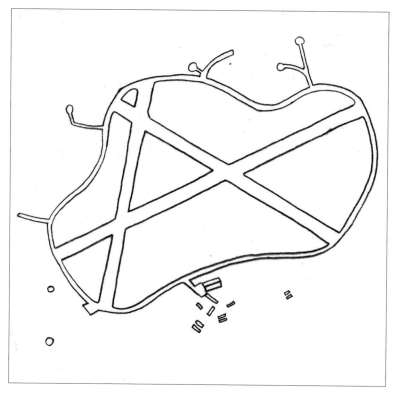

Thruxton

The opening of the airfield was thereby delayed until August while tarmac was laid

4 August: No. 225 Squadron arrived from Tilshead with Westland Lysanders for ASR work

November: No. 1526 (BAT) Flight arrived from Andover

## 1942

February: No. 51 Squadron dispersed Whitleys at Thruxton for Operation Biting, the first operational paratroop drop mounted from the UK

27 February: C Company of the 2nd Parachute Battalion and Flight Sergeant C. W. H. Cox, an RAF radar expert, in 12 Whitleys led by Wing Commander Pickard successfully found the Würzburg radar station at Bruneval, near Le Havre

19 August: No. 226 Squadron with Bostons and Nos 13 & 614 Squadrons with Blenheims arrived for Operation Jubilee, the Dieppe raid, where they were engaged in smoke-laying. One No. 13 Squadron Blenheim was lost and the Bostons suffered considerable damage

24 August: No. 298 Squadron formed with 10 Whitley Vs

August: No. 297 Squadron arrived from Hurn with Whitleys and Albemarles for paratroop exercises by day and Nickelling over France by night

October: No. 298 Squadron was disbanded

## 1943

Early in 1943, No. 297 Squadron started bombing operations

March: Horsa glider towing commenced. This training was put to good use 2 months later when Whitley/Horsa combinations started moving units from one airfield to another

September: The Glider Pilot Exercise Unit arrived, and a part of No. 3209 Servicing Commando arrived to do modifications on Typhoons

October: The GPEU departed to allow room for 123 Airfield's Nos 168, 170, 268 & 63 Squadrons with Mustangs to use Thruxton for winter accommodation

10 November: Nos 168, 170 & 63 Squadrons departed for Sawbridgeworth. The GPEU returned with its Masters and Hotspurs, and was renamed as the Operational Refresher Training Unit before moving to Hampstead Norris

## 1944

3 January: Thruxton was transferred to the USAAF 9th Air Force

February: No. 1526 (BAT) Flight departed

29 February: The 366th FG of the 71st Fighter Wing arrived from Membury with P-47 Thunderbolts

14 March: The 366th FG flew its first operation and gradually built up its experience in the months running up to D-Day

6 June: The first sorties were made at daybreak in the fighter-bomber role, each Thunderbolt carrying two 1,000-lb bombs targeting the coastal batteries near the beachhead. Later they turned their attention to attacking enemy armour

20 June: The 9th Air Force moved to France and were replaced by the Anson ambulances of No. 1311 Flight from Aston Down in anticipation of numerous casualties

July: No. 1311 Flight became No. 84 Group Communications Squadron

No. 43 OTU started using the airfield for Auster AOP flying and Thruxton was also used to house Mobile Parachute Servicing Units

## 1945

With the completion of glider operations in Europe, the number of Horsas in open storage on the north side of the field increased. By the end of 1945, the gliders were being slowly broken up

## Closure:

In 1946, Thruxton was declared surplus to RAF requirements and closed. It was leased by the Wiltshire School of Flying.

## Current status:

Thruxton has one hard runway and a grass runway situated inside the Thruxton racing circuit. There is limited aircraft movement on race days, but flying and training still go ahead during practice and test days.

## *Haunted RAF Thruxton*

*Source: Keypublishing Aviation Forum, 1 November 2011*
John Green commented that certain airfields have an unusual feel to them, and
Thruxton is one of these. A sense of unease is often felt in the passage from the
cafeteria where, over the years, some individuals have glimpsed people in Second
World War uniform moving to the small rooms that lie off the passage.

# Thurleigh

No. 2 Bomber Group
No. 8 Bomber Group
USAAF 8th AF

| | |
|---|---|
| County: | Bedfordshire |
| Location: | 5 miles N of Bedford |
| OS Ref.: | TL 042601 |
| Opened: | 1941 |
| Closed: | 31/03/1994 |
| Pundit code: | TL |
| USAAF Station: | 111 |
| Control Tower: | A. Watch Office with Met Section 518/40 |
| | B. Post-war ATC building, type not known |
| Condition: | A. Demolished in 1946 |
| | B. Not known |
| Runways: | 3 concrete/tarmac, (240) 2,000 x 50 yards, (180) 1,400 x 50 yards, and (300) 1,400 x 50 yards; (180) & (300) extended to 1,800 and 1,700 yards |
| Hardstandings: | Originally 36, extended in 1942 to 51 frying pan and loop types |
| Hangars: | T2 – 4 |
| Bomb, ammunition, and fuel stores: | All located to the W of the airfield |
| Ad., tech. & barr.: | 16 temporary living and communal sites were dispersed in the countryside to the E of the airfield and N of the village |
| Population: | USAAF Officers – 443, OR – 2,529 |

In total, the 306th Bomb Group lost 171 B-17s and crews.

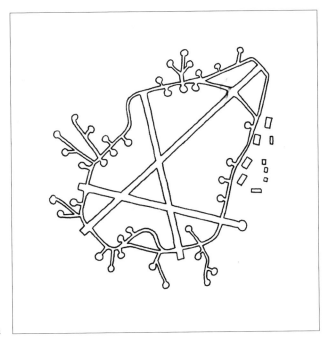

Thurleigh

## History to 1946:

### 1941

The airfield was built for No. 2 Bomber Group on farmland 1 mile north of Thurleigh village

24 July: RAF Thurleigh opened

9 October: Thurleigh was transferred from No. 2 Bomber Group to No. 8 Group

### 1942

15 January: No. 160 Squadron formed and was equipped with B-24 Liberator IIs

12 February: 524 men of No. 160 Squadron were sent to India, leaving the squadron with just 96 personnel

16 February: No. 18 OTU arrived and the cadre of 160 Squadron moved to RAF Polebrook

1 March: 127 Polish airmen of No. 18 OTU arrived

3 June: No. 18 OTU moved to Bramcote

4 June: Thurleigh was among 28 fields listed for use by the US 8th Air Force and was tentatively designated station B-4

10 August: Thurleigh passed to the US 8th Air Force and its runways were lengthened and increased in thickness, and additional hardstandings were constructed

7 September: The 306th Bombardment Group, comprising the 367th, 368th, 369th & 423rd Squadrons, arrived from Wendover AFB in Utah with B-17s and was assigned to the 40th Combat Wing

## 1943

27 January: The 306th carried out its first mission, attacking U-boat yards at Wilhelmshaven

16 April: The 306th suffered severe losses in attacks on Bremen

17 August: The 306th suffered severe losses in attacks on Schweinfurt

## 1944

11 January: The 306th was awarded a Distinguished Unit Citation for a mission against aircraft factories in central Germany without fighter escort

22 February: The 306th received a second DUC during 'Big Week', the intensive campaign against the German aircraft industry, when it bombed an aircraft assembly plant at Bernberg

## 1945

19 April: The 306th flew its 342nd and final mission

## 1946

Construction work began on the airfield to turn the site into what became known as the Royal Aircraft Establishment (RAE), Bedford

**Closure:**

In 1997, the airfield was closed, the RAE having become the Defence Evaluation and Research Agency (DERA). DERA consolidated its experimental flying operations at Boscombe Down, moving aircraft from Farnborough as well as Bedford.

**Current status:**

The southern part of the site is now Thurleigh Business Park and includes the runway, currently used for the mass storage of new cars. The northern part houses the Bedford Autodrome as well as the 306 Bombardment Group Museum. (Website: www.306bg.co.uk)

## Haunted RAF Thurleigh

*Source: Keypublishing Aviation Forum*

Hangar 4 at Thurleigh was one of the old 306BG hangars moved from its original location. A couple of the old MT guys wouldn't go in there as it definitely had a different feeling to the other hangars; this was most pronounced towards the office end.

*Source: bedfordshire.gov/AirfieldGhosts*

In the early 1990s, a civilian staff member of the MoD witnessed the door to the reading room in the Officers' Mess opening wide and then closing all by itself. Another incident in the same room saw a light bulb fall from its fitting and land on the coffee table next to the man's hand, with the feeling of a presence in the room. The empty corridors have also echoed with the sound of footsteps. Keith Paull detected a strong smell of frying bacon and eggs, which became very strong in one area of the car park and then suddenly disappeared.

*Source: WWII Re-enacting Forum, 9 October 2004*
An RAF policeman related that every so often the apparition of an American in full flying gear riding a bike round the route of the old perimeter track had been spotted. The figure, seen a number of times by different people, would apparently reach a certain point and then just disappear. The account given to explain the apparition is that in December 1943 a waist gunner of a B-17, who was convinced he wasn't going to make his 25th (and last) mission, rode out to the hardstanding and shot himself.

*Source: Luton Paranormal Society*
Keysoe Road was the administrative quarters used by the 306th Bombardment Group of the USAAF and later became an RAF Officers' Mess. Michael Cook was living in the Mess whilst working for the Defence Research Agency, and on numerous occasions he would hear footsteps outside his door after he had gone to bed. Every time he investigated the sounds he would find nothing to account for the footsteps. When he talked about it with the other residents, he was told that the Mess was haunted by an America airman. On another occasion, when Michael was in the reading room, he watched as the door to the bedroom slowly opened and then slowly closed by itself.

*Source: Luton Paranormal Society*
When the airfield became part of the Royal Aircraft Establishment it was regularly patrolled by MoD policemen. Patrols had repeatedly reported seeing wartime aircrew playing cards through the windows of a lit hut. However, when they went around the hut to the door to investigate, they would always find the hut empty and in darkness. One policeman with his dog during an evening patrol spotted a man on a bicycle who turned off towards a hangar. Thinking it was an intruder on the airfield the policeman went round the other way to cut him off, but could find no sign of either man or bicycle.

# Turweston

92 Group

| County: | Buckinghamshire |
| Location: | 3 miles NE of Brackley |
| OS Ref.: | SP 615383 |

| | |
|---|---|
| Opened: | 11/1942 |
| Closed: | 23/09/1945 |
| Pundit code: | TW |
| Control Tower: | Watch Office for Bomber Satellite and OTUs 13726/41 |
| Condition: | Derelict |
| Runways: | 3 concrete, (100) 2,000 x 50 yards, (040) 1,400 x 50 yards, and (160) 1,100 x 50 yards; (040) later extended to 1,750 yards |
| Hardstandings: | Heavy Bomber type – 27 |
| Hangars: | T1 – 1 |
| Ad., tech. & barr.: | Temporary buildings |
| Population: | RAF Officers – 93, OR – 934, WAAF Officers – 3, OR – 179 |
| Sat. airfield(s): | Satellite to Chipping Warden; satellite to Silverstone |

## History to 1946:

### 1941
23 November: Turweston replaced Gaydon as satellite to Chipping Warden, and 'A' Flight of No. 12 OTU arrived with Wellington Ics and Ansons

### 1943
April: No. 12 OTU moved to its permanent satellite at Edgehill

30 April: Turweston became a second satellite to No. 13 OTU with Mitchells

1 May: No. 307 FTU's Bostons arrived but stayed only until 18 May

3 July: Turweston became a satellite to Silverstone

August: No. 17 OTU conversion and general handling squadrons arrived with Wellington IIIs

24 November: No. 17 OUT's Gunnery Flight formed with Wellingtons and Martinets

### 1945
July: No. 17 OUT's Wellingtons were withdrawn from Turweston

August: Gunnery Flight moved out

2 November: All flying ceased at the airfield

### Closure:
On 21 January 1946, RAF Turweston closed and was transferred to the War Office.

### Current status:
Turweston Aerodrome reopened for business in 1994, having been rebuilt as a combined airfield, aero-club, flight school, and rally track.

## Haunted RAF Turweston

*Source: Bruce Barrymore Halpenny,* Ghost Stations, *1986 (pp. 20-1)*
In 1958, in the early hours of one morning the duty cook, who lived out of the base and cycled in, when entering the billet was confronted by an airman in full flying kit with a silk scarf. For a few moments the cook stared at the airman before letting out a yell. As he did so, the ghost airman disappeared.

*Source: Personal communication, 20 July 2011*
Damien Dyer wrote that as a kid in the mid to late 80s, he and his friends used to explore the local airfields around Brackley including RAF Turweston. One day, while exploring the old tower, they heard noises and felt that they should not be there so left the place very quickly. Damien has only been back in the last couple of years as a pilot, and still finds the place spooky.

*Source: Luton Paranormal Society*
The society conducted an investigation on the airfield on 15 April 2011. Following a walk of about ten minutes around the site of the former airfield, the group began the investigation with a walk along the length of the NW-SE runway, following the line of the public footpath, and experienced a feeling of a great many people around. The name 'Wilson' was picked up. The first vigil, of 40 minutes' duration, was conducted at the SE end of the runway and fairly quickly voices were heard which sounded fairly close but no one was visible. This was soon followed by the

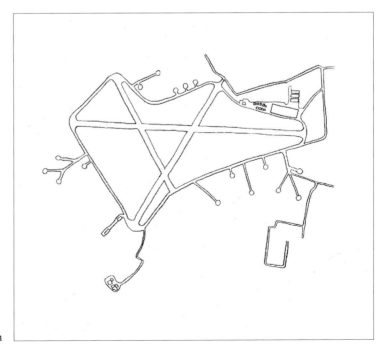

Turweston

sound of footsteps on gravel, which gradually receded. Still no one was visible. This lasted for around seven minutes. The camcorder infra-red light began to fail when filming the grass area but was fine when filming up the track. Two very black figures huddled together were seen on the grass about twenty metres away from the NW-SE runway and then vanished. The second vigil took place at the intersection of E-W and NW-SE runways and was of 30 minutes' duration. A noise like crunching gravel was heard and a white flash of light was seen just to the right of the portacabin door. Something was seen moving very fast in a straight line and parallel with the fence in the area of the runway. One of the team sensed someone standing behind her and heard whispering. Another had an image of a man lying on the tarmac, and a vision of fire and debris that vanished. The only sound recorded on this vigil was of an aircraft, which was described as odd as the sound went on for several minutes.

(www.lutonparanormal.com/investigations/pdf/2011_04_15.pdf)

# Twinwood Farm

No. 12 Group, Fighter Command

| | |
|---|---|
| County: | Bedfordshire |
| Location: | 4 miles N of Bedford |
| OS Ref.: | TL 035550 |
| Opened: | 1941 |
| Closed: | 14/06/1945 |
| Pundit code: | TF |
| Control Tower: | Watch Office for Night Fighter Stations 12096/41 |
| Condition: | Preserved as museum |
| Runways: | Grass; 1942, 3 concrete, wood and rubber chippings, (330) 1,600 x 50 yards, (242) 1,400 x 50 yards, and (278) 1,100 x 50 yards |
| Hardstandings: | 22 |
| Hangars: | Blister – 6 |
| Bomb stores: | Located to the SE beyond the perimeter track |
| Ad., tech. & barr.: | Temporary buildings to the N and NE |
| Population: | RAF Officers – 70, OR – 858, WAAF Officers – 1, OR – 149 |
| Sat. airfield(s): | Satellite to Cranfield |

## History to 1946:

Before the war the site had interested Bedford councillors as a possible location for a municipal airport.

**1941**

Cranfield's SFTS with Oxfords was using the grass-surfaced airfield

August: Cranfield's SFTS moved to Lyneham, and Twinwood Farm had a major upgrade whilst remaining under Cranfield's control

August: No. 51 OTU formed to train night fighter crews

**1942**

9 April: Twinwood Farm opened as a 3-runway satellite. Thereafter it served No. 51 OTU with Blenheims and then Beaufighter Is

**1943**

March: Twinwood Farm had a brief period of intense fighter activity when Nos 164, 169, 239, 268 & 613 Mustang I Squadrons arrived before leaving during Exercise Spartan

17 September: The Advanced Training Squadron at Twinwood Farm was given the designation No. 551 Squadron

**1944**

15 December: Glenn Miller took off for France in a Norseman. It crashed into the sea somewhere off the Cherbourg peninsula

**Closure:**

On 14 June 1945, No. 51 OTU and RAF Twinwood Farm closed.

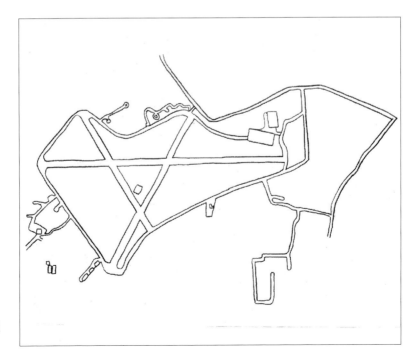

Twinwood
Farm

**Current status:**

Most of the site has returned to agriculture, but the Control Tower has been restored and houses the Glenn Miller Museum. (Website: www.twinwoodairfield. co.uk)

## Haunted RAF Twinwood Farm

All sorts of phenomena have been witnessed at Twinwood Farm, from noises, voices, balls of light travelling down corridors, physical sensations, light switches clicking, and apparitions seen. In 2002, two builders were working in the Control Tower when they ran out, saying that they were never going back in because of the evil presence. However, they did return a few days later to complete the job after they calmed down.

*Source: Adrian Perkins,* Ghost Detective II, *2006*

This excellent book contains many stories about paranormal events at Twinwood Farm, and accounts of investigations held there in 2005. I urge you to seek this volume out and read the accounts for yourselves.

Robert Allen remembers that whilst restoring Building 54, the Armoury, everyone involved with the project had the distinct feeling of being watched. On numerous occasions, when the double doors were opened, members of the team had caught a glimpse of the outline of someone standing in the doorway. Every time they investigated to see who was there, nobody could be found.

On other occasions, a discarnate muffled voice has been heard in the building. At about 8.30 p.m. on an August evening in 2003, Robert, Paul, and John were cutting timber with a rotary saw when they all heard the loud voice of a woman whose words were indistinguishable. John said there was a woman standing in the doorway, but when they all looked, no one was there. About a week later, during a Glenn Miller festival, a medium told them that she had just picked up the presence of a woman, named 'Vera' who had served as a WAAF. There are two stories in wide circulation that may apply to this spirit contact. In the first, a WAAF was taken up in a plane to do a circuit of the airfield but the aircraft crashed, killing both her and the pilot. In the second, a WAAF was knocked down by a vehicle in the local village and died from her injuries.

Nigel wrote about his experiences in Hut 55 in 2003. He had been preparing the main room for the militaria fair and on one occasion, while locking up, he saw a man at a desk in one of the side rooms. However, when he entered the room to challenge him, there was no one there. On another occasion, again whilst locking up, he heard talking from one of the rooms and assumed that some people were still in the building. In the same room he saw the same man, who again vanished.

*Source: Luton Paranormal Society*

Paranormal activity, including a lot of inexplicable electrical activity, has been reported in most of the surviving buildings on the airfield. At one time a strange ball of light was seen to fly around one of the huts. Ghostly footsteps have regularly been heard in the middle of the night, and the apparition of an elderly man in RAF uniform has been seen.

*Source: Keypublishing Aviation Forum, 11 January 2009*

Several times when the contributor was working in the old armament building he heard a woman whispering and many times whistling has been heard, although no one else was round. One evening just at lock-up time, after switching off all the lights, he saw something fly past at knee height and hit a door. By the light of a torch the area was investigated but nothing found. Ghost hunters have spent nights there and have witnessed strange lights in one of the buildings.

*Source: Keypublishing Aviation Forum, 22 June 2010*

Three individuals spent a night in the old MT block. The building was securely locked from within by them. They were awoken at about 5.25 a.m. by the sound of footsteps walking briskly outside the door. Having fallen back to sleep, they were awoken at abut 6 a.m. by what was likened to the sound of hammers on steel, which ceased abruptly when one of the group spoke. In a peculiar twist, one person had a dream involving one of the other participants where he 'woke up and saw a man standing over J'. Sometime later, J said aloud, 'What a weird dream. I dreamed that I woke up to see a man standing over me.' Another oddity was that a wind-up Baygen radio would only pick up dance band music.

*Source: WWII Re-enacting Forum, 7 October 2004*

Matt Price wrote that certain members of his Second World War group heard noises in the barrack room at Twinwood Farm. Three of them swear that they heard a dog in the room, but there was none present.

*Source: WWII Re-enacting Forum, 8 October 2004*

Another incident occurred in the Control Tower in early June of 2004 when, looking at the casualty log on the main table, our witness noticed the telephone and other electronic equipment starting to make a buzzing noise. On closer inspection it was seen that none were connected to the mains. In addition, there seemed to be a static charge in the room. When asked about the ghost sightings, the two ladies in the shop downstairs said that neither of them had experienced anything but that all those who had, said they encountered an electric charge in the air before people materialised.

A further account comes from the owner's daughter, Alice, who helps run the site. She left the office to go to the Admin building, now called the long hut. As she was halfway down the corridor she passed a room with the door open and thought she saw someone in the office. Thinking it was one of the volunteers doing some work, she turned and walked back to the room and saw sitting behind a desk an RAF officer, who looked up when she stood in the doorway. Even then she thought it was a re-enactor, until she realised this was midweek and no re-enactors were known to be on site, especially in uniform. She was out of that building like a shot. Another chap spent a Friday night there on his own, waiting for the rest of the re-enactors to turn up the following morning. He was found locked in the company office after a night in which he swears he heard someone walking around the Motor Pool picking up and setting down a jerry can. The next day there was spilt water throughout the building.

There have also been countless sightings of figures in the Tower.

*Source: Adrian Perkins,* Ghost Detective II, *2006 (pp. 43-55)*
On 7 October 2005, an investigation was conducted at former RAF Twinwood Farm.

At 8.30 p.m. in the lecture hall, conversations were heard between men and women outside and to the rear of the hall yet no footsteps were heard to account for people walking around. At 10.45 p.m. voices were heard from within the corridor, a clock ticking, and then laughter. Sometime after midnight, in Hut 55, footsteps were heard outside, but on investigation there was nobody to be found. A green flash was seen from outside and noises were again heard from down in the corridor. A door was heard to slam, but it could not be traced, and voices in conversation were heard again in rooms that were empty. The sound recording equipment did not pick it up. In the Ops Room, the shadow of a person was seen moving across a window and a light source observed by at least two of the team moved across a wall and around a door. At a ouija board session in the orderly room, one of the team received information of personal relevance. There was also a message from an old friend of one of the team to go into the corridor. On entering the corridor, one of the men was pushed from behind and a conversation occurred between the man who was pushed and the spirit. As the conversation ended, the cameraman saw two lights appear above his head. They remained for a second or two before vanishing.

*Source: Adrian Perkins,* Ghost Detective II, *2006 (pp. 59-76)*
A second investigation saw two small teams at former RAF Twinwood Farm. Team A was to go to the Control Tower and Team B was to stay in Hut 55 and later swap at 12.10 a.m.

Team A began their investigation at 10.25 p.m. by walking around the ground floor of the Tower. On the first floor, two team members picked up on the spirit of an RAF sergeant. In the R/T room they experienced chest pains and heart palpitations, and in the control room a pendulum swung violently and a team member started to pick up on the spirit of an officer called Andrew who seemed to have a head injury. In the small cafeteria attached to the building, all of them heard muffled conversations coming from the museum part of the Tower. The voices were both male and female, and continuous. This was followed by strange bleeping noises and clicks. Later a male voice was heard talking upstairs. In a solo vigil upstairs, a team member heard the sound of fingers tapping on one of the desks, and muffled conversations coming from the direction of the museum. As they left the Tower, they found that all the doors they had closed were now open again.

In Hut 55 at 10.25 p.m. one member of Team B was video monitoring the long corridor, another was filming in night vision, one was checking for any unusual sounds, and the other person was observing. At the far end of the corridor, two of them heard a loud hissing noise behind them which was caught on tape. A few mumbled voices in the distance were heard later.

After Team B entered the Control Tower at 12.10 a.m. they locked the door. While they were downstairs, movement was heard upstairs and they decided to investigate, but nothing was found. Later one of them started to feel uneasy and cold, and began to shake and shiver; it seemed as though the temperature had plummeted.

The spirits were then asked for a sign and immediately the sound of fingers tapping on a desk was heard. One of the cameras then switched itself off and on again. The team moved into the dance hall, where one of them noted the temperature was freezing cold and that his camera had stopped working.

In Hut 55 after 12.10 a.m., two members of Team A picked up on spirits. Communication was made with a Jose Hayes who said she was a corporal in the WAAF who had been stationed at RAF Cranfield and was killed in a mid-air collision between a Dominie and a Beaufighter flying from Twinwood Farm to Cranfield on Thursday, 11 November 1943. She also gave her service number. The information later proved correct. A voice-activated tape recorder that had been placed in the Armoury, because noises had been reported from there in the past, was checked and found to have activated and at least two minutes of tape used up. The recorder had picked up a heavy metallic banging, then gunfire, followed by a man's voice saying, 'Michael's place', or 'My cool place'. The recorder was replaced and reset, with another ordinary recorder for comparison should noises be detected later, and the room relocked. On several occasions, members of the team saw movement across windows and heard voices or footsteps but all searches outside found nothing. At 4.30 a.m. an end was called to the investigation, and the recorders in the Armoury were collected and rechecked. The tape on the voice-activated unit had run for 30 seconds. The other recorder had a full 45 minutes of recording which, when checked, was just tape hiss.

*Source: Adrian Perkins,* Ghost Detective II, *2006 (pp. 77-86)*

A further investigation was conducted at Twinwood Farm on 3 March. On this vigil the locations were the Tower, Armoury, and Flight Offices (Hut 55). Four members of the team set off to the Tower where the communication equipment failed, a camcorder stopped operating, and there were sudden drops in temperature. Two other members were in Hut 55. When one of them called out, immediately there were loud bangs in response. At 10 p.m. an investigation began in the old canteen. Two people reported cold air drifting into their faces and could find no reason for it. Another heard music and muffled female voices through an earpiece connected to his recorder in the Armoury. Bangs and knocks were heard down the corridor, and spirit communication was received. When team members went to the Armoury to collect the tape recorder and video camera, they found that the voice recorder had not recorded the sounds previously heard. One member's tape had caught a woman's voice having a discussion. Towards the end of the investigation, one person saw a light on in Hut 49. which had been locked up earlier. Going to investigate, two members of the team witnessed a white figure glide through the trees and suddenly shoot down into the ground. On closer investigation, nothing was found. In Hut 49 all the rooms were empty and the doors were locked, but the room at the end had its light on. It was not on a timer and one assumes from the response that it had not been on earlier. The rest of the vigil produced no phenomena.

*Source: Luton Paranormal Society, 17 February 2012*
The society investigated parts of Twinwood Farm at the end of February 2012. When at the north-west corner of the airfield, one member of the team experienced a sudden blinding headache. Anomalous lights were seen on the landing area of the airfield and an odd sound was heard. Another member witnessed a black shape and heard a thud. At the eastern side of the airfield, one person experienced a feeling of cold with shivers and sickness. Another member of the team at this location witnessed orange dots in diagonal shapes, heard a whistling sound, and smelt something that was mustard-like. At the south-east corner of the airfield, a short burst of music was heard and a shadowy shape was witnessed crossing the field. An uneasy feeling at the pig farm was experienced, as were cold shivers, one member experiencing the feeling of being drawn towards the woodland and also feeling that there was something coming down the path towards them. At the same location, one member saw a whitish/grey fog-like shape, whilst another heard the sound of voices and possibly distorted radio equipment. In the wood, a little later, the same member experienced the feeling of being watched and saw a black shape floating briefly above the field.

# Upavon

No. 3 Group
No. 23 Group
No. 38 Group

| | |
|---|---|
| County: | Wiltshire |
| Location: | 9 miles N of Amesbury |

| OS Ref.: | SU 152542 |
|---|---|
| Opened: | 19/06/1912 |
| Closed: | 03/08/1993 |
| Control Tower: | Watch Office for all Commands 12779/41 |
| Condition: | In use |
| Runways: | Grass, E-W 1,150 yards, N-S 625 yards, NE-SW 1,300 yards; Sommerfeld tracking, (240) 1,250 x 50 yards |
| Hangars: | A Type – 2, C Type – 1, Blister – 10 |
| Ad., tech. & barr.: | Permanent accommodation |
| Population: | RAF Officers – 142, OR – 745, WAAF Officers – 6, OR – 352 |
| Sat. airfield(s): | Overton Heath, New Zealand Farm |
| Decoy airfield(s): | All Cannings Q |

## History to 1946:

### 1912

April: An airfield was constructed near the village of Upavon

19 June: The completed buildings were taken over and the Central Flying School of the Royal Flying Corps arrived

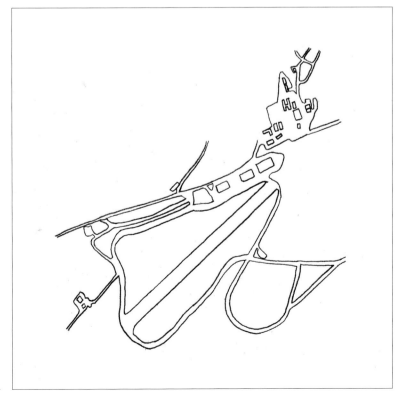

Upavon

**1914**

November: The Aeroplane and Armament Experimental Establishment was formed

**1917**

January: The A&AEE moved to Martlesham Heath whilst Upavon trained pilots

**1920**

26 April: The Central Flying School re-formed with Avro 504Ks and Snipes for advanced training

**1926**

1 April: Upavon came under the newly formed No. 3 Group
7 October: The Central Flying School moved to Wittering

**1934**

May: Upavon became a shore base for Fleet Air Arm units

**1935**

September: The FAA units moved to Gosport, and Upavon was transferred to No. 23 (Training) Group
2 September: The Central Flying School returned from Wittering

**1937**

November: Oxfords arrived at Upavon

**1938**

Squadrons: CFS & Handling Flight
Work started on improvements to the station
August: The training course length was reduced from 10 to 9 weeks and the student strength rose from 40 to 50 on each intake

**1939**

Squadrons: CFS & Handling Flight
3 September: All the training aircraft were dispersed around the perimeter and guarded at night by armed RAF personnel

**1940**

Squadrons: CFS & Handling Flight
April: The Refresher Flight took over the new C Type hangar to house a varied collection of aircraft to write pilots notes
6 May: Under Operation Banquet, Upavon was to be prepared to provide Ansons to fly the personnel and equipment of No. 1 Flying Training School, Netheravon,

to Scampton where its Harvards were to operate as part of the anti-invasion force

Upavon was in constant daytime use, while much of the night flying training was being carried out at RLG Overton Heath and, later, New Zealand Farm

October: The Handling Flight left for Boscombe Down

## 1941
Squadrons: CFS

## 1942
Squadrons: CFS & No. 7 Flying Instructors School

January: A 1,250-yard Sommerfeld track runway had to be laid on the rutted and boggy airfield

1 April: The CFS disbanded and became No. 7 Flying Instructors School giving 4-week OTU instructor courses

August: No. 7 FIS became an (A)FLS for 8-week flying instructor courses with Magisters

August: A Horsa from Netheravon crash-landed

## 1943
Squadrons: Nos 7 FIS & 1537 Beam Approach Training Flight

9 January: The crew of a 295 Squadron Whitley were killed when it stalled whilst overshooting

April: No. 1537 BAT Flight formed using the Lorenz Blind Approach system

22 December: Oxford LX595 attempting a night landing hit a flagpole, plunged into the roof of a hangar, and burst into flames

## 1944
Squadrons: Nos 7 FIS & 1537 BAT Flight

## 1945
Squadrons: Nos 7 FIS & 1537 BAT Flight

## 1946
Squadrons: Nos 7 FIS & 1537 BAT Flight, Transport Command Communication Flight & No. 38 Group Communication Flight

7 April: No. 7 Flying Instructors School disbanded and the staff became part of the re-formed Central Flying School at Little Rissington

July: The HQ of 38 Group, Transport Command arrived at Upavon and activity was confined to its Communications Flight

## Closure:
On 3 August 1993, the RAF officially handed over Upavon to the Army.

**Current status:**
The site is now HQ Land Forces.

## Haunted RAF Upavon

A figure wearing Second World War airman's kit allegedly walks around the camp at night. The bust of Lord Trenchard in the Officers' Mess spooks dogs at night who bark ferociously at it for no apparent reason. Many have commented on the strange atmosphere at the old airfield, and there are tales of seeing pilots in First World War costume.

*Source: Bruce Barrymore Halpenny, Ghost Stations, 1986 (pp. 77-8)*
In August 1939, Archie Pratt arrived at Upavon and was detailed for midnight watch guard duties on his second day. Archie was standing at a fence looking at a white bull, when he noticed a human shadow which he took for another guard. He watched as the shadow walked right across the bulk of the bull and by the light of the moon, which was in front of him at the time, he perceived a phantom figure which had, as he recounts, an eerie glow. Suddenly the figure vanished.

*Source: Army Rumour Service Forum, 16 January 2004*
In the Sergeants' Mess, there is an upstairs room used only for storage where someone once hanged themselves. The contributor was working in the Mess and needed replacement bags for the hoover, which were kept in the storage room upstairs. He got the bags and came down again but discovered that he had left the keys in the room and so had to go back up the stairs to get them. There he found that the door was locked, although no one but himself had been there, and he knew that the keys had been left inside the room. A spare set of keys was obtained from the Mess manager, and upon unlocking and opening the door, the keys were seen on the floor at the opposite end of the room.

# Upper Heyford

No. 1 Group
No. 2 Group
No. 6 Group
No. 92 Group

| | |
|---|---|
| County: | Oxfordshire |
| Location: | 5 miles NW of Bicester |
| OS Ref.: | SP 515268 |
| Opened: | 1917 |

| | |
|---|---|
| Closed: | 1994 |
| Pundit code: | UH |
| Control Tower: | A. Office for Duty Pilot 2072/26 |
| | B. Watch Office with Met Section 518/40 |
| | C. Watch Office 5223a/51 |
| Condition: | A. and B. Demolished |
| | C. Current status not known |
| Runways: | 3 concrete, (220) 1,911 x 50 yards, (270) 1,453 x 50 yards, and (310) 1,453 x 50 yards |
| Hardstandings: | 7 loop types, 23 pan types |
| Hangars: | Coupled – 3, A Type – 6, ARS – 1 |
| Ad., tech. & barr.: | The OTU was using accommodation in Aynho Park, Fritwell Manor, Fewcott House, Middleton Stoney, sundry stone cottages, and Nissen huts around the station |
| Population: | RAF Officers – 202, OR – 1,816, WAAF Officers – 12, OR – 388 |
| Sat. airfield(s): | Brackley (Croughton), Barford St John, Hinton-in-the-Hedges |
| Decoy airfield(s): | Otmoor Q |

## History to 1946:

### 1918
Upper Heyford opened as a landing ground

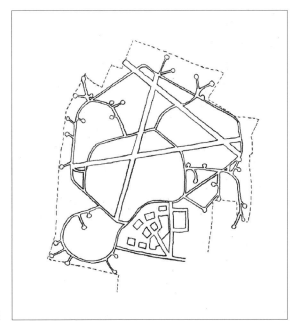

Upper Heyford

**1932**

5 September: No. 57 Squadron arrived from Netheravon with Hawker Harts

**1936**

Upper Heyford was in No. 1 (Bomber) Group

16 March: No. 218 Squadron formed from 'A' Flight of No. 57 Squadron

**1937**

4 January: No. 108 Squadron re-formed from 'B' Flight of No. 57 Squadron with Hinds

19 February: No. 108 Squadron moved to Farnborough

15 March: No. 226 Squadron formed from 'B' Flight of No. 57 Squadron with Audaxes

16 April: No. 226 Squadron moved to Harwell

18 May: No. 113 Squadron re-formed with Hinds

31 August: No. 113 Squadron moved to Grantham

**1938**

March-April: No. 57 Squadron received Bristol Blenheim Is

22 April: No. 218 Squadron moved to Boscombe Down

May: No. 18 Squadron received Blenheims

11 July: No. 34 Squadron arrived from Lympne and received Bristol Blenheim Is

**1939**

January: Upper Heyford moved into No. 2 Group

2 March: No. 34 Squadron moved to Watton. The Upper Heyford Blenheim I squadrons were to provide aerial reconnaissance for the British Army in France

23 September: SHQ Finningley arrived with Nos 7 & 76 Hampden squadrons to become the No. 5 Group Pool

24 September: Both Blenheim squadrons departed for France

September: Upper Heyford and its satellite at Brackley (Croughton) were moved into No. 6 Group and a training role

**1940**

4 April: Nos 7 & 76 Squadrons merged to form No. 16 OTU

7 May: No. 16 OTU received the first of 19 Handley Page Herefords. A month later, more Ansons arrived

13 August: Two Hampdens, L4138 and P4339, collided just after take-off

25 July: Hampdens set off on leaflet-dropping sorties

27 July: More leaflet-dropping sorties

**1941**

Upper Heyford housed No. 16 OTU, training up to 24 one-pilot crews for Hampdens each month

April: The Herefords were moved to No. 5 B&GS

**1942**

Barford St John and Hinton-in-the-Hedges replaced Croughton as satellites

25 April: No. 16 OTU began receiving Wellington Ics

30/31 May: 14 Wellingtons and 16 Hampdens of No. 16 OTU took part in the Cologne 1,000-bomber raid

1/2 June: A mixed force of 30 crews flew on the Essen 1,000-bomber raid. Wellington DV763 crashed at Brabant

25/26 June: 23 Wellington Ics flew on the Bremen 1,000-bomber raid. Wellington X9982 was lost without trace

28/29 July: Wellingtons L7894-U2 & YR1450-Y1 were lost on a raid to Hamburg. Only 3 crew survived to be interned

31 July: Wellingtons DV736-F2 & HF852-C2 were lost on a raid to Düsseldorf. There were no survivors

September: Wellington IIIs started to arrive for No. 16 OTU

November: Group ordered that 4 Nickelling sorties be flown per fortnight

27/28 November: Leaflet dropping was resumed with drops in the Nantes area

17 December: No. 1505 BAT Flight's Oxfords of No. 92 Group provided beam approach practice from Upper Heyford

20/21 December: Between Bullseyes, propaganda leaflets were dropped on Paris

**1943**

Training, Bullseyes, and Nickelling sorties continued throughout the year

20 February: No. 1505 BAT Flight disbanded

March: No. 16 OUT's strength was 57 Wellington Ics, 6 Ansons, 1 Defiant, and 2 Lysander target towers. Wellington Xs joined the OTU

**1944**

Training, Bullseyes, and Nickelling sorties continued throughout the year

December: No. 1655 Mosquito Training Unit arrived from Warboys with 37 Mosquito bombers, 11 Mosquito trainers, and 24 Oxfords

**1945**

1 January: No. 16 OTU was disbanded and re-formed by renaming No. 1655 Mosquito Training Unit as No. 16 OTU in 92 Group. Barford St John was again the satellite field

March: No. 16 OUT's nominal strength stood at 45 Mosquitos of Mks 3, 4, 6, 20 & 25, and 32 Oxfords, for navigation and light bombing training

The immediate post-war period witnessed a rapid reduction in strength

**1946**

1 March: No. 16 OTU moved to Cottesmore

**Closure:**

On 7 December 1993, the last USAF F-111s were removed; soon afterwards, the whole site was transferred back to the RAF and Upper Heyford was closed.

**Current status:**

The airfield is now abandoned, with the majority of the residential buildings now let out as rented accommodation and some of the shops and services having reopened for the local community.

## Haunted RAF Upper Heyford

*Source: Army Rumour Service Forum, 23 December 2006*

A security guard patrolling and securing buildings at Upper Heyford suddenly felt really cold at one spot in a particular building which was otherwise warm. One of his colleagues had an identical experience on this patrol.

*Source: WWII Re-enacting Forum, 7 October 2004*

A former employee for a car company at the airfield wrote that the place was huge, so it was very easy to get lost. He used to be on the early shift, and says that it was always creepy coming into the converted hangar and making sure all the computer systems were up for the early shift. On many occasions, he saw things out of the corner of his eye or heard unexplained banging at 3 a.m.

# Upwood

No. 6 Group
No. 7 Group
No. 92 Group
No. 8 Group
Transport Command

| | |
|---|---|
| County: | Huntingdonshire |
| Location: | 2 miles SW of Ramsey |
| OS Ref.: | TL 269842 |
| Opened: | 1937 |
| Closed: | 1994 |
| Pundit code: | UD |

| Control Tower: | A. Watch Office with Tower (Fort Type) 207/36 Concrete |
| | B. Watch Office for all Commands 343/43 |
| Condition: | A. Demolished in 1943 |
| | B. Demolished in the 1970s |
| Runways: | Grass, the landing ground allowing runs of 1,000 yards in any direction; and 3 concrete/tarmac, (240) 2,000 x 50 yards, (190) 1,400 x 50 yards, and (290) 1,600 yards x 50 yards |
| Hardstandings: | In 1940, 36 Heavy Bomber type tarmac hardstandings were put down round the airfield boundary, together with a perimeter track. In 1943, only 6 of the square hardstandings were considered usable and 30 of the loop type were added, together with a completely new concrete perimeter track |
| Hangars: | C Type – 4; 3 fronted the bombing circle, with the other situated behind and on the W side |
| Bomb stores: | Originally on the NW side of the landing area |
| Ad., tech. & barr.: | The camp of Expansion Period permanent buildings of steel and brick with roofs was located in the SW corner adjacent to the village of Bury |
| Population: | RAF Officers – 201, OR – 1,884, WAAF Officers – 5, OR – 333 |

Total losses from Upwood were 33 Lancasters and 33 Mosquitos.

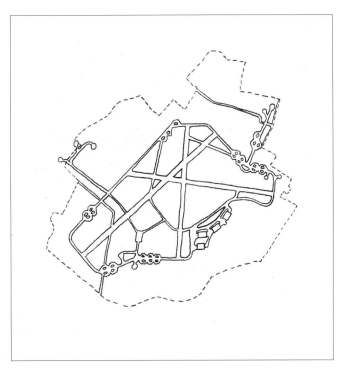

Upwood

*History to 1946:*

**1916**

Upwood was first used as an aeroplane landing ground when the Royal Flying Corps established a training station for night flying. A few huts and temporary aeroplane sheds were erected, only to be quickly removed when the RAF vacated the site in 1919

**1935/36**

The former landing ground was converted into a permanent RAF station of some 250 acres

**1937**

1 March: Upwood opened with the arrival of No. 52 Squadron from Abingdon with Hinds

3 March: No. 63 Squadron arrived from Andover with Hinds

May: No. 63 Squadron received Battles

November: No. 52 Squadron received Battles

**1939**

16 September: No. 90 Squadron arrived from West Raynham with Blenheims and Upwood became a training establishment for Blenheim crews

17 September: No. 63 Squadron moved to Benson for operational training in No. 6 Group

18 September: No. 52 Squadron moved to Benson for operational training in No. 6 Group

**1940**

1 February: No. 35 Squadron arrived from Bassingbourn with Ansons and Blenheim IVs

6 April: Nos 35 & 90 Squadrons disbanded to form No. 17 OTU

15 July: No. 17 OTU was transferred to No. 7 Group

**1941**

30/31 July: Hampden AE266 of No. 61 Squadron attempted to land at Upwood after a raid on Cologne but crashed short of the runway

22 September: No. 11 Blind Approach Training Flight formed for bad weather and night flying training

October: No. 11 BAT Flight became No. 1511 BAT Flight

**1942**

May: No. 7 Group was renumbered No. 92 Group

**1943**

17 April: No. 17 OTU moved to Silverstone

28 April: No. 1511 BAT Flight moved to Greenham Common, and Upwood was upgraded with concrete and tarmac runways

**1944**

1 February: The station reopened into No. 8 Group and No. 139 Squadron arrived from Wyton with Mosquito XXs

5 March: No. 156 Squadron arrived from Warboys with Lancaster IIIs

**1945**

27 June: No. 156 Squadron moved to Wyton

29 June: No. 105 Squadron arrived from Bourn with Mosquito XVIs

**1946**

1 February: No. 105 Squadron disbanded and No. 139 Squadron moved to Hemswell; Upwood was transferred to Transport Command

July: Upwood reverted to Bomber Command and No. 7 Squadron arrived from Mepal with Lancasters

July: No. 49 Squadron arrived from Mepal with Lancasters

4 November: No. 148 Squadron re-formed at Upwood with Lancaster B.Is; No. 214 Squadron re-formed at Upwood with Lancaster Is

**Closure:**

In 1994, the USAF NCO college closed; RAF Upwood was declared surplus to requirements by the Ministry of Defence and closed.

**Current status:**

Much of the airfield is unused since it was closed. Most of the station was vacated and the land and buildings sold off to civil ownership. In 2004, Turbine Motor Works purchased a large amount of property on the former base, including the four C Type hangars. The Nene Valley Gliding Club and local ATC Squadrons still use Upwood, and a part of the airfield is now used by Urban Assault to play Airsoft every other Saturday.

## *Haunted RAF Upwood*

*Source: Facebook, Phantoms of the Rhur, 22 April 2011*

Ian Williams wrote that he had documented two sightings of a phantom padre or a priest, in modern clothing, which was seen by three people. The figure has also been sighted in the former chapel, which is now a canteen for an engineering company. He also noted that the sound of marching men has been heard around the hangars.

**The Georgian style Guardhouse at RAF Upwood**
The guardhouse to the airfield (and many other buildings) was vandalised before the locked gates were installed. This is the location where GJS Ghosthunting heard voices and witnessed an iron bar moving without any physical contact. It is located on private property off Ramsey Road at OS TL 2742 8338. (© *Chris Huff*)

**The Nissen Huts at RAF Upwood**
The Nissen hut in the foreground is the upgraded building incorporating a dining area, kitchen and a classroom where the former airfield padre was seen. This is largely the reason why the hut is believed to have served as the airfield's chapel. The Nissen hut behind, in original condition, is believed to have served as the airfield's mortuary. It is located on private property off Ramsey Road OS TL 2738 8346. (© *Chris Huff*)

**Operations Board at RAF Upwood**
The condition of the former operations board in the station HQ is indicative of how the weather and general vandalism are taking their toll on the buildings. Soon the plaster on the wall will have peeled off completely and another piece of aviation history will be lost. It is Located on private property off Ramsey Road at OS TL 2748 8337. (© *Chris Huff*)

*Source: Facebook, GJS Ghost Hunting, 2011*
Upwood was found to be a strange place when the group visited, and many things happened to them while they were there. In the guardroom one member of the group was overcome and felt that he could not move was, having no energy at all and feeling very sick. In the same room there was an iron bar hanging down that started to move on its own. Everyone in the group heard voices in the room as well. Outside, and on the airfield, the group were followed by footsteps.

*Source: The Airfield Information Exchange, 10 July 2008*
Jason wrote that his grandfather was at Upwood during the Second World War. He went back to the airfield in 2005 to see what his former airfield looked like, and the company that refurbish jet engines in the hangars allowed access and showed them around the area. The restored briefing room is currently used as a classroom, and while at the airfield they learned that this area is reputed to be haunted.

*Visit to RAF Upwood, Saturday 9 June 2012*
I was met at the locked main gates by Sean Edwards who took me first to the former guardhouse, which had previously been cleaned up and slightly renovated but had subsequently had the windows removed and, prior to the gates being fitted to the airfield, had suffered damage from vandals. This was the location where GJS Ghost Hunting had witnessed various phenomena in 2011, so I was keen to see if

anything would happen during my visit. The HQ building opposite had suffered a similar fate, with much of the former parquet flooring ripped out, and general vandalism and graffiti everywhere. Of interest in this building was the black-painted wall for the missions board still just visible, although in very bad condition and peeling off the wall.

There were no feelings or experiences of a paranormal nature whilst in these two buildings.

The two Nissen huts I was allowed access into on this visit were very interesting paranormally. Nissen hut A had been revamped and the interior converted into a classroom at one end with an office by the former middle entrance (connected to Nissen hut B by a short corridor) and a kitchen with dining area comprising a number of pine tables and benches taking up the rest of the structure. Sean informed me that this was the chapel of the airfield at one point during its long history. In addition to the account by Ian Williams of a phantom chaplain witnessed in the building, Sean related the account of a workman seeing the same figure who looked at him whilst the renovations were taking place in the building. He ran out of the hut, refusing to go back in. It was certainly a very interesting location: there was a definite and strong 'hairs on the back of the neck' presence at the office by the classroom, the area identified by Sean as the location where the chaplain had been witnessed. In the dining area there was the very firm impression of airmen on wooden chairs in rows chatting and singing 'Bless 'em all'. Then all went quiet as a stoutish man in RAF uniform pulled back a curtain and started pointing at a map on the wall outlining targets. There was at this point a change in the atmosphere to one of 'some of us are not coming back' and a general sadness. There was no feeling of the area having been a chapel.

Nissen hut B was structurally sound and untouched by any modern decoration or restoration. The far end of the hut had a very unpleasant feel to it and this, Sean informed me, was the former mortuary of the base. There were a lot of jumbled images to sift through in there. One was of a young ginger-haired man with a single wing on his uniform who I thought was a navigator; another figure, standing in the corner staying out of contact, was completely burned. There were images of bodies on stretchers in various states. Sean admitted that he didn't like being in this area on his own. Whilst we were in this area, I heard footsteps, as though someone was walking around the outside of the hut on gravel – but no one was there.

# Warboys

No. 3 Group
No. 8 Group

County:              Huntingdonshire
Location:            S edge of Warboys village

| OS Ref.: | TL 290795 |
|---|---|
| Opened: | 1941 |
| Closed: | 1964 |
| Pundit code: | WB |
| Control Tower: | Watch Office with Ops Room for Bomber Satellite Stations, 15898/40, 7344/41, 13079/41 |
| Condition: | Demolished |
| Runways: | 3 tarmac, (122) 1,250 x 50 yards, (179) 1,100 x yards, and (069) 1,100 x 50 yards. In early 1942, before the airfield was finished, the runways were extended to 2,097, 1,447 & 1,350 yards respectively |
| Hardstandings: | Originally 24 pan types but 2 were lost to hangar construction; 18 loop types added in 1942. The total of aircraft standings was 39 |
| Perimeter track: | The original peritrack was reworked in early 1942 to connect the ends of the new runway |
| Hangars: | T2 – 2, B1 – 1. One T2 was on the SE side of the technical site near the start of the new bypass road, with another on the N side; the Bl was E of runway 18 head |
| Bomb stores: | L off the W side of the airfield |
| Dispersed camp: | Eleven domestic, Mess, and communal sites were dispersed either side of the A141 S to Old Hurst |
| Population: | RAF Officers – 256, OR – 1,503, WAAF Officers – 4, OR – 287 |
| Sat. airfield(s): | Satellite to Upwood; satellite to Marham |
| Decoy airfield(s): | Benwick Q |

In total, 99 aircraft were lost on operations from Warboys: 16 Wellingtons and 83 Lancasters.

## History to 1946:

### 1941/42
Warboys airfield was constructed to the W of the A141 Huntingdon to Chatteris road, opening late in 1941 into No. 3 Group

### 1942
17 April: No. 17 OTU dispersed at Warboys as a satellite to Upwood

5 August: No. 17 OTU moved to Steeple Morden

15 August: No. 156 Squadron arrived from Alconbury, which was then being turned over to the USAAF, with Wellington IIIs

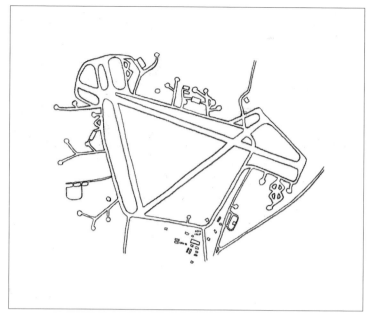

Warboys

## 1943

January: No. 156 Squadron converted to Lancasters as part of the new No. 8 Pathfinder Force in No. 8 Group. Its role was to mark targets with incendiary bombs and flares

13 March: No. 1507 BAT Flight arrived from Finningley with 4 + 1 Oxfords

17 June: No. 1507 BAT Flight moved to Gransden Lodge

1 July: No. 1655 Mosquito Conversion Unit at Marham started using Warboys as a satellite

## 1944

5 March: No. 156 Squadron moved to Upwood; thereafter Warboys became an operational training station. No. 8 Group's Pathfinder Navigation Training Unit arriving from Upwood with 9 Halifaxes and 9 Lancasters

7 March: No. 1655 Mosquito Conversion Unit arrived from Marham with 4 + 1 Mosquitos

June: No. 1655 MCU establishment was 37 Mosquito IV/XVI/XXs, 11 Mosquito T.3s, and 24 Oxfords

December: The PNTU establishment was 14 Lancasters, 14 Mosquitos, and 15 Oxfords

30 December: No. 1655 Mosquito Conversion Unit departed for Upper Heyford

## 1945

1 January: No. 1323 Automatic Gun Laying Turret Flight arrived from Bourn with Lancasters

18 June: The PNTU was disbanded

22 June: No. 128 Squadron arrived from Wyton with Mosquitos

28 June: No. 1696 Bomber Defence Training Flight arrived with 12 Spitfires, 6 Hurricanes, and 1 Oxford

20 July: No. 571 Squadron arrived from Oakington with Mosquito XVIs

20 September: No. 571 Squadron disbanded; No. 128 Squadron was transferred to No. 2 Group

30 September: No. 1323 AGLT Flight & No. 1696 BDT Flight were disbanded

8 October: No. 128 Squadron moved to B.58 Melsbroek

RAF Warboys closed to flying, but the airfield was kept open

**Closure:**

In 1964, the air-to-air missiles were removed and the airfield was sold.

**Current status:**

The technical site buildings were taken over by a transport firm and the airfield itself was returned to agricultural use.

## Haunted RAF Warboys

*Source: Bruce Barrymore Halpenny,* Ghost Stations, *1986 (p. 177)*

An unusual wartime apparition was reported from RAF Warboys. Aircraft returning from raids were seen to make a good approach but after reaching a certain distance along the runway they would invariably swerve off the landing line (sometimes, it is said, with disastrous consequences). After each incident, the pilots were questioned, but they would not say exactly what made them veer off the approach. Eventually one pilot owned up to the cause of the poor landings. He said that as he was making his approach, the figure of a small girl suddenly appeared in front of him and walked straight across the runway. Other pilots were then questioned about their landings, and they too admitted that they had all seen the girl on the runway. Some time after this, the partially exposed skeleton of a child was found by the side of the haunted runway. The remains were never identified but were taken away for burial in a nearby churchyard. From that time onwards, it is said, there were no more sightings.

*Source: The RAF Upwood website*

The website gives the same information as above regarding the girl witnessed on the runway. However, Phil Jackson wrote to the website regarding another apparition at former RAF Warboys, and Sean Edwards kindly passed it on to me. Phil wrote that a woman who used to work in one of the RAF buildings next to the café at Old Hurst, on one occasion when she was collecting some printing tape, saw a figure in the doorway which she thought was a motorcyclist with a helmet on. The figure entered the building and promptly disappeared. When she later approached her boss, who was in the building, he knew all about the apparition and told her, 'That wasn't a motorcyclist; that was our ghost pilot.'

# Warmwell

No. 25 Group
No. 10 Group
No. 11 Group

| | |
|---|---|
| County: | Dorset |
| Location: | 4 miles E of Dorchester |
| OS Ref.: | SY 765885 |
| Opened: | 05/1937 |
| Closed: | 11/1945 |
| Pundit code: | XW |
| USAAF Station: | 454 |
| Control Tower: | A. 1937 - 1941 Air Traffic Watch Office, not known |
| | B. Watch Office for all Commands 12779/41, medium windows to 343/43 |
| Condition: | A. Demolished |
| | B. Converted into house |
| Runways: | Grass, NE-SW 900 yards, WNW-ESE 1,680 yards, NW-SE 900 yards |
| Hardstandings: | Single-Engine – 6, Twin-Engine – 12 |
| Hangars: | Pre-war – 1, Bellman – 2, Blister – 8 |
| Ad., tech. & barr.: | Temporary buildings to the E & SE of the airfield |
| Population: | RAF Officers – 103, OR – 1,356, WAAF Officers – 4, OR – 212 |
| Sat. airfield(s); | Satellite to Middle Wallop |
| Decoy airfield(s): | Knighton Q |

During 15 weeks of operations from Warmwell, the 474th FG lost 27 P-38s, all but 5 known or suspected lost due to ground fire.

## History to 1946:

### 1937

1 May: The airfield (then known as Woodsford) opened for No. 6 Armament Training Camp

July: A Station Flight was formed with Tutor and Wallace target tugs. Nos 206 & 220 Squadrons arrived for the annual coastal defence exercise

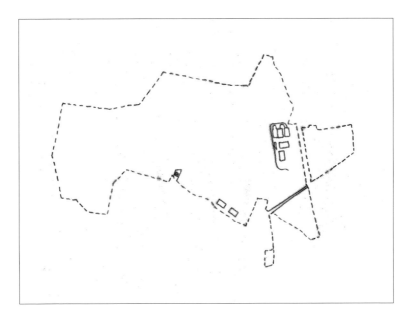

Warmwell

1 August: The practice range at Chesil Bank opened and soon a constant stream of operational squadrons were flying in for training

1 December: No. 6 Armament Training Camp transferred to No. 25 Group

## 1938

January: The Flying Training Schools began using the airfield

1 April: No. 6 Armament Training Camp was renamed 6 Armament Training School under No. 25 Group command, equipped with Seals, Henleys, Wallaces, and Magisters

July: The station was renamed RAF Warmwell

26 September: No. 217 Squadron arrived from Tangmere with Ansons to patrol the English Channel

5 October: No. 217 Squadron returned to Tangmere

## 1939

25 August: No. 217 Squadron returned to Warmwell

2 September: No. 10 AOS was formed from No. 6 ATS

2 October: No. 217 Squadron moved to St Eval

6 November: The Central Gunnery School was formed for gunnery instructor training

## 1940

1 January: No. 10 AOS was renamed No. 10 Bombing and Gunnery School

March: Warmwell was chosen as a forward operating base for Middle Wallop

4 July: Warmwell was declared operational in No. 10 Group

5 July: No. 609 Squadron detached flights to Warmwell and was lodged in temporary tented accommodation on the north edge of the airfield

13 July: No. 10 B&GS moved to Dumfries

25 August: Ju 88s dropped 7 bombs on the sick quarters and 2 hangars on the north side of the main camp; there were 9 unexploded bombs in the camp area but fortunately no casualties

29 November: No. 609 Squadron arrived from Middle Wallop with Spitfire Is

## 1941

24 February: No. 609 Squadron moved to Biggin Hill and was immediately replaced by No. 234 Squadron from St Eval on convoy patrols and bomber escort

26 March: A single Ju 88 dropped 4 bombs on Warmwell

1 April: The station workshops received a direct hit from 3 He 111s, killing 7 and injuring 18

11 May: Nine bombs were dropped near the Control Tower but the majority exploded between the northern boundary and the railway line. This proved to be the Luftwaffe's last attack on the airfield

23 June: The CGS departed for Castle Kennedy

10 July: Twelve bombers and 3 fighter squadrons left Warmwell for an attack on radar sites in France

31 October: No. 276 Squadron arrived from Harrowbeer with Walrus Is & IIs

1 November: No. 10 Group Target Towing Flight was formed at Warmwell and squadrons started to arrive for air-firing practice

6 November: No. 402 (RCAF) Squadron arrived from Rochford with Hurricane IIs to pioneer the use of the aircraft as a fighter-bomber

## 1942

3 March: No. 175 Squadron formed at Warmwell for the same task as No. 402 Squadron, with most of the squadron's attacks on shipping

4 March: No. 402 Squadron moved to Colerne

15 May: Of 3 minesweepers found off Cap de la Hague, 2 were sunk

13 September: No. 263 Squadron arrived from Colerne with Whirlwinds to concentrate on Roadstead missions

10 October: No. 175 Squadron moved to Harrowbeer

## 1943

February: No. 263 Squadron began night Rhubarbs

22 September: The 4th Fighter Group with P-47 Thunderbolts arrived, setting off early next morning to escort 60 bombers attacking Vannes airfield in France

December: No. 263 Squadron converted to Typhoons

**1944**

19 March: No. 263 Squadron moved to Harrowbeer

12 March: Warmwell became Station 454 of the 9th AF and the personnel of the 474th Fighter Group arrived from Oxnard, California, with Lockheed P-38s

3 April: No. 276 Squadron moved to Portreath

25 April: The 474th FG conducted fighter sweeps along the French coast

14 April: No. 275 Squadron arrived from Eglinton for ASR duties with Walrus Is & IIs

May: The 474th FG conducted bombing and strafing attacks in France

7 May: Three P-38s were lost to a bounce by Fw 190Ds while escorting B-26s

5/6 June: The 474th FG flew patrols over the invasion fleet, losing 2 aircraft, believed to have collided

18 July: A 474th formation, led by Lieutenant Colonel Henry Darling on an armed reconnaissance, surprised a force of bomb-carrying Fw 190s and shot down 10 Luftwaffe aircraft with the loss of a single P-38

5 August: The 474th FG flew its 108th and last mission from Warmwell

6 August: The 474th FG moved to St Lambert in France, and Warmwell was returned to the RAF

27 August: No. 17 APC arrived from North Weald

22 November: Warmwell was transferred from No. 11 to No. 10 Group, and No. 14 APC arrived

**1945**

19 September: The last air-firing course was completed

14 October: Nos 14 & 17 APCs disbanded

**Closure:**

In November 1945, Warmwell was reduced to care and maintenance, and this marked the end of the site as an active airfield.

**Current status:**

The land is now used for agriculture and housing. In 1973, the airfield itself was purchased by ECC Quarries.

## Haunted RAF Warmwell

*Source: Bruce Barrymore Halpenny,* Ghost Stations, *986 (pp. 116-20)*

In July 1940, Squadron Leader Ingham was killed when Defiant L.6982, whilst on approach to land, stalled and crashed. A few days later the ashes of Ingham were scattered over the airfield from a Wellington. During the summer of 1940 there had been many rumours about Ingham's ghost which, it was said, would visit the Flight Office and change the flying rosters. Some of the night Duty Crew claimed to have heard the noise of a Defiant taxiing out.

One night in early December, LAC Joyce was Duty Armourer, which entailed sleeping in the Armoury Office. At about 6.30 p.m. he left the NAAFI and headed to the Armoury Section. The only entrance to the office part was a door opening to a hallway giving access to four offices formed in a square around it. Joyce had the keys to all the offices and the key to the outer door. As he was about to fall asleep, he heard footsteps coming down the concrete path to the outer door. It opened and someone came in, walked across the hall to the door of an office, opened it, and went inside. Then all was quiet once more. However, soon after, the sound of footsteps was heard again in the office, then the sound of the opening of drawers and of rummaging around inside them. Joyce called out a challenge and all went silent again, but soon afterwards the shuffling noise started again. By now, Joyce was out of bed, and picking up his keys he went into the hallway lit by the blue light and found all doors locked. Opening up the office, he saw it was empty. Then someone moved swiftly behind him, walked over to the light switch, and switched the light off. The figure then hurried down the hallway, flung the outer door open, and walked very quickly up the concrete path into the night. Checking the outer door once his nerve returned, Joyce found it was still locked.

In charge of the photographic section in 1940 was Squadron Leader Goodhart. Across the corridor from his room was Squadron Leader Ingham's room, unoccupied since the Defiant crash in July. Late one evening, Goodhart was lying on his bed in the Officers' Mess reading when, to his utter astonishment, he heard Ingham's door open and somebody walk down the corridor to the bathroom. All the time the figure was heard whistling. When Goodhart looked down the corridor to see who it was, Ingham was walking in shirt and trousers with a towel over his shoulder heading for the bathroom, which he then entered. Goodhart followed him, opened the bathroom door, and put the light on only to find no one there.

# Welford

No. 8 Air Support Command

| | |
|---|---|
| County: | Berkshire |
| Location: | 2 miles E of Great Shefford |
| OS Ref.: | SU 415745 |
| Opened: | 09/1943 |
| Closed: | N/A |
| Pundit code: | WZ |
| USAAF Station: | 474 |
| Control Tower: | Unknown Watch Office |
| Condition: | Demolished |
| Runways: | 3 concrete and wood chippings, June 1943: (330) 2,000 x 50 yards, (030) 1,400 x 50 yards, and (370) 1,400 x 50 yards |

| Hardstandings: | 46 loop types and 4 pan types |
| --- | --- |
| Hangars: | T2 – 2 |
| Bomb stores: | Located outside the peritrack to the E of the airfield |
| Ad., tech. & barr.: | Dispersed temporary accommodation mostly in the park area to the N. The Base Commander's residence was in The Priory |
| Population: | USAAF Officers – 470, OR – 1,898 |

## History to 1946:

Welford was another of the airfields originally surveyed and accepted for construction as an RAF bomber OTU, only to be allocated for USAAF use with transports.

### 1943
10 June: RAF Welford opened

6 September: No. 8 Air Support Command took charge

6 November: The 315th Troop Carrier Group transferred from Aldermaston with the 34th & 43rd Troop Carrier Squadrons, with C-47 and C-53 transports

10 December: The squadrons of 434th TCG arrived at Welford for a month for parachute training on Salisbury Plain

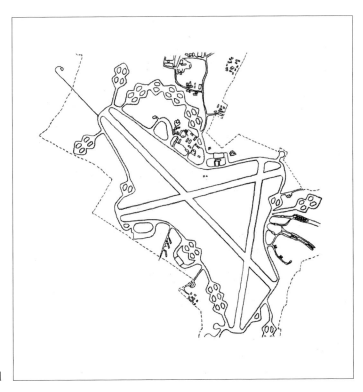

Welford

**1944**

10 January: The 434th TCG returned to Fulbeck

January: At the end of the month, the 315th was ordered to move to Spanhoe

23 January: The 435th TCG with its 75th, 76th, 77th & 78th TCSs began arriving from Langar

6 February: The 435th took part in the first joint airborne exercise when British and US paratroops were dropped at Winterbourne Stoke. Intensive training activities continued, dropping paratroops and towing assault gliders

23 March: Winston Churchill and General Eisenhower visited Welford to observe an exercise by the 101st Airborne Division in preparation for the liberation of France

5/6 June: The 435th TCG dropped the 101st Airborne Division paratroop south of Cherbourg in the early hours of D-Day, losing 3 of its 45 aircraft. In the afternoon, 50 C-47s towed 38 Horsas and 12 Waco CG-4As, losing another 3 aircraft. The group received a Distinguished Unit Citation

Summer: The movement of personnel and supplies to France and the evacuation of wounded were the group's main activities

Glen Miller is said to have played one of his last concerts at Welford before he disappeared

6 August: The aircraft of the 90th TCS & 438th TCG operated from Welford up to the 28th

15 August: Half the crews and aircraft were sent on detachment to Tarquinia in Italy for the invasion of southern France

17 September: The 435th dispatched flights of 36 and 28 aircraft for the airdrops in Holland with paratroops of the 101st Airborne. Heavy flak knocked down 2 and damaged 10 C-47s in the first flight, and damaged another 8 in the second

18 September: Two flights of 30 aircraft, each towing gliders, were sent out with reinforcements; 17 aircraft were flak damaged but all the C-47s returned

19 September: More gliders were towed and 3 C-47s were lost

20 September: Parapacks were delivered by 45 aircraft to Overasselt, and after this intensive period of operations, the group returned to hauling tasks to and from the Continent

**1945**

13 February: The 435th began to move to A.48 Brétigny

As with the other airfields in the 53rd Wing area, Welford was retained by IX TCC as a transit base

June: Welford was handed back to the RAF and Transport Command took over

**1946**

Training activities ceased and the airfield was then little used by aircraft, although an RAF presence in the form of HQ Radio Navigational Aids, originally HQ Southern Signals Area, was in residence until the summer of 1952

October: The station was transferred to No. 90 Signals Group

**Current status:**
The airfield is currently used by the USAF.

## Haunted RAF Welford

Welford was built around an Augustinian priory in use between 1150 and 1525, with the formal title of the Priory Church of St Margaret, Welford. The building became the official residence of the Base Commander until 1995.

The Priory is reported to be haunted, but as the site is an active USAF airfield, it is difficult to get confirmation of this.

# West Malling

No. 11 Group, Fighter Command

| | |
|---|---|
| County: | Kent |
| Location: | 5 miles W of Maidstone |
| OS Ref.: | TQ 680555 |
| Opened: | 1930 |
| Closed: | 1969 |
| Pundit code: | VG |
| Control Tower: | A. 1930-39, Air traffic control building |
| | B. Watch Office with Met Section 5845/39 |
| Condition: | A. Demolished |
| | B. Disused/derelict in 2009 |
| Runways: | Grass, then Sommerfeld tracking; 1945: (264) concrete runway 2,000 x 50 yards |
| Hardstandings: | 13 pan types, 3 Spitfire, 4 Blenheim and 12 Tempest |
| Hangars: | J Type – 1, Blister – 16 |
| Ad., tech. & barr.: | Permanent buildings to the W of the airfield by the A228 |
| Population: | RAF Officers – 68, OR – 1,334 |
| Sat. airfield(s): | Biggin Hill Sector Station |
| Decoy airfield(s): | Collier Street Q, Hammer Dyke Q |

By the end of the Second World War, West Malling had accounted for 165 enemy aircraft including 34 probably destroyed and 59 damaged.

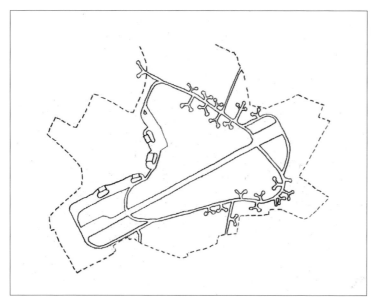

West Malling

## History to 1946:

**1930**

West Malling aerodrome was a grass-surfaced private landing ground housing the
  Maidstone School of Flying

**1940**

Squadrons: 26, 66, 141 & No. 421 Flight

June: An RAF SHQ was formed at West Malling under the administration of
  Fighter Command and designated a satellite to Kenley

8 June: No. 26 Army Co-Operation Squadron arrived from Lympne with Lysanders
  to carry out reconnaissance and photographic sorties. No. 51 Wing arrived for
  2 days

25 July: West Malling was used as an advanced aerodrome for both Kenley and
  Biggin Hill

10 August: A raider dropped 14 bombs on the landing surface and among the
  new workhouse block, which was extensively damaged. Other buildings
  suffered only superficial damage but 17 workmen and 3 sappers were injured,
  a workman dying later

15 August: A bombing raid caused considerable damage to the station, in particular
  to wooden structures. One ambulance was written off and 2 airmen killed

16 August: The J1 hangar roof was hit and badly damaged; 3 aircraft of No. 26
  Squadron were badly damaged but fortunately there were no casualties

18 August: Dive-bombing attack caused damage to hangars and 3 Lysanders were
  written off but there were no casualties

3 September: No. 26 Squadron departed for Gatwick. About 30 bombs were dropped by 6 enemy aircraft, causing 20 craters on the airfield, slightly damaging the parachute section, and wounding a civilian. Several unexploded bombs lay around the airfield

8 September: The telephone service was put out of action

9 September: A Do 17 dropped 6 anti-personnel bombs, gutting by fire 2 temporary buildings, 1 bomb scoring a direct hit on an Army post resulting in 6 soldiers being killed and 3 injured. An airman was injured through falling down a trench

17 September: An anti-personnel bomb fell near the SHQ, damaging hangars and blowing out a number of windows

28 September: Aircraft dropped several anti-personnel bombs and numerous incendiary bombs, wounding an airman and 2 soldiers

31 October: No. 421 Flight arrived from Gravesend and received Spitfires to report on bomber formation build-up over the Channel

6 November: No. 421 Flight moved to Biggin Hill

## 1941
Squadrons: 29, 264, No. 1452 Turbinlite Flight & No. 1528 BAT Flight

## 1942
Squadrons: 26, 32, 29, 264, 485, 486, 531, 610, 616, No. 1452 Flight & No. 1528 BAT Flight

5 May: No. 32 Squadron arrived from Manston to undertake offensive fighter sweeps over France

## 1943
Squadrons: 3, 29, 64, 85, 96, 124, 130, 234, 350, 410 & 531

July: West Malling began to accept the heavy bombers of the RAF and USAAF upon returning from raids over Europe. Thunderbolts of the 8th AAF arrived to escort the American bombers

## 1944
Squadrons: 29, 41, 80, 85, 91, 96, 124, 157, 274, 316, 322, 409, 610 & 616

23 April: No. 91 Squadron arrived from Drem to mount anti-Diver operations with Spitfire XIVs

1 May: No. 85 Squadron transferred to Bomber Command

6 May: HQ, No. 148 Airfield to 12 May

12 May: HQ, No. 148 Wing to 19 June

5 July: No. 274 Squadron arrived from Gatwick to mount anti-Diver operations

30 August: Workmen arrived to carry out extensive improvements including the construction of a new concrete runway

**1945**

Squadrons: 29 & 287

June: Station improvements and the concrete runway completed

**1946**

Squadrons: 25, 29, 91, 247, 287, 500 & 567

**Closure:**

The US Navy facility flight departed in 1963, and West Malling was closed to
flying.

**Current status:**

RAF West Malling is now the site of the Kings Hill residential and business
development. A number of H-block accommodation buildings are in use as
offices and the Control Tower is a listed building.

## Haunted RAF West Malling

*Source: Bruce Barrymore Halpenny,* Ghost Stations, *1986 (pp. 83-5)*

In 1954, Norman Skinner was stationed at West Malling. At that time the Officers'
Mess ante-room had a pair of glazed, French window-type doors leading to the
outside. One particular evening, a group of officers were sitting in the ante-room
talking, when suddenly one of them noticed a figure clad in 1940s flying gear
peering in through the glass. Skinner asserts that this figure was sighted many
times and although investigated immediately, no one was ever found. The phantom
airman was the subject of considerable barrack room conversation.

*Source: Bruce Barrymore Halpenny,* Ghost Stations, *1986 (pp. 83-5)*

From 1979 until 1982, George Kimber was in charge of security at West Malling
airfield. There are four H blocks on the airfield, one of which is said to take on a
very strange atmosphere when entered. Cleaners, council staff, and security guards
when alone in the building have all have commented that there is a feeling of
someone walking alongside them. During the three years that Kimber was in charge
of security, the intruder alarms would activate in the early hours of the morning at
least twice a week. Each time the building had to be searched in case of intruders,
but no one was ever found, and although the alarms were often checked for faults,
none were ever identified. Kimber also states that the security guard had to do the
search without a guard dog, as no dog would go any further than the door.

    When two security guards were on a shift, one would stay in the control room,
located in the wartime guardroom, and the other would be out on mobile patrol.
Many times the inside guard would call the outside guard on the radio to check
on an airman seen standing under a lamppost or walking past the guardhouse.

**RAF West Malling Control Tower**
The Grade II listed building and former Control Tower is now in the middle of the Kings Hill residential and business development, which includes two schools, local retail units and an 18-hole golf course. The tower was left disused and boarded up for many years and the development enveloped it. However, at the time of writing, the it is being renovated with plans to turn it into a coffee shop and conference centre with a display dedicated to the former airfield. It is located off Fortune Way at OS TQ 6745 5500. (*Courtesy of Lee Hall © Lee Hall*)

**RAF West Malling Officers' Mess**
The former Officers' Mess (the Gibson Building) is used as Tonbridge and Malling Borough Council offices. It was built in 1939 to a typical expansion period design and is a Grade II listed building. The exterior of the brick-built building still shows traces of the painted camouflage dating to the Second World War. This is the location for the investigations by Kent group, Ghost Connections. (*Courtesy of Lee Hall © Lee Hall*)

However, the guard on mobile patrol never found anybody around. One security guard who saw the apparition described it as wearing Second World War period RAF uniform, complete with a gas mask. On two occasions, a security patrol van was hit by a house brick with sufficient force to make a large dent in the top of the van but nobody was seen in the area to account for this.

*Source: Bruce Barrymore Halpenny,* Ghost Stations, *1986 (pp. 83-5)*
Two airmen and one WAAF have been observed by staff on the airfield. A dramatic sighting occurred in 1981, when filming for the *We'll Meet Again* television series was being undertaken. While some 30 staff, actors, and film crew were standing by the Control Tower waiting for filming to start, the airmen and WAAF were observed on the airfield ahead of them, looking into the engine of a Jeep. When the film director asked if they could be moved out of shot and one of the film crew approached them, they and the Jeep, in full view of the assembled cast, vanished.

*Source: Tonbridge & Malling newsletter*
Accounts of paranormal activity in the old building have been reported for many years, and include footsteps, deathly chills, and close encounters with a wandering airman. Eve Smith started working at the former Officers' Mess in 1980. One evening, the caretaker had arrived to lock up and as they left the building and the last door was locked, Eve turned to him and said, 'Are you going to leave that man in there?' The caretaker asked who she was talking about and Eve described the man she had seen through the window. He was in uniform and holding a big bunch of keys on a large ring. This prompted the caretaker to re-enter the building and check every room, all the doors and windows of which were still securely locked. When he returned to Eve he said, 'I think you've just seen a ghost.' On another occasion, Eve was dusting the desk when suddenly a chill fell across her and she heard a sliding noise. She looked down and watched as a large glass paperweight moved from one end of the desk to the other.

A former employee once had a scare working at her desk when the door swung open to reveal an airman standing in the doorway in full uniform. The image was so real that she was able to describe the uniform down to the very last button to her war veteran friend, who confirmed it was indeed the uniform of a Second World War airman.

Sid Hurst was working here alone, repairing a server in the computer room. The glass door of the server had been removed and was leaning against the wall, reflecting the room, and Sid happened to glance at it while he was working. He saw the reflection of a figure behind him leaving the room via the open door. However, when he checked the other room, there was no one there and all the doors were locked from the inside. On another morning, Sid and a colleague were working when they heard first the outside door and then an office door open and close. Thinking nothing of this, as they often heard their colleague arriving at work, they expected her to walk in to their office as usual while waiting for her PC to start up. But she didn't, as there was no one there.

On another occasion, an anonymous member of staff, walking down a corridor in the old building towards the toilet, stopped briefly to speak to a colleague and then turned to continue down the corridor. As she did so, for just a split second she is adamant that she saw someone disappear into the toilet. There is only one toilet in the room, but she decided she would go and wait until it was free. Entering the room, she found there was nobody there.

Late one night, there were only three people working in the wing. Two of them were walking down a corridor and as they passed an office they both heard a deep voice say 'Hello'. Turning to see who had followed them up the corridor, they found it deserted. The occupant of the office confirmed that she had not uttered a word.

*Source: The Airfield Information Exchange, 30 April 2008*

Lee wrote that there have been numerous accounts of hauntings/paranormal activity at West Malling. In the 1950s, an airman in Second World War costume was sighted through the window of the Officers' Mess on many occasions. One of the RAF accommodation H blocks has a strange atmosphere and staff working there have stated that they have felt a presence. The site's security guards were called numerous times to investigate the alarms going off but no one was ever found inside the building and the guard dogs would not enter. Airmen in Second World War uniforms have been seen by security staff on many occasions in various places around the airfield but, again, no one has been found. The sound of Merlin engines has been heard over the airfield; indeed Lee has heard this himself twice in the early hours, and on the second occasion his girlfriend also heard it. In the 1980s, a cadet and his mates sneaked onto the airfield to stay overnight in one of the buildings. During the time they were there they heard footsteps approaching, and thinking it was security and that honesty was the best policy, they went to speak with them but found that there was no one there to account for the sound.

*Source: Keypublishing Aviation Forum, 16 March 2004*

West Malling has a number of ghosts including the sound of what is believed to be a de Havilland Mosquito. Visitors to the area have occasionally reported being buzzed at night by a very low flying piston-engined aircraft, although no aircraft is ever seen. In 1993, footsteps were heard coming along the corridor towards the bar but no one was there. 'George', as the phantom has been named, has been heard on a number of occasions but only ever made noises and is never seen. About the same time, Group 4 Security rang from the old guardroom to report that they had a visitor to the airfield. The adjutant went down to see who had arrived, but by the time he got there only the security guards were present; the visitor had gone. He was described as a young officer in a greatcoat and a peaked hat, wearing leather gloves, and smoking a cigarette. Greatcoats had not been worn for a few years, and by this time there were no RAF visitors to West Malling. The figure's appearance at the former airfield remains unaccountable.

*Source: Keypublishing Aviation Forum, 11 April 2005*
Keith wrote that at around 1 a.m. during the early Great Warbirds air displays at West Malling, a colleague was checking around one of the hangars where the BBMF were parked when he heard the sound of footsteps and saw two men. Both were dressed in Second World War era flying clothing and were just walking around in the hangar. They approached him and asked if he could direct them to the Officers' Mess, as they were late for supper. He explained that there was no longer an Officers' Mess at West Malling, and with that the two men said, 'Thank you', turned around, and began to walk away. As they did so, he noticed that there was no sound of footsteps, and then they just vanished.

*Source: Keypublishing Aviation Forum, 4 July 2006*
In November 1976, five of the local ACF platoon gained access to an empty billet on the far side of the airfield, intending to spend the night inside. One was awoken in the early hours by footsteps walking down the corridor, which suddenly stopped. He waited for a security guard's torch to be flashed around the room but there was no torch and no further footsteps.

*Source: Keypublishing Aviation Forum, 19 March 2011*
Irene got up one morning at around 3 a.m. to go to the toilet and as she was entering the toilet block she tripped over a young man, probably only 18 or 19 years old, in wartime uniform in the doorway. His features were rather indistinct but he definitely spoke to her in a broad American accent and was very understandable and very polite, though slightly dishevelled. He called her 'Ma'am' and apologised for having frightened her, before leaving. During the next twenty-four hours no one on the site matched this young man's description, and nobody knew of anyone it could possibly have been. Although extensive enquiries were made, it was never established who or what this polite young American airman was.

*Source: Army Rumour Service Forum, 15 November 2002*
A senior RAF officer, having arrived at West Malling only the previous evening, was woken up at 3 a.m. by someone who looked in and said, 'Oh sorry, old boy' and walked out again. The Wingco thought about it for all of thirty seconds, until it dawned on him that the figure was wearing a yellow Mae West and sheepskin flying boots. He spent the rest of the night sleeping in his car. On another occasion, at night in the old Officers' Mess, one of the doors shut of its own accord with no one nearby.

*Source: Ghost Connections UK*
The Ghost Connections team have witnessed a variety of phenomena in the Officers' Mess including camera batteries frequently failing although fully charged at the start of the investigation, and cameras shutting themselves down unaccountably. Lights and shadows have been witnessed in various parts of the building. Taps,

thuds, and bangs, including a loud bang similar to an explosion, have been heard emanating from empty areas, as well as the sound of whispering and shuffling feet. On one occasion, a knock was heard and a breath followed by a voice possibly saying 'Armstrong' or 'I'm trying'.

On 3 June 2005, the team arrived at 11.30 p.m. to investigate various locations during the night and witnessed a number of unaccountable phenomena. In the corridor there was the smell of pipe tobacco, shadows were seen moving in the dark, a tall uniformed man was sensed, and a camera unaccountably shut down in the East Wing loft, whilst in the West Wing loft the hand of one team member was touched and a feeling of uneasiness was experienced by everyone.

The team again investigated at West Malling, on 3 March 2007, beginning at 8.30 p.m. in the northern end of the East Wing loft. During the course of multiple sessions a movement was noticed near the access hatch, cold draughts were experienced, everyone started feeling very cold, and one member was shaking with the cold. Flickering lights and a flash of light were observed near the southern end of the loft. In response to calling out, there were four clear bangs captured on video footage as though from the metal shelving that lines the loft, numerous taps were heard, and an odd, unnatural noise was heard on the reviewed footage that was not heard by the team at the time. At the southern end of the loft, the temperature was noticed to drop drastically and the team all felt drained and weak. Flashing lights were seen in the central area of the loft and, slightly later, shadows were observed in the same area. One team member thought he saw the head and shoulders of a figure move from left to right across the loft by the entrance. Everyone had the feeling of not being welcome and stated that the whole area began to feel very nasty and oppressive. In a later session, footsteps were heard shuffling around their seating position. When the investigation ended at 3.20 a.m., one member of the team felt that she was being followed down the corridor.

In June 2008, the investigation started in the former Mess hall where the atmosphere underwent a noticeable change to a chill. In the main corridor, by the entrance to the hall, the sound of shuffling was heard and movement was seen, followed by the loud slam of a door from down the corridor towards the West Wing, which upon immediate investigation revealed no one and nothing out of place. When attempting to get into the West Wing loft later, the coded key card was suddenly not functioning, although it had worked fine up to the point when it had been tried on the loft door. (Website: www.ghostconnections.com)

# Weston-on-the-Green

No. 7 Group, Training Command
No. 23 Group, Training Command
No. 3 MU
No. 38 Group, Transport Command

| County: | Oxfordshire |
|---|---|
| Location: | 3½ miles SW of Bicester |
| OS Ref.: | SP 535205 |
| Opened: | 1939 |
| Closed: | N/A |
| Pundit code: | WG |
| Control Tower: | Basic FTS/RFTS Tower |
| Condition: | Demolished |
| Runways: | Grass; in February 1943 Sommerfeld tracking and peritrack laid for 2 runways of 1,510 & 1,050 yards |
| Hangars: | Blister – 6, Double Blister – 4, Bessonneau 12-bay – 2, Bessonneau 9-bay – 2, T2 – 1 |
| Ad., tech. & barr.: | Temporary buildings; 6 dispersed accommodation sites for airmen and NCOs in huts, whilst officers were billeted at Kidlington. The communal site was 1½ miles away from the airfield |
| Population: | RAF Officers – 47, OR – 650, WAAF Officers – 8, OR – 126 |
| Sat. airfield(s): | Satellite to Brize Norton, Bicester, RLG to Kidlington |

## History to 1946:

### 1918
27 July: No. 28 Training Depot Station opened with 6 aircraft sheds and a repair shed

### 1919
No. 28 TDS closed

### 1921
All activity ceased at the site and it reverted to grazing land

### 1939
Weston opened as the satellite to Brize Norton within No.7 Group
2 September: No. 90 Squadron temporarily dispersed Blenheims to Weston

### 1940
April: No. 13 OTU at Bicester used Weston for its Ansons and Blenheims
9 August: Weston was the first Oxfordshire airfield to be bombed when 5 HE bombs hit the landing ground without causing damage
25/26 August: Incendiaries were dropped on the airfield
26/27 August: Seven more bombs fell on the flying field
1 November: Weston became an RLG for No.15 SFTS at Kidlington, using it for the Harvards and Oxfords of 'J' and 'K' Flights

**1941**

20 February: A detachment of 30 men from No. 15 SFTS moved to Weston to service the aircraft based there

12 August: A German raider joined night flying Oxfords of No. 24 Course, opening fire and destroying one before dropping 6 light bombs and strafing the airfield, damaging 7 Oxfords

22 December: No. 2 GTS was transferred from No. 70 Group Army Co-operation Command to No. 23 Group, Training Command. No. 2 GTS had 8 Hectors for glider towing duties; 4 were swapped for 2 dual-control examples at Thame and 2 more were used for pilot training. (Maintenance of these biplanes was a problem.) Hawker Hinds started to arrive

23 December: No. 15 SFTS withdrew 'J' and 'K' Flights from Weston but a Blister hangar was set aside for the use of any night flying Oxford that might need servicing

28 December: The first trainees arrived

29 December: The first 4 gliders arrived from No. 15 MU at Wroughton but tailplane warping was discovered and 2 gliders had to be borrowed from Thame

**1942**

January: Winter brought a deterioration of the airfield surface. The Hectors needed a replacement so a Hawker Audax arrived. Establishment was 30 Hotspur gliders, 16 tugs, 2 Tiger Moths and 1 Hind

2 January: The first 6-week course for glider pilots commenced

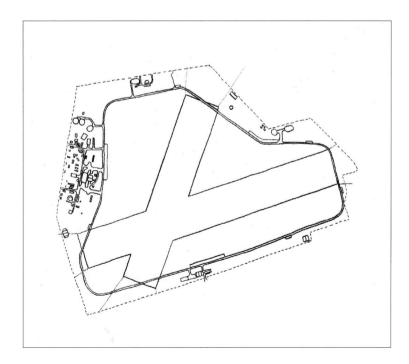

Weston-on-the-Green

7 March: Five Audaxes arrived, with others later in the month; a few Hectors remained for full load towing

16 June: The first Miles Master arrived for towing equipment

28 June: Three dual-control Master IIs arrived and conversion training was undertaken with the assistance of instructors from No. 9 (P)AFU

August: The glider establishment had doubled and the tug strength set at 40 aircraft

2 September: Master DL425 was towing HH518 from Weston when the combination smashed into Witney church steeple. All survived the crash but with serious injuries

**1943**

Intensive glider pilot training continued

February: The conditions at Weston were so bad that the unit was detached to Cheddington

20 March: Flying resumed at Weston

6 April: No. 2 GTS ceased to function; No. 20 (P)AFU in 23 Group at Kidlington used Weston as its satellite

15 May: An Oxford crashed into the roof of a cottage on the airfield boundary; the pilot survived

September: Sommerfeld track runways and peritrack were laid at Weston. Thereafter day and night flying training with Oxfords took place

**1945**

31 May: No. 20 (P) was disbanded

1 October: Weston was passed to No. 3 MU

**1946**

15 March: Weston was passed to Upper Heyford as a part of Transport Command in 38 Group and was used as a drop zone for parachutists by No. 1 PTS. There was also an LZ (Low Zone) Kite Balloon daily above Weston from which parachute training took place

**Current status:**

The site is still an active RAF airfield: Weston-on-the-Green is the home of the Joint Service Parachute Centre.

## Haunted RAF Weston-on-the-Green

*Source: The Paranormal Database*

In 1995, an officer encountered several dark shapes whilst taking part in a night exercise with a group of ATC cadets on the perimeter track on the south-west side of the airfield. As one of the shapes ran towards him, he side-stepped the figure and it vanished as it passed. When he later mentioned his experience to a colleague, he was overheard by an airman who said that he had also had a similar encounter.

# Whitchurch

No. 2 ATA

| | |
|---|---|
| County: | Somerset |
| Location: | 3 miles S of central Bristol |
| OS Ref.: | ST 595686 |
| Opened: | 1929 |
| Closed: | 1957 |
| Control Tower: | Civil Watch Office |
| Condition: | Demolished |
| Runways: | Grass; an E-W tarmac runway 1,016 yards long was completed in 1941 |
| Hangars: | During the war, 5 large hangars were built on the N side of the airfield |
| Ad., tech. & barr.: | Temporary buildings in the SE corner |
| Population: | Unknown |

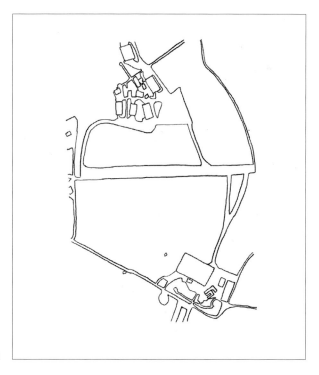

Whitchurch

## History to 1946:

**1929**
Bristol Corporation bought 298 acres of farmland to the south of the city for a new municipal airport

**1930**
31 May: The airport was officially opened by HRH Prince George, Duke of Kent, and handled 915 passengers in its first year of operation
The Wessex Aeroplane Club relocated from Filton airfield and together with Bristol Corporation managed the facilities, which included a hangar, a clubhouse for the flying club, and an aeroplane showroom. Early services offered by air ferry were to Cardiff, Torquay, and Teignmouth. Access was from Whitchurch Lane until Airport Road was built, when a private access road was also built on the east side of the airport

**1932**
Two air taxi firms were based at the site

**1934**
Bristol Air Taxis had become Western Airways and was soon joined by Railway Air Services, a subsidiary of Imperial Airways offering connections to Plymouth, Birmingham, London, Southampton, and Liverpool

**1935**
July: A new terminal building was opened and regular international services started with flights on the Cardiff-Whitchurch-Le Touquet-Paris Le Bourget route

**1937**
Irish Sea Airways, the precursor of Aer Lingus, and Great Western & Southern Air Lines commenced operations from Whitchurch

**1938**
1 December: No. 33 Elementary and Reserve Flying Training School was established in No. 26 Group at Whitchurch to prepare RAFVR pilots

**1939**
1 February: No. 33 ERFTS transferred to No. 50 Group
August: The airport was requisitioned by the Air Ministry and declared a Restricted Area; No. 33 ERFTS closed
3 September: No. 33 ERFTS was disbanded
September: Imperial Airways and British Airways Ltd evacuated 59 aircraft from Croydon and Heston airfields to Whitchurch. The two airlines, in the process

of merging to form the British Overseas Airways Corporation, were to be the nucleus of National Air Communications to undertake war transport work. Airport security was increased with barbed-wire fencing and Air Ministry police posts and a runway and taxiways were constructed

5 November: No. 2 Ferry Pilots' Pool of the Air Transport Auxiliary was formed from B Section of No. 3 FPP. It was responsible for ferrying Blenheims, Beaufighters, and Beauforts built by the Bristol Aeroplane Company at Filton, Hurricanes built by the Gloster Aircraft Company at Brockworth, and Whirlwinds and Spitfires produced by Westland Aircraft at Yeovil

## 1942/43

Civil services to Shannon Airport and an extension of the Lisbon route to Gibraltar developed, with Lisbon and Shannon providing connections to the US. Famous passengers who used these services included Bob Hope, Bing Crosby, Queen Wilhelmina of the Netherlands, and Eleanor Roosevelt

## 1943

1 June: BOAC Flight 777 was shot down en route to Whitchurch from Lisbon; among those lost was the well-known actor Leslie Howard

## 1944

The Bristol Aeroplane Company had an engine maintenance facility in hangars on the airfield; 57 Douglas DC-3s were based at Whitchurch

November: BOAC moved out to Hurn, Bournemouth, as the runways there were capable of accommodating larger aircraft and the success of the invasion of Normandy had lessened the danger from the Luftwaffe

## 1945

September: No. 2 FPP was disbanded and Whitchurch was transferred to the Ministry of Civil Aviation. A number of flying clubs used the airport but it did not attract many scheduled services

## Closure:

The airport closed in 1957 and services were transferred to Lulsgate Bottom.

## Current status:

All that remains of Whitchurch Airport are a few street names and a short length of runway visible in Hengrove Park. It was announced in 2009 that part of the former airport was to be developed as South Bristol Community Hospital, a Skills Academy, and a leisure centre

## Haunted Whitchurch

*Source: Peter Underwood,* Guide to Ghosts & Haunted Places, *1996 (p. 154)*
At Hengrove Park, which used to be part of the aerodrome at Whitchurch, a cleaner and other personnel have witnessed the apparition of a Second World War Luftwaffe officer.

*Source: Richard McKenzie,* They Still Serve, *2008 (p. 116)*
McKenzie mentions the apparition of a Luftwaffe pilot who presumably crashed in the area, though no records have yet been found to prove this.

# Witchford

No. 3 Group

| | |
|---|---|
| County: | Cambridgeshire |
| Location: | 1 miles SW of Ely |
| OS Ref.: | TF 028025 |
| Opened: | 06/1943 |
| Closed: | 1945 |
| Pundit code: | EL |
| Control Tower: | Watch Office for all Commands 12779/41 |
| Condition: | Demolished |
| Runways: | 3 concrete, (100) 2,010 x 50 yards, (160) 1,408 x 50 yards, and (220) 1,418 x 50 yards |
| Hardstandings: | 36 loop types |
| Hangars: | B1 – 1, T2 – 2; the B1 and a T2 were located on the technical site on the NW side of the airfield between runway heads 10 and 16, close to Witchford village, a second T2 lying between runways heads 04 and 34 |
| Bomb stores: | Located near Bedwell Hey Lane |
| Ad., tech. & barr.: | A total of 14 dispersed sites, NW of the airfield and Witchford village |
| Population: | RAF Officers – 125 OR – 1.377, WAAF Officers – 2, OR – 228 |

A total of 99 aircraft and crews were lost on operations from Witchford: 8 Stirlings and 91 Lancasters.

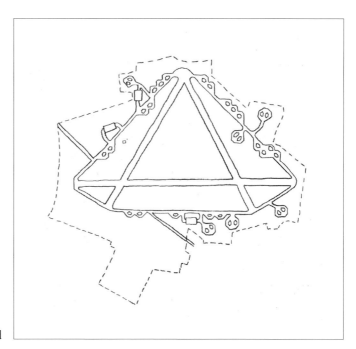

Witchford

## History to 1946:

### 1942

Construction on a Class A standard airfield began with three intersecting runways on a 10-foot rise of stable soil south-south-west of Ely near the junction of the A10 and A142 roads

### 1943

June: RAF Witchford was officially opened into No. 3 Group, Bomber Command

19 July: No. 196 Squadron arrived from Leconfield and No. 4 Group with Wellington Xs and converted to Stirlings

August: No. 196 Squadron commenced operations from Witchford. The increasing vulnerability of the type to the enemy's night defences reinforced No. 3 Group's plan to re-equip with Lancasters

November: No. 196 Squadron moved to Leicester East for troop transport duties with its Stirlings

26 November: No. 115 Squadron arrived from Little Snoring with Lancasters and was the only squadron based at Witchford for the duration of hostilities

### 1945

25 April: No. 115 Squadron flew its last operation from Witchford

August: No. 115 squadron left for Graveley

15 October: No. 29 Air Crew Holding Unit arrived at Witchford

**Closure:**
On 31 March 1946, No. 29 Air Crew Holding Unit was withdrawn and RAF
    Witchford was closed.

**Current status:**
The technical site hangars were retained for some years for military storage and
    currently one T2 remains on the former technical site, which now forms
    Lancaster Way Business Park. An area of the runways is used for poultry units,
    the landing ground area having been reclaimed for arable farming.

## Haunted RAF Witchford

*Source: Keypublishing Aviation Forum, October 2009*
Bill wrote that he and his wife had an experience at Witchford when returning
from Ely. At about 10.30 p.m. they parked the car near the squadron memorial
and walked a short way down the road to the industrial estate, on the site of the
former airfield. In the moonlight they looked over to the site of the former runway
and suddenly became aware of the growing sound of aero engines all about them.
Then shadowy figures passed close by them and all around there was a feeling of
great activity going on. This continued for a few minutes and then, as suddenly as it
started, it was over and all was peaceful again. Questioning his wife over what she
had experienced, she described pretty much the same thing to him. He then asked
her if she had been frightened and she said, 'No, it's as though we were meant to be
here to witness it.' A few minutes later, a security guard rode up on a bicycle and
asked them if it was their car parked on the roadway and what they were doing
there at that time of the evening. He did not seem the least bit surprised when he
was told that they had just stopped to look over the old airfield.

# Wittering

No. 12 Group

| | |
|---|---|
| County: | Cambridgeshire |
| Location: | 3 miles SE of Stamford |
| OS Ref.: | TF 045025 |
| Opened: | 1916 |
| Closed: | N/A |
| Pundit code: | WI |
| Control Tower: | Watch Office with Tower 207/36 |
| Condition: | In use |
| Runways: | Grass, E-W 4,500 yards, NE-SW 1,450 yards |

| | |
|---|---|
| Hardstandings: | 16 pans |
| Hangars: | C Type – 2, GS – 1, Extra-Over Blister – 1 |
| Ad., tech. & barr.: | 1920s Expansion Period brick buildings for technical, administrative, and domestic accommodation |
| Population: | RAF Officers – 186, OR – 2,70, WAAF Officers – 20, OR – 498 |
| Sat. airfield(s): | Collyweston |
| Decoy airfield(s): | Alwalton Q/K, Maxey Q |

The station's wartime record was the destruction of 151 aircraft and 89 flying bombs.

## History to 1946

### 1916
The site, then known as Stamford landing ground, was allocated for Home Defence use, and was one of the flight bases for No. 38 Squadron

### 1919
The airfield was kept under care and maintenance

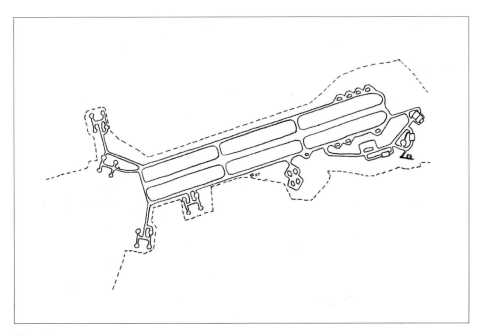

Wittering

**1924**

May: It was reopened as RAF Wittering and upgrading of the station commenced

**1926**

7 October: The Central Flying School arrived from Upavon with assorted aircraft

**1935**

30 August: The CFS returned to Upavon

1 October: No. 1l Flying Training School formed with Harts, Furies, and Audaxes

**1938**

15 May: No. l1 Flying Training School departed for Shawbury, and Wittering returned to operational status in No. 12 Group

**1940**

Squadrons: 1, 23, 25, 32, 74, 151, 229, 266 & 610 rotated

**1941**

Squadrons: 25, 151, 266, No. 1453 Flight & No. 1529 BAT Flight

14 March: Wittering was bombed, resulting in 17 deaths and some minor damage. During the course of the war, the station was bombed 5 times, none of which caused much damage

7 November: No. 1529 BAT Flight formed with Masters

**1942**

Squadrons: 25, 152, 486, 532, No, 1453 Flight, No. 1529 BAT Flight, No. 1530 Flight & PGITW

27 February: The Pilot Gunnery Instructors Training Wing formed with Masters

28 March: The PGITW moved to Sutton Bridge

5 April: No. 1529 BAT Flight moved to Collyweston

During 1942 and early 1943, the airfield was involved in offensive operations, various squadrons taking the attack to the enemy with patrols over the North Sea, although the night fighter role remained a key one

**1943**

Squadrons: 91, 118, 141, 288 (det), 349, 438, No. 1530 Flight, AFDU, AFDS & USAAF 55th FS

25 March: The Air Fighting Development Unit, for operational trials and evaluation, arrived from Duxford, and the Air Fighting Demonstration Squadron arrived from Fowlmere

August: The USAAF 55th FS briefly appeared at Wittering when the 20th FG arrived at Kings Cliffe, which could not accommodate 3 squadrons

**1944**

Squadrons: 438, No. 1530 Flight, AFDU, AFDS, DFDW, DFLS, CFE & USAAF
   55th FS

15 February: The AFDS disbanded

3 April: The USAAF 55th FS moved out and the Fighter Interception Unit arrived
   from Ford

16 October: The AFDU became part of the Central Fighter Establishment under
   the title of Air Fighting Development Squadron

**1945**

Squadrons: 68, DFDW, DFLS, CFE & FTCIS

January: The CFE moved to Tangmere

17 December: The Flying Training Command Instructors' School arrived from
   Brize Norton

**1946**

Squadrons: 19, 23, 41, 219 & FTCIS

24 May: FTCIS moved to South Cerney

**Current status:**

The site is an active RAF airfield.

## Haunted RAF Wittering

*Source: Bruce Barrymore Halpenny, Ghost Stations, 1986 (pp. 128-9)*
In August 1944, Private Easters was guarding D dispersal at about 8 p.m. when
suddenly he heard a whoosh as though a shell had passed over him. Looking up, he
saw a bomber about 30 feet in the air above the runway, heading straight towards
the Control Tower. The aircraft made no engine noise apart from a quiet whoosh
that alerted him to its presence, and it vanished before reaching the Tower.

*Source: Bruce Barrymore Halpenny, Ghost Stations, 1986 (pp. 128-9)*
In the early 1970s, Flight Lieutenant Len Devonshire was in the Control Tower
with the WAAF Duty Officer. He remembers that she had just made them both a
cup of coffee when suddenly they heard footsteps coming up the stairs. The WAAF
accused Devonshire of not locking the outside door properly (for security reasons,
the door into the Control Tower and Ops Block was always locked). As they went
to the landing to see who had got into the Control Tower building, they witnessed
a man in a Second World War period flying suit, fur-lined boots, and leather helmet
coming up the stairs towards them. He passed them, seemingly oblivious to their
presence, and made no attempt to communicate. His footsteps were heard on the
landing as he went into the Senior Air Traffic Controller's office, and after a few

minutes he came out and went downstairs again. They checked the outside door together and found that it was still securely locked. Devonshire was convinced that the apparition they both saw in the Control Tower was part of the crew of the bomber that had crashed into the Control Tower.

*Source: Fighter Control Forum, 12 November 2010*
During the Second World War, an Army officer driving from London stopped for the night at RAF Wittering. The airfield was bombed that night and the officer was among those killed. Many people have since claimed to have seen someone walking round the rebuilt building at night.

*Source: D. W. Hauck, The International Directory of Haunted Places, 2000 (p. 29)*
Hauck also mentions that a bomber seemingly attempts to land on the runway with only a whistling sound. Perhaps linked to this are the sightings since the 1940s of an airman wearing Second World War uniform in the Control Tower. The manifestations allegedly date back to an accident in which a badly damaged bomber attempted to land at Wittering but crashed. This was perhaps Wellington DV839 of No. 14 OTU on 24 October 1943. The rear gunner (the sole survivor) was dragged from the burning aircraft by WAAF Corporal Holden.

*Source: The Paranormal Database*
Ghostly airmen have been witnessed at the site of the crash, and a former MP reported feeling a presence and witnessing lights coming on and loud bangs in the Control Tower. It is also alleged that footsteps have been heard in the empty hangar for No. 1 Squadron, together with shadows seen moving around.

# Wratting Common

No. 3 Group, Bomber Command

| | |
|---|---|
| County: | Cambridgeshire |
| Location: | 3 miles NW of Haverhill |
| OS Ref.: | TL 645500 |
| Opened: | 05/1943 |
| Closed: | 1946 |
| Pundit code: | WW |
| Control Tower: | Watch Office for all Commands 12779/41 & 343/43 |
| Condition: | Demolished |
| Runways: | 3 concrete, (308) 2,000 x 50 yards, (197) 1,400 x 50 yards, and (252) 1,400 x 50 yards |
| Hardstandings: | 36 loop types |

| Hangars: | T2 – 4, B1 – 1; one T2 and the B1 hangar were erected at the main technical site between runway heads 13 and 07, and the other T2s for gliders on the N side of the airfield between 13 and 20 |
| Bomb stores: | Located W of the site at Skippers Hall Farm |
| Ad., tech. & barr.: | The technical site was on Weston Woods Farm and the 10 dispersed domestic and Mess sites were in fields towards Weston Green |
| Population: | RAF Officers – 164, OR – 1,961, WAAF Officers – 6, OR – 342 |
| Sat. airfield(s): | Satellite of Stradishall |

In total, Wratting Common lost 43 aircraft and crews: 34 Stirlings and 9 Lancasters.

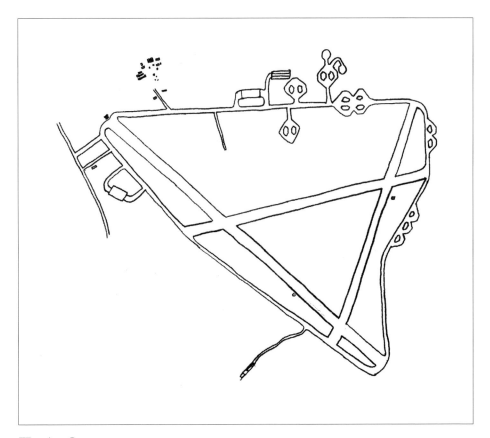

Wratting Common

## *History to 1946:*

### 1942/43
A bomber airfield was built to Class A standard located on the Cambridgeshire side of the county boundary with Suffolk and officially named RAF West Wickham.

### 1943
31 May: No. 90 Squadron arrived from Ridgewell with Stirling IIIs at a very incomplete West Wickham to make room for the USAAF units that had been allocated the station

21 August: Notice was received that the official name of the station would change from West Wickham to Wratting Common

13 October: No. 90 Squadron moved to Tuddenham when No. 3 Group decided to concentrate Stirling conversion units in the Stradishall clutch, No. 31 Base, of which Wratting Common was a satellite or sub-base

November: No. 1651 Heavy Conversion Unit arrived from Waterbeach with Stirling Is, soon to be replaced by Stirling IIIs

### 1944
9 November: No. 1651 HCU moved to Woolfox Lodge where crews were trained for transport squadrons

13 November: No. 195 Squadron arrived from Witchford where it had been re-formed from 'C' Flight of No. 115 Squadron a few weeks earlier. No. 195 Squadron grew to 3 full Flights with 30 Lancasters, remaining at Wratting Common to see out the war.

After VE Day the squadron was involved in supply drops over the Netherlands and transporting prisoners of war to the UK from Germany and Italy

### Closure:
On 14 August 1945, No. 195 squadron was disbanded at Wratting Common and no further flying units were based at the station. Wratting Common was soon reclaimed for agriculture, with much of the concrete taken for hardcore.

### Current status:
Most of the site is part of Thurlow Estates owned by the Vesty family. The hangars survived, as did many of the larger Nissen huts, now serving as cover for commercial enterprises.

## Haunted RAF Wratting Common

*Source: Bruce Barrymore Halpenny,* Ghost Stations II, *1990 (pp. 105-6)*

In July 1987, Peter Giles working for the Metal Box Company was delivering new paint tins for storage in a modernised Second World War hangar at the airfield. As the lorry was being unloaded, Peter had a walk around the former airfield. Stopping at a hangar, he went inside. He immediately became aware of how cold it was in there, and had the distinct feeling that he was not alone. Unlike his encounter at Full Sutton (see RAF Full Sutton in Volume 3), the overriding fear that he felt on this occasion meant that he left the hangar as fast as he could and returned to his truck. On seeing his frightened look, the site manager asked him if he was all right. When Peter told him about what he had experienced inside the hangar, the site manager replied that although he had never seen anything untoward in there, he admitted that he would not hang about after dark or go up to the airfield unless he had to. The hangar had formerly been used to repair combat-damaged aircraft during the war years.

# Operations of the Second World War

**Argument** (20-25 February 1944)
The USAAF launched a series of missions that became known as 'Big Week'. The Luftwaffe was lured into a decisive battle for air superiority against massive attacks on the German aircraft industry by USAAF bombers, protected by squadrons of P-47 Thunderbolts and P-51 Mustangs.

**Banquet** (July 1940)
A British plan to use every available aircraft in a last-ditch effort to repel an expected German invasion in 1940 or 1941. On 13 July 1940, the Air Officer Commander-in-Chief, Training Command was ordered to plan to make the maximum practical number of aircraft available for operations. Aircraft allocated under Banquet would, in many cases, lack bombsights, armour for the protection of the crew, defensive guns and self-sealing fuel tanks. RAF instructions were very clear that no aircraft was to be considered unfit, anything that could fly and drop bombs would suffice.

**Banquet Light** (July 1940)
The most ominous of the Banquet plans which would see the formation of forces composed of De Havilland Tiger Moth biplanes and other light aircraft of the Elementary Flight Training School. The scheme required trainee pilots to be introduced to bombing at an early stage of their instruction. The Banquet Light strike force would be employed in an Army cooperation role and sent to bomb concentrations of airborne troops or soldiers landing on the beaches. Most of the pilots would be students, comprising a strike force of about 350 aircraft. The Moths and their inexperienced pilots would have been very vulnerable to enemy aircraft and the plan was widely regarded as virtually suicidal.

**Bellicose** (20/21 June 1943)
The RAF bombed Friedrichshafen, landing in Algeria where they refuelled and rearmed and bombed the Italian naval base at La Spezia on the return to Britain. This was the first 'shuttle raid' where bombers fly from their home base to bomb

an initial target and continue to a different location where they are refuelled and rearm.

**Biting** (27-28 February 1942)
Also known as the Bruneval Raid. On the night of 27 February a small detachment of airborne troops parachuted into France a few miles from the German radar installation at Bruneval. The force then proceeded to assault the villa in which the radar equipment was kept, killing several members of the German garrison and capturing the installation after a brief fire-fight. A technician that had come with the force proceeded to dismantle the Würzburg radar array and remove several key pieces to take back to Britain. The raiding force then retreated to the evacuation beach, and encountered Germans guarding the beach. After another brief fire-fight the raiding force was picked up by a small number of landing craft and transferred to several Motor Gun Boats which took them back to Britain. The raid was entirely successful.

**Carpetbagger** (4 January 1944-April 1945)
USAAF aerial resupply of weapons and other material to resistance fighters in France, Italy, and the Low Countries.

**Carthage** (21 March 1945)
An RAF raid on the Shellhus, the Gestapo headquarters in Copenhagen, that was repeatedly requested by members of the Danish resistance in the hope of freeing imprisoned members and destroying Gestapo records. The attacking force comprising RAF de Havilland Mosquitos of Nos 21, 464 & 487 Squadrons of No. 140 Wing were organised in three waves of six aircraft with two Mosquitos to record the attack and thirty Mustangs to give cover from German aircraft and attack flak sites out and back.

**Catechism** (12 November 1944)
The last of nine attempts to sink the *Tirpitz* by thirty Avro Lancasters from Nos 9 & 617 Squadrons, plus a film unit aircraft from No. 463 RAAF Squadron. The aircraft took off from Lossiemouth, each equipped with a Tallboy bomb. At least two hit the *Tirpitz* in Tromsø Fjord, Norway, the battleship suffering a violent internal explosion, capsizing, and remaining bottom upwards.

**Chastise** (16/17 May 1943)
A low-level attack with Barnes Wallace's Bouncing Bombs on three German dams by No. 617 Squadron, subsequently known as the Dambusters. The Möhne and Edersee Dams were breached, while the Sorpe dam sustained only minor damage. Of the nineteen Lancasters employed on the raid, eight failed to return.

**Cooney Party** (7 June 1944)
Nine aircraft of No. 38 Group dropped elements of the 4th Free French Parachute Battalion or 2eme RCP (Regiment de Chasseurs Parachutistes) to disrupt enemy communications between West Brittany and the remainder of France.

**Corona** (October 1943)
To confuse German night fighters during RAF bomber raids on German cities, native German speakers impersonated German Air Defence officers, initiating communications via radio with German night fighter pilots and countermanding previously given orders. The operation was first launched during the attack on the German industrial centre of Kassel on the night of 22/23 October 1943. The Luftwaffe responded by replacing male fighter controllers with female ones, to which the RAF then responded by using German-speaking WAAF personnel.

**Cromwell** (1940)
Codename to warn that a German invasion of Britain was imminent.

**Crossbow** (1943-1944)
Codename of the campaign of Anglo-American operations against all phases of the German long-range weapons. It included missions targeting research and development of the weapons, their manufacture, transportation, the launch sites, and against V-1s in flight.

**Crucible** (1940)
Codename to warn of a potential Luftwaffe attack on London.

**Diver** (1944)
Defence of London against German V-1 rockets.

**Doomsday** (May 1945)
The British 1st Airborne Division acted as a police and military force during the Allied occupation of Norway following the German surrender on 8 May. The 1st Airborne Division landed near Oslo and Stavanger between 9 and 11 May. The majority of the transport aircraft carrying the division landed safely, but one crash caused a number of fatalities.

**Gomorrah** (July 1943)
A campaign of air raids for eight days and seven nights on Hamburg created one of the greatest firestorms raised by the RAF and USAAF in the Second World War.

**Hydra** (17/18 August 1943)
An RAF attack on the Peenemünde Research Centre which opened the bombing campaign against the Nazi V-weapon programme, at the cost of forty bombers,

and hundreds of civilian deaths in a nearby concentration camp. The raid killed two V-2 rocket scientists and delayed test launches for seven weeks.

## Jericho (18 February 1944)

A low-level raid by Mosquitos of No. 140 Wing 2 TAF, based at Hunsdon. It comprised eighteen Mosquitos from No. 464 RAAF Squadron, No. 487 RNZAF Squadron and No. 21 Squadron led by Group Captain Percy Charles Pickard on Amiens prison with the objective of freeing French Resistance and political prisoners. When two Allied intelligence officers were also captured and sent to Amiens prison, a precision air attack on the prison was requested. The Mosquitos flying at rooftop height succeeded in breaching the walls and buildings of the prison, as well as destroying guards' barracks. Of the 717 prisoners, 102 were killed, 74 wounded, and 258 escaped, including 79 Resistance and political prisoners, although two-thirds of the escapees were recaptured.

## Jubilee (19 August 1942)

Combined operations raid on the occupied port of Dieppe. The assault began at 5 a.m. and by 10.50 a.m. the Allied commanders were forced to call a retreat. Over 6,000 infantrymen, predominantly Canadian, were supported by limited RN and large RAF contingents. The RAF's main objective was to throw a protective umbrella over the amphibious force and beachheads. Fifty-one fighter squadrons of Spitfires, eight squadrons of Hurricanes, four squadrons of reconnaissance Mustang Mk Is and seven squadrons of light bombers were committed to the attack. RAF losses amounted to 106 aircraft, 88 fighters destroyed or damaged, and 18 of the bombers. Against this total, forty-eight Luftwaffe aircraft were lost.

## Juggler (13 August 1943)

After being postponed several times by unfavourable weather, a strike by 376 bombers of 16 bomb groups was carried out against the Regensburg heavy industry plants, beyond the range of escorting fighters. Although inflicting heavy damage on the target, it was catastrophic for the RAF, with sixty bombers lost and many more damaged beyond repair.

## Ladbroke (9 July 1943)

A glider landing of British airborne forces near Syracuse that began on as part of the Allied invasion of Sicily, carried out from Tunisia with a force of 144 Waco gliders and 6 Horsa gliders. Sixty-five gliders released early by the American and British towing aircraft crashed into the sea, drowning approximately 252 men. Of the remainder, only eighty-seven men arrived at the Pont Grande bridge, though they successfully captured the bridge and held it beyond the time they were to be relieved. Finally, with their ammunition expended and only fifteen soldiers remaining unwounded, the Allied troops surrendered to Italian forces.

**Magic Carpet** (June 1945-February 1946)
A USAAF operation to transport American servicemen back to the US. Hundreds of Liberty ships, troop transports, aircraft carriers, battleships, and hospital ships were used.

**Mallard** (6 June 1944)
A British airborne operation by the 6th Airborne Division as a part of Operation Overlord to airlift glider infantry of the 6th Airlanding Brigade and divisional troops to reinforce the 6th Airborne Division on the left flank of the British invasion beaches.

**Manna** (1945)
An Allied parachute drop of food to the German-occupied Netherlands.

**Market Garden** (17-25 September 1944)
The combined force had 1,438 Dakota transports (1,274 USAAF and 164 RAF) and 321 converted RAF bombers. Market Garden delivered over 34,600 men of the 101st, 82nd and 1st Airborne Divisions and the Polish Brigade, landing 14,589 troops by glider and 20,011 by parachute; 1,736 vehicles and 263 artillery pieces were landed by glider and 3,342 tons of ammunition and other supplies were brought by glider and parachute drop.

**Millennium** (30/31 May 1942)
The first 1,000-bomber raid by the RAF on Cologne, using bombers and men from bomber squadrons, OTUs, Coastal Command, and by crewing forty-nine aircraft with pupil pilots and instructors, 1,047 bombers took part in the raid. In addition to the bombers attacking Cologne, 113 other aircraft on Intruder raids harassed German night fighter airfields, destroying 3,330 non-residential buildings, seriously damaging 2,090, and lightly damaging 7,420. The number reported killed was between 469 and 486, of whom at least 411 were civilians and 58 military. The RAF lost forty-three aircraft, twenty-two over or near Cologne, sixteen by flak, four by night fighters, two in a collision, and two Blenheims in attacks on night fighter airfields.

**Obviate** (29 October 1944)
RAF Bomber Command's first attack on the *Tirpitz* at Tromsø by eighteen Lancasters of No. 617 Squadron, eighteen of No. 9 Squadron, and a film unit aircraft from No. 463 Squadron from Lossiemouth at 1 a.m. Cloud arrived over the *Tirpitz* just 30 seconds before the Lancasters and they were forced to bomb blind. Thirty-two bombs were released but no direct hits were scored.

**Paravane** (15 September 1944)
Twenty-eight Lancasters set off from Yagodnik in Russia. Twenty carried 5-ton Tallboy bombs, seven carried 400-500-lb Johnny Walker mines

designed for use against ships in shallow water, and one was fitted for photo reconnaissance. A smokescreen obscured the *Tirpitz* from the attackers, many of whom did not release their bombs. One Tallboy however struck the ship 50 feet back from her prow, pierced her bow compartments without detonating and exited under the waterline on the starboard side before exploding.

## Pointblank (1943-1944)
Allied combined bomber offensive intended to cripple or destroy the German aircraft fighter strength, thus drawing it away from frontline operations.

## Quick Force (1941)
After Dunkirk, 3,000 men of No. 21 Aircraft Depot were withdrawn to Henlow, where they worked on unpacking, assembling, testing, modifying and repairing Hurricanes. Fifty to 100 fitters were serving on HMS *Furious* and other carriers, dismantling Hurricanes for transport to Malta.

## Strangle (March 24-Spring 1944)
A series of air operations during the Italian Campaign by the USAAF 12th and 15th Air Forces to interdict German supply routes in Italy north of Rome. The aim, to prevent essential supplies from reaching German forces in central Italy and compel a German withdrawal, was not achieved.

## Tablejam (1940-1945)
Under Operation Tablejam the RAF/SOE made 677 sorties delivering weapons and material to the Danish Resistance. From 436 successful missions, the RAF/SOE delivered 6,300 containers and 581 packets with about 650 tons of weapons at a great number of dropping places. The RAF/SOE weapon flights were carried out by RAF squadron Nos 138, 161, 196, 295, 298, 299 and 570. On the night of 26 April 1945, seven aircraft took part in an operation code named 'Tablejam 343' and were assigned to different targets in Denmark. The defences were reputed to be severe and the instructions were to 'go in low'.

## Tonga (5-7 June 1944)
A British airborne operation by the 6th Airborne Division as a part of Operation Overlord. The paratroopers and glider-borne airborne troops landed on the eastern flank of the invasion area near Caen, aiming to capture two strategically important bridges over the Caen Canal and Orne River.

## Torch (November 1942)
The Anglo-American invasion of French North Africa during the North African Campaign. Aerial operations were split into two: east of Cape Tenez in Algeria by RAF aircraft, and west of Cape Tenez by USAAF aircraft.

**Varsity** (24 March 1945)

A successful Anglo-American airborne operation. In the early hours, 541 transport aircraft containing airborne troops, and a further 1,050 troop-carriers towing 1,350 gliders, began to take off from airbases in England and France and rendezvous over Brussels, before turning north-east for the Rhine dropping zones. This immense armada took 2 hours and 37 minutes to pass any given point, and was protected by some 2,153 fighters from the RAF & 9th AF.

# Glossary of Abbreviations

AAC: Army Air Corps
AACU: Anti-Aircraft Co-operation Unit
A&AEE: Aeroplane and Armament Experimental Establishment
AAF: Auxiliary Air Force
A&IEU: Armament and Instrument Experimental Unit
AAS: Air Armament School
AATT: Anti-Aircraft and Target Towing (Flight)
ADF: Air Defence Squadron
AEF: Air Experience Flight
AFDS: Air Fighting Development Squadron
AFDU: Air Fighting Development Unit
AFS: Advanced Flying School
AFTS: Advanced Flying Training School
AGS: Air Gunnery School
ALG: Advanced Landing Ground
ANS: Air Navigation School
AOC: Air Officer Commanding
AONS: Air Observer Navigation School
AOS: Air Observer School
APC: Armament Practice Camp
ASH: Narrow-beam radar used for low-level operations
ASR: Air-Sea Rescue
ASU: Aircraft Storage Unit
ASV: Air-to-Surface Vessel (radar)
ATA: Air Transport Auxiliary
ATC: Air Training Corps or Air Traffic Control
ATS: Advanced Training Squadron
BAT Flight: Blind or Beam Approach Training Flight
BCBS: Bomber Command Bombing School
BCIS: Bomber Command Instructors' School
BCDU: Bomber Command Development Unit

BDTF: Bomber Defence Training Flight
BDU: Bomber Development Unit
BFTS: Basic Flying Training School
BG: Bomb Group (USAAF)
B&G: Bombing and Gunnery (Flight)
BLEU: Blind Landing Experimental Unit
BS: Bomb Squadron (USAAF)
BSDU: Bomber Support Development Unit
CCDU: Coastal Command Development Unit
CFE: Central Fighter Establishment
CFS: Central Flying School
CGS: Central Gunnery School
C&M: Care and Maintenance
CNCS: Central Navigation and Control School
CPF: Coastal Patrol Flight
CTW: Combat Training Wing
CU: Conversion Unit
EATS: Empire Air Training Scheme
EBTS: Elementary and Basic Training School
ECFS: Empire Central Flying School
EFTS: Elementary Flying Training School
EGS: Elementary Gliding School
EGTS: Elementary Gliding Training School
ELG: Emergency Landing Ground
ERFTS: Elementary and Reserve Flying Training School
E&WS: Electrical and Wireless School
FAA: Fleet Air Arm
FIS: Flying Instructors' School
FIU: Fighter Interception Unit
FLS: Fighter Leaders' School
FPP: Ferry Pilots' Pool
FTS: Flying Training School
FTU: Ferry Training Unit
GRU: Gunnery Research Unit
GS: Glider School (ATC)
GTS: Glider Training School
HCU: Heavy Conversion Unit
HGCU: Heavy Glider Conversion Unit
HTCU: Heavy Transport Conversion Unit
LFS: Lancaster Finishing School
MCU: Mosquito Conversion Unit
MRU: Mountain Rescue Unit
MT: Motor Transport

MU: Maintenance Unit
NLG: Night Landing Ground
OADU: Overseas Aircraft Despatch Unit
OCU: Operational Conversion Unit
OFIS: (Operational) Flying Instructors' School
OTU: Operational Training Unit
(P)AFU: (Pilots) Advanced Flying Unit
PAMPA: Long-range weather reporting sortie
PRU: Photographic Reconnaissance Unit
RAAF: Royal Australian Air Force
RAF: Royal Air Force
RAFVR: RAF Volunteer Reserve
RAT Flight: Radio Aids Training Flight
RAuxAF: Royal Auxiliary Air Force
RCAF: Royal Canadian Air Force
RFC: Royal Flying Corps
RFS: Reserve Flying School
RLG: Relief Landing Ground
RNAS: Royal Naval Air Station or Service
RNZAF: Royal New Zealand Air Force
RNEFTS: Royal Navy Elementary Flying Training School
RNVR: Royal Naval Volunteer Reserve
ROC: Royal Observer Corps
SDF: Special Duty Flight
SFTS: Service Flying Training School
SLG: Satellite Landing Ground
SofAG: School of Aerial Gunnery
SofTT: School of Technical Training
TCDU: Transport Command Development Unit
TCU: Transport Conversion Unit
TCW: Troop Carrier Wing
TFW: Tactical Fighter Wing
TRE: Telecommunications Research Establishment
TRG: Tactical Reconnaissance Group
TTF: Target Towing Flight
UAS: University Air Squadron
USAAF: United States Army Air Force
WAAF: Women's Auxiliary Air Force
WRNS: Women's Royal Naval Service

# Glossary of Wartime Terms

Anti-Diver Patrol: Mission to intercept and shoot down V-l flying bombs

Anti-Rhubarb: A patrol to intercept low-level intruders

Armed Recce: Armed Reconnaissance, search and attack missions

Aphrodite: The use of aged B-17s as radio-controlled bombers

Baedeker raid: German reprisal attack delivered on smaller, historic cities such as Canterbury

Bullseye: A night training exercise for bomber personnel to resemble an operational night flight

Carpet: A supply-dropping operation to resistance forces

Carpetbagger: An operation to airdrop supplies to underground patriot forces in Western Europe

Channel Stop: Air operations intended to stop enemy shipping passing through the Strait of Dover

Circus: Bomber attacks with fighter escorts in the daytime. The attacks were against short-range targets with the intention of occupying enemy fighters and keeping their fighter units in the area concerned

Darkie system: The method of homing in at night on radio signals

Day Ranger: A daytime operation to engage air and ground targets within a specified area (see also Ranger)

Dicer: A low-level photo reconnaissance sortie

Distil: A fighter operation to shoot down enemy aircraft minesweeping, usually off Denmark

Diver: The V-1 flying bomb

Drem lighting: A system of markers and approach lights

Eric: A daytime training exercise involving both bomber and fighter crews

FIDO: Fog Investigation and Dispersal Operation

Firebash: Sorties by Mosquitos of No. 100 Group with incendiaries or napalm against German airfields

Flower: Patrols in the area of enemy airfields with the intention of preventing aircraft from taking off and attacking those aircraft that were airborne

Foxhunt: A bombing mission using Microwave Early Warning radar control

Fuller: The prevention of *Scharnhorst* and *Gneisenau* from moving out of Brest

Gardening: A mission to disrupt transportation on or near rivers by mining, sometimes accompanied by attack; laying mines in coastal waters

Gee: A medium-range radio aid to navigation using ground transmitters and airborne receivers

Highball: A smaller version of the Bouncing Bomb fitted to Mosquitos

H2S: Airborne radar navigational and target location aid

Instep: A mission to restrict attacks on Coastal Command aircraft by maintaining a presence over the Western Approaches

Intruder: Offensive patrols usually carried out at night intended to destroy enemy aircraft over their own territory

Jackpot: A mission against enemy airfields

Jim Crow: Coastal patrols to intercept enemy aircraft crossing the British coastline, originally intended to warn of invasion in 1940

Kipper: Patrols to protect fishing boats in the North Sea against attack from the air

Lagoon: A shipping reconnaissance operation off the Dutch coast

Leigh light: The searchlight used for anti-submarine operations

Lindholme gear: Survival equipment dropped from ASR aircraft to crews ditched in the sea

Mahmoud: Sorties flown by Mosquitos equipped with backward-facing radar; when enemy aircraft were detected an unexpected 180-degree turn enabled a surprise attack

Mandolin: Attacks on enemy railway transport

Mandrel: An airborne radar jamming device used by No.100 Group

Moling: Nuisance raids by individual aircraft in bad weather with the object of harassing the German air-raid warning system

Nickelling: During the 'Phoney War' the RAF carried out small bombing raids, and a large number of propaganda leaflet raids (codenamed 'Nickels') were dropped

Noball: V-1 Launch sites

Oboe: A ground-controlled radar system for blind bombing

Popular: A general Tactical Reconnaissance mission against coastal targets

Pundit code: Lights or letters displayed giving the airfield ID

Q-site: A dummy airfield with flashing lights

Ramrod: Short-range bomber attacks to destroy ground targets, similar to Circus attacks

Ranger: A freelance flight over enemy territory by units of any size, the intention being to occupy and tire enemy fighters

Rhombus: A weather reporting flight

Rhubarb: An operation when sections of fighters or fighter-bombers, taking full advantage of low cloud and poor visibility, would cross the English Channel and then drop below cloud level to search for opportunity targets such as railway locomotives and rolling stock, aircraft on the ground, enemy troops, and vehicles on roads

Roadstead: Bomber/fighter-bomber escort mission against transport shipping targets

Rodeo: A fighter sweep over enemy territory/fighter mission using bombers as bait/ diversion

Rover: An armed reconnaissance flight with attacks on opportunity targets

Serrate: A sortie with airborne radar to locate and destroy enemy night fighters, combined with night bomber raids

Starfish: A dummy fire simulating bombing activity to attract enemy bombers away from the real target

Stopper: A Coastal Command patrol outside Brest harbour

Sweep: A fighter mission to an area without a specific target

Thum: A weather reporting flight

Tinsel: Equipment carried by RAF bombers used for jamming Luftwaffe night fighter controllers' speech radio-frequencies during the Second World War

Turbinlite: An airborne searchlight for night fighter operations

Window: A radar countermeasure in which aircraft spread a cloud of small, thin pieces of aluminium which appeared as a cluster of secondary targets on radar screens or swamped the screen with multiple returns

X-raid: Approaching unidentified aircraft

Y-Service: Monitoring of German radio transmissions to and from aircraft

# Bibliography

Ashworth, C., *Action Stations 5: Military Airfields of the South-West* (1982).
—*Action Stations 9: Military Airfields of the Central South and South-East* (1985)
Beck, P., *Keeping Watch* (2004).
Bentine, M., *The Door Marked Summer* (1981).
Bivona, G. S., M. Whitington, and D. McConachie, *Haunted Encounters: Ghost Stories from Around the World* (2004).
Bowyer, M. J. F., *Action Stations 1: Military Airfields of East Anglia* (1979).
Bowyer, M. J. F., *Action Stations 6: Military Airfields of the Cotswolds and the Central Midlands* (1983).
Brooks, J., *The Good Ghost Guide* (1994).
Brooks, R. J., *Sussex Airfields in the Second World War* (1993).
Burks, E. and G. Cribbs, *Ghosthunter: Investigating the World of Ghosts and Spirits* (1995).
Caidin, M., *Ghosts of the Air* (1994).
Cameron, J., *Haunted Kent* (2005).
Cheshire, L., *The Face of Victory* (1961).
Chorley, W. R., *Royal Air Force Bomber Command Losses of the Second World War, 1941* (1993).
—*Royal Air Force Bomber Command Losses of the Second World War, 1942* (1994).
—*Royal Air Force Bomber Command Losses of the Second World War, 1944* (1997).
—*Royal Air Force Bomber Command Losses of the Second World War, 1945* (1998).
—*Royal Air Force Bomber Command Losses: Operational Training Units, 1940-1947* (2002).
—*Royal Air Force Bomber Command Losses: Heavy Conversion Units and Miscellaneous Units, 1939-1947* (2003).
Codd, D., *Haunted Lincolnshire* (2006).
Currie, J., *Echoes in the Air* (1998).
Curry, D., *The Men That Never Clocked Off: Ghost Stories from Cambridge Airport* (2004).
Delve, K., *The Source Book of the RAF* (1994).
—*Military Airfields of Britain: Southern England (Kent, Hampshire, Surrey and Sussex)* (2005).
—*Military Airfields of Britain: East Anglia (Norfolk and Suffolk)* (2005).
—*Military Airfields of Britain: South-Western England (Channel Islands, Cornwall, Devon, Dorset, Gloucestershire, Somerset, Wiltshire)* (2006).
—*Military Airfields of Britain: Northern England (Co. Durham, Cumbria, Isle of Man, Lancashire, Merseyside, Manchester, Northumberland, Tyne & Wear, Yorkshire)* (2006).
—*Military Airfields of Britain: Northern Home Counties (Bedfordshire, Berkshire, Buckinghamshire, Essex, Hertfordshire, London, Middlesex, Oxfordshire)* (2007).

—*Military Airfields of Britain: Wales and West Midlands (Cheshire, Hereford and Worcester, Northamptonshire, Shropshire, Staffordshire, Warwickshire, West Midlands, Wales)* (2007).
—*Military Airfields of Britain: East Midlands (Cambridgeshire, Derbyshire, Leicestershire, Lincolnshire, Nottinghamshire)* (2008).
—*Military Airfields of Britain: Scotland and Northern Ireland* (2010).
Desmond, K., *Aviation Ghosts* (1998).
Dobinson, C., *Fields of Deception* (2000).
Freeman, R. A., *Airfields of the Eighth Then and Now* (1978).
—*UK Airfields of the Ninth Then and Now* (1994).
—*Bases of Bomber Command Then and Now* (2003).
Gardner, P., *Ghostly Tales from an English RAF Base* in Bivona, G. S., M. Whitington, and D. McConachie (2004).
Halley, J., *The Squadrons of the Royal Air Force* (1980).
Halpenny, B. B., *Action Stations 2: Military Airfields of Lincolnshire and the East Midlands* (1981).
—*Action Stations 4: Military Airfields of Yorkshire* (1982).
—*Action Stations 8: Military Airfields of Greater London* (1981).
—*Ghost Stations* (1986).
—*Ghost Stations II* (1990).
—*Ghost Stations V* (1991).
—*Ghost Stations VI* (1994).
—*Ghost Stations VII* (1995).
Hauck, D. W., *The International Directory of Haunted Places* (2000).
Jenkins, V., 'A "Strange Presence" at the Old Airfield' in *Flak News* Vol. 10, No. 4, October 1995.
Jennings, P., *Haunted Suffolk* (1996).
King, C., *Haunted Essex* (2009).
Lakin, T., *Haunted Middlesbrough* (2007).
Llewelyn, K., *Flight into the Ages* (1991).
McKee, A., *Into the Blue* (1981).
McKenzie, R., *They Still Serve: A Complete Guide to the Military Ghosts of Britain* (2008).
Middlebrook, M. and C. Everitt, *The Bomber Command War Diaries* (1985).
Ogley, B., *The Ghosts of Biggin Hill* (2001).
Perkins, A., *Ghost Detective II* (2006).
Quarrie, B., *Action Stations 10: Supplement and Index* (1987).
Smith, D. J., *Action Stations 3: Military Airfields of Wales and the North-West* (1983).
—*Action Stations 7: Military Airfields of Scotland, the North-East and Northern Ireland* (1983).
Spencer J. and A., *The Encyclopedia of Ghosts and Spirits* Vol. 1 (1992).
Sturtivant, R., J. Hamlin, and J. J. Halley, *RAF Flying Training and Support Units Since 1912* (2007).
*True Ghost Stories from WWI & WWII* (2005).
Underwood, P., *Guide to Ghosts & Haunted Places* (1996).
Willis, S. and B. Holliss, *Military Airfields in the British Isles 1939-1945* (1987).
Wood, A. C., *Military Ghosts* (2010).
Woodhouse, R., *Supernatural Cleveland (And District)* (1990).

## Information Sources Online

Air of Authority – A History of RAF Organisation: www.rafweb.org
Bob Baxter's Bomber Command: www.bomber-command.info
Control Towers: www.controltowers.co.uk/listing.htm
Haunted RAF Airfields: http://rafg.moonfruit.com

History of War: www.historyofwar.org/subject_RAF_units.html
Lost Bombers: www.lostbombers.co.uk (defunct)
RAF Commands: www.rafcommands.com/home.html
The Stars and Stripes: www.stripes.com

## Online Forums

The Airfield Information Exchange: www.airfieldinformationexchange.org/community/
    forum.php
Army Rumour Service: www.arrse.co.uk
Castle of Spirits: www.castleofspirits.com
Cornish Paranormal Group: http://cornishparanormalgroup.org.uk/forum
Dark Knights Paranormal: www.dkparanormal.com
E-Goat: www.e-goat.co.uk/forums/index.php
East Kent Paranormal Investigation Group: http://btmekpg.myfreeforum.org
Fighter Control: www.fightercontrol.co.uk/forum
Flak News: www.398th.org/FlakNews/Articles/index.html
Fortean Times Online: www.forteantimes.com/forum
G503: www.g503.com
Ghost Finder Paranormal Society: www.ghostfinderukforum.com
Ghost Haunted: www.ghosthaunted.com
Ghosts UK:
www.ghosts-uk.net/modules/newbb/viewtopic.php?topic_id=6412&forum=17&post_
    id=61750#forumpost61750
Ghostvillage: www.ghostvillage.com
Kent History Forum: www.kenthistoryforum.co.uk
Keypublishing Aviation Forum: http://forum.keypublishing.co.uk
PPRuNe Professional Pilots Rumour Network: www.pprune.org
Spook Central: http://spookcentral.webs.com/apps/forums/topics/show/7612515-ghosts-
    of-the-air
Unexplainable.Net: www.unexplainable.net
World War 2 Talk: www.ww2talk.com
WWII Re-enacting: www.wwiireenacting.co.uk

## Other Websites

Bedfordshire County Council: www.bedfordshire.gov.uk/AirfieldGhosts (defunct)
Dover Kent Archives: www.dover-kent.com/Mayfly-Hawkinge.html
Facebook: GJS Ghost Hunting
Facebook: Phantoms of the Rhur
Ghost Connections UK: www.ghostconnections.com
Luton Paranormal Society: www.lutonparanormal.com
The Molesworth Pilot: www.303rdbg.com/news/2010-09-05.html
The Paranormal Database: www.paranormaldatabase.com
Paranormal Pondering: http://soulwrangler.wordpress.com/2008/07/28/raf-tangmere
Paranormal Tours: www.paranormaltours.com
Peterborough City Council: www.peterborough.gov.uk (defunct)
Psychic Investigations: www.psychicinvestigations.net/index.html
Rachel Keene: www.rachelkeene.co.uk/rivenhall.html
RAF Upwood: www.rafupwood.co.uk
Supernatural Shires: www.supernaturalshires.co.uk/HERTS-PLACES.html
Sussex Paranormal Research & Investigations Team: www.paranormal-research.co.uk
Vale and Downland Museum, Wantage: www.wantage.com/wantage-life/vale-and-
    downland-museum
Wings Museum: www.wingsmuseum.co.uk